Saving the Children

BERKELEY SERIES IN BRITISH STUDIES

Edited by James Vernon

Saving the Children

HUMANITARIANISM, INTERNATIONALISM, AND EMPIRE

Emily Baughan

UNIVERSITY OF CALIFORNIA PRESS

*The publisher and the University of California Press
Foundation gratefully acknowledge the generous support of
the Ahmanson Foundation Endowment Fund in Humanities.*

University of California Press
Oakland, California

© 2022 by Emily Baughan

Library of Congress Cataloging-in-Publication Data

Names: Baughan, Emily, 1988- author.
Title: Saving the children : humanitarianism, internationalism, and empire /
    Emily Baughan.
Other titles: Berkeley series in British studies ; 19.
Description: Oakland, California : University of California Press, [2022] |
    Series: Berkeley series in British studies ; 19 | Includes bibliographical
    references and index.
Identifiers: LCCN 2021014315 (print) | LCCN 2021014316 (ebook) |
    ISBN 9780520343719 (cloth) | ISBN 9780520343726 (paperback) |
    ISBN 9780520975118 (epub)
Subjects: LCSH: Save the Children Fund (Great Britain)—History. |
    Humanitarianism—Political aspects—20th century.
Classification: LCC BJ1475.3 .B37 2022 (print) | LCC BJ1475.3 (ebook) |
    DDC 361.2/6—dc23
LC record available at https://lccn.loc.gov/2021014315
LC ebook record available at https://lccn.loc.gov/2021014316

Manufactured in the United States of America

31 30 29 28 27 26 25 24 23 22
10 9 8 7 6 5 4 3 2 1

For my mum
Annie Baughan (née Rutherford)
1958–2019

CONTENTS

ACKNOWLEDGMENTS

A monograph—especially one that has taken this long—is a scrapbook of formative conversations, intellectual communities, and treasured friendships. Many will recognize their contributions folded into the text and its notes. It is a pleasure to make these, and my gratitude, more visible.

This book's series editor, James Vernon, made it a more ambitious project than I had originally imagined and pushed me to say what I meant. I am grateful for everything, especially his kindness and patience when life delayed writing. The very first iteration of this project was forged in conversation with my PhD supervisor, James Thompson. I would never have considered postgraduate study, much less a career in academia, without his encouragement. My co-supervisor, Kirsty Reid, modeled how to live authentically within and beyond the university—a lesson as valuable as her contribution to this project's beginnings. Seth Koven and Robert Bickers, who examined my PhD thesis, raised fresh questions and possibilities.

The Department of History at the University of Bristol made me a historian. I arrived there as an undergraduate and left as a lecturer, having learned so much about the scholar, teacher, and colleague I wanted to be. I am grateful to the entire department—rare in its commitment to distributing time and resources downward—and especially to Tim Cole, Su Lin Lewis, Josie McLellan, Margery Masterson, and Rob Skinner. Jess Farr-Cox read and edited every word of this book: I could not have finished it without her.

At the University of Sheffield, my enthusiasm for this project was reawakened by the History, Politics and Culture Reading Group, and the Red Deer Writers' Collective. Exploring the contours of work, life, politics, and scholarship together was the encouragement I needed to finish this project, and it sparked my excitement to move on to new questions. I am especially grateful

ix

for the commentary and camaraderie of Eliza Hartrich, Tom Johnson, Rosie Knight, Erin Maglaque, Chris Millard, Simon Toner, and James Yeoman. During my time at Sheffield I have learned as much standing outside the university as I did inside. I have our local UCU branch and its members to thank for that. I am grateful to Adrian Bingham for his support as head of department and his insight as a reader of this book. Dan Brockington and Amy Ryall made it possible for me to have conversations about this work beyond the department and the university.

Both Bristol and Sheffield were springboards for the international travel and academic fellowships that made writing and researching this kind of history possible. I acknowledge the support of the Fulbright Commission, the Worldwide Universities Network, the Mellon Foundation, the Arts and Humanities Research Council, the British Institute of East Africa, the Max Batley Peace Studies fund, the Economic History Society, and my unearned privilege in benefitting from these awards. I am especially grateful to mentors across the world, and the energy they poured into this project. Vivian Bickford-Smith was a generous host at the University of Cape Town in 2013. It was a dream to study with Susan Pedersen at Columbia University in 2013–14. I had to pinch myself often during a summer spent on Capitol Hill with the Decolonization Seminar in 2015. I am grateful to all the seminarians and faculty, in particular Philippa Levine and the late Marilyn Young. Many of the arguments that follow were worked out in conversation with Laura Lee Downs during long runs on the banks of the Arno during my year as a Max Weber Fellow at the European University Institute in 2015–16. I spent two summers, in 2012 and 2018, as a Kluge Fellow at the Library of Congress. The friendship of Bronwen Colquhoun, Oliver Cox, and Hazel Wilkinson is infinitely more precious to me than any of the words written there. It was such luck to share H Street with Sophie Jones twice, six years apart.

Then, there are the mentors and friends whose contributions cannot be tied to a particular moment or place. None of this—the book or the life lived alongside—would have made sense without Anna Bocking-Welch, Charlotte Riley, Tehila Sasson and Natasha Wheatley. I treasure their sisterhood and solidarity. Helen McCarthy has supported me and this book from the very start. Jordanna Bailkin and Michelle Tusan were my dream readers: along with an anonymous reviewer, they improved this text enormously. It has been a pleasure to learn from so many historians of development and international-isms over the years, including Arthur Asseraf, Muriam Haleh Davis, Kim Lowe, Matthew Hilton, Kara Moskowitz, Eva-Maria Muschik and Stephen

Wertheim. Conversations with Eleanor Davey about the material conditions and political imperatives of writing histories of aid have been a tonic.

I owe many thanks to staff at Save the Children, most of all to Juliano Fiori. He has lived with this book and its interwar liberals almost as long as I have, alongside the long shadows they cast in our present moment. Our conversations and collaborations have been a joy. The time and trust of the Humanitarian Affairs Team at Save the Children was a gift. I am profoundly grateful to Gareth Owen, Fernando Espada, Jessica Field, Sophie Dicker, Millie Cooper, and Anna Wyatt. I have learned so much from Mike Aaronson, whose institutional memory begins where this book leaves off. I hope he recognizes at least something of his experiences in the few years of overlap! Countless members of the legal team enabled my access to archives and images over the years. I want to thank particularly Michael Weaver, Mizan Choudhury, and Amy Banks. I am profoundly grateful to Mark Eccleston at the Cadbury Library, for all he did to enable my continued access to Save the Children's archives during its move, an ongoing cataloging project, and during three UK lockdowns. Jamie Perry often visited the Cadbury Library on my behalf: I owe a lot to his meticulousness and creativity. Particular thanks are also due to the staff of the Archives d'État de Genève for many enjoyable hours spent with the collections of the Save the Children International Union. Jack Lundin, Ben Buxton, and Adeoye Agunlejika generously shared personal papers.

The years spent living a stone's throw away from Save the Children's London offices with Kat and Tom Newton were such happy ones, as have been all adventures we've shared before and since. The company of Eve Young, Jess Franses, and Patrick Nation on trips back to London has been sustaining.

Families are conspicuously absent from this book about children, but it would never have been written without mine. My dad, Chris, has been a steadfast source of love and encouragement, as well as a careful editor and valued sounding board. My brothers, Jack and William, haven't read this: I appreciate that (and them) deeply, too. My expansion-pack sister, Rebecca Smith, has held me through all the years spent on this project, most especially the last. I owe more than I can say to the generosity and love of Jane and Gary Franses. I ended many working days in Oxford at the kitchen table of my parents-in-law, Margaret and Richard Stevens, where I was always welcomed with warmth.

I met Simon Stevens in 2010, at the moment this project started to take shape. The footnotes of this book are a travelogue of adventures—mostly together, sometimes apart—in a decade in which we, and our work, grew up together. His intellectual contribution to this book is incalculable. So too is his contribution of care, for me and, in the final months of writing, for our small son Alec. It was never the plan to be finishing this book in lockdown with a baby. Simon made this time not only possible, but precious.

The pages that follow hold so many memories of my mum, Annie. Of summer evening strolls after the close of archives and libraries across the world, of penciled comments in the margins of drafts, of my small frustrations exchanged for her vast love and pride. She died suddenly as this project was entering its final stages. I miss her every day. Written in the light of her love and with the gifts she gave, this book is for her.

Introduction

IN THE SUMMER OF 1968, my mother, Annie Rutherford, stole her sister's stamp collection. She gave it to the Belfast branch of the Save the Children Club, which sold the stamps to raise money for "Biafran babies." Aged eleven, Annie didn't know where Biafra was, but she felt keenly that it was her duty to respond to suffering in far-off places. The proceeds from her stamps— along with millions of pounds raised by the British public and donated by the British government—were used to purchase high-protein drinks for children on the front lines of the conflict, including another eleven-year-old girl named Affiong, at a Save the Children feeding center in the war-ravaged region of Calabar.[1]

The Biafran famine is remembered as the foundational moment of contemporary humanitarianism.[2] However, that the mechanisms existed to turn stamps stolen by Annie in Belfast into a high-protein drink for Affiong in Biafra was due to an aid and development sector that had been fifty years in the making.[3] This book charts those fifty years—years in which the contemporary aid sector was born and grew up during an era of international collaboration and imperial decline. To do so, I follow Save the Children from its foundation in the aftermath of the First World War, through a further period of global conflict and decolonization, and into the era of postcolonial international aid. I argue that British humanitarianism was inseparable from— and sheds new light upon—the two defining features of Britain's twentieth century: the loss of empire and the rise of the welfare state.

Contemporary British humanitarianism was born out of the peculiarity of Britain's imperial role in an era of internationalist cooperation. In the nineteenth century, British humanitarianism was a product of imperialism. It sought to rescue the victims of colonial cruelty, and in doing so demonstrate the benevolence of British imperialism. After the First World War, a new imperative to save Europe (and particularly its children) altered the geography of British humanitarianism, shifting its focus beyond the British Empire into a new "international" area. A new generation of humanitarians styled their work as an internationalist attempt to create mutual peace and prosperity across Europe in the aftermath of war. They downplayed Britain's imperial ambitions, reconfiguring Britain as a champion and exemplar of collaborative internationalism. Despite this, British international humanitarianism was an attempt to create conditions favorable to British imperial rule and free trade.[4] This became explicit when, after the Second World War, British aid organizations increasingly relocated their efforts from Europe to Britain's colonies—the space in which British humanitarianism had first been forged—in a bid to slow the disintegration of British imperialism. After empire's end, humanitarian internationalism became a means of performing Britain's ongoing global role.[5]

British world leadership, and the emergence of its modern welfare state, were biopolitical projects. Children were central to both. British humanitarians worked to create physically healthy, mentally disciplined, and emotionally well-adjusted children across the globe. Drawing on the emerging medical, psychological, and even eugenic "knowledge" that undergirded the rise of Britain's welfare state, humanitarians believed that children's bodies and minds could be molded to create a world in Britain's economic and political image. The young would grow up to be the workers of European or colonial economies, and the peaceful democratic citizens (or docile colonial subjects) of an interconnected world.[6] This imagined world was unequal: the future roles that humanitarians envisaged for children—and thus the forms of education and intervention they received—were determined by imperial attitudes to race, bourgeois views of class, and Protestant visions of productivity.

This study of Save the Children (SCF), one of Britain's oldest, largest, and most influential aid organizations, is an experiment in writing an international, institutional history. By focusing on a single institution across a turbulent fifty-year period in the twentieth century, we can draw together the international and imperial contexts of Britain's global engagement. A study of Save the Children also connects domestic and international developments in child welfare. It reveals not only how Britain exported ideas about the welfare of children and families but also how child welfare practices that became embedded in Britain's welfare state were contingent upon innovations overseas. Annie in Belfast and Affiong in Biafra were connected by both the pennies raised by stolen stamps and a vision of global childhood that had emerged from imperial Britain in the twentieth century.

HUMANITARIANISM, CAPITALISM, AND IMPERIALISM

The rise of humanitarianism is inseparable from the rise of capitalism and imperialism. Historians have understood humanitarianism as "concern for distant others," identifying the campaign against the trade in enslaved peoples in the late eighteenth and early nineteenth centuries as the first humanitarian campaign.[7] For Britain, the first state to partially abolish the trade in enslaved people, the success of the campaign marked the beginning of an imperial superiority complex. British rule was cast as uniquely benevolent colonization.[8] The British Empire not only freed the enslaved, but also claimed that colonization was a tool for civilization and Christianization. The apparently "humanitarian" basis of empire went hand in hand with its primary function: the accumulation of capital. Missionary schools and hospitals were preparing colonized minds and bodies to produce goods for an imperial market in which the profits of imperial natural resources could be extracted and channeled to British businesses and the British state.[9]

Humanitarianism did not spring entirely from colonial empires. In 1853, the International Committee of the Red Cross (ICRC) was founded by Swiss businessman Henri Dunant. Aiding the military victims of wars, the ICRC claimed to be impartial, neutral, and independent.[10] The two distinct strands of nineteenth-century humanitarianism—the colonial tradition and the continental tradition—met in the aftermath of the First World War. Missionary organizations and Red Cross societies alike worked together to halt the spread of epidemic disease, mass famine, endemic poverty, and the postwar refugee crisis in Europe.[11] From 1920, humanitarian organizations such as the SCF and the ICRC were aided in their war relief and disease control efforts by the newly founded League of Nations, an international, intergovernmental organization created to build a lasting peace through collective security and cooperation in social, economic, and humanitarian matters.[12] This was because the health of Europe's workers was understood as integral to the health of the international economy which was, in turn, a necessary condition for "international peace."[13]

The League of Nations—dominated by Britain and France—also cast colonialism as part of an international peace effort. Through colonization, the natural resources and labor of colonized territories were opened to the wider world in the name of international prosperity. At the same time, colonized territories were being "tutored" in the norms of participatory democracy, and would become ready to, eventually, take up their position in an international order based on stable, liberal governance. As a recent wave of historical work has shown, the "liberal internationalism" of the League of Nations upheld, rather than challenged, imperialism.[14] In this book, I examine a particular humanitarian iteration of liberal internationalism. Doing so uncovers how the relationship between internationalism and imperialism was understood by the British public, and experienced "on the ground" by the objects of their benevolence. Recent histories of liberal internationalism have, broadly, centered on international intergovernmental institutions (the League of Nations and the United Nations) and their subsidiary organizations, tending to begin or end with the Second World War, as the League of Nations declined and the United Nations was founded.[15] Examining the interaction between internationalism and imperialism through Save the Children, I disrupt this periodization. Save the Children's version of humanitarian internationalism, while it might have been born from the interwar international order, outlasted it.

In the aftermath of the Second World War, "humanitarian" interventions became ever more integral to both the external image and the internal operations of the British Empire. Britain, still paying off its war effort, sought new ways to make the empire profitable, fitting more colonial subjects for labor through education and healthcare. Welfare interventions were also designed to stymy anti-colonial resistance at a moment when, in the context of the Cold War and the rise of American power, the international community was increasingly sympathetic to calls for democracy and territorial sovereignty. However, postwar colonial welfare interventions proved too little too late.[16] By the end of the 1960s, the British Empire, which had once spanned one-fifth of the world's land, was little more than a handful of territories.

The end of the British Empire led to a rupture in the ideas and practices of British humanitarianism. Save the Children's utopian optimism about the world had hinged on growing international cooperation but also, more crucially, on British world leadership. In a world without empire, they ceased to imagine a more prosperous future was possible for the world's poorer nations. Despite this, British humanitarianism continued to grow, even while the empire contracted, as new development projects were launched in colonial territories preparing for independence.[17] New humanitarian organizations, such as Oxfam and Christian Aid, brought fresh optimism and idealism to the doctrine of "development."[18] These organizations employed former colonial officials to lend their "expertise," and enlisted the British public in ongoing attempts to build friendship and to "develop" Britain's former colonies.[19] After decolonization, humanitarianism became a means through which the British public and the British state sought to address problems of poverty, inequality, and underdevelopment caused by imperialism, while seeking to invent empire's positive legacy.

GLOBALIZING BRITAIN'S WELFARE STATE

Like the British Empire, the modern British welfare state sought the maximization of economic productivity through the creation of a healthy workforce.[20] Its architects, with their diverse origins in the interwar labor movement, late nineteenth-century philanthropy, and liberal politics, shared beliefs about the inherent moral worth of work and the immorality of idleness. Assistance, either from the public purse or private charity, was not a universal right, but was owed in times of need to those who had demonstrated they were "deserving" through industry and thrift in earlier stages of life.[21] After 1945, entitlement to the full complement of state services was based on contributions made by the employed via taxation, or services were intended for those experiencing brief spells of unemployment: the modern-day "deserving poor" who had proven their will to work.[22] The British state venerated not only production, but reproduction. Through pro-natalist policies, it ensured the creation of the citizens of the future, while marginalizing individuals and lifestyles that deviated from heterosexual, reproductive norms.[23]

Across twentieth-century Europe, children were the first beneficiaries of emerging welfare states.[24] Whereas adults' welfare entitlement depended on willingness or ability to work, almost all children were imagined as potential future contributors to society.[25] For the children of the British poor, this future contribution was imagined in biological and economic terms: children were white imperial settlers, soldiers, or future producers (and reproducers).[26] Moments when the British Empire's military strength or economy were under threat produced rapid advances in child welfare. In the aftermath of the Boer War, when mass enlistment revealed the "physical degeneration" of Britain's lower classes, a raft of child welfare legislation sought to save children's bodies from the ravages of poverty.[27] In the early twentieth century, European powers competed not just to amass warships, but to invigorate future soldiers, workers, and mothers through expanded state child welfare provision.[28]

 Although healthy children had the potential to transcend the poverty of their parents, this was by no means seen as a certainty. Poverty was seen as a moral as well as material condition. It arose through lack of self-discipline and so could be prevented in the next generation through appropriate socialization.[29] Mass education in Britain aimed to "civilize" the children of the working classes, viewed as savage not only due to their social position but also because, as children, they were seen as closer to nature.[30] Curricula were designed to inculcate discipline, self-control, and punctuality alongside reading, writing, and arithmetic.[31] State education, increasingly organized and planned after the 1944 Education Act, aimed to eradicate unemployment (and its attendant "idleness") by matching the abilities of children to the needs of the economy.[32] Children with bodies that were deemed incapable of contributing to society were often excluded from mainstream education or medical care, lest they transfer their perceived physical or intellectual limitations to the next generation.[33]

In the aftermath of the First World War, humanitarian organizations scaled up arguments about the importance of children's health for national strength in a new international era. If the present health of children forecast the future abilities of future workers, then the international economy—and therefore international peace—depended on "all the world's children." Despite their universalist claims, international humanitarian organizations continued to exclude from their care children they deemed unfit. In the early twentieth century, humanitarians not only globalized British welfare policies, but operationalized British eugenics. After the defeat of Nazism discredited eugenics, humanitarian organizations directed racialized psychiatry to the same ends: the creation of productive imperial subjects.

Britain imported as well as exported child welfare practices. New forms of knowledge, such as psychoanalysis and sociology, which underpinned advances in welfare and childcare in Britain, were often formulated elsewhere. British child welfare experts watched the rise of the social sciences in Germany and the United States keenly, eager to adapt new innovations to a British context.[34] In the first half of the twentieth century, the British Empire functioned as a "laboratory" in which innovations could be tested and measured before they were implemented in British working-class communities.[35] These flows of knowledge and practice were multidirectional: child welfare workers trained in Britain took themselves and their methods to far-flung parts of the empire.[36] Through the apparatus of international humanitarianism the British welfare state—and its moral underpinnings—have been writ global. Through the figure of the innocent child, Victorian notions of deserving and undeserving poor were understood worldwide—never challenged, but rather entrenched, by international aid.

CHILDREN AND FAMILIES

Affection within families and the special status afforded to the young by societies is not—as many scholars have claimed—uniquely modern. Before the twentieth century children were important participants in family economies: their "innocence" and inherent Romanticism had been celebrated in the Renaissance humanist movement, in the eighteenth-century Romantic movement, and in Protestant religion.[37] Yet the particular way that children were valued—and who they were valued by—shifted in Western Europe and North America over the last two hundred years. During campaigns against child labor, beginning in the late eighteenth century, humanitarians identified the treatment of children (along with the abolition of slavery) as a key measure of British humanity. The abolition of child labor in the nineteenth century lent industrial capitalism ethical authority (in the way that the abolition of slavery legitimated British imperialism). The abolition of child labor in the nineteenth century, and the decline of multigenerational family living in the twentieth, also meant that children's economic value as earners or future caretakers for their parents declined. Instead, children's value within families was imagined in emotional terms. As in campaigns against child labor, children were imagined as objects of affection, which placed them "above" economic calculations of their worth (or, as was increasingly the case for the bourgeois consumerist family, their cost).[38] At the same moment, the economic value of children to nation-states at large, rather than the family as a singular unit, became an organizing principle for emerging welfare states.

In the twentieth century, Save the Children understood the value of children in the economic (or indeed biopolitical) language of welfare states. However, when explaining its work to would-be supporters, it spoke of children's special emotional value, using the metaphors of the family, calling upon potential donors to honor maternal or paternal obligations to children far away. Yet, while these organizations drew on familial metaphors, they tended to overlook the children's existing families. They viewed children as emotive objects, rather than emotional subjects. Privileging physical needs over emotional preferences, early international aid organizations often removed children from their communities, placing them in orphanages, boarding schools, or sanatoria away from violence or urban poverty.[39] These settings were designed with the intention of maximizing children's future economic potential, creating strong minds and healthy bodies, rather than replicating the emotional regimes of bourgeois family life.

During the Second World War, mass evacuations of children from towns and cities across Europe prompted a new wave of psychological and psychoanalytical studies, which argued that children's emotional stability was dependent on secure attachment to their parents, particularly their mothers.[40] When reports of juvenile delinquency spiked across Europe after 1945, fears about the potential of emotionally insecure children to create social and political upheaval became widespread.[41] The observations of wartime psychoanalytic studies—as much as the process of evacuation itself—profoundly reshaped the relationship between children and families. The protection of the nuclear family, and in particular the bond between mother and child, was enshrined in the organization of emerging welfare states. Postwar employment policies and family benefits pushed mothers out of work and back into their homes. In Britain, the 1950s and the 1960s saw a dismantling of institutional forms of childcare, while (newly professionalized) social work interventions increasingly sought to ensure that children were raised in (ideally biological) families.[42] The emotional culture of middle-class families shifted, as popular child-rearing advice literature foregrounded children's need for secure attachment and affection, in contrast with earlier approaches that emphasized training and discipline.[43] It was mothers who shouldered the burden of these new emotional imperatives.

Mothers also shouldered blame.[44] While many nineteenth- and early twentieth-century philanthropists preferred to focus on the image of the child in isolation, mothers shifted into focus when they could be used to explain bad behavior or ill health. In Britain, early twentieth-century childcare movements focused primarily on education for mothers, imagining that malnourished children were improperly fed rather than lacking access to food.[45] Fifty years later, professional social workers found the cause of children's behavioral problems to be in their mothers' "neglect" rather than rising levels of urban deprivation.[46] Throughout the twentieth century, at moments when local philanthropists and international humanitarians faced the most ingrained challenges (declines in birthrate, global depression, the economic exploitation of postcolonial states), they sought maternal solutions to structural problems.[47] From the slums of East London to the rural Gold Coast, humanitarian interventions with mothers involved "teaching" standards of childcare and affection that were simultaneously declared to be natural, instinctive, and universal.[48]

Throughout the twentieth century, humanitarian organizations designated other people's children as valuable to Western donors while often discounting how children were valued in their own communities and families. In the first part of the twentieth century, aid organizations denied the emotional attachment of parents to their own children, disrupting familial connection in favor of forms of mass shelter and education designed to enhance children's economic value as future workers. In the second half of the twentieth century, humanitarian organizations sought to export new emotional imperatives drawn from around child attachment and maternal bonding into the Global South. In doing so, they denied the economic value of children to their communities, seeking to abolish child labor and early marriage.[49] Thus, they insisted on a modern, Western childhood as universal: protection, education, and family life became the "rights" of all children.[50] In this way, humanitarian organizations created the norms of childhood and family life that they claimed to uphold.[51]

CHILDREN AND THE ANTI-POLITICS OF AID

A common feature of humanitarian organizations across the last two centuries is the claim to be above, beyond, or otherwise separate from "politics." Concerned with the transcendent cause of humanity, humanitarians cast their interventions as impartial and nonpolitical. However, humanitarianism desires not just to help people, but also to shape the world in which they live. Rather than conceptualizing humanitarianism as a political ethos in and of itself, I read it as a set of practices that express political visions.[52] In Britain, humanitarian internationalism emerged from late Victorian liberalism.[53] Early twentieth-century British humanitarians held a series of core liberal beliefs in common: the rationality of markets, the importance of self-reliance, and the duties of communities to their less well-off members. Many of these individuals were Quakers and nonconformist Protestants who viewed work as inherently good but profit and accumulation as distasteful.[54] Their support for British colonialism stemmed from a desire to extend the liberal virtues of self-reliance and trade to the wider world as well as a Christian-influenced imperative to "steward" natural resources.[55] They therefore understood colonialism and capitalism as moral (rather than political) issues.

Humanitarianism was about saving individual subjects as well as upholding normative global systems. Aid organizations attempted to "depoliticize" both aid itself and its recipients, through the construction of the ideal humanitarian subject: the inherently valuable and innately innocent child.[56] Children were thought to lack the self-interested calculation required to be political actors. As political objects, their innate value rendered them a universal and unifying concern.[57] Children, of course, have more political capacity than has been recognized either in the past or at the present moment, though that is not the focus of this book.[58] This is not a study of children as actors, but rather an examination of how children were constructed and acted upon by humanitarians.

The founders of Save the Children were women, as were many of its early relief workers. These women used their femininity and "maternal compassion" for children to distance themselves, and humanitarian work, from politics. Yet the majority of female humanitarians had in fact emerged from the women's suffrage movement and saw humanitarian action as a form of political participation.[59] Aid organizations were able to draw on the expertise and rhetoric of women's suffrage campaigns while casting humanitarianism itself as nonpolitical. The women's suffrage movement had claimed women's right to vote by invoking the transcendent maternal compassion that women would bring to the degraded political arena.[60] Aid organizations relied on these discourses of maternalism to give an impression of political impartiality in controversial interventions. However, in the field, as well as back in British headquarters, aid work became an intensely masculine profession, dominated by ex-military and former colonial officials.[61] Women's contributions, cast as expressions of emotion rather than expertise, were easily marginalized. This, until recently, has been as much the case in the historiography on humanitarianism as in the contemporary humanitarian movement. By reading politics through humanitarianism we can recover women's political visions for international order.[62] Doing so restores ideas about children and their bodies to the central space that they occupied in internationalist political thought.

The ability of British aid organizations to forge relationships with the British government during the twentieth century (and indeed the twenty-first) has rested on their claims to be nonpolitical. The use of domestic tax revenue to aid people outside the national or imperial community has been a controversial matter since it first occurred during the Russian famine in 1921. Yet the British government has continued to make regular grants during crises in the last century, including, at the time of writing, to the food crisis in Yemen, conflict-affected communities in Somalia, and Syrian refugees in Jordan.[63] Since 1921, many of these government-funded programs have been administered by nongovernmental humanitarian organizations. The British government has now become one of the largest sources of funding for major British aid organizations. To protect revenue streams, aid organizations have avoided overt criticism of government policy, even when these policies are worsening the very crises in which aid organizations are intervening. Partnerships between aid organizations and states—partnerships that Save the Children pioneered—have made the performance of distance between the humanitarian and the political spheres all the more vital.[64] In a century that had seen secularization and the decline of the role of the Anglican church in British politics, aid organizations have come to speak as a national moral voice by presenting the cause of humanity as elevated above political concerns.[65]

Humanitarian non-politics (or even "anti-politics") gave aid organizations proximity to power, but limited their ability to leverage it.[66] Anti-politics also limited the ability of many humanitarian organizations to identify the structural conditions in which they operated. At the beginning of the twentieth century, aid organizations worked to uphold and support capitalism and colonialism, unquestioningly viewing both as inherent goods. Just a few decades later, a new generation of aid workers within the same organizations were coming to an understanding that colonialism and capitalism were generating rather than alleviating poverty. They engaged with critiques of (post) colonialism and global capitalism and demanded solutions to inequality that went beyond Western aid.[67] This was a moment of self-reflection that Save the Children did not participate in. With its own anti-politics firmly established, colonialism and capitalism were never named by Save the Children as causes of poverty, war, or environmental crises.[68]

HISTORIES OF SAVE THE CHILDREN

This book is about British humanitarian internationalism, its relationship with empire, and how children became its objects. It shows how British humanitarians created a vision of international responsibility based on British imperial power, and then failed to adapt this vision to a post-empire world. It is, then, the story of the rise and slow decline of a particular form of humanitarian internationalism that did not outlast the imperial world order it had been created to uphold. Each chapter examines a distinct phase in British humanitarian foreign relations with the wider world and asks two questions: What did internationalism mean to the British at this moment, and how was this vision to be realized through "saving" particular types of children?

Save the Children is an organization able to bear the weight of this questioning. It is unique as a self-styled international aid organization with a hundred-year history, during which time it has remained vast and influential.[69] From its foundation in 1919, SCF was global not only in ambition but presence. In its first three years, it worked in twenty-seven countries. By 1970, that had risen to forty-nine. In 1920, the British Save the Children Fund founded the Save the Children International Union, an umbrella body that drew together child welfare agencies across Europe, the British Empire and, from 1934, North and South America. In the Second World War and its aftermath, Save the Children played an active role in intergovernmental reconstruction programs. It became the first of Britain's international aid organizations (that is, those founded to work in Europe) to begin projects in the British Empire in the 1950s, and in the 1960s it spearheaded many of the initiatives that characterized the global "development decade." During this time, hundreds of thousands of British citizens donated regularly via weekly subscriptions or child sponsorship programs; gave gifts and left legacies; and attended fundraising events at schools, churches, synagogues, and local branches.[70] In moments of crisis, Save the Children also drew donations (in kind or cash) from the British state, which enabled, for example, mass famine relief programs in Russia in 1921 and Nigeria in the late 1960s.

In spite (or perhaps because) of its scale, it is difficult to determine what Save the Children was and did. The Fund's claims to be working "in" a certain country meant very different things at different times. Humanitarian organizations have the "map-coloring" proclivities of the empires that birthed them. Grand claims about global reach need to be closely interrogated. Between the two world wars the Fund claimed to "work in Hungary" where, for example, it was funding a single school. Korea in the 1950s claimed the largest proportion of the Fund's income, and yet only a handful of British Save the Children Fund staff ever set foot on Korean soil in this decade. Meanwhile, in Russia in 1921, the Fund was one of only two British organizations on the ground and its operatives distributed the aid of the British government and a host of other British and European humanitarian organizations.

What was meant by a "Save the Children" intervention is further complicated by the diversity of the Fund's staffing arrangements and decision-making processes. From the 1920s to the 1950s, the Fund paid local workers, from maids to chefs to nannies, and informal contacts whom they never regarded as "staff." In the 1960s, the number of de facto employees mushroomed as postcolonial states demanded that foreign aid and development organizations employ local personnel. Very few Save the Children interventions featured the stereotypical lone British aid worker, a "man on the spot" arriving able to implement a mission worked out in London or Geneva. The Fund's decision-making process was complex and often opaque. Each month from 1919 to 1970 (and beyond), the Fund's executive council met to discuss major matters of policy, planning, and strategy. A host of subject-specific committees, some long-standing (the Education Committee), some more ad hoc (the Emergency Nursery Schools Committee, 1933–45) were convened. Despite complex, top-down governance structures, decisions were often taken by workers on the ground, influenced by local community members. There was no single model of a "Save the Children" intervention.

It is also often impossible to tell where a Save the Children intervention ended and that of another organization began. Save the Children grew up alongside a host of international aid organizations in the aftermath of the First World War, and its work was dependent on the existence of other agencies. Many of the Fund's early interventions were in fact grants that it made to other relief organizations. Despite this, Save the Children saw other humanitarian organizations as competitors. Concerned with promoting the role of the British in the international relief movement, the Fund's leaders were always frustrated by the size and scale of American relief efforts and spent the interwar period seeking to match them. Save the Children competed not only for British dominance of the international aid movement, but also within Britain for its own position in an emerging aid sector. The Fund's early leaders prided themselves on running the charity "like a business" and sought the largest possible market share of British donors.[71] This approach became ingrained not only in the Fund but in an increasingly professionalized and bureaucratized British relief sector more broadly.[72] While overseas, Save the Children relief workers often lived and worked alongside, for example, staff of the American Near East Relief organization in 1920s Constantinople, or Oxfam in 1960s western Nigeria, they competed for donations and prestige.[73] In telling the story of Save the Children's interventions, this book also shines a light on the rise of an international aid sector, in which the Fund played a leading (but not unmatched) role.

The extent to which Save the Children can be said to have intervened in the lives of children and their families across the world also varies widely. During the Russian famine in 1921–22 and again during the Nigerian Civil War in 1968–69, the Fund distributed daily rations and medical care to upwards of a million children. During the wartime evacuation of children within Britain, and the postwar evacuations of children from occupied Berlin, every evacuee, to some extent, was impacted by policies that the Fund had designed. From interwar France to 1960s Uganda, some children received over a decade of sponsorship, including correspondence, educational support, and clothing. Others received an occasional bar of soap, infrequent visits from social workers in their villages in Caribbean Islands or rural Czechoslovakia, or a single can of condensed milk as they passed along the well-worn refugee routes. Children spent anything from a single week to entire childhoods in Save the Children–sponsored orphanages, schools, sanatoria, and holiday homes.

Save the Children's relationship with the British public was also an ever-changing one. At moments it was highly visible, with advertisements appearing on billboards, buses, in newspapers, and on television. Between 1919 and 1970, the Fund was lauded in Parliament, satirized in novels, and derided in the right-leaning popular press for forgetting that "charity begins at home." Sustained support for the Fund, requiring a degree of disposable income, was certainly tied to affluence, but humanitarianism was by no means a purely middle-class preoccupation: from 1948, over one million "working men and women" across Britain, from factory workers to typists, contributed through the Penny-a-Week scheme.[74] Throughout much of the interwar and postwar period, the Fund relied on both the financial and practical support of the trade union movement, which raised funds for the children of German miners in the Ruhr valley in the mid-1920s, and organized the hosting of hundreds of children evacuated by the Fund from Spain in the 1930s. At the same time, the Fund drew support from the British establishment and the British media. In 1970, the Fund secured royal patronage from the teenage Princess Anne, whose trip to Kenya with the Fund was broadcast to two million British children on the popular BBC television program *Blue Peter*. If Save the Children was not (as it claimed) a "real national movement," it was certainly a household name with an international footprint.[75]

The history of Save the Children, then, is as vast and heterogeneous as the organization itself. In this telling, I do not provide an exhaustive account of all the Fund's interventions. Rather than writing the history of an institution,

I have tried to write a history of British humanitarian internationalism *through* an institution. In this telling, I focus for the most part on two groups. First, the Fund's leaders: to begin with, a tangle of Quakers, feminists, liberals, and socialists, and then later a coterie of former colonial officials, retired military officers, and a growing number of career humanitarians. The ideas and attitudes of these leading figures are important because of their profound influence in Britain and beyond via ever-deepening ties to successive British governments, widespread press coverage, and mass publicity campaigns.[76] The second group I focus on is a diverse array of humanitarians and social workers, many of whom were not working on behalf of "distant others" but in their own communities. These men and women "on the ground" did not passively implement the visions of their London-based leaders, but often subverted the instructions they received, frequently due to their interactions with the recipients of aid.

Save the Children did not solely provide relief, but also sought to "rehabilitate" or later "develop" the communities it worked in. When communities received material support from Save the Children, they were usually expected to change the way they fed, clothed, and educated their young in line with prevailing British customs. Humanitarian intervention often upended family economies, inverted generational hierarchies, or (at its most extreme) separated children from parents. The imbalance of power between giver and receiver meant that aid was not exchanged for lifestyle change in any form of "transaction"; "choices" were often determined by life-or-death need. Nevertheless, the recipients of aid were never passive. Interventions met resistance, and recipients were alert to the political and economic motivations of their "humanitarian" benefactors. Time and again in the archives, I found children disrupting notions of innocence by giving fascist salutes or going on strike at humanitarian "work schools," and mothers pouring donated milk on the ground or throwing stones at aid workers' white jeeps. It is difficult to get a picture of how widespread such instances of pushback were. Communities in crisis are seldom well-represented in archives, and there were not enough fragments through which to reconstruct local responses to many Save the Children interventions. I have tried, though, to allow those voices to speak in my sources whenever I have heard them.[77] In doing so, I do not want to reproduce the simultaneously sensationalized and inadequate accounts of human suffering used by aid organizations to raise money. Rather, I am interested in moments when communities in crisis, and their self-appointed advocates, shaped or disrupted the humanitarian enterprise.

To an extent, I have been guided by Save the Children's archives, but I have also moved beyond them. The institutional archive of Save the Children is vast and underused. This is because, like the archives of many cautious aid organizations, Save the Children's internal records were not publicly available until recently. The first time I viewed the papers, they were kept in a disused munitions mine in Chippenham, and I carried an emergency oxygen mask with me. Opening those first boxes was a historian's dream. The vast and varied collection held the personal correspondence of founders and staff, national files spanning the globe over a seventy-year period, snapshots of fundraising efforts from across Britain from the 1920s to the 1990s, humanitarian ephemera (badges, money boxes, posters), and an astonishing collection of humanitarian photography, a genre that the Fund itself helped to create in the last century. The official archive is a rich resource for historians not only of humanitarianism, but politics, society, and culture, both in modern Britain and across the world in the twentieth century.

The official archive is an asset to the present-day organization. Obsessed with how they would be remembered by "historians of the future," the early leaders of Save the Children meticulously compiled a catalog of triumphs, imagining themselves the harbingers of a "new world order" to be celebrated and memorialized.[78] To understand more than the founders' and leaders' vision of themselves, I traveled to the archives of Save the Children's collaborators and competitors, international institutions, national governments, and private individuals. Remnants of the Fund's work are scattered as widely as its interventions were, and I have read as many perspectives as possible. The history that follows is not one I could have drawn from institutional archives alone: it is not a celebration, nor an account of advancing operational logistics or technical expertise. It is, instead, a critical history of the emergence of a particular model of British international aid set against a backdrop of a changing world, where conflict and controversy shed light on changing norms.

This, then, is a story of Save the Children told from the outside in. It is a history of modern Britain told from the outside in, too: an account of how an organization adapted ideas about welfare and internationalism to suit national needs and sought to export British norms and values to the wider world. Historians writing in a new vein of scholarship on "Britain and the world" have shown both how British people understood their place in the wider world and how people lived global changes at home in their everyday lives.[79] They have situated their stories within the British Isles and shown that events in "the world" created modern Britain.[80] Accounts of the British outside Britain are usually situated either within or without the British Empire.[81] In this account, I build on (but depart from) existing scholarship, reading interventions within and beyond the British Empire alongside one another. Told across Central and Eastern Europe, Southeast Asia, and Africa, it is a multi-local history of British internationalism.[82]

In six chapters, I explore British humanitarian interventions in eighteen countries over a fifty-year period. I follow a group of actors characterized by their tendency to turn up at moments of crisis around the globe and, often with scant knowledge of local cultures and customs, propose universal solutions to particular problems. They would then just as confidently assert that they had "transformed" the communities they had worked in. Unlike my actors, I have tried to realize (but also expand) the limits of my competence. I have also avoided replicating their claims that British humanitarianism made or transformed the modern world in any straightforward way. There is still much work to be done if we are to fully understand how far Western humanitarian interventions impacted the communities and children on which they were focused. What follows is an account of the overlapping histories of internationalism, imperialism, welfare, and the family, told through the life of an institution and its staff across a long sweep of the twentieth century.

ONE

British Internationalisms and Humanitarianism

IN JANUARY 1919, a group of British feminists breached the Allied powers' ongoing blockade of recently defeated Germany by sending packages full of baby's bottles to German women. When the bottles arrived, they remained empty due to milk shortages in war-ravaged Berlin, but this did not matter to their senders. The purpose of the gift was to make a government-defying gesture of solidarity on the part of the Women's International League for Peace and Freedom, an anti-war campaigning body.[1] Four months later, in April 1919, these women went on to found a new organization, aimed at fusing political protest with humanitarian provision: the Save the Children Fund. Their leader, Dorothy Buxton, believed that publicizing the plight of children suffering in the aftermath of the Great War would draw the British public into a broader protest against the inequalities of the postwar world order. Buxton saw humanitarian action as a gateway to radical politics. It was only political change, not humanitarian aid, that could end suffering in Europe and create peace.[2]

Buxton and her vision of political humanitarianism were soon forgotten. In its first four years, Save the Children moved from being a small propagandizing body administered from Buxton's living room to a professional international charity that drew donations on an unprecedented scale. In 1919 it had been founded to protest against the postwar policies of the Allied powers; by 1922 it was acting as the "accredited agent" of the British government, distributing relief to Russian famine victims. In this period, the Fund gained a new leader, Eglantyne Jebb, who is now popularly remembered as the founder of the worldwide Save the Children movement. Jebb embedded the traditions of early twentieth-century domestic British philanthropy within international aid, while at the same time creating a movement that broke radically with the established methods of overseas aid. Save the Children worked outside Britain and its empire, advocating a new "internationalist" duty to suffering populations in Europe in the aftermath of war. It positioned children not only as the primary victims of war, but as future citizens of a new international order. This chapter analyzes the early transformation of the Save the Children Fund, and how in turn the Fund transformed ideas about humanitarianism and the role of Britain and its empire in the emerging international order.

DOROTHY BUXTON AND THE POLITICS OF HUMANITARIANISM

Dorothy Buxton (née Jebb) and her sister Eglantyne were born into an upperclass family in rural Shropshire in 1881 and 1876, respectively, at the height of the Victorian era. Their mother, Eglantyne Louisa Jebb, was an Irish social reformer who founded the Home Arts and Industries Association as a means to prevent rural poverty through training in traditional crafts.[3] Energetic and independent, Eglantyne Louisa played a leading role in the education of her five daughters, and she made sure that each became involved in philanthropic work from an early age. The Jebb women were often to be found visiting ailing villagers or tutoring local children. This strong charitable ethos was commonplace for aristocratic women in the late nineteenth century. Regarded as an appropriately compassionate, feminine concern, philanthropy was a sphere in which the women of the Victorian era found intellectual stimulation, independence, and citizenship.[4] Charity was also regarded as the duty of the upper classes. It was an important means of preserving a social order in which it was believed that the lower classes felt a sense of gratitude and duty toward their social superiors. It was intended to inculcate the values of industry and self-sufficiency among the poor.[5] This patrician view of charity was held by the patriarch of the Jebb family, the deeply traditional country aristocrat, Arthur Jebb. Arthur Jebb was a member of the local Board of Guardians, an institution created by the 1834 Poor Law, which administered workhouses and gave out small discretionary grants to struggling families, based on their perceived moral character.[6]

Despite the conservatism of their father, the daughters of the Jebb family were also brought up participating in political debate. They were well acquainted with the internationalist thought circulating among elite liberals in Victorian Britain. Liberal internationalism was a broad church with some key shared beliefs: that a peaceful world order should be built on cooperation between autonomous nation-states; that an intergovernmental organization should be founded to arbitrate disputes without the need for war; and that the prosperity of nations could best be attained through a system of free trade.[7] Victorian internationalists included campaigners for the rights of "small nations," such as Eglantyne Louisa, a campaigner for Irish independence.[8] The belief held by many Victorian internationalists that some "civilized" (i.e., white and Christian) nations should be independent did not conflict with their faith in the British imperial project. Author and journalist Richard Jebb, for instance, the cousin of Eglantyne and Dorothy, believed that the British Empire was not only capable of peaceful international cooperation with other nations, but was in fact a model of it.[9] For John Maynard Keynes, a close childhood friend of the family and later Dorothy's tutor at Cambridge, internationalism was primarily an economic question. Mutual security needed to be based on a system of integrated, international trade.[10]

Of all the children of the Jebb family, Dorothy was the most influenced by the internationalist principles she encountered growing up. Born in 1881, she was a "passionate" young woman with "large eyes, a long nose and large opinions." Like her mother, she bristled against the conservatism of her father and (against his wishes) began studying at Newnham College, Cambridge, in 1900. She joined the Political Debating Society and fell in with a set of radicals, idealists, and vegetarians.[11] In 1902, on a "reading holiday" in the Lake District, Dorothy met Charles Roden Buxton. The grandson of antislavery champion Thomas Fowell Buxton, Charles Roden Buxton came from a dynasty of liberal politicians and humanitarian activists. His lifelong friend Virginia Woolf described him as "a rather thin, water-blooded sort of a man," "more at home in the nineteenth-century than the twentieth" and nicknamed him, "the Rodent."[12] Dorothy was won over by his earnestness and left-wing political commitments, and they married in 1904. Dorothy and Charles enjoyed a companionate marriage of equals, referring to each other as "dear comrade." Their home life in Golders Green, where they moved to "live amongst the workers," was very different from their respective upper-class upbringings.[13] They refused to buy new clothes; became vegetarians; and, to the horror of their families, renounced the extravagance of holiday celebrations, feeding their two young children toast and eggs for Christmas dinner. Through their encounters with poverty in North London, and their experience of (self-inflicted) personal austerity, both became increasingly persuaded by socialist principles.[14]

The Buxtons were further radicalized by the First World War. At the start of the conflict, the couple and their two children left Golders Green, moving to a cramped flat in Hampstead in order to allow German refugees to live in their family home.[15] Both Charles and Dorothy devoted themselves to urgent realization of internationalist principles as a path to lasting peace.[16] They became founder members of the Union of Democratic Control (UDC) in 1914. Influenced by the ideas of British economist J. A. Hobson, UDC members believed that the British working classes were being manipulated by a jingoistic press to support a war they had not chosen. They hoped that if the British public realized that their interests were better served by cooperation and peace and were given more democratic control of foreign policy, this would usher in an era of internationalism. The UDC sought to educate the British public about the consequences of war and to lobby Parliament to publicly examine war aims and to end involuntary conscription.[17] In 1915, Charles and Dorothy Buxton became Quakers, and this further deepened their commitment to pacifism. In 1917, Charles left the Liberal Party to become a candidate for the Independent Labour Party, a section of the parliamentary left that remained opposed to the war and supportive of the Russian Revolution in 1917 for its potential to bring about international socialism.[18] For Dorothy Buxton, internationalism remained the polestar within an ever-shifting constellation of personal and political convictions.

In 1915, drawing both on her new Quaker conviction in the "oneness of humanity," and a UDC-informed desire to educate the public about the evils of war, Dorothy Buxton decided that "humanising the enemy in the eyes of the British public" was the fastest means to end the war. She began a weekly feature in the *Cambridge Magazine* called "Notes from the Foreign Press," reproducing accounts of everyday life in the territories of the Allied and Central powers to provide an alternative account of the conflict to that presented by the "jingoistic press."[19] She did this from their small living room, while juggling childcare and a host of other wartime commitments. In 1915, Buxton became a founder member of the Women's International League for Peace and Freedom (WILPF), an international organization of pacifist feminists with branches across Europe.[20] The pacifism of the WILPF was based on the belief of contemporary feminists that women were the natural opponents of war.[21] Though WILPF members were ardent campaigners for women's suffrage, many also felt that women's exclusion from high politics rendered them less contaminated by the warlike ambitions of politicians.[22]

When the war came to an end, Buxton was bitterly disappointed. The German surrender did not mean that German suffering lessened: in fact, it got worse. Keen to secure German admission of their "war guilt" and reparations payments in what would eventually become the Versailles Treaty, the Allies continued their naval blockade, preventing fresh food from entering the country, with broad support from the British public.[23] The widespread nationalism and xenophobia of the war years remained deep seated. The public will, as First Lord of the Admiralty Sir Eric Geddes famously described it, was that Germany should be squeezed "like a lemon until the pips squeak."[24] In 1918 the Representation of the People Act, granting electoral representation to men of all social classes over the age of twenty-one and property-owning women over the age of thirty, did not lead to a more peaceful foreign policy. Rather, the "Khaki election" of 1918, won by Lloyd George's coalition government, seemed to confirm popular support for militarism, patriotism, and anti-German slogans such as "Hang the Kaiser."[25] The democratization of British politics had resulted in a more nationalist political culture.[26]

Buxton believed that any attempt to challenge the conditions of the armistice in Germany had to start with public opinion in Britain. In January 1919 she founded the "Rubber Teats for German Babies Fund." The Fund sent over £2,150 in cash (around £90,000 in today's terms) and milk-bottle tops to mothers in Berlin, where a rubber shortage meant that many were having to feed their children with dangerous, bone-tipped bottles. It drew on a long tradition of feminist solidarity based on shared, maternal concern for the young. Though the Rubber Teats Fund had little impact on conditions in Germany, Buxton judged it a success, as it informed the British public about the plight of former enemies, cultivated friendly relationships with German women, and mounted a practical political critique of the ongoing blockade.[27] For Buxton, charity was a means to a political end.

January 1919 also marked the start of the Paris Peace Conference: a meeting of all the major wartime powers to discuss blueprints for a world after war.[28] Negotiations, which went on until June, resulted in the signing of the Versailles Treaty that contained the infamous German "war guilt" clause, in which Germany accepted responsibility for the war and for reparations payments. Buxton and her set of liberal-left internationalists had desperately hoped to avoid this outcome, seeing it as an extension of the damaging blockade policy that would depress the German economy and thus undermine peace. In the same month as the start of the Peace Conference and the founding of the Rubber Teats Fund, Buxton became a founder member of yet another initiative, the Fight the Famine Council (FFC). Drawing together over a hundred suffragists, trade unionists, Labour politicians, and prominent liberal thinkers, the Council crusaded against the government's use of "hunger as a weapon."[29] The Council organized petitions, public meetings, and public demonstrations, alongside a tide of newspaper editorials and advertisements in major national broadsheets. These publications highlighted the scale of hunger in Germany and the cruelty of the British government in allowing it. One pamphlet argued that, with over eight hundred people per day dying for lack of food, "it would be more humane to turn machine guns onto the people of Germany than to let them starve."[30] It warned the British public that the conditions proposed by the Versailles Treaty were likely to be just as damaging as the ongoing blockade.[31]

The Fight the Famine Council's meetings and publications primarily focused on the "economics of the hunger problem."[32] Hunger weakened workers, the Council argued, and caused economic depression in former enemy states. Animated by the principles of free trade internationalism, the Council argued that for true peace to be realized, all states needed to be prosperous enough to trade with one another.[33] The Council reminded British workers that, even now, their economic fortunes were linked to those of their neighbors, as the price of goods across Europe rose when the Continent lost out on the labor of hungry workers in Austria and Germany.[34] The Fight the Famine Council also warned against the longer-term effects of poverty in Germany. Advancing an argument most famously made by founder member John Maynard Keynes, the FFC warned that economic depression in Central Europe would give rise to political extremism and future war.[35]

As the signing of the Versailles Treaty approached, Buxton feared that the campaigning of the FFC was not having enough impact.[36] Claiming that "something more must be done," Buxton and her fellow WILPF members led a public march to Trafalgar Square on 6 April 1919, distributing leaflets that featured a large photograph of starving Austrian children under the caption, "Our Blockade Caused This."[37] This was not the first time that the suffering of children had been used to generate political capital in the campaign against the blockade. The Fight the Famine Council often focused upon the damage that the blockade caused to children's health, arguing that it would hamper the productivity of the "workers of tomorrow."[38] In contrast, the WILPF drew upon Victorian tropes that represented children as objects of innocence and purity.[39] The leaflets presented ending the blockade as a matter of humanitarian conscience and drew widespread attention after their distributor, veteran suffragette Barbara Ayrton Gould, was arrested in contravention of the War Communications Act for distributing anti-government propaganda.[40]

Images of suffering children had a profound effect on Dorothy Buxton. She had "frequent nightmares from which she could not escape" about child famine victims.[41] At the next public meeting of the FFC, Buxton insisted that the collection should be used for humanitarian provision rather than more pamphlets. This led to the creation of an autonomous body to undertake the "humanitarian function of the council's work," while the Council devoted its attentions to political lobbying against "the causes of food scarcity."[42] The new humanitarian body was the Save the Children Fund or, as its early members began to refer to it, the SCF. The slogan "Save the Children" had been a regular refrain in propaganda produced by the women's suffrage, free trade, and labor movements.[43] All of these campaigns, by drawing on the iconography of the child, situated their causes as compassionate and future facing, in the interests of society's most vulnerable members. "Save the Children" was both a call to action and a nod to many of the campaigns that its early supporters had been involved with before the war, embedding the Fund within a tradition of progressivism and protest. Buxton believed that the work of Save the Children, like that of the Rubber Teats Fund, would help to build permanent peace by fostering relationships between British donors and famine victims.[44] More important in Buxton's view was the role that the Fund would play in "kindling human sympathy" in Britain, drawing people into a political critique of the "unfair peace."[45] Believing that communicating the plight of famine victims was the best means to ensure popular opposition to the blockade and to the conditions of the Paris Peace Treaty, Buxton was adamant that Save the Children would be directed toward "winning [the public] over to a modified point of view rather than merely raising money."[46]

While Buxton hoped to draw people into politics through the SCF, she also realized that she would have to make the Fund's political objectives less overt. She stepped down from her role as secretary and invited her older sister, Eglantyne, to take over.[47] Jebb had prior experience of philanthropic work but lacked Buxton's reputation for political radicalism. In early May, in a bid to catapult Jebb into the limelight, the women of the WILPF organized further leafleting in Trafalgar Square, during which Jebb was predictably arrested, as Gould had been a few weeks prior. The two sisters tried to use the arrest to whip up public indignation, with Jebb penning impassioned accounts of her bravery for London papers.[48]

The Paris Peace Treaty was eventually signed in June 1919. It cemented German war guilt and reparations payments, but also announced the creation of a new international organization, the League of Nations. For Buxton, the League of Nations promised by the Versailles Treaty had fatal flaws that made a fair and lasting peace impossible. The former Central Powers were excluded, Russia was not invited, and ultimately the United States would not join. Buxton believed that the objective of the League was not peace but the "holding down of Germany and her allies."[49] The shortcomings of the League of Nations alienated a generation of early internationalists who had fought for a more equitable world order than the one that came into being in 1919.[50]

After handing leadership of the Fund over to her sister, Buxton made a series of last-ditch attempts to protest the Paris Peace Treaty via the SCF. However, her suggestions, such as the executive council of the Save the Children going on a suffragette-inspired hunger strike to protest German reparations payments, were unpopular with the Fund's new council and especially with her sister.[51] By midsummer 1919, the Fund was receiving a steady stream of donations, and Jebb felt that, rather than focusing on political stunts, it needed to devise a convincing program for helping the malnourished children of Europe.

ORGANIZING CHARITY: EGLANTYNE JEBB AND THE LEGACIES OF BRITISH PHILANTHROPY IN OVERSEAS AID

Save the Children had been founded by Dorothy Buxton as a small protest and propaganda organization; it became Britain's largest international humanitarian organization due to the influence of her older sister, Eglantyne Jebb. Jebb was a serious, often solitary woman with long white hair and a "delicate" constitution. Like Buxton, she had attended university against her father's wishes and, when she left Oxford just after the turn of the twentieth century, she volunteered for the Cambridgeshire branch of a nationwide philanthropic initiative, the Charity Organisation Society (COS). Jebb had initially viewed the poverty she encountered during her COS work as a result of a moral failure and, like her parents, believed that hardship could be overcome through individual effort. Her concern, which mirrored that of the COS more broadly, was to prevent recipients from becoming "dependent" on charity, ensuring that they found work.[52] When claimants did not meet rigid criteria, interventions took on a more punitive character. Those deemed lazy and idle were billeted to workhouses (a system that, though in decline in the early twentieth century, still existed), or left to rely on family.[53]

Jebb's early philanthropic efforts were interrupted by her mother's illnesses. It fell to her, as the family's only unmarried daughter to accompany her mother to a series of European spa retreats.[54] Buxton, who worried constantly about the toll that caring for their mother had on her sister's mental well-being, encouraged her to take up a new humanitarian endeavor in the form of the Macedonian Relief Fund. In 1913, Jebb traveled to Macedonia to work in a hospital for six weeks and became a fundraiser for the Macedonian Relief Fund on her return.[55] Despite her enthusiasm, Jebb's involvement with the Macedonian Relief Fund was short-lived. On her return to Britain, Jebb suffered a series of personal losses. An intense romantic friendship with Margaret Keynes, the sister of John Maynard Keynes, ended when Margaret married in 1913. In 1914, a close friend died, and Jebb claimed to be able to communicate with him in nightly séances. Jebb then became severely unwell with a chronic thyroid condition and spent the years that followed in a small cottage in the Scottish Highlands. When she was eventually well enough to return to London at the end of 1917, she moved into the home of Charles and Dorothy Buxton. The two sisters were close, but Jebb did not become involved with the radical political movements that filled Buxton's days.

Save the Children's early work was informed by Jebb's background in the British social work tradition. Her vision for the SCF was that it should function much like the COS, collecting funds from British donors and distributing them to organizations already at work on the Continent to prevent duplication or inefficiency.[56] By funding and coordinating the efforts of other charities, the SCF could position itself as an "expert" body, even in its early days when an ever-changing cast of volunteers were working from a shabby, one-room office in Holborn.[57] In December, Jebb made the Fund's first professional hire. Russia-born British businessman Lewis Golden, who had fled Russia during the Bolshevik revolution, had also worked as a foreign correspondent for the *Daily Mail* in wartime Europe. Golden became the Fund's secretary, and Jebb took the title of honorary secretary, separating the Fund's administration from its policy-making.

For Jebb, "professionalizing" and depoliticizing the Fund went hand in hand. She worked to diversify the Fund's council—its main decision-making body—comprised in 1919 mostly of Fight the Famine Council and WILPF members, inviting individuals such as conservative feminist Lady Norah Bentinck (who refused, stating that she did not desire the "saving" of German children or "Bolshie" babies).[58] Jebb created the figurehead post of president, which pacifist Liberal Lord Weardale was invited to take up. Though a staunch supporter of internationalism, Weardale was known for his conservative views (such as his opposition to women's suffrage), and his anti-Bolshevism. Rumors then spread among SCF volunteers that Jebb had gone so far as to invite Margaret Lloyd George, wife of the prime minister, to undertake the role of vice president ("as if a murderer were to head the public subscription for a coffin for its victim," one complained to Dorothy).[59] Jebb conflated the bipartisanship of the Fund's growing organizational machine with the nonpolitical nature of its cause: children could draw wide-ranging support because they were a universal cause.

Jebb married the discourse of "nonpolitical" support for aid at home with "impartial" delivery overseas. Drawing on the tradition of the Red Cross movement's providing of aid impartially to both sides in wartime, Jebb described impartial aid in peacetime as help for children "regardless of race, nationality or creed."[60] While the Buxtons' personal preference was for giving to German children, Jebb ensured that the Fund demonstrated impartiality by giving to a host of programs for children of different nationalities across continental Europe. In Save the Children's first year, grants were made to emergency feeding centers in Austria and Germany run by British Quakers; sanatoria in France and Belgium organized by local child welfare organizations; and a traveling British humanitarian, Lady Muriel Paget, in Eastern Europe.[61] Working through existing organizations allowed the Fund to have an international reach from the outset. To publicize its interventions, it founded "the most melancholy magazine in existence," *The Record*, which, like "Notes from the Foreign Press," sought to educate the British public about the living conditions of noncombatants overseas.[62]

In its early years, the greatest proportion of the Fund's resources was channeled into Austria. Giving to Austria—a former enemy power—enabled the Fund to fulfill Buxton's vision of peace building through international friendship. It also satisfied Jebb's desire to avoid controversy, as the new Austrian state was not popularly held "responsible" for the war in the same way that Germany was.[63] Jebb wanted to ensure that donations were spent on the "right sort" of children in Vienna. The challenge in efficient relief work, she explained to the SCF's supporters, was to separate the "ordinarily poor" from those who were "poor only as a result of the war": the hard-working middle classes. It would be more efficient to help this group, Jebb believed, because they would soon be able to "help themselves." Seen by Jebb as bastions of stability and productivity, strong middle-class populations across central and eastern Europe would prevent political unrest and future war. Donations were used almost exclusively for the benefit of children of artisanal and middle-class parents, who would provide the "best return for their investment," as they were likely to take on the stable professions of their parents.[64] In these calculations, the SCF embedded the ethos of the COS—and the connection between receiving relief and performing disciplined labor—into the burgeoning international aid sector.

Adapting a model pioneered by the American Red Cross in wartime France, from January 1920 the Fund began what they termed "financial adoption," an early iteration of the highly popular child sponsorship programs now run by major aid organizations the world over.[65] The schemes functioned in 1920, as they do now, by matching individual (Austrian) children with (British) adults with whom they would correspond and from whom they would receive a monthly allowance for food and clothing.[66] The children were those of doctors, lawyers, government officials, former army officers and traders.[67] In cases where the "wrong type of child" appeared to have been selected, sponsors were encouraged to call upon local relief workers in Austria to "investigate."[68] In this model, the four thousand child sponsors recruited by Save the Children between 1920 and 1922 became, in effect, a vast army of untrained social workers, policing the productivity and morality of far-off families.

In May 1922, for example, a Quaker relief worker coordinating Save the Children "financial adoptions" received a complaint from the sponsor of a young boy named Johann Bernardz, "who had received a nice little communication from her child, but is disappointed, declaring that you have given her a Jew, when she specifically desired otherwise."[69] The relief worker visited Johann's house, in the hope that "some details of the boy's situation might soften her toward him." She reported back that the child's family were "not Jews, but of Polish peasant type and Roman Catholics ... the father's pension now represents under 10 shillings a month. Frau Bernardz tries to earn a little by doing plain sewing, but she finds it difficult to keep herself and the boy aged 8 years, and has been very glad to have the food parcels."[70] In spite of the family's obvious need, however, the relief worker concluded that "the case is not one that particularly appeals to our sympathies and if the adopter would prefer to give her help to another child, I could certainly give her one who would probably interest her more."[71] Johann was dropped from the Fund's list of recipients.

Jebb was inspired by the International Committee of the Red Cross principle of "impartiality": the idea that the only condition of receiving aid should be suffering, and that no group should be either privileged or excluded as recipients. When the Fund removed Johann Bernardz from its list of recipients, it claimed to do so not due to his religion, but his class. Jebb did not view this as contradicting the principle of impartiality, but rather as a means to make aid more efficient, and thus save more children.[72] Concentrating resources on middle-class children seemed to her the perfect balance of practical utilitarianism with "impartiality."[73] Not all of the Fund's partners agreed. Dr. Macfie, head teacher of a school in Vienna from which the Fund selected recipients of child sponsorship, pointed out the hypocrisy of an organization that, while it claimed that "relief should be given without bias according to religion, politics or creed," focused its efforts almost exclusively on the middle class.[74] One of the Fund's early council members, Frank Hodges, the general secretary of the Miners' Federation of Great Britain, was furious that the children of Austrian workers were being overlooked by the Fund, which had received £10,000 from his union, as well as financial support from the Trades Union Congress. Hodges resigned from the Fund's council.[75]

The fund's exclusive focus on middle-class children in Vienna was not replicated in its work elsewhere. Working in partnership with other agencies rather than training and sending its own operatives meant that work carried out under the "Save the Children" banner had a different character in every locale. The diversity of the Fund's council, which by 1920 incorporated individuals such as socialist feminist Ethel Snowden and Conservative Foreign Secretary Lord Curzon, also meant that a host of often contradictory ideas about relief work coexisted at its highest level. For example, while Buxton shared Jebb's concern about the most efficient ways to distribute relief, her vision of internationalism rested upon the restoration of international trade, which depended on the labor of the working classes. Buxton was particularly concerned about the effect of malnutrition in later life, and she believed that feeding working-class children was more important than educating their middle-class counterparts.[76]

Many sections of the left in Britain continued to oppose the conditions of postwar peace even after the Treaty of Versailles had been signed. They especially opposed reparations payments, which depressed living standards in Germany into the 1920s, even as conditions broadly improved throughout the rest of Europe.[77] When the Ruhr district was invaded by French and Belgian armies in 1923 in order to seize the coal owed to them under the

FIGURE 1. Cartoon drawn for Save the Children Fund by David Lowe of *The Star* (a left-leaning evening newspaper). *The Record of the Save the Children Fund*, December 1920.

Versailles Treaty, leading lights of the British left flocked to the Save to Children Fund to express their concern for the children of unemployed German miners. A Save the Children subcommittee headed by Lady Cynthia Mosley (the first wife of the politician Oswald Mosley, then in his pre-fascist, socialist days) sought donations to prevent the "physical and moral degeneration" of the children of the Ruhr, whose malnutrition, they argued, would retard trade with Germany for years to come.[78] With limited funds available due to ongoing public reluctance to give to the children of "former enemies," Cynthia Mosley, like Jebb, argued that relief should be directed selectively and efficiently at the children most likely to contribute to German reconstruction in adulthood. For Mosley, it was children's health that determined their deservingness. Influenced by eugenic ideas prevalent in the left at the time, she cautioned that they should not be "making special provision for 'cripples' or 'halfwits.'"[79] Mosely, like many early members of the Fund, understood internationalism as a biopolitical project: it required strong bodies and minds. In the aftermath of the First World War, Save the Children exported not just the innovations of British philanthropy but also its limitations and exclusions.

BUILDING AN INTERNATIONAL RELIEF MOVEMENT: SAVE THE CHILDREN IN GENEVA

For Jebb, internationalism was a project of feeling. She believed peace would be built upon the friendships forged between people from across Europe, and especially the bonds of friendship forged between humanitarians from across the world who were, in turn, guiding the general public toward greater sympathy for people of different nationalities. To promote affective ties between aid workers, as well as to coordinate their work, Jebb founded the Save the Children International Union (SCIU), an umbrella body that drew together the efforts of child welfare societies from across Europe. Jebb chose Geneva as the home for the International Union because of its historic connections to humanitarianism, after the foundation of the International Committee of the Red Cross (ICRC) there in 1863, and because of its new role as the home for the newly established League of Nations.[80] Through ICRC vice president Frédéric Ferrière, a regular contributor to "Notes from the Foreign Press" during the war, Jebb was introduced to his niece, Suzanne Ferrière, president of a newly-formed Swiss child welfare organization, the Comité International de Secours aux Enfants. They became lifelong friends. The leaders of the ICRC were supportive of an attempt to create a Geneva-based child welfare movement, as part of their ongoing battle for influence against the American humanitarian movement. In 1919, the American League of Red Cross Societies had been founded, and it claimed that it would bring the spirit of the Red Cross movement into constructive peacetime work. It did so in part through the foundation of an international network of child welfare and education societies. Save the Children was imagined by the Geneva-based ICRC as a European competitor that would divert support away from American-led aid.[81] The endorsement of the ICRC was crucial to Jebb, who regarded the organization as the origin of the humanitarian ideals that Save the Children sought to embody: the ICRC was intended to be independent of political influence, neutral in war, and impartial in the delivery of relief.

Alongside the Swiss Comité, Jebb and Buxton recruited child welfare societies from across Europe and the British Empire to join the International Union, most often calling upon old friends from the Women's International League (WILPF). Like Buxton, many WILPF members had founded child welfare organizations in the aftermath of the war. Many of these were domestically focused, and those that provided international relief tended to be much more narrowly focused than the SCF. The French SCIU affiliate, for example, concentrated on a small collection of child sponsorships for German former enemy children as an act of postwar peace-building. Like the early SCF, the humanitarian work of WILPF women across Europe was as much about its symbolic function as the practical help it provided. It promoted conciliation between women where, it was felt, male diplomacy was failing.[82] Through child welfare organizations, the women of the WILPF were claiming their space in international politics through maternalism, in the tradition of national "votes for women" campaigns."[83] Buxton invited radical socialist and WILPF member Gabrielle Duchêne to represent France; WILPF member Anna-Lenah Angstrom represented the Swedish child welfare society Rädda Barnen, and WILPF member Elizabeth Rotton secured the affiliation of German child welfare society Vereinigung für Kinderhilfe.[84] The membership of Vereinigung für Kinderhilfe was especially important to both sisters, showing that, unlike the League of Nations, the SCIU embodied "genuine reconciliation" by including former enemies. Buxton and Jebb hoped that the work of the SCIU might serve as an example to statesmen at the League of Nations of how much more could be possible through "true" international collaboration.[85]

The success of the Save the Children International Union was secured in December 1919, before it had been formally launched, when Eglantyne Jebb was invited to an audience with Pope Benedict XV. Jebb impressed the pope, who issued the first ever papal encyclical to name a non-Catholic organization as the beneficiary of donations from Catholic churches worldwide. This raised over £350,000 for the Save the Children International Union in

Geneva.[86] William Mackenzie, a British Catholic and crime fiction writer, was appointed as professional secretary to manage this central SCIU fund and act as the pope's representative on the SCIU Council.[87] The international Save the Children movement was ecumenical, even multifaith, rather than secular. In Britain, alongside drawing on Catholic supporters, the SCF was also close to the Jewish community, securing an endorsement from the chief rabbi in 1920. Both sisters had moved away from their Anglican upbringing, embracing spiritualism (Jebb) and Quakerism (Buxton). Other delegates to the International Union from elsewhere in Europe were a mixture of Catholics, Quakers, atheists, and Protestant nonconformists. The Save the Children movement's ecumenical aid, which would transition into the secular humanitarianism of the mid-twentieth century, made it possible for it to adapt and benefit from the traditions of religious philanthropy while not being constrained by it.

Member societies of the SCIU were required to pay into the central SCIU fund varying amounts each month according to the relative resources of each society and the extent of postwar poverty in their country. Even the very poorest member societies (such as the Latvian affiliate of SCIU) had to give a minimum contribution of 5 percent of their income. Jebb claimed this was to "teach internationalist spirit" to "young European nations."[88] These nations were also meant to receive "training" from the British Fund in the social work tradition. Seeking to export British welfare norms and standards to existing organizations, Save the Children often failed to recognize that these groups had expertise and local knowledge that the Fund itself lacked. The Council of the International Union was dominated by British delegates, and while national societies donated funds into a shared pot, when it came to distribution, funds were most often sent to British aid organizations.[89] In Germany, for example, donations from across Europe were channeled through the SCIU to British Quaker organizations, whose methods Jebb believed were superior.[90] The International Union may have built fellowship between humanitarians across Europe, but it also diverted internationally gathered funds away from local organizations and into British-led aid. While the SCIU focused on international cooperation (in the form of sharing ideas and practices) between mostly domestically operating child welfare organizations, international *action* remained the preserve of Britain.

Despite British dominance of the international Save the Children movement, and the high cost of membership, national societies from across Europe vied to become SCIU members.[91] From the outset, Jebb sought to extend membership beyond Europe to the British Empire.[92] Australian peace campaigner Celia John, who had met Buxton and Jebb on a visit to London in the summer of 1919, founded the first "colonial" chapter of Save the Children. Canada, Australia, and South Africa followed in 1920. The existence of these dominion societies strengthened the position of the British Fund within the International Union. In the SCIU the "British Empire" voted together on key decisions. Donations from the British dominions to the SCIU were also counted as "British." Jebb, like many international thinkers at the time, imagined imperial unity as an "example" of international collaboration that the rest of the world could learn from and aspire to.[93] Drawing on the practices of the Charity Organisation Society, the Women's International League, the League of Nations, and the International Committee of the Red Cross, the SCIU represented an elite idea of internationalism. It sought to foster affective bonds among internationally mobile elites, entrench British leadership, evangelize to "less advanced" nations about child welfare standards and the importance of international collaboration, and place children at the center of a new world order, with (elite) women as their protectors.[94]

BUILDING AN INTERNATIONAL
RELIEF MOVEMENT IN RUSSIA

In Geneva, Jebb had tried to create a blueprint for an international humanitarian movement. Over three thousand miles east, in Russia, she had the opportunity to realize her vision. Rumors of an impending famine in Russia had been circulating since the winter of 1920. After the Bolshevik revolution in October 1917, a civil war raged between the anti-Bolshevik White Army and the Bolshevik Red Army until October 1922. Peasant grain was regularly requisitioned by both sides, leading to widespread food shortages, and in many areas crops had failed.[95] The Bolshevik government was reluctant to allow foreign aid, fearing it would be used to undermine their precarious rule. Buxton had been keeping abreast of developments in Russia via the Hands Off Russia Committee, an organization founded to lobby against British support for the White Army, and was eager that Save the Children should help Russian hunger victims.[96] In the spring of 1920, Charles Roden Buxton and Philip Snowden (husband of Ethel Snowden, a founding member of the Save the Children council) had visited Russia as representatives of the Independent Labour Party, spending two months in a peasant commune near Moscow to experience "live socialism" and meet Soviet officials.[97] It was through these connections that Save the Children became one of the few British organizations granted access to Russia by the Bolshevik government when it appealed for international aid in July 1921.[98]

While the socialist sympathies of some leading Fund members cleared the Fund's path into Russia, once the campaign began, Jebb resolved that political connections must be kept "strictly out of the public eye."[99] Aid to Russian famine victims was a controversial cause. Antisocialist sentiment in Britain ran high, and editorials in right-wing tabloids warned Britons that famine relief was a "revolutionary not humanitarian matter"—it would ultimately help the Bolshevik state to keep its grip on Russia.[100] Some would-be donors feared that aid for Russia was being funneled directly to the Red Army by left-wing aid workers.[101] Any hint that the Fund might be supportive of Russian socialism, and might be using famine relief as an expression of that support, would undermine the Fund's carefully curated "nonpolitical" image, and the entire Russian famine relief effort. Jebb countered any accusation or speculation about the Fund's "pro-Bolshevik" leanings in the strongest possible terms: humanitarianism, she insisted, was separate from or, indeed, "above," politics.[102]

Dorothy Buxton did not agree with Jebb's "nonpolitical" approach to Russian famine relief, believing that solutions to the famine were political and economic. Rather than aid, Buxton argued, Russia should be granted trade credits that would allow the Soviet government to buy grain from neighboring European states. This would draw Russia into the international economy—a precursor to peace. Buxton also believed that the British working class stood to gain. In the five years prior to the First World War, Britain had received ten million tons of grain from Russia.[103] Speaking on the famine at Quaker meetings, Labour Party branches, and women's groups, she argued that "feeding a Russian child today guarantees a cheap loaf tomorrow."[104] In September 1921, when the British government refused to grant trade credits to the Bolshevik regime, Buxton denounced the decision as an attempt to "starve [the Russians] into submission."[105] She feared that the British policy showed that the "internationalist spirit" of the immediate postwar era was faltering.[106] Exhausted and disillusioned, Buxton had a nervous breakdown in 1922 and withdrew from the day-to-day running of Save the Children.[107]

Although she was also concerned about the dissipation of a "great internationalist moment," Jebb continued to hope that humanitarian internationalism would prevail despite the failings of national governments. For

Jebb, the Russian famine marked the starting point of "the greatest international relief movement the world has yet seen."[108] Between September 1921 and April 1923 Save the Children opened almost a thousand feeding centers across Russia's Saratov Province.[109] Ten-year-old Boris Chernigov was one of two hundred fifty thousand children who received daily meals from Save the Children during this period. Boris's meal of bread and condensed milk was exactly 650 calories: the minimum ration that a new cadre of nutritional scientists had determined would sustain a malnourished child.[110] Boris claimed his meal by presenting his personalized ration card to a Russian supervisor, who was answerable to the SCF's Russian operative, Lawrence Webster, for all rations distributed down to the last ounce. A former soldier and fluent Russian speaker with a "keen business sense," Webster typified an emerging class of professional relief workers.[111] He fit comfortably into an emerging humanitarian masculinity, where guns were essential equipment and sympathy was considered an unnecessary distraction from efficiency.[112] By the time Boris's ration reached him, it had traveled in a sealed train across the Russian tundra stored under the guard of watchmen with orders to shoot thieves.[113] Boris was not allowed to take his meal outside the feeding center, in case he shared it with his family or was accosted by starving members of his community. Instead, Boris ate his 650 calories under a Union Jack, portraits of the British King and Queen, and a large plaque proclaiming in Russian that St. Christopher's Methodist Church in Grimsby had supplied the donations. Boris's mother, who had sold her winter coat and begged on the streets to feed her children, apparently told a Save the Children representative that even though she did not know where England was, it "must be a very good country to send us food."[114] Jebb's vision was being realized: Russian peasants and the British public were being drawn into relationship via a humanitarian response of unprecedented scale, and these relationships were made possible by advances in science, international travel, and the rapidly professionalizing aid sector.

In addition to flying Union Jacks, Save the Children flew the flags of France, Belgium, Norway, Sweden, Canada, and New Zealand: countries whose affiliates of the Save the Children International Union had contributed funds to the relief effort.[115] Many SCIU affiliates were reluctant to send their own operatives into Russia, where mortality rates for relief workers were high (causes of death included typhus, typhoid, and suicide).[116] Others had been unable to secure access. Jebb believed it was important to display the national banners of many countries above feeding centers in Saratov, both

FIGURE 2. A kitchen funded by Rädda Barnen, the Swedish branch of the Save the Children Fund in Saratov, 1921. Save the Children Photo Collection, Save the Children Archives, Birmingham, UK.

for the esteem of donor countries (whom she did not want to feel "swallowed up by the wolf of international relief") and so that the Russian people could see the "strength of international effort on their behalf."[117] The famine was an opportunity to showcase international collaboration and the spirit of the Save the Children movement.

The "patchwork of national banners" that hung above Save the Children's thousand feeding centers was "hemmed on every side" by American flags. Stars and stripes were displayed in American Relief Administration (ARA) feeding centers west of Saratov across the River Volga, and east of Saratov across the Ural mountains.[118] In the aftermath of the First World War, the resources and reach of American humanitarian organizations drastically outstripped those of their European counterparts. The American Red Cross (ARC) had ended the First World War with a surplus of $100 million, which was spent on postwar reconstruction in Europe. In February 1919, the congressionally funded ARA was founded to distribute a further $100 million in food aid to Europe. A further grant of $20 million was given to the ARA for distribution in Russia between 1921 and 1923. These American humanitarian organizations sought to civilize and stabilize Europe's war-torn and famine-stricken nations to ensure ongoing peace and international security. Both the

ARA and ARC believed that meeting people's material needs would lessen the appeal of communism across Europe.[119]

The SCF, the SCIU, and the ICRC regarded the American presence in Europe as a threat to the international relief movement. The United States had entered the war late and had lost little in terms of men and money compared to Britain and France. Although President Woodrow Wilson had been a key architect of the League of Nations and laid out a vision of postwar "Wilsonian" internationalism that the League embodied, the United States did not join the League, undermining its legitimacy. Nevertheless, the Americans were winning the hearts and minds of Europeans through humanitarian intervention, which was resented by many within the European humanitarian community.[120] Jebb viewed American aid as inherently "nationalist," whereas European aid, to her mind, had sprung from the ICRC tradition of impartiality and international collaboration.[121] The Russian famine was not just a site where humanitarian internationalism was realized, but where its meanings—and its leadership—were contested.

During the Russian famine, Jebb also fought to protect her vision of international relief from the encroachment of other British aid organizations. Save the Children was not only considered to be a "left-wing" organization: with its pacifist origins and close ties to continental relief organizations, it was also cast as "unpatriotic" by other British relief organizations.[122] In the middle of 1920 a number of public figures who considered themselves to be of "more conservative opinion" than the leaders of the SCF inaugurated a new charity, the Imperial War Relief Fund.[123] This new fund would, like the SCF, give to victims of hunger and disease in war-torn Europe. Unlike the SCF, it would collaborate only with aid organizations from the British dominions. Its leaders hoped that by doing so, it would show that the British Empire could compete with the scale of American relief and was not reliant on European collaboration. Jebb, who viewed the role of the British as ensuring both European and imperial collaboration, saw this as another challenge to her dream of a "truly international" aid movement. It was, ironically, Save the Children's connections to the Soviet government that canceled the threat of British organizations criticizing their left-wing politics. The Imperial War Relief Fund was, unlike Save the Children, unable to secure visas for its operatives to enter Russia, and all donations it received for Russian famine relief were ultimately transferred to the SCF.[124] Given the scale of American aid, Britain did not emerge as the leader of the international relief movement during the Russian famine. Save the Children, however, did emerge as the leader of the British relief movement.

"BOLSHEVIK BABIES" AND THE ANTI-POLITICS OF INTERNATIONAL AID

Raising funds for Russian famine relief was Save the Children's most challenging task to date. Would-be donors were put off by the thought of "Bolshevik babies" who "might rise up and kill us thirty years hence."[125] Seeking to overcome these fears, Save the Children struck upon a winning fundraising formula that bolstered the Fund's finances and shaped the way that international aid was understood and operated in the century to come. Before the famine, SCF leaders had feared that the initial postwar sympathy for Europe was "drying up" as the average monthly donations the Fund received fell from £47,000 in September 1920 to £21,000 in March 1921. But between August 1921 and April 1923, £1.3 million was donated to the SCF's famine appeal: an average of £65,000 each month. Four hundred fifty SCF local branches were founded during the upsurge in support caused by the Russian famine appeal, ensuring the long-term support of first-time donors. Prior to the Russian famine the downturn in donations had made Jebb question whether Save the Children would outlast the initial phase of postwar reconstruction. By the end of the famine appeal in 1923, the Fund could plausibly claim to be, in Jebb's words, "a real national movement."[126]

The SCF Council attributed this surge of donations to new fundraising methods.[127] This shift in the Fund's fortunes was largely down to another of the SCF's early professional hires, its business-minded press secretary Edward Fuller. Fuller—the architect of the Fund's Russian famine appeals—capitalized on the increasing availability of film and photography to "show" the "reality" of suffering. Captions alongside images read: "Having now even seen [the Russians] suffering so very clearly, how would we not help?"[128] Placing his faith in the connection between witnessing pain, and responding to it, Fuller devoted 17 percent of Save the Children's income to its "propaganda" department, well beyond the spending of other British relief bodies at the time. He took out full-page spreads in national newspapers and had famine appeals printed on the side of London buses and in underground stations. He commissioned documentary maker George Mewes to travel to Russia

FIGURE 3. George Mewes in Saratov, filming his Russian famine film, 1921. Like Suzanne Ferrière on her fact-finding mission to Moscow, he is surrounded by interested children hoping to be included in his filming. "Filming the Famine," *The Record of the Save the Children Fund*, January 1921.

to make a film of the famine, which was then shown in cinemas, churches, and school halls across the country. (The silent film was accompanied by a macabre script with lines such as "bring out the bodies" to be called out by a fundraiser from behind the screen.)[129]

Fuller believed that seeing the "truth" of the famine would produce an automatic instinct to help. He elided the extent to which the Fund editorialized the images of the famine's "truth." The Fund paid journalists to send them "typical" famine images, but humanitarians imagined famine images in a particular way—featuring young children, especially girls, at a late stage of hunger. They sifted through the images they received to find the most "heartrending" examples.[130] When Save the Children deployed its own relief workers with cameras, the extent of their composition of images became even more clear. When Swiss SCIU delegate Suzanne Ferrière visited Russia in the spring of 1922, she wandered famine-affected areas for hours searching for a so-called "typical" victim, refusing the requests of children who begged to have their photos taken but were not "thin enough."[131] When the "right" kind of hunger victim was located, camera-wielding humanitarians were ruthless in their posing of the "correct" kind of photo: a child isolated from its parents and wearing as little as possible to show the full extent of its hunger.[132] Children were stripped naked and posed for photographs outdoors, where the lighting was better, despite the freezing conditions.[133]

Posing and editing famine images was as much about exclusion as inclusion. Right down to clothing, famine photography removed all context from suffering children that might have identified them as Russian peasants (or indeed young Soviet citizens). Landscape was usually cropped, though sometimes snow—to emphasize the cold that hungry children faced—was shown. Pictures of children were captioned with text such as: "The individual child is quite apart from nationalism, and we do not ask him what his parents' views are on the political or economic questions of the day."[134] Donors were assured that child relief was "a humanitarian matter which is far removed from politics."[135]

Children in Russian famine appeals were rarely depicted with their parents or other adult community members. This was only partially a new development. Even before the famine, Save the Children appeals had never featured fathers: they were the former enemy soldiers that the Fund was asking its donors to forget in favor of the nonpolitical, extra-national child. Save the Children's earliest appeals had, however, focused on the plight of mothers. Newspaper line drawings often depicted Madonna-like figures, with covered heads cradling their emaciated children. These images were intended to provoke British parents to imagine what they would feel if they could not feed their own young. This technique had been prominent in prior British humanitarian campaigns dating back to the abolition movement in the late eighteenth century.[136] It had been used, for example, by philanthropist Emily Hobhouse (who in 1920 was working for Save the Children in Liepzig) in her campaign against British concentration camps during the Boer War. In these campaigns, the suffering of children was a vector through which identification with an adult, their mother, was forged. This identification between adults, particularly women, around the suffering of children was the essence of the internationalist maternalism that had underpinned the Women's International League and Save the Children's predecessor, the Rubber Teats for German Babies Fund.

The Russian famine marked the culmination of a subtle but significant shift away from humanitarian identification with mothers in favor of children. Russian children were described routinely as "orphans," and appeals focused disproportionally on runaway or abandoned children. Seeing children depicted alone, donors were asked to imaginatively *become* Russian children's parents (though few were, in fact, actually parentless). This insistence of the solitary status of children, in turn, impacted the way relief was given, as Save the Children ensured the donating public that *only* the young would benefit from supplies, which they ate while separated from family members in special kitchens. Any individual or group that raised over £100 in donations to the SCF appeal was given its own "named kitchen," and children would eat under a banner declaring the names of their benefactors. They were told that they could know the "exact names and addresses" of the children that they, specifically, had fed.[137] These structures, of course, made the orphaning or abandonment of children more likely, as parents sent children vast distances from their homes to receive relief, and themselves succumbed to hunger as disease while their young were fed. The Fund also launched a version of the "child adoption" scheme they had piloted in Austria: if organizations or individuals could not raise the £100 needed for their own kitchen, they were paired with a Russian "orphan" with whom they could "correspond and connect." For one school class in Manchester, this was ten-year-old Olga, who wrote to thank them for their "good food and attention."[138] During the Russian famine, hungry children became orphans—first in the humanitarian imagination and then practically, as children departed their families to travel to kitchens where only the young could be fed.[139]

Children were ideal humanitarian victims, not just because of their removal from the political contexts of crises but also because of the special vulnerability of their bodies. Images of child hunger were especially powerful at a moment when new scientific knowledge had established and popularized understandings of childhood malnutrition. In Britain, at the turn of the century, the physical condition of recruits to fight in the Boer War had revealed mass malnutrition among the working class, and a raft of welfare reforms in schools and maternity care had aimed to adequately nourish young children—the imperial citizens and soldiers of the future. Research into the lifelong effects of malnutrition on the young continued apace during and after the First World War, and the popularization of its findings—that infant hunger produced lifelong poor health—made the figure of the malnourished child especially abhorrent to viewing publics. Margaret Kelleher argued that, in the nineteenth century, famine was feminized: the figure of the mother, in particular, was used to convey the far-reaching effects of famine on the entire national body.[140] In the twentieth century, portrayals of famine were infantilized. Children's hungry bodies became emblematic of the long-lasting danger of famines for international society. In the early 1920s—a moment of epidemics and refugee crises—it was not just the child, but the hungry, orphaned child that emerged as the ideal humanitarian subject.

The image of the hungry, orphaned child was embedded at the heart of Save the Children. The Fund's emblem, selected by Jebb in 1920, was an image of a swaddled baby, created by Renaissance artist Andrea della Robbia to decorate a foundling hospital in fifteenth-century Florence. The image connected the child-saving movement of the early twentieth century with its historic organs: the foundling hospital had been a symbol of humanist compassion for children in early modern Europe. The hospital cared for orphaned or abandoned babies, referred to as "innocents," who were trained in trades, or as wives and nuns, to become useful future citizens.[141] With its arms outstretched in a crucifix position, and swaddling bands wrapped up to its waist, the "bambino" (as Save the Children referred to it) was Christ-like, calling on donors to "do unto" Europe's hungry as if they were the Christ Child. Save the Children adapted the image from della Robbia's original rendering, making the child thinner and appearing on the brink of death: ghostly rather than ethereal. In a testament both to the influence of Save the Children, and to the imaginative pull of the orphaned child in the early-twentieth century, organizations across the world began to use the della Robbia bambino emblem. Between 1920 and 1940 it was adopted not only by the member societies of the SCIU, but the American Association of Pediatrics, and the Brussels-based International Office of Child Protection.[142] Over the next five decades, the bambino would become plumper again and have its feet unbound as child-rearing guidelines changed. In the early twentieth century the bambino became as recognizable as the iconic Red Cross. The bambino symbolized a universal child, owed care by all.[143]

The child-saving impulse after the First World War was as much an American as a European phenomenon. The American Near East Relief Fund, and the American-dominated League of Red Cross Societies, (founded in 1915 and 1919 respectively) also urged special parental compassion for children on the part of the American public. Like Save the Children, these organizations used adoption metaphors, casting the United States as a "father" of European "orphans."[144] Save the Children was often irritated when other organizations focused their appeals on children, imagining that they had a monopoly on child-centered relief. It was a lucrative monopoly to which to aspire. Children were, according to the Fund's press secretary, a "good product," and child relief

FIGURE 4. Russian famine victims receiving their daily ration under the bambino logo. From its earliest days, Save the Children was aware of the importance of branding in fundraising shots. This marketing image was widely circulated. "Filming the Famine," *The Record of the Save the Children Fund*, January 1921.

"sold."[145] Throughout the course of the Russian famine, the Fund honed its "marketing" of child hunger, zeroing in on powerful motifs—the child alone, orphaned, starving, and naked. Working with the ICRC, Save the Children shared curated famine images, as well as how-to guides describing the best way to appeal to different sections of the general public, with child welfare societies across Europe and the British Empire.[146] By doing so, it standardized depictions of human suffering in ways that defined a genre of humanitarian film and photography for a century to come.[147]

Save the Children's conscious "marketing" efforts were described in terms of "capturing" compassion, rather than creating it. The Fund's president, Lord Weardale, saw the decision to focus solely on children as a reluctant response to the fact that existing public sympathy was for the young.[148] What he and his colleagues failed to acknowledge (perhaps even to themselves) was that their actions were not only capturing but also limiting public sympathy.[149] Fixing "the innocent child" as the humanitarian cause of the day, the Fund and its supporters tacitly endorsed the idea that European adults—perhaps former enemies, perhaps Communist, perhaps "idle" or unemployed—were beyond sympathy. In 1918, the Rubber Teats Fund had sought to capitalize on people's sympathy for hungry children in order to draw them into a wider critique of the postwar suffering of all ages. In Russia, humanitarianism began, and ended, with the starving child.

HUMANITARIAN INTERNATIONALISM
AND THE BRITISH PUBLIC

Save the Children was both an architect and a beneficiary of growing internationalist sentiment in Britain and the changing of public and parliamentary attitudes to overseas aid. After initial victory celebrations in 1918, as the human and economic costs of the war hit home, there was a widespread disavowal of the militaristic and "pugnacious nationalism" felt to have caused the conflict.[150] Virtues such as peacefulness and fairness were extolled as quintessentially British.[151] At a moment when the meaning of Britishness was being softened and feminized, Britain's global power was presented in terms of concern for humanity, rather than conquest and domination.[152] Britain's participation in "internationalism," such as its leading role in the League of Nations, was presented by politicians and the press as a natural extension of the collaborative and compassionate virtues that had animated the British Empire.[153] International collaboration was not a threat to, but an expansion of, British power.[154]

In this climate, a host of popular internationalist institutions sprang up, and organizations such as schools, churches, and trade unions took a new interest in international affairs. Groups such as Rotary International and Toc H sought to build international friendship through voluntary service, organizing foreign exchanges and visits overseas.[155] The League of Nations Union, a mass membership internationalist lobby, was founded in 1918 to educate and inform the British people about internationalism, and then to organize popular support for the League of Nations.[156] These groups promoted internationalism as a broad, unifying creed, removed from party politics. The League of Nations Union, in particular, had been derided by Dorothy Buxton as an organization that celebrated, rather than challenged, the "unjust" international order created by the Versailles Treaty. Yet the nonpartisan, popular internationalism of groups such as the LNU played an important part in ensuring the success of the Save the Children Fund.[157] They served to defang internationalism. They made it a cause of educated, genteel middle classes, rather than fringe socialists and pacifists, and removed it from the sphere of partisan politics (viewed as "degraded" by the mass enfranchisement of men and some women after 1918).

While internationalist lobbies became a feature of emerging middle-class sociability, humanitarian internationalism had a much broader, cross-class appeal. Save the Children's 450 local branches, while they have left little behind in terms of records, seem to have shared members and meeting places with typically working-class trade unions and nonconformist churches. Donations to the famine appeal were often made collectively, by factory workers, miners, shop girls, working-class-friendly societies and local trade union branches. Buxton had always believed that the most important constituency to win over to the internationalist cause was the working class: they stood to gain the most from economic cooperation, or lose the most if they were sent to the front lines of a war. For her, Save the Children was an attempt to harness working-class radicalism and democratize elite internationalism. Through the Labour Party and the trade union movement, the Fund sought to tap into the "progressive enthusiasm" and "internationalist outlook" of the working class, whom they viewed as their natural supporters.[158]

Save the Children's supporter base grew exponentially during the Russian famine appeal. Throughout 1921 and 1922, the *Guardian* and *Observer* launched national appeals, while local newspapers including the *Yorkshire Post* and the *Lancashire Evening News* organized separate collections.[159] Even when Save the Children was not mentioned as a direct beneficiary, donations invariably ended up in the Fund's hands since—aside from a small Quaker initiative—it was the only British organization distributing aid in Russia.[160] The total donations to the Fund—£55 million in today's terms—outstripped both the Biafra famine appeal of the late 1960s and Band Aid in the early 1980s. The Russian famine appeal was Britain's first and largest international humanitarian effort.[161]

Against the backdrop of growing public support for international aid, In March 1922, a governmental grant in aid to the famine-stricken regions was debated in Parliament. Hotly contested but eventually approved, this was the first instance of overseas disaster aid granted by the British government outside the British Empire. The grant was supported by Liberal and Labour members of the House of Commons and in the House of Lords, as well as a handful of internationalist Conservatives. Like Buxton, Labour Party members saw internationalism as a working-class tradition. They argued that mass public support for famine relief had been clearly expressed through the widespread support of charitable appeals, and that it was the duty of the government to reflect the will of the people. Liberals were less concerned that donations to charitable appeals necessarily reflected the will of the entirety of the British public but argued that the government had a role in guiding public sentiment: it should grant aid even if the majority of the people did not will it, leading the British public toward higher principles. For Liberal Party members, international aid not only demonstrated the civilization of the British people but could also play a part in civilizing British political life.[162]

With the support of both Liberal and Labour members of Parliament, the sum of £100,000 proposed by Lloyd George was granted for famine relief. Labour's calls for the grant to be increased to/by half a million pounds were not put to a vote, after vocal dissent from members of the Conservative Party. The government grant consisted mostly of gifts in kind that were useless to famine victims: leftover army supplies from the First World War such as old tins of bully beef and half a ton of out-of-date lime juice.[163] The granting of state aid was symbolic, expressing the belief that the public mood had shifted in favor of overseas aid. For Save the Children, the government grant was also a critical moment, as the Fund became "the government's accredited agent in relief distribution in Russia."[164]

While the public and political mood was ever more favorable to the work of the Save the Children Fund, support for overseas aid was far from universal. With postwar poverty and unemployment at its peak in Britain, and reconstruction to the tune of £12.5 million already promised to war-torn European states at the Paris Peace Conference, politicians and press to the right of the political spectrum argued that "charity begins at home."[165] When they took the controversial decision to send relief to Russia, members of Save the Children's council anticipated that their work would be subject to "attacks from every side."[166] Attacks came in the form of a campaign waged against the Fund in the *Daily Express*, which from November 1921 published a series of articles claiming that the Fund's description of conditions in Russia was melodramatic and inaccurate. *Express* editorials argued that even if the famine was as bad as Save the Children said, the Fund was ignoring the plight of the poor children in Britain. The *Express* urged its readers to donate to the impoverished children of unemployed Cornish miners, who should have "the first claim upon the public concern."[167] Jebb and Edward Fuller relished the "cheap publicity," and the opportunity to expand upon their vision of international duty to an unconverted audience.[168] Jebb wrote repeatedly to the editor of the *Express*, urging that it was "a matter of national pride . . . to carry British standards of child welfare into foreign lands."[169] Despite its "present hardship," Britain, she argued, could not deny its long-standing "duty to those more desperate than ourselves."[170] Fuller meanwhile published his own series of editorials in the Fund's monthly magazine, *The Record*, righteously defending the Fund against the predictable critiques that the SCF was pro-Bolshevik, that the famine was exaggerated, and that the British were not responsible for Russian children.[171]

The hours that Jebb and Fuller poured into indignantly "defending" the Fund against the *Daily Express* were well spent. While international relief would always remain a target of Britain's populist right, public opinion on the issue had undeniably shifted. International aid was no longer a sectional, left-wing cause; it was now a function of the British state (even if reluctantly and feebly). This was, in part, due to Save the Children's novel "marketing" of child hunger victims, as well as the growing popularity of internationalism, which Save the Children had helped to build. A shift had taken place between 1918 and 1921: "saving" foreign children, even Bolshevik babies, was now an acceptable part of mainstream culture.

The nature of internationalism had shifted too. After the signing of the Versailles Treaty in 1919, there were ongoing negotiations about the borders of nation-states, the conditions of reparations, and the membership of the League. By the mid-1920s, many of the aspects of the Paris Peace Treaty that Buxton and the Fight the Famine Council had opposed had been revised. The Locarno Treaty of 1925 restored the Ruhr areas to Germany and halted steep reparations payments, and in 1926 Germany and Russia were both admitted to the League. These shifts placated left-leaning internationalists such as Buxton, whose faith in the possibility of a peaceful international order led by the League of Nations was revived. These concessions did not alienate more conservative opinion in Britain, which was placated by the realization that the new international order would shore up British imperial power. Internationalism ceased to be a radical creed when it became clear that it would entrench the status quo, and it became a rare point of consensus in the turbulent politics of the 1920s.

HUMANITARIANISM, CHILDREN, AND INTERNATIONALISMS

Save the Children placed the young at the center of the internationalist moment that followed in the wake of the First World War. Its "marketing campaign" drew upon religious and romantic portrayals of children as innocents, alongside new scientific understandings of childhood that underlined the particular vulnerability of early years. In a divided, impoverished Europe, internationalism was a future-building project. It was children, the citizens of tomorrow, who could realize it. By placing the young at the center of the international order, Save the Children also claimed a special role for Britain, as the parent and provider for "the world's children." It drew upon the paternalist ethos of the British Empire, and directed it toward the war-torn European continent, represented in the image of the starving child.

Within its first three years, Save the Children moved from Dorothy Buxton's living room in Golders Green to a large office in well-heeled Soho. It formalized ties between elite pacifist women through the founding of an international organization in Geneva. Its early cast of left-wing council members was joined by a professional secretarial staff and prominent Conservative public figures. Under the leadership of Eglantyne Jebb, it moved from being a grant-giving organization, in the style of the Charity Organisation Society, to being a "fully operational" employer of its own professional relief workers, some of the first of their kind.[172]

The Save the Children Fund was an undoubted success, though not in the terms its founder, Dorothy Buxton, had imagined for it. Humanitarian concern for children had not radicalized the British public, drawing them into protest against the inequities of the international order. Instead, by allying children with the cause of internationalism, the Fund had worked to depoliticize internationalism, making it a cause of "humanity" and the British its champions and exemplars. As Russian famine relief wound down in 1923, both Jebb and Buxton feared that the public enthusiasm for internationalism was fading. In the next chapter we see how, through an attempt to place children at the center of the fledgling League of Nations and international diplomacy, the leaders of Save the Children tried to reinvigorate the desire for peace and cooperation that had grown from the ruins of the First World War.

TWO

The Geneva Declaration of the Rights of the Child and Stateless Children

ON A SUMMER DAY IN 1922, Eglantyne Jebb climbed a mountain just across the border from the city of Geneva. She sat on a rock, ate a "simple lunch," and experienced what was later styled by her biographers as a moment of divine inspiration. She descended, like Moses, with a draft of the Declaration of the Rights of the Child. The Declaration proclaimed the entitlement of all children to welfare provision, education, and emergency relief "beyond all considerations of race, nationality or creed."[1] The adoption of the Declaration by the League of Nations in 1924 was widely reported and celebrated across Europe and North America. Yet not everyone was optimistic: Save the Children relief worker William Kennedy, based in a refugee camp outside Constantinople, doubted whether the Declaration would ever apply to stateless refugees, as in practice it was the nation-state that took responsibility for children's education and welfare. Kennedy wondered whether, in its absence, the international community would step in.[2]

In an era when states across Europe were making increasing commitments to child welfare, the Declaration of the Rights of the Child sought to fix child welfare as an international concern. Despite its universalist language, the Declaration should be read as an attempt to enshrine the connection between a child's present care and future productivity, expanding biopolitical nationalist child welfare discourses internationally. It sought to fix the rights of children as international citizens: individuals who would grow up to contribute to the international economy, and therefore could make claims upon the international community for care and protection. The health of children, Save the Children's leaders imagined, would enable a prosperous future, mutual trade, and lasting peace. Yet the Declaration of the Rights of the Child remained ambiguous about the rights of children deemed "a burden" to their societies, and about refugee children who had no nation to which they could contribute. On the one hand, child rights expressed an expansive vision of liberal internationalism, and on the other, clearly demarked its limits. The Europe that humanitarians envisaged was made up of ethnically homogenous nation-states, comprising strong, healthy workers. Children who appeared likely to grow up to fulfill this vision were the "raw material" of the international order, while those who would not fell outside the imagined international community and beyond the boundaries of humanitarian concern.

THE SAVE THE CHILDREN FUND AND THE EVACUATION OF RUSSIAN REFUGEE CHILDREN FROM CONSTANTINOPLE, 1920–1922

Children, Save the Children believed, were the ideal "international citizens."[3] They could contribute to all nations through an interconnected international economy and therefore should draw support from the international community at large. Save the Children's leaders began to form their ideas about children's international citizenship through their experience of working with Europe's growing population of refugees. In the immediate aftermath of the First World War, while the Save the Children Fund (SCF) had been fighting famine in central Europe and in Russia, another humanitarian crisis was unfolding in Constantinople. In 1920 the city was overflowing with Russian refugees who had fled the new Bolshevik state, following the defeat of the counterrevolutionary White Army. Arriving either by "trudging barefoot and starving over-land" or aboard "disease ridden, over crowded boats," refugees needed immediate care and had no means of providing for themselves.[4] Indeed, it was not clear who should care for refugees, or how. Refugees were "capable," "able bodied," and normally found in places of relative plenty: their hardship was a consequence of their political position, rather than any physical or practical constraint.[5] Although "statelessness" was not itself a new phenomenon, in the years after the First World War it was on a scale never previously seen. As the Allied powers sought to contain old empires and create new, ethnically homogenous nation-states, national borders were redrawn and populations exchanged. Millions of Europeans found that they were no longer citizens of the states in which they lived and either chose or were forced to move elsewhere.[6] Russians and Armenians who had fled their homes due to violence or persecution added to their numbers. Mass postwar

movements of people were accompanied by new attempts to regulate populations via passports, registration, and work permits. Refugees had their movements and employment prospects drastically restricted, and many became
stranded in ports, unable to work. The response to this new refugee crisis
was improvised. It involved a range of actors, including relief organizations,
national governments, and the League of Nations, and it was the product of
varying degrees of communication, cooperation, and conflict between these
agencies.[7]

Over seven hundred thousand refugees were congregated in Constantinople alone, and many (though there are no exact figures) were children.[8]
Save the Children's refugee relief began there, as a series of small grants channeled through the "exiled" Russian Red Cross, an organization patronized
by influential émigrés and prominent Europeans who opposed the Bolshevik
government.[9] Many of Save the Children's founding members, including
Dorothy Buxton, were sympathetic to Russian socialism. Very few of Save
the Children's council and their left-liberal ilk went so far as to hope that
Russian Communism would "spread" across Europe, however: they still imagined that liberal democracy and free trade were the foundations of peace.
Rather, they saw Russian socialism as an "interesting experiment" that should
be allowed to play out without the inference of foreign powers.[10] Yet the
Fund's leadership also contained a powerful White Russian lobby, headed by
Lord Weardale. Weardale's support for the exiled Russian Red Cross was a
mark of his opposition to socialism (an opposition born largely from his anti-
Semitism) and an act of solidarity with White Russians.[11] For Eglantyne Jebb,
meanwhile, support for White Russian children was a means to illustrate
the "nonpolitical" nature of child welfare work. For her, it was symbolically
significant that both White and Red children were being provided with the
"exact same rations" on both sides of the Russian border.[12]

As well as making grants for refugee relief, the SCF threw its weight
behind the International Committee of the Red Cross (ICRC) campaign
for the League of Nations to declare its formal responsibility for refugees.
Issuing a joint statement with the ICRC, the Fund proclaimed the postwar
refugee crisis to be a problem that "far surpassed the competence of humanitarian organizations." Charities could provide "simple material relief" to
refugees, but the crisis could only truly be resolved if refugees were repatriated or resettled elsewhere on a long-term basis. The League of Nations
was the "only supranational political organisation" with the "authority" to
reach these long-term solutions.[13] This appeal marked the end of the Fund's

consciously cultivated distance from "official diplomatic channels."[14] By 1920, Fund leaders, in line with left-leaning opinion in Britain, had become more supportive of the League of Nations, as the League incorporated more of the designs of a left-leaning internationalist lobby. Jebb believed that if the League took on a humanitarian role in refugee relief and resettlement, this would enhance its popularity and legitimacy, demonstrating its "true capabilities" and "benevolent character" to the European public.[15]

The League of Nations refugee relief work began with the inauguration of the High Commissioner for Refugees (LNHCR) in August 1921. Headed by Norwegian polar explorer Frijdof Nansen, whom the Fund also worked with in his role as High Commissioner for Russian Famine Relief, the LNHCR focused on the repatriation and resettlement of Russian refugees, leaving "material assistance" to humanitarian organizations.[16] Despite Jebb's hope, the League remained one step removed from humanitarian relief work, focusing instead on the legalities and practicalities of resettlement. Thus, the LNHCR had no resettlement or aid programs that targeted children specifically, believing that they would resettle alongside their parents. Unaccompanied or orphaned refugee children, or those whose parents had not yet been resettled by the LNHCR, would be entirely dependent on charity.[17]

Seventeen-year-old Mira and her eleven-year-old sister Lalia were among thousands of unaccompanied Russian children in central Europe. The daughters of a rural doctor, they were the only family members to survive a Red Army attack on their home in December 1920. Following the rape and murder of their mother and the fatal shooting of their father and brothers, the two girls fled to Kiev. The White Russian Red Cross funded their onward passage to Constantinople, where they met Reverend Kolomsy, an American Baptist minister of Russian descent who had established a series of schools in the nearby countryside.[18] These schools were "safe havens" where Russian children could "rediscover" their childhoods while learning industrial crafts and performing arts. The schools received large donations from Kolomsy's US-based Russian Education Society, while the attendance fees of orphan children such as Mira and Lalia were underwritten by "adoptive parents": British benefactors who could provide food and clothing for individual children at the cost of a shilling a week. These "adoptions" were organized by Save the Children.[19]

As in Save the Children's Austrian adoption schemes (discussed in chapter 1), in Constantinople both orphans and children with parents were selected for "adoption." In Austria, where the Fund's adoption scheme was piloted, the scheme's purpose had been to keep families together, because, in the view of Save the Children relief workers, having the responsibility of childcare removed by relief workers "demoralised" parents (adoptive parents funded food rations, which children could eat in their homes). This Victorian discourse of demoralization had two meanings: a literal loss of morals, as parents were said to become irresponsible and dependent on outside help to raise their children; and a state of emotional despondency experienced by people who had had their role in society removed. In line with late nineteenth-century liberal philanthropic beliefs, the Fund held that demoralized Austrian adults would become unproductive, burdensome citizens, unable to contribute to the reconstruction of their nation, and thus it was vital to preserve adults' sense of responsibility both to their children and society at large.[20]

In Constantinople, by contrast, SCF relief workers were concerned about the demoralization of children. Here, adult refugees were seen as a lost cause. With no immediate prospects of employment, relief workers believed the demoralization of Russian adults to be unavoidable, claiming that "idleness" would soon lead to "vice and crime," activities that (it was assumed) would soon be "imitated by their children."[21] With the "mean streets as their only playground," Jebb claimed, refugee children "consort with undesirable elements and join street gangs," speeding their slide into dependence on aid and/or crime.[22] This concern was shared with organizations in Constantinople, in particular Near East Relief, the major American humanitarian body founded in 1915 in response to mass dislocation and violence against minorities in the Ottoman Empire. Descriptions of the effects of unemployed parents and urban living on refugee children mirrored both late nineteenth-century philanthropists' descriptions of British and American slums and their practices, which included removing hundreds of thousands of British slum children from environments of poverty and adult unemployment to place them in rural boarding schools or sending them to the British dominions. It was believed that green, open spaces would allow them to grow up free of the "moral taint" of cities.[23] Similarly, to "protect" refugees from their own parents, donations from "adoptive" parents funded their education in one of Dr. Kolomsy's boarding schools outside Constantinople.[24]

Although the LNHCR had no formal responsibility for the relief of children, their education was a "special concern." In the early 1920s, many assumed that Russian socialism would be short lived. Russian refugee children were viewed, in the words of High Commissioner Nansen, as "the foot soldiers of the economic army," necessary for "Russian reconstruction" after Bolshevism. Nansen claimed that all League of Nations members had a duty of care toward Russian refugee children, on the grounds that they would contribute to the economic recovery of Russia from socialism.[25] Nansen was "particularly impressed" by the forward-thinking policies of the new state of Czechoslovakia in this regard. In addition to granting asylum to 500,000 Russian adults between 1919 and 1925, the Czech foreign minister offered "education and shelter" to Russian refugee children currently resident in other nations.[26] The first of these were 1,635 children attending schools funded by Save the Children and Dr. Kolomsy outside Constantinople, who would be relocated to Czechoslovakia in November 1921 while their parents remained in the city.[27] What had begun as a practice of removing children from urban "slums" to rural boarding schools culminated in their "evacuation" to another state altogether. In 1921, the Czechoslovakian foreign minister also offered to "care for" 469 children from the famine-stricken province of Saratov in Russia, who were to be moved to Czechoslovakia and adopted by local families.[28] The humanitarian "evacuation" of children from Saratov and Constantinople was not unprecedented. The SCF had previously organized the temporary relocation of children from several famine-stricken European cities to schools, sanatoria, and foster families elsewhere on the continent. For example, in 1920, four hundred German children were evacuated from Leipzig to SCF-funded French summer camps (*colonies des vacances*) for six months, to escape the "degenerative conditions" of the war-torn city.[29] Similarly, between August 1919 and November 1921, twenty Austrian schoolboys attended an English country boarding school at Save the Children's expense. When they returned home, school caps on heads and cricket bats in hands, a Save the Children donor praised them as "little English schoolboys" and remarked without regret that many had "forgotten their native tongue."[30]

While Save the Children's fundraising appeals (examined in chapter 1) insisted on the value of children to the international economy and to British donors, they forgot children's value to their own families or communities. Child sponsorship programs, the Fund's most successful fundraising initiative, deliberately obscured children's existing family ties, presenting them as "orphans" in need of financial "adoption" by benevolent Britons. It seems that the Fund came to believe its own fiction, rhetorically removing children from families by presenting them as "orphans" and then literally removing them through its resettlement programs. Given a choice between family life in a war-torn city and institutional care in the "healthy" countryside, relief workers always chose the latter on the behalf of children, with no discussion or consideration of the preferences of children themselves. If children could be sent to another country, even farther from their parents, so much the better.

As we saw in chapter 1, Save the Children's mode of child-focused relief had initially been a pragmatic choice: the Fund found it easier to rally concern for "innocent" children than former enemy adults. However, what had begun as pragmatism quickly became an ideological preference. For Jebb, internationalism represented the possibility of a "new world order" and a definitive break with the allegiances and political grievances of the past. A generation of adults who had participated in the violence of the First World War was tainted, "demoralised" by poverty in its aftermath. Children were the ideal international citizens: malleable and free of the prejudices of their parents, they would build a new world order within a generation. Separating children from families was thus the fastest path to a lasting peace, since they could learn new languages and assimilate into new cultures more quickly than adults. Separating children from their parents and moving them across Europe would create a new class of international citizen, building bonds across Europe as they settled into new cultures, illustrating the similarities between people of all nations as they did so.[31]

For the Czech government, which requested the first cohort of Save the Children–sponsored Russian refugees, child resettlement was not about forging a new international order. Rather, it was a nation-building opportunity. Czechoslovakian officials believed that the Bolshevik government would soon topple and hoped that Russian children raised in Czechoslovakia (many of whom were thought to have been members of the former Russian intelligentsia or upper classes) would return to post-Bolshevik Russia fit to lead, while remaining loyal to the state that had cared for them.[32] Further, even if these children did not return to Russia, Czechoslovakia stood to benefit, as a healthy, young population was seen as integral to the stability of the newly created Czechoslovak state.[33] Having seen the eagerness of the Czechoslovakian government to receive Russian refugee children, in November 1921 a representative of the Save the Children International Union (SCIU), Monsieur Gehri, was dispatched to Bulgaria in the hope of making similar arrangements. Bulgaria also shared a border with Russia, and thus (Gehri assumed), its leaders would also want new, young citizens to ward off the threat of communism. Bulgaria had also received adult refugees, resettled by the LNHCR, signaling its willingness to accept new citizens. After

negotiation, the Bulgarian government agreed to provide residential schooling for the five thousand children remaining in Constantinople, donating a
substantial sum to meet the costs.[34] The Bulgarian government also informed
Gehri that they would be prepared to care for eight hundred Russian famine
children from Saratov by moving them to orphanages in Sofia.[35]

The evacuation of refugee children from Constantinople to Bulgaria took
place in December. It was an unusually harsh winter, and many of the children were dressed in ragged clothes and leaking shoes. Relief workers were
much more concerned by these material hardships than the emotional distress that the removal of their children caused many Russian parents. The
child relief committee of Constantinople, headed by Lewis Golden and
Dr. Kolomsy, informed those coordinating the evacuations that they must
do their "best to soften the processes of family separation and adaptation to
unfamiliar environments," but that they should "not waver" in their resolve
to complete the evacuations. Kolomsy and Golden withheld relief from any
children who, having been offered an education in Bulgaria, chose to remain
in the city. Informed that they would have to take "full responsibility for their
children's nourishment and education," and lacking the resources to do so,
the majority of parents waved their children off on a train bound for Sofia in
December 1921.[36]

The Russian children "evacuated" to Bulgaria and Czechoslovakia from
Constantinople in 1921 were the vanguard of a wider trend. Despite the
reluctance of many Russian refugee parents, the Russian Union of Zemstovs
(a Russian émigré association) began a more extensive evacuation scheme,
removing eight thousand children from Constantinople and other Near Eastern cities to France, Czechoslovakia, and Bulgaria between 1921 and 1930.[37]
These children became a source of humanitarian concern and journalistic
interest. In 1922, the ICRC sent a delegate to Sofia to inspect the orphanages
of Russian children evacuated from Constantinople. The children were found
in "poor condition," subjected to "harsh discipline" and, in some cases, fed
only 350 grams of soup each day.[38] Members of the French and British press
also sought out the evacuated children, in hope of publishing "sensational
stories."[39] They were often disappointed when, instead of recounting narratives of "red terror" and dramatic escape, children either claimed that their
stories were "too boring" or invented details such as having been "eaten by
lions."[40] A number of schoolteachers also published accounts of their work
with refugee children. Less concerned with the children's past experiences,
they viewed them as unique subjects for pedagogical experiments designed

to determine "national feeling." This was a subject of enduring importance as, although the Czech and Bulgarian governments were keen to secure the loyalty of their young wards, exiled Russian parents and charitable organizations were reluctant to see children "de-nationalised or "assimilated" into a new culture.[41]

The findings of two surveys, carried out at a Russian-language secondary school in Moravská Třebová in Czechoslovakia and a Russian-language primary school in Umen, Bulgaria in early 1924, revealed that children's "assimilation" depended on how much of their lives had been spent outside Russia. The older, secondary-school children who were studying in Třebová, most of whom would have spent at least ten years in Russia, strongly identified as Russian and with Russian culture.[42] In the Bulgarian primary school, relative identification with Bulgaria and Russia depended on age. At the time the survey was conducted in 1924, most children had not seen Russia for four years, and so the youngest had little memory of their time there. Whereas children aged eight and nine uniformly claimed to "love Russia" and said they "did not love Bulgaria" (one stated that this was "because they speak Bulgarian there"), children under the age of eight felt ambivalent about Russia ("Russia is large. Bolsheviks live there. They can kill you.") The younger children professed to "love Bulgaria" and some claimed to be Bulgarian, "since we live on the land here."[43]

Only around half of the Russian refugee children in Bulgaria and Czechoslovakia attended specialized Russian-language schools.[44] Others attended Czech or Bulgarian schools, some living with foster parents and others in state orphanages, and for these groups assimilation and "denationalization" were far more rapid. Writing in June 1924, a reporter for the "International Bulletin" of the SCIU noted that the Saratov famine children with living parents, who had been relocated to Czechoslovakia just three years earlier, were being returned to Russia after a long campaign by their communities. Save the Children noted the sadness that this caused to their birth families because most had become "Czech in all but origin," had "forgotten their Russian tongue" and regarded their foster families as their own.[45]

While Russian children were able to move and adapt to new nations and cultures, the situation for refugee adults was very different. Unable to return to Russia, and with migration to other nations dependent on work, which was scarce, a large, unemployed adult Russian refugee population remained in Constantinople. The SCF became infuriated with the LNHCR, which it felt had failed to uphold its commitment to find "long-term solutions" to the refugee crisis.[46] Against the advice of the LNHCR, which did not wish to see

Russians permanently settled in already crowded Constantinople, the Fund began to plan work schemes for refugee adults, such as carpet making. These schemes targeted the mothers of infants under five, thought to be too young to be moved away from Constantinople, and provided nursery schools as well as vocational training.[47] They focused on teaching women "traditional" crafts and found markets for them among liberal middle-class donors in Britain, for whom "refugee carpets" were a fashionable form of moral consumption, and a symbol of the internationalism of the owner.[48] This replicated the practices of the late Victorian Arts and Crafts movement, of which Jebb's mother had been a proponent, and which fetishized rustic, "traditional" feminine labor as a way to inculcate self-discipline in poor women.[49] Rarely did the refugee carpets schemes result in economic self-sufficiency: the price of materials and shipping carpets to buyers in Britain meant that a profit was seldom raised. Instead, carpet-making refugees remained dependent on Save the Children for their meals and a small amount of spending money. For Save the Children (and a host of American organizations in Constantinople who adopted similar models), carpet making was not about "independence" or self-sufficiency, but instilling self-discipline through labor.[50] It was a last-ditch attempt to prevent the "social degradation" of mothers so that, eventually, their children could become independent citizens.[51]

The Fund took important lessons from its work in Constantinople. Through its evacuation schemes, the Fund had witnessed the enthusiasm of "small nations" for healthy children. Refugee children had offered a blueprint for children's international citizenship. This was citizenship not dependent on nationality or children's present contributions to the community. In its work with refugee adults, Save the Children staff believed that they had witnessed the demoralizing effects of unemployment and came to promote a vision of citizenship built upon the idea of adults making a contribution to society in labor and children's potential to contribute such labor to national and international economies in their adult life. Save the Children would seek to build citizenship through labor again in its refugee relief work in Greece, where it created model communities designed to resettle and rehabilitate refugee families.

THE SAVE THE CHILDREN FUND IN GREECE, 1922–1924

In the summer of 1922, as the last battles of the Greco-Turkish war over the partitioning of the crumbling Ottoman empire raged, eight hundred thousand Armenian and ethnically Greek residents of the former Ottoman Empire fled into Greece. Arriving either on foot with only what they could carry or on crowded ships rife with typhus and malaria, these refugees were destitute and, in many cases, deeply distressed, having witnessed the slaughter of family members and neighbors. The American Red Cross (ARC) was first on the scene, receiving Greek refugees who flocked to Athens and Salonika. According to Sophie Nelson, an ARC nurse from Boston, Massachusetts, the chaos the refugees found when they arrived in Greece was little better than the violence they had left behind. Food was scarce and malaria was rampant. Children "died in swarms." Babies died and were buried minutes after birth. Families huddled in disused army barracks and under canvas for shelter; a lucky few slept in churches or the national theater. The situation, Nelson claimed, was far worse than anything she had witnessed on the Western Front.[52]

The bulk of refugee relief in Salonika and Athens was carried out by the ARC and the SCF, under the leadership of Dr. William Kennedy, a former British Army medic. Kennedy and newly appointed Save the Children president Percy Alden, were granted permission by the British government to set up feeding centers in disused British army barracks, run along the same lines as the Russian famine feeding centers. The leadership of the Fund was, however, reluctant to commit to another long-term feeding scheme due to the belief that they had "pauperized" Russian refugees in Constantinople, making them dependent on charity without providing long-term employment opportunities. They also doubted that donations for another emergency feeding scheme would be forthcoming so soon after the Russian famine.[53] According to SCIU secretary William Mackenzie, Greek refugees were not as emotive as famine victims: "They all look too cheerful."[54]

The situation of refugees in Greece differed from those in Constantinople in that they were recognized as "citizens" rather than stateless persons. They were able to move around Greece and find work. In July 1922, the Greek government appealed to the League of Nations to help with the long-term settlement of refugees on vacant, fertile farmland. However, that summer, the loan of £10 million that the Greek government would eventually receive from the League for refugee resettlement had yet to materialize, so any efforts had to be made under the auspices of the underfunded LNHCR.[55] That Save the Children decided to start a major refugee relief scheme in Greece was due mostly to its friendly relations with the newly hired LNHCR representative for Greece, Colonel Proctor.

A former Australian army colonel, Proctor shared many of the Fund's fears about the demoralizing effect of "idleness." "Under the current system," he cautioned, refugees' "bodies would be fed but their characters ruined," and they would become "utterly worthless citizens convinced of their divine right to receive food and flatly refusing work when it is offered."[56] He was keen to keep emergency relief to a minimum and to accelerate the resettlement of refugees. With minimal funds at his disposal, Proctor proposed a resettlement scheme for ten thousand refugees, who would be moved from the camps in Salonika to the fertile, underpopulated lands of Western Thrace in northern Greece. Here, Save the Children would be responsible for the provision of food, shelter, and relief workers, while the refugees themselves would set about the construction of permanent homes and smallholdings. Proctor declared that it would be "better to feed a smaller amount of people and put them on their feet" than to "demoralise many" with "indiscriminate charity."[57]

The scheme appealed to Percy Alden, the chairman of the Save the Children Fund from 1922. A former Labour MP and trade unionist, Alden saw work as the only way to restore "self-respect" to impoverished refugee men. Like the LNHCR, Alden viewed the "problem" of refugees in gendered terms. If men could be given work, he believed, then the care of women and children (whom he termed "dependents") would be met by male community members. Rather than male refugees being "forced into positions of dependence" as had been the case in Constantinople, the Western Thrace scheme placed refugee men at the center of a family economy and, by enabling them to work, the Fund sought to improve the "lot of [their] children."[58] Built in 1922, the Western Thrace settlement scheme was therefore a form of child relief that preserved family units and did not undermine paternal authority or self-esteem. It was also the first Save the Children scheme that took fathers into account at all. True to the roots of the SCF in the Victorian philanthropy of the Charity Organisation Society, the "deserving poor" did not include idle men or their families. Charity often called upon paternalistic sentiments to provide for those who lacked a "male provider." In much the same way as Save the Children imagined all children as orphans, all mothers were imagined as war widows. When families were described to donors (if at all), fathers were absent. In Alden's view, however, men were central to the Western Thrace scheme. Rather than taking on the role of male provider, the SCF would enable men to fulfill their own "familial duties" through the creation of work, making them "productive citizens" who would benefit the

FIGURE 5. A home in Save the Children's model village for refugees, Atolvo, Bulgaria, 1926. Simple bungalows had a connected pig pen, and wood stove. "Atolvo," *The World's Children*, June 1926.

Greek economy. Contributing to a wider community or nation, refugees would, in his eyes, be "rehabilitated."[59]

Following the success of the Western Thrace settlement scheme, the Fund constructed two more villages for refugee families in Bulgaria, where their previous child resettlement programs had ensured friendly relationships with Bulgarian government officials. Named Atolvo (after the Fund's president, the Duke of Atholl) and Xhebba (for Eglantyne Jebb), these villages provided a small two-bedroom hut each for one hundred families. They also provided work for adult men, such as pig breeding and charcoal burning ("for what good is a home if a man goes on starving?" Alden asked). The villages were based on a British fantasy of rustic, rural life: they were set up to create agriculturists and artisans, with no reference to refugees' past occupations or existing skills.[60] More importantly, both schemes provided men with labor and the ability to meet the needs of their dependents—two mechanisms for controlling the refugee population. The LNHCR and host governments feared that unemployed "gangs" of adult men would bring "unrest" to their new nations. Children and work were seen as inherently stabilizing. Later, in the aftermath of the Second World War, craft activities, other forms of manual labor, and family reunification schemes were promoted in displaced persons camps in Europe, again as a means of containing the resentment (and, it was feared, violence) that might arise from the boredom or isolation of adult men.[61] Save the Children's villages provided a blueprint for later initiatives.

Atolvo, Xhebba, and the Western Thrace Scheme were praised in the fundraising propaganda of the Save the Children Fund, but these "model" projects were far from typical of the Fund's refugee work in the 1920s. Just one hundred families were housed in these villages, whereas tens of thousands passed through orphanages and boarding schools provided for by the SCF.[62] Nonetheless, the Western Thrace and Bulgarian villages put into practice SCF leaders' deeply held belief that work was stabilizing and a necessary contribution to the wider community. It was this contribution to national economies through labor that anchored refugees to their new nations. This connection between economic contribution and entitlement to citizenship was the cornerstone of the Fund's vision of children's international citizenship, later enshrined in its Declaration of the Rights of the Child.

THE SAVE THE CHILDREN FUND, LEAGUE OF NATIONS, AND THE GENEVA DECLARATION OF THE RIGHTS OF THE CHILD

The SCF's work for refugees took place against the backdrop of its changing relationship with the League of Nations. Save the Children's leaders, particularly Dorothy Buxton, had initially been deeply disappointed by the League. Buxton viewed it as an expression of the elitist "old diplomacy" that had caused the war, and was doubtful that the League's Allied-dominated, exclusive and hierarchical structure would enable the "open exchange" necessary to prevent future conflict. However, by 1920 the Save the Children Council had become more optimistic about the League's role in the "new world order." This shift in opinion was due in part to their approval of the work the League had done in preventing the spread of typhus in Eastern Europe and repatriating prisoners of war. The Fund regarded both initiatives as acts of humanitarian diplomacy, enhancing international cooperation between different relief organizations and governments and creating political stability in war-torn nations.[63]

Save the Children's leaders hoped that the League might also take an interest in child welfare. Like the League's refugee resettlement and disease prevention programs, they saw this as an "implicit part of its peacekeeping work" that would enhance the League's "moral authority."[64] "Destitute and degraded children," Jebb believed, were as much a "menace to peace and prosperity" as impoverished adults.[65] Jebb therefore proposed that the

League should intervene in "standards of child life" across Europe and the wider world. She also hoped that child welfare work would democratize the League, making space within the League's apparatus for humanitarians and campaigners, whom Jebb saw as more organic internationalists than the League's detached diplomats and politicians.[66]

In June 1920, child welfare was discussed in the first General Assembly of the League of Nations. Giuseppe Motta, president of the Confederation of Switzerland and a personal friend of Jebb, proposed that "child rescue" seemed "almost obligatory upon the League" and might be "one of its noblest tasks."[67] There was widespread support, in principle, for the notion that the League should perform concern for children, but resources to do so were limited.[68] Motta proposed that the League would uphold the "moral authority" of existing child welfare agencies, but grant them neither financial nor organizational support. This meant nothing to an organization like Save the Children in practice, though it boosted their claim that saving children was a matter of international importance. In a debate on the role of the League in the lives of Europe's children, it was pointed out that the League was already supporting children through a variety of means: the World Health Organization was combatting child mortality and the International Labour Office was working to abolish child labor. In 1921 the League Assembly approved an International Convention for the Suppression of the Traffic in Women and Children, but there was neither the capacity nor the will to do more.[69]

Many prominent feminists and humanitarians shared Jebb's belief that the League needed children more than children needed the League. The American president of the WILPF, Jane Addams, echoing a claim that Jebb had made before the Russian famine, stated in 1921 that the internationalist "golden moment" that followed the First World War was fading.[70] Addams, like Jebb, believed that with the League's immediate successes in the containment of disease and fostering reconciliation established, the Assembly needed to make a new, grand gesture, to remind ordinary people that internationalism was a moral cause worth supporting. Addams, along with Gustav Ador, the president of the International Committee of the Red Cross, imagined that the League of Nations would harness a moment when children were especially valued due to fears of population decline in the aftermath of war.[71] For wider membership of the WILPF, the League proclaiming an interest in childhood would also expand women's interest in international politics, and herein lay the "great future of internationalism."[72] Furthermore, the Swiss and Belgian governments were keen for an international intergovernmental organization dealing with child welfare to be founded at the League: firstly, because child welfare seemed so popular in their own nations; and secondly, because they believed the medical, physiological, and legal innovations in child welfare were easily replicable across different national contexts. They wanted to formalize transnational flows of ideas around childhood in the same way that, via the League, governments now pooled information on labor, economics, and health.

Jebb, who had founded the SCIU in Geneva precisely because of its proximity to the League of Nations, began developing her own vision for a League of Nations child welfare committee. What she wanted was some form of international treaty, perhaps similar to the 1906 Red Cross Convention for the Amelioration of the Condition of the Wounded and Sick in Armies in the Field, in which signatory states would take on responsibilities for children, enforced by the League. She set about writing this "treaty" in 1922 on a mountain outside Geneva.[73] Jebb's draft, which underwent many alterations, revisions, and committees, eventually read:

1. The child must be given the means requisite for its normal development, both materially and spiritually.

2. The child that is hungry must be fed, the child that is sick must be nursed, the child that is backward must be helped, the delinquent child must be reclaimed, and the orphan and the waif must be sheltered and succoured.

3. The child must be the first to receive relief in times of distress.

4. The child must be put in a position to earn a livelihood, and must be protected against every form of exploitation.

5. The child must be brought up in the consciousness that its talents must be devoted to the service of its fellow men.

It was later prefixed by the SCF with the statement that it applied to all children, "beyond and above considerations of race, nationality or creed," and titled, "The Geneva Declaration of the Rights of the Child."[74]

Work on the Declaration had begun in March 1922, several months before Jebb ascended the mountain, in an SCF subcommittee headed by British novelist Ethel Sidgwick. The initial aim of the Declaration had been to see off competition from the International Council of Women, which had just announced it was creating its own Children's Charter. The Charter contained forty-three clauses (in contrast to the Save the Children Fund's five), setting out standards for a wide range of areas including healthcare, education, living conditions, and even access to wildlife. Stemming from a tradition of maternalism, it placed children within families, linking the welfare of the young to family allowances and maternal health.[75] For Jebb, it set standards for children and mothers that could only be realized through increases in state-funded welfare services, and this, she argued, would make it "too socialistic" to gain widespread support in Europe. Jebb also felt that the prescriptive nature of the Charter would make it inapplicable to the world's "less developed nations."[76] By contrast, the SCF hoped their deliberately vague Declaration of the Rights of the Child would draw popular support in Europe and beyond. Many historians of human rights have been keen to locate the antecedents of the 1948 Universal Declaration of Human Rights at earlier moments. They have pointed to the Declaration of the Rights of the Child as proof of a universalist tradition within interwar internationalist thought in which all are valued equally and individually by sole virtue of their humanity.[77] However, the Declaration of the Rights of the Child was concerned not with universal value of children as individuals, but with the value of healthy, educated children to their communities.

Jebb had initially envisioned the Declaration as a "children's charter" that would "deal with the duties of the community to the individual, [and] the duties of the individual to the community."[78] However, once the document, drafted by the SCF in London, was taken to the SCIU in Geneva, her original plan to term the document a "charter" was set aside. A Dutch SCIU delegate claimed that the term *charter* would not hold the same meaning when translated across all European languages, while *rights* would.[79] The matter became controversial: several SCIU delegates objected to the term *rights* because they believed it cast children as citizens with entitlements. This was "almost heresy" because children did not work, vote, or serve in armies, the markers of (male) citizenship. These delegates would have preferred the term *charter* as it cast children as benevolently protected, rather than claiming citizens' "rights" per se.[80] Jebb ignored this concern. Whether her document was termed a "rights declaration" or a "charter," its purpose had always been to fix children as international citizens. Children's claims would be based not on their innate humanity, but on a special form of children's citizenship that matched contribution and entitlement, claiming entitlements for the present while delaying contributions until the future. The Declaration was popular because these ideas were already widespread. In an era of reconstruction and nation-building, children took on renewed importance to their nations as "citizens of tomorrow," or "the economic army of the future," and (to internationalists) the "raw material of the League of Nations."[81]

Jebb also liked the term *rights declaration* because she believed it would appear "more historic" than a simple charter, akin to the Magna Carta of 1215 or the French Declaration of the Rights of Man and Citizen of 1789.[82] A shrewd publicist, she took what she imagined would be the path to greater press interest. She was keen to point out that the first three claims expressed commitments that had already been made by most European states to their children. A raft of welfare legislation across European societies (as well as North America and the British dominions) ensured most children's access to education and healthcare. The Declaration was, however, careful not to prescribe *by whom* children must be "succoured," "fed," or "nursed," meaning that civil society organizations and governments alike could *seek* to fulfill it without being strictly *bound* by it.

In the last two clauses of the Declaration, which focused on children's "duties to [their] fellow man," the Declaration sought to ensure that the young would "pay back" the care they received in their youth. This balancing of "rights" with duties was a continuation of the liberal tradition from which the Fund's founders hailed, which situated the individual within the community, seeing them as mutually supportive.[83] In her extensive writings on the Declaration, Jebb explained the interconnected nature of rights and duties. She illustrated the importance of Clause Three—that the child should be the first to receive help in times of distress—by drawing on the example of British children during the First World War, who were "nurtured under conditions of widespread shortage . . . and are today a charge upon the country as mental and physical defectives because of the privations of their infant years."[84] Jebb claimed that Clause One—that the child must be given all they need for their material and spiritual development—found its "corollary" in Clause Four, that all children must "be placed in a position to earn a living and taught a trade." Drawing on the discourse of demoralization, Jebb argued that "a child who, as an adult, is unable to work, becomes a burden not only to his community but himself, degraded, demoralized and victim of our lack of foresight."[85] Learning a trade was, therefore, a form of "spiritual development," in the interest of both child and community.

On the basis of Clauses One and Four, Jebb lobbied for increased "vocational training schemes" to be instigated in schools across Europe as the "foremost response" to the Declaration.[86] Her thinking was shaped by a number of the Fund's staff across Europe, in particular Hungarian schoolmistress Julia

Vajkai. In 1920, Vajkai had founded a network of "work schools" for Hungarian war orphans, initially funded by the SCF. The schools quickly became self-funding, training children in profitable crafts such as weaving baskets for local fruit growers, cobbling boots, lace making and sewing clothes for other children. Vajkai, who had urged Jebb not to include anything in the Declaration of the Rights of the Child that could be seen to prohibit child labor, believed that work had a disciplinary function for poor Hungarian children. Repetitive, intricate crafts would endow children with "self-mastery" that would in turn make them peaceful, productive citizens.[87] While the language of labor and trades that the SCF repeated seemed gendered, proclaiming the entitlement of boys to adult professions, Vajkai's schemes focused entirely on girls. For her and Jebb, the self-discipline that work taught children was as important as the specifics of the trade itself. It is possible, though they never openly articulated this belief, that Jebb and many of her fellow leaders of Save the Children (mostly women who had not married and many of whom had done some form of work during the First World War, when a host of industries opened up to women) believed in the importance of women's education training due to their own experiences. Save the Children seldom, if ever, spoke of children's biological capacities as the *re*productive citizens of the future. They were interested in the productive role of boys and of girls through practical training, and the social benefits that this would confer on the children themselves, as well as their wider communities.

Vajkai's model was replicated across Europe and when local markets could not be found for children's products, they were used for the Fund's own work. Boys and girls in Austrian orphanages made baby clothes and wicker baby baskets that were distributed by Save the Children to new mothers.[88] Children were not compensated for their labor beyond their bed and board at the schools. Indeed, in one work school in Serbia, a Save the Children visitor found that the children were living *too* comfortably on their earnings ("I daresay they have even been given bedsteads to sleep on!") and, fearing that a scandal would break if Save the Children beneficiaries were seen to be living better than the British working class, the Fund redirected their earnings into the Fund's other projects.[89] The fruits of labor were, after all, intended to be as much spiritual as material.

Stressing the role of today's children as future workers, the Save the Children's rights agenda dovetailed with the concerns of nationalist and eugenicist groups, who were also worried about the health of future British workers, including soldiers. For example, the Fund took a leading role in the

FIGURE 6. Hungarian girls making lace at Julia Vajkai's workroom school, 1923. Lace making was highly intricate and intensive labor, requiring a high level of skill and precise, sometimes painful, repetitive fine movements. "Austria and Hungary," *The World's Children*, July 1923.

British Association for Nursery Education alongside organizations such as the Maternal and Child Welfare Council, which was at the time committed to lowering the birth-rate of the lower classes to improve the balance of "British stock."[90] Until the publication of the Declaration, the Fund had never explicitly expressed an interest in reproduction: a desire to increase or decrease birth-rates.[91] However, after the Declaration was adopted by the League of Nations, Jebb reflected further on questions of biological citizenship. Should the Fund recognize that not all children would be productive workers, and should it therefore limit its provision for these groups, as a way of limiting "unproductive populations" altogether?

In a series of articles for *The World's Children*, Save the Children leaders grappled with this problem through a discussion of "the question of Child Rights, as applicable to the United Kingdom." In one article, Jebb stated her concern that if the Declaration was applied to children "indiscriminately," it would lead to "the degeneracy of certain sections of the population owing to the fact that people who, in a harder age would have died off in childhood now survive, and transmit to their numerous descendants tendencies to disease and crime."[92] Jebb was also uncertain about what provision should be made for "mentally deficient children," a group that she explained were not the same as the "backwards children" addressed in the Geneva Declaration because their condition could not be improved.[93] The model of social citizenship that the Fund laid out, in which all children could contribute to their societies, still had clear biological limits.[94]

There was a profound ambivalence at the heart of children's rights. On the one hand, it was feared that the states that did the most to uphold the rights of children might be weakened by promoting the health of "bad stock." On the other hand, the extent to which a state implemented the Declaration was read as a marker of that state's "civilization." In a posthumously published essay, Eglantyne Jebb explained that the principles underpinning the Declaration were not new: it simply "enumerated those duties towards children which are universally acknowledged by the conscience of mankind."[95] In a volume examining child rights around the world, published in 1925 by SCF press secretary Edward Fuller, children's rights were proclaimed to be "as much the ethics of the jungle" as the logic of "civilized" Western states.[96] At the same time, Fuller's volume showed that more "advanced" nations had attained these principles more fully.[97] It then used societies' fulfillment of "child rights" as a benchmark for civilization and progress. It was, he stated, the duty of "older nations," such as those that made up the Council of the League of Nations, to "guide younger and less experienced nations towards the principles of the Declaration."[98] The Declaration would need to be adopted by the League, he argued, to illustrate that "more civilized" states were willing to protect not only their own children, but also other people's.

The League of Nations did indeed formally adopt the Geneva Declaration of the Rights of the Child in 1924. How did this come to be, when the organization had proven so reluctant to take on any responsibilities for children? First, by the time that the Declaration made its way before the General Assembly of the League in September 1924, the SCIU had laid groundwork for its acceptance through its own informal channels. At a conference hosted by the SCIU, delegates were encouraged to return to their home countries and examine the extent to which the articles were upheld there.[99] Nineteen countries in Europe, North and South America, and the British dominions were represented, and hundreds of newspaper reports followed across the globe as delegates used the Declaration to assess how far their countries went to uphold children's rights. Second, Jebb exploited her contacts with

British politicians to bring it before the Council.[100] In 1924, Britain had its first short-lived Labour government, meaning that Save the Children leaders were suddenly in close proximity to political power. Prime Minister Ramsey MacDonald, a close friend of Charles and Dorothy Buxton, brought the Declaration before the General Assembly of the League of Nations.

Since his initial hesitation about committing the League to child welfare, Giuseppe Motta had become a "close friend" of the SCIU, attending conferences and socializing with its members. Motta agreed to the suggestion of another SCIU supporter, the Hungarian Delegate Comte Apponyi, that a special plenary session of the Assembly should be held for the Declaration to be approved. Meanwhile, the SCIU sent copies to the thirty-seven Assembly member states' delegations translated into their native languages, and SCIU representatives roamed the parquet corridors of the Palais Wilson drumming up support from diplomats and permanent League staff alike. The Declaration was rapidly approved on 26 November 1924 and was greeted by applause. Most of those applauding did so safe in the knowledge that the Declaration gave them no new responsibilities. Humanitarian groups, feminist organizations and religious groups used the Declaration to petition their own national governments. Similarly, governments from France to Poland and Britain to Czechoslovakia experienced the Declaration not as an additional burden, but a useful propaganda tool that could be used to highlight existing provisions for the young. As we'll see in the next chapter, everyone agreed that if children's rights were not being upheld, it was in "backward" nations in colonial empires that had not been permitted to join the League of Nations.

The permanent secretariat at the League of Nations, meanwhile, made sure that its existing work would not be substantively altered by the Declaration and its authors. It inaugurated a Child Welfare Committee, tasked vaguely with "promoting" the Declaration, but insisted that the work of the Child Welfare Committee was to be "strictly limited."[101] It was to focus only on documenting, researching, and discussing the "experiences of different countries" in five areas (child marriage, child health, child labor, family allowance, and the repatriation of foreign minors) in order to prevent "inefficient overlap" with the League's other subsidiary bodies. It was also agreed that the Child Welfare Committee would meet just once a year, for five days at the end of April.[102] Typically, the Committee discussed hypothetical questions (what depth would the ideal swimming pool be?) or moral problems (what was the appropriate level of censorship when children attended the cinema?).

Jebb quickly became frustrated: she had a grander vision for the League and Children's Rights.

CHILD RIGHTS AND STATELESS CHILDREN

If the Declaration of the Rights of the Child was to be realized primarily within the context of nation-states, it had an obvious flaw: it did not address children without a "national government to act as their protector."[103] Responsibility for stateless children had also been discharged by the LNHCR, which transferred the care of refugees to the International Labour Office in 1924. Thereafter, the League's resettlement policies were directed at adult men and, as in the Western Thrace settlements, their movement to and citizenship of new nations would depend on their labor.[104] Believing that attention to male refugees would improve the situation of refugee families, the LNHCR made no provision for "unproductive women or children."[105] Of the estimated one million refugee children in Eastern Europe, however, the majority were thought to be orphaned or in families with no "male breadwinner."[106] Many such children became the subjects of controversial or misguided charitable interventions. Allegations of children being sold by orphanages into "white slavery" were commonplace.[107] One orphanage for Armenian children proudly boasted that it had halved its numbers by allowing local men to choose "attractive wives" from its charges.[108] In 1925 Eglantyne Jebb and the secretary of the SCIU, William Mackenzie, contended that an international convention, endorsed by the League of Nations and its members, was needed to deal with "alien" children in foreign lands.[109] It would formalize the type of arrangement that the Fund had made when it resettled Russian children in Czechoslovakia and Bulgaria, opening up paths to national citizenship for refugee children.

Here, Jebb saw a purpose for the newly inaugurated League of Nations Child Welfare Committee. She proposed a comprehensive charter (a Convention for the Assistance or Repatriation of Foreign Minors) to guide the settlement and naturalization of children outside their countries of origin.[110] In Jebb's view, this charter, in contrast to the "strictly limited" interests addressed by the Committee, would be something that "the health or even lives of many children might depend on."[111] The charter, which was the work of Mackenzie and Jebb, was imbued with familiar SCF internationalist rhetoric. In particular, it stressed the link between the welfare of stateless children and international peace and stability. It cast those states deemed more "advanced" as the "protectors" of stateless children and the promoters of universal humanitarian principles, stating that any "civilised country owes all children the same care within its borders, irrespective of race, nationality or creed."[112]

Jebb did not regard the proposed repatriation convention, which urged states to devote their resources to "foreign children," as "unduly utopian."[113] Its lofty language was underpinned by practical proposals for child resettlement which, based on the Fund's success in settling children in Czechoslovakia and Bulgaria, set out a number of incentives for states that agreed to naturalize foreign children.[114] Most notably, the convention would create a centralized, international account devoted to child repatriation and resettlement. All states would enter this account as either creditors or debtors, decided on the basis of an assessment of each nation's financial capacity and the number of foreign children cared for by a particular state at any one time. Any new child taken in by a state would count as "credit" and would therefore either lessen its debt to the international account or result in payment from the "debtor" nations.[115]

Jebb and Mackenzie believed that the burden of this account could be "easily born" by the League's member states.[116] They did not, however, discuss any of the costs involved, nor what the financial recompense for resettling a child would be, because they regarded the incentives created by the Fund as secondary to a greater benefit to be received by nations that resettled foreign children: the children themselves. The convention rested on a vision of children as citizens, who would pay back any entitlements granted by their host state through their duties to its community in adulthood. To ensure this, Jebb proposed that the Charter should contain a "five-year clause," stipulating that a child who received the welfare benefits of a nation for a period of five years would "repay the state that raised him" by becoming a naturalized citizen. Jebb reasoned that this would appeal to the "natural self interest" of national governments, guarding against the ultimate injustice: a scenario in which a soldier might go to war against a state that had "succoured him" in his youth.[117] Of course, as Jebb herself admitted, there might be occasions when these requirements would go against the wishes of a child, although she believed this would be rare. She argued that children's gratitude to their host state would outweigh any desire to return to their homeland, and in any case, there were simply so many children in mid-1920s Europe of "uncertain nationality as a result of changing frontiers, flight caused by political disturbances and invasions, lost documents, or without civil status in their own country of residence."[118]

The proposed convention codified the principles that had underpinned the Fund's resettlement programs for Russian refugees in Eastern Europe in

1921. These prompted care for children based on the contribution they might eventually make to the nations that raised them, irrespective of nationality. The nationality of children was seen as flexible and contextual, determined by the "state that succoured them" rather than their place of birth or ethnicity. For Jebb and Mackenzie, this flexibility was the greatest asset of child refugees, making them ideal international citizens.[119] Mackenzie regarded "attachment to nationality" as the most problematic aspect of the "refugee mentality," on the grounds that it prevented the successful resettlement and integration of stateless adults. In his view, the solution to the refugee problem lay in the "next generation," unfettered by "national attachments."[120]

The Fund's desire to actively assimilate refugee children into new nations nevertheless flew in the face of the relief efforts for child refugees, spearheaded by both exiled Russian organizations and the League of Nations. For the Union of Zemstovs, the primary goal of child relief programs was to preserve children's "national identity" so that they would willingly return to "reconstruct" Russia after the (anticipated) fall of the Bolshevik government.[121] The Union of Zemstovs had supported the removal of refugee children from Constantinople to Bulgaria and Czechoslovakia in the early 1920s under the impression that children would attend specialist Russian schools in these nations, thus preserving their Russian identity. Disapproving of Save the Children's willingness to place refugee children with non-Russian families and in local schools, the Union of Zemstovs devoted an ever-increasing percentage of its funds to establishing Russian schools and by 1929 had sponsored over eight hundred such institutions throughout Europe. Believing that the needs of Russian children had been met in these institutions, rather than by the states in which they resided, the Fund withdrew from "the Russian refugee question."

The relief efforts of "League of Nations House," an LNHCR-led initiative, also privileged the preservation or restoration of children's national identity. After Russians and Greeks, the third major group of refugees in the Near East in the 1920s was Armenians. The SCF did not directly fund the needs of Armenian refugee children, transferring funds to the Lord Mayor's Armenian Fund headed by Save the Children council member Magda Coe, and to the US-led Near East Relief Fund. These organizations were particularly well-funded because, in the early twentieth century, Armenia had become a cause célèbre among British and American liberals and evangelicals in its capacity as a small nation threatened by the Ottoman Empire and later the Bolsheviks and as a Christian country in a predominantly Islamic region. Between

1915 and 1922, during the genocide waged against Ottoman Armenians by Ottoman Turks, an untold number of children were forcibly removed from their families and adopted into Turkish homes. Between 1922 and 1926, two thousand of these children were "rescued" by League of Nations–funded social workers and placed in specialist orphanages, where they were "renationalised." Much like the Russian refugee schools, these efforts focused on teaching children the languages, cultures, and crafts necessary to restore and preserve their national identity. Both the Armenian rescue efforts and the initiatives run by Russian émigré organizations were therefore centered on protecting the national identities of children.

Ethnicity, if not nationality, was important to the societies that received refugee children, too. In Save the Children's programs in Czechoslovakia, Russian children had been accepted because they were Slavic, like their hosts. This perceived shared heritage made them biologically and economically desirable for a population trying to increase its numbers. Indeed, Save the Children had based its child refugee resettlement schemes on British imperial child migration programs that operated on similar principles. In these schemes, between 1618 and 1967 as many as one hundred fifty thousand children from poor British communities were sent to "white" dominions.[122] Jebb thought of this as new societies readily accepting new workers, but white children were being accepted as settlers for their reproductive capacity as much as (or more than) their productive capacity, expanding white communities that imagined themselves under threat from indigenous populations. In proposing an economic case for refugee resettlement, Jebb ignored the fact that, in the contexts where her idea seemed to have worked, there were racial reasons that Slavic children were desired. Child migrants were valued for their white (or indeed White Russian) bodies, as much as their future labor.

In cases where children were desired by new nation-states, Jebb viewed the fastest route to resettling (and often renationalizing) refugee children was to remove them from their parents and communities.[123] Fund leaders did not seem to expect children and parents to object to the schemes, nor did they regard preserving family units as a priority. William Mackenzie frequently expressed "surprise" at petitions from parents who wished their children returned from distant boarding schools. Neither Jebb nor Mackenzie imagined that children might be valued by their own families as they were by humanitarian organizations. Like Jebb, Mackenzie believed that one of the Charter's prime benefits was that it would allow the removal of refugee children from incompetent and unstable parents, even when a space in a privately funded school or foster family could not be found. If a child became a naturalized citizen of the state, Jebb noted, then they would be eligible for care in state-funded orphanages. In a case file presented to the Child Welfare Committee in June 1926, Jebb detailed the situations of over forty families who, in her view, would benefit from the Charter. One was that of "B.A.," a "backward," motherless boy whose father was thought to be of Czechoslovak origin and who was then resident in Austria. As the boy was not recognized as Austrian, he could not be admitted to an institution to "escape" his feckless father. A similar case was that of "M.N.," a child thought to be of Romanian origin and who, along with five siblings, was inadequately cared for by "destitute" parents, and would be better placed in a state orphanage.[124]

Jebb's meticulously compiled case files reflected her background in the "scientific" and "professional" Charity Organisation Society. However, she did not convince the League of Nations Council to endorse her proposed Repatriation Convention. Between 1925 and 1929, the League of Nations Council rejected the Charter four times: British delegates refused to endorse it, fearing that it might subject imperial child migration schemes to international scrutiny.[125] The desire to keep the League from meddling in imperial affairs was ironic, given that the Fund had modeled its proposals on these imperial schemes.[126] Undaunted, the ever-pragmatic Jebb set about revising the convention to simply address the repatriation (rather than the long-term settlement) of foreign children, which would help to identify the national status of children and return them to "their" state. However, this revision also provided insufficient when the Charter came before the Council of the League for a fifth and final time in 1930 and was relegated to a "policy recommendation."[127] The General Council informed the Child Welfare Committee that the convention would be sent to the League's member states in order to allow them to make bilateral treaties between themselves if they so desired. None did.[128]

REFUGEE CHILDREN'S "RIGHT TO HAVE RIGHTS"
IN INTERWAR EUROPE

When Dr. William Kennedy, the Fund's relief worker in Constantinople, looked across crowded refugee camps and questioned the applicability of child rights to stateless children, he anticipated the later work of Hannah Arendt. Arendt observed that, after the signing of the 1948 Universal Declaration of Human Rights, millions of "displaced persons" were still not entitled to employment and were excluded from the provisions of postwar welfare states. For refugees, universal rights were a fiction. While the Universal Declaration sought to enshrine rights for individuals (rights that did not depend upon membership of a particular state or community, but the simple fact of humanity), it could not do so. There was, Arendt famously wrote, a "right to have rights," which in practice could only be conferred by states upon their own citizens.[129]

Jebb would have seen Hannah Arendt's later critique of universal rights as self-evident: Jebb had never imagined that children could make claims upon society based on their innate humanity. She viewed child rights as the rights of citizens, who would be cared for by states. Her concern was to convince states of the expediency of upholding children's present entitlements based on future potential. In the 1920s, she was pushing at an open door. Across Europe, North America and beyond, states and civil societies had been expanding and extending provision for children since the mid-nineteenth century. The novelty of Jebb's vision was its attempt to claim the international nature of children's citizenship by appealing, not to universal sentiment, but to the world economy. If children were the productive workers of the future, then their health mattered to the entire international community.

Because children's rights were about the good of international society, rather than children as individuals, any child that might undermine the biological health of the community was excluded. While some states were prepared to accept the care of children of different nationalities, they were more suspicious of children whom they believed did not share a common ethnicity with the wider population. While recognizing this, Save the Children did not deal with the racial limits of their social and economic vision of children's citizenship. Save the Children's vision of child rights only worked in a context in which states had bought into how the Fund valued children: as productive future citizens. Thus, the Declaration of the Rights of the Child did not incite nations to care for Jewish refugee children or critique Nazi eugenics in the 1930s. If there was a "right to have rights" for interwar children, then it was conferred not only by nation-states but by healthy, ethnically desirable bodies.

THREE

Empire, Humanitarianism, and the African Child

IN JULY 1931, two hundred conference delegates squinted into the sun as they posed for a photograph near the banks of Lake Geneva. Kenyan nationalist and future president Johnstone Kenyatta stood alongside Lord Lugard, the former colonial governor of Nigeria, while the West Indian delegate of the League of Coloured Peoples, Mitra Sinanan, was positioned near British missionary anthropologist Dora Earthy.[1] This group met at Save the Children's 1931 Conference on the African Child, at which the Fund outlined its vision of humanitarian internationalism extending into a new continent. The official account of the conference by feminist journalist Evelyn Sharp described "friendliness and mutual respect" in a "sunlit conference hall." In reality, though, tensions ran high and new humanitarian groups and old missionary organizations, representatives of imperial powers, and anti-colonial activists came to blows (at one point, literally) over the best interests of the African child. These tensions were elided by Earthy, who celebrated how "men and women of all nations" could come together around a shared cause: extending the "rights of the child" to the children of Africa.[2]

Save the Children's Declaration of the Rights of the Child framed children as universal subjects, worthy of care regardless of race, nationality, or creed. Extending the Fund's work into Africa seemed to be an exercise in universalizing child welfare beyond Europe. However, as in Europe, humanitarian ideas about the best interests of children were bound up with ideas about the economy, geopolitics, and the utility of individual children's bodies. When the Fund was talking about African children, it was also, of course, talking about European colonialism and children's place within it. Through their discussion of African children, British humanitarians were formulating (and performing) their vision of a new ethical imperialism, which they believed

FIGURE 7. Participants at the Conference on the African Child at a reception at Le Reposoir, a grand home on the banks of Lake Geneva owned by a Save the Children supporter. Archives de l'Union Internationale de Protection de l'Enfance, Archives d'État de Genève, 92.4.11

was fit for an era of international cooperation. In this model, Africa and its children would be integrated into the global economic order through rapid industrialization, which would enable them to furnish Western powers with the raw materials needed to maintain a prosperous, peaceful world order. The role of imperial powers was to prepare the continent and its people for this new economic role, and—by matching economic "progress" with wider forms of social development—ensure that African people benefitted from their labor.

Save the Children's move into Africa represented an attempt to graft old imperial ideas and traditions onto the "new international order" of the interwar years, but the Fund's work in Africa also marked a key shift in the assumptions of colonial philanthropy. In the interwar years, the enlightenment view that humans were essentially the same—separated only by their relative position on a hierarchy of civilization that all societies could, one day, attain—was falling out of vogue. It was being replaced by a view that races were biologically different and that this difference would be reflected in the roles played by Europeans and imperial subjects in the new international order. Save the Children's council imagined that African children had fundamentally different capabilities from their European counterparts. African children were being invited to play a part in the global economic order not as citizens, but as servants.

INTERNATIONALISM, IMPERIALISM, AND "WORLD RESPONSIBILITY"

The liberal internationalism of the interwar years upheld the existence of colonial empires, but it was always clear that this would be the case. In 1919, the League of Nations promoted the Wilsonian principle of "self-determination": that the boundaries and legitimacy of a state should be determined by the will of its inhabitants. Across the globe, colonized peoples—many of whom had fought alongside their European colonizers during the war—hoped that the principle of self-determination would also spell the end of colonialism. It did not. Self-determination, enacted through plebiscites over contested national boundaries in central Europe, was imagined only to apply to white, European minorities and not the colonized people of Africa and Asia.[3] For the British radical internationalists who made up Save the Children's early leaders and supporters, internationalism had seemed to imply a critique of imperialism, not because imperialism threatened the principle of self-determination, but because it threatened peace. The Union of Democratic Control (the organization that spawned the Fight the Famine Council and later Save the Children, as we saw in chapter 1) had been most influenced by the influential socialist thinker John Hobson, who argued in *Imperialism: A Study* that imperialism was as detrimental to British workers as it was to colonized people, because it drew them into wars of expansion that were in the interests of a capitalist elite.[4] Empires were, in this formulation, a threat to international peace.

The left-leaning internationalists who had founded Save the Children had been involved in campaigns against imperial expansion during the 1899–1902 Boer War, and against the unfettered imperial capitalism and violence of Congolese rubber production.[5] After the First World War, however, many of these former critics of empire wavered in their opposition to imperialism. Their earlier critique of colonialism was not necessarily grounded in a belief in the right of colonized peoples to self-determination, but rather in a critique of colonial capitalism. It was possible for them, therefore, to imagine that an acceptable model of colonial rule could exist, if it exploited neither British workers at home nor colonized people overseas. In line with a long mission-ary tradition, they imagined that empire was, or at least could be, a civilizing force.[6] At the same time, they were influenced by liberal and left-wing visions of imperialism (like that of the Fabian society, or of liberal free trade advo-cates) that focused on the potential benefits of an imperial economy for the British working classes.[7] Charles Roden Buxton, husband of SCF founder Dorothy Buxton and the son of a colonial governor, was especially prominent in debates within the Labour Party about the possibilities for what he termed "ethical imperialism" as a feature of the "new world order."[8]

Charles Buxton was by no means alone in his desire to create an ethical model of imperialism after the First World War. The question of how to create an internationalist form of colonialism was one of the very first chal-lenges that faced the Allied powers in the aftermath of the First World War. The delegates to the Paris Peace Conference had considered what to do with the former German colonies and the ex-Ottoman Middle East. The Confer-ence had created the Permanent Mandates Commission, a body intended to oversee these territories and ensure that governance was in the interest of the "well-being and development of [their] peoples." Mandated rule was described by the Covenant of the League of Nations as a "sacred trust of civilization," intended to support colonized people in the "strenuous condi-tions of the modern world" until they were ready for self-government.[9] Each year, governments ruling mandated territories delivered reports to the League of Nations Council on their rule. The Mandates Commission studied these and heard petitions made by colonized peoples or outside interest groups (such as humanitarian organizations) concerning the conduct of colonizing powers. While it was concerned only with the former territories of the Axis powers, the Mandates Commission embedded imperial rule at the heart of the League of Nations.[10] The Mandates system not only extended the empires of Allied colonial powers but legitimated imperialism, reconciling it with the international norms of the twentieth century.[11]

For Charles Buxton and many of his associates in the Labour Party, the Mandates Commission epitomized ethical imperialism, and they argued that it be extended so that all colonized territories could be overseen by the League of Nations.[12] The Mandates Commission codified the principles of trusteeship through a series of checks and balances in the form of reports, petitions, and surveys to hold colonizing powers to account. Though the practice of accountability rarely matched the principle, Charles Buxton believed that all colonial powers should be encouraged to apply the principles of trusteeship in their territories. In this model, he envisioned the "outdated" concept of colonialism being replaced by a modern, international form of "world responsibility" in which the world's leading states, via the League, would take on collective trusteeship for those he referred to as "backwards peoples."[13] The existence of the League of Nations, and in particular the Mandates Commission, deepened the support of previous imperial skeptics, such as Charles Roden Buxton, for British colonialism. Imperial rule was to be finessed and improved, not abolished or challenged.

While Buxton proposed an alternative model for empire, he could not envisage a near future in which colonized states were independent. Instead, he admired the vision of trusteeship laid out by the former colonial governor of Nigeria and British appointee to the Mandates Commission, Lord Lugard, in *The Dual Mandate* (1922).[14] *The Dual Mandate* described the twin pillars of ideal imperial rule: to hold the land and resources of colonized states in trust for the wider world, developing industry in order to unlock these resources for the good of the international economy, and to hold colonized land in trust for its inhabitants while advancing their education and systems of governance to such an extent that they would (eventually) be ready to take on the mantle of independence.[15] In this vision, imperialism benefitted both colonized people and Western people, raising standards of living and education for the former, and producing economic benefits for the latter.[16]

While impressed by the vision laid out in *The Dual Mandate*, it seemed to Charles Buxton that it would be "impossible to fulfill one mandate without betraying the other."[17] Rapid industrialization in colonial territories that unlocked natural resources for the good of the wider world would, he feared, lead to the abuse of indigenous workers. Optimistic as ever about the capacity of informed public opinion, Buxton believed that humanitarian efforts, alongside parliamentary interventions, could keep "native protection" firmly on the imperial agenda.[18] He also hoped that, even in the absence of a scaled up Mandates Commission, the League of Nations would respond to appeals from the public on behalf of colonized people and intervene to stop the worst abuses of power.[19] It would, then, fall to humanitarian organizations like Save the Children to step in: first working to overcome the lack of a formal independent overseer of imperial practice at the League by keeping colonial living conditions on the public and political agenda; and second, imagining an imperial capitalism that fulfilled both mandates, protecting colonial subjects while modernizing the colonial economy.

In the years after the First World War, humanitarian organizations embraced these challenges willingly. As discussed in the introduction, imperial humanitarianism—usually in the form of missionary-led schools and hospitals—was as old as formal imperialism, but in the interwar years, humanitarian practices began to shift. Increasingly, as Charles Buxton had envisaged, British humanitarians with concerns about the treatment of colonized people looked to Geneva. Britain's oldest and most prominent imperial humanitarian organization, the Anti-Slavery and Aboriginal Protection Society (ASAPS), regularly petitioned the Mandates Commission; its chair, John Harris, was even briefly considered for a formal post.[20] A new generation of British imperial feminists also took their campaigns to the League, determined that the new representation of women in Parliament would lead to the uplift of their sisters in colonial subjecthood.[21] In the age of so-called "ethical imperialism," humanitarians and feminists fought practices such as child slavery, child marriage, and female genital mutilation, and diplomats at the League of Nations could be formidable allies in securing the compliance of the Colonial Office and bettering the lives of colonized peoples.[22]

At a moment when imperially focused humanitarians were turning toward the League of Nations to further their work, Save the Children, a self-styled "international" organization founded to work in war-torn Europe, began to debate extending its work into the British Empire. It seemed the opportune moment to do so. As the decade drew to a close, the European refugee crisis seemed to be on its way to "liquidation," and the famines and epidemics of the immediate postwar period had been (briefly) replaced with widespread economic prosperity.[23] The Fund's leader, the cerebral and otherworldly Eglantyne Jebb, had become interested in "Eastern religions" and, shortly before her death at the age of forty-one in 1928, she had proclaimed that the Fund must extend its work to "all the world's children," beginning in India. At an Extraordinary General Meeting of the Save the Children Council in January 1929, Dorothy Buxton communicated this final message from her sister, urging the Fund to realize Jebb's dying wish.[24]

It was not Dorothy (overcommitted as ever to a host of political campaigns) who led the Fund in fulfilling Jebb's dream of expansion, but Dorothy's sister-in-law, Victoria de Bunsen. An "adventurous, plucky and highly intelligent woman," Victoria de Bunsen had been involved in humanitarian ventures since the prewar years when, with her brothers Charles Roden Buxton and Lord Noel Buxton, she had traveled to the Balkans to tend to Macedonian victims of Turkish violence.[25] She had volunteered for the Fund since 1921 and served on the committee that authored the Declaration of the Rights of the Child. In 1928, de Bunsen's eldest brother, Lord Noel Buxton, had become the Fund's president, and de Bunsen had taken up a seat on the Fund's Council. Pragmatic and unsentimental, de Bunsen had been bemused by Jebb's exploration of Eastern religion and was unenthusiastic about working in India. Instead, she saw an opportunity to align a new venture for the SCF with the interests and history of the Buxton family. The centenary of the abolition of the slave trade was approaching, and de Bunsen and her brothers were the great-grandchildren of Thomas Fowell Buxton, "who along with William Wilberforce was the liberator of the African slaves."[26] The family had "historical ties to Africa" through generations of missionaries, and so de Bunsen believed that Africa, rather than India, should be the Fund's next site of intervention.[27] The situation in Africa was also more urgent: the Buxtons, like Lord Lugard, believed that Africa was poised on the brink of an industrial revolution due to its abundant natural resources and cheap labor. If the Fund acted now, it could prevent some of the worst effects of economic advance—child labor, unsanitary urban slums—from impacting African children, as they had impacted European children in the nineteenth century.[28]

De Bunsen was also persuaded to devote the Fund's attention to Africa by missionaries already working there. Throughout the nineteenth century, British missionaries had often been at the forefront of educational and medical interventions across the empire, and their presence served to confirm the benevolent character of colonialism to the British public. For many Britons, missionaries had been a vector of engagement with the empire, and donations to them had been a way of participating in the humanitarian imperial project.[29] In the interwar period, donations to missionary organizations and church attendance were declining as Britain inched toward the secularization that would characterize the post-1945 decades. Missionaries were in search of new sources of revenue and a new image. Large missionary organizations such as the London Missionary Society and the Church Missionary Society were increasingly emphasizing the medical and educational nature of their work, realizing that this drew more money than evangelism. Partnership with Save the Children, a modern, non-faith-based "expert" aid organization, would enhance this new image. Dr Alfred Cook, a prominent medical missionary, also made the case for an African intervention to his close friend, Victoria de Bunsen. Save the Children would be aided by Africa's many British missionaries, he claimed, and missionaries in Africa had more influence than their counterparts in India or Southeast Asia because "there was no great organized religion whose teachings we find ourselves in conflict with." He continued, "Whilst in Asia the Hindu, the Malay, the Chinese and the Japanese are proud of their civilization, the African does feel an irresistible attraction for the new way of living which the white man brings him."[30]

Keen to build connections with missionaries, de Bunsen hosted an "information evening" attached to the 1930 Lambeth Conference of the Church of England where she outlined her vision for Save the Children's entry into Africa: a conference in Geneva. Holding a conference about African children in Switzerland was, at least, consistent with the approach taken to questions of race and globalization at the Lambeth Conference itself, where an entirely white church leadership passed resolutions that urged the church to work against the "exploitation of the weaker races," and build "friendly race relations."[31] Supporting the newly proposed Save the Children conference seemed a way to fulfill these new resolutions to many of the missionaries present, and offered an opportunity to align missionary endeavor with a modern, humanitarian organization.[32]

While Anglican missionaries were hoping to share some of the popularity of Save the Children's humanitarian work, Edward Fuller, the Fund's press secretary, was similarly hoping that the Fund would claim a stake in the popularity of "Africa," conceived of as a signifier for exotic fantasies and savior complexes, rather than any specific geographies within the continent. Fuller imagined that Africa would provide an exotic change from the European refugees and reconstruction programs that, ten years since the end of the First World War, were boring donors. In 1928, Fuller began "testing the waters," reprinting reports on African child welfare drawn from missionary publications in the Fund's now bimonthly magazine. Drawing on classic imperial tropes, these reports described Africa as a single, homogenous space: "captivating" and "enthralling," a backdrop for sensational tales of "tribal customs" and "native taboos." These reports, designed more to shock than to educate SCF supporters, explained how "savage" and "amusing" African practices could end in the tragic deaths of African children.[33]

Fuller's early attempts to interest Save the Children supporters in Africa were unsuccessful. By the end of the 1920s, as the global economy entered the depression of the 1930s, the Fund could barely draw in donations sufficient to continue existing projects, let alone launch new ventures. Undaunted, de Bunsen proposed a model designed to allow the Fund to exert its influence in Africa at minimal cost. She proposed that Save the Children and its International Union should become centers for "information and propaganda on African children," which they would provide to other parties interested in Africa as a means of directing their work.[34] De Bunsen's main focus was colonial governments and missionaries, who would be invited to attend a Conference in Geneva in July 1931, hosted by the International Union. At the conference, she intended to draw together a host of experts to "meet on a common platform" to determine the best interests of African children and thus maximize child welfare.[35] De Bunsen was fortunate to be organizing the conference while the Labour Party was in government: Charles Buxton was an MP and Lord Noel Buxton served in Ramsay MacDonald's cabinet as the minister for agriculture. Lord Passfield, the Labour government's colonial secretary, was the brother-in-law of founder member and staunch supporter Kate Courtney, and a personal friend of the Buxton family. De Bunsen used these connections to secure the formal support of the Colonial Office for the Conference.[36]

IMPERIALISTS, HUMANITARIANS, AND "THE AFRICAN CHILD"

Preparations for the Conference on the African Child began in June 1930, when 1,500 questionnaires on "the conditions of child life" were sent to missionaries and British colonial officials in Africa. The questionnaire contained 128 questions on topics ranging from the accessibility of schools to the diet of children in different age groups. Only 358 questionnaires were returned, including 315 from missionaries.[37] De Bunsen was concerned by this low response rate and the bias toward missionaries, as she had hoped that "people concerned with trade, hygiene and demography" might also provide information.[38] De Bunsen also noted with disappointment that the completed questionnaires did not come from as "geographically dispersed" an area as the Fund had hoped, with the majority originating from eastern and southern Africa and coastal regions. Despite this, conference organizers did not doubt their ability to pronounce on Africa as a whole: "The needs of a baby in Kenya or Basutoland (or for that matter a London slum)," they blithely remarked, "are basically the same."[39]

Missionaries were not only the foremost respondents to the questionnaire, but also the most enthusiastic attendees of the conference, making up half the delegates.[40] The League of Nations was also well represented, although this was largely because Eric Drummond, secretary-general of the League and a personal friend of Noel Buxton, had ordered officials from the Mandates Commission and the Health and Social Sections to attend.[41] Further delegates came from the British SCF, the International Union, and the ICRC. Academics, anthropologists, doctors, British colonial officials, and governmental representatives from Belgium, Spain and Italy joined them.[42] The composition of the conference reflected the Fund's attitude: European humanitarians (rather than Africans or people of African origin) were best qualified to determine the needs of the continent. "Expertise" was more important than experience. The vast majority of the European delegates were British. This, de Bunsen claimed, was because of the particularly humanitarian quality of British imperialism. While the conference was framed as a space for sharing concerns and innovations, in reality de Bunsen intended it to showcase the superior quality of the British Empire and universalize British welfare practices in non-British colonial territories.[43]

Lord Lugard became patron of the conference, and his concerns framed its discussions. In the context of an imminent industrial revolution in Africa, the conference discussed the duty of European empires to prevent this from "damaging" native life and customs. Whereas in Asia industrialization had occurred over a longer period, beginning in the late nineteenth century, in Africa Lugard felt this process would be more rapid. Conference attendees were consequently urged "never to forget the baffling pace at which civilization has sprung upon [Africans]."[44]

Despite noting the "damage" it might cause, SCF leaders were nevertheless enthusiastic about the predicted industrialization of Africa. In the phased progress narrative laid out in the Fund's 1924 *International Handbook of Child Care and Protection*, it was claimed that nations must pass through an industrial phase in order to attain higher standards of child welfare. Assuming that the European experience served as a blueprint for African industrialization, European humanitarians attending the Conference felt confident that they could predict the problems that would be faced in Africa. They aimed to prevent "what had happened in Europe, where the industrialization preceded the regulation of child labor, with consequences it has taken a generation to repair."[45] The conference formally proposed that the legislation laid down by the International Labour Office for the regulation of child labor in "civilised countries" should be adapted specifically to protect African children.[46]

While industrialization was deemed a force from which African children required protection, it was also Africa's changing economic circumstances that made African children so valuable. As before, children were regarded as future workers. Because it upheld an internationalist vision in which economic interdependence led to mutual peace and prosperity, the Fund believed that ensuring the fitness of children for labor was an investment that would benefit the wider international community. In a worldview in which African economic development was essential to Western prosperity, African children became important players in the global economic system. Indeed, Lugard believed that charity directed at African children had the potential to be even more valuable than that directed at European children in terms of the future contribution they were likely to make. He wrote in the preface to the Conference Report, "I have sometimes wondered whether the self-sacrifice of noble lives devoted to saving malformed children and those afflicted with incurable disease . . . as well as the feeble minded child who can never 'make good' is either kind to the individuals or wise from the point of view of the community. . . . But saving children in Africa is, or should be, quite a different matter. The infant mortality recorded in some regions is so appalling . . . a great proportion of children [die] who might have grown up into healthy manhood or womanhood."[47] Colonial Secretary Lord Passfield agreed: "An improvement in the health of African children, and a reduction of infant mortality," he explained, was not "simply a humanitarian question" but one of "future prosperity," which might be viewed from a "materialistic point of view."[48] The Fund's interest in Africa was rooted in the same principles as its interest in children in Austria and Germany: child health was an international concern, with consequences not only for children's own immediate communities, but also for European peace and prosperity.

At the opening session of the conference, while delegates sat fanning themselves packed into a crowded hall on a hot summer's day in Geneva, Lord Noel Buxton framed their shared endeavor as the expansion of the principles Child Rights across the globe. As we saw in the previous chapter, in 1924, Save the Children's "Declaration of the Rights of the Child" was formally adopted by the League of Nations and considered the rights of children in relation to the contributions that they would make as citizens in later life. Despite the apparently universal nature of the five child rights it laid out, Lord Noel Buxton claimed that the two articles most integral to their capacity to work applied to African children: the first clause (that "The child must be given the means requisite for its normal development") and the fourth ("The child must be put in a position to earn a livelihood, and must be protected against every form of exploitation").[49] Speaking in a later session, Archdeacon Owen of the Church Missionary Society (CMS) in Kenya objected to this "narrow" approach, contending that article five (that the "child must be brought up in the consciousness that its talents must be devoted to the service of fellow men") was also vital. Arguing that this was "already secured for children so far as the life of the tribe is concerned," he observed, "we belong to a world community, and what we want to do is have the child serve a larger community than that of the tribe."[50] Owen failed to grasp the implicit assumption of Conference organizers that in fitting African children for labor, they were simultaneously ensuring their service to the "world community."

While the Declaration of the Rights of the Child had also claimed children's right to "spiritual" development, religion was seldom mentioned by the delegates at the Conference, despite the fact that over half of the delegates there represented evangelizing, Christian organizations. Save the Children and its International Union were not "secular" institutions. Because of the diversity of European Christianity, along with the religious diversity of the Council of the British Fund (largely composed of Quakers and nonconformists, as well as increasing numbers of Jews, theosophists and Bahá'í), the movement presented itself as nondenominational. Its appeals sometimes used religious images or evoked Christian notions of duty and responsibility, but its work on the ground had no obviously religious character. Missionaries took their cues from their hosts, speaking in firmly practical terms about the well-being of African children and the economic reasons for their interest, while seldom mentioning the religious nature of their work.[51]

The early sessions of the conference discussed the value of African children to international prosperity. On its second day, delegates examined how these valuable African children could be kept alive and healthy. Many of the discussions focused on infant mortality: the deaths of children under one year of age. A number of missionary delegates alleged that as many as 70 or 80 percent of African children died before the age of one. This "appalling slaughter of innocents" was claimed to be due to a large and often contradictory range of factors, including "poor hygiene, overhandling, chill, lack of sleep, overfeeding and paradoxically, malnutrition, bad housing, bad aid, parental neglect, and infectious diseases."[52] Practices such as the murder of children by "being placed in the bush to be eaten alive by vultures and other kinds of ants and creatures" were also proclaimed as the norm by a number of other delegates, who drew similarly firm links between supposedly high rates of infant mortality and (often imagined) African cultural practices.[53] Most often, the "ignorance" of African mothers was blamed. Delegates agreed that the quickest way to improve child welfare was maternal education, urging women to abandon "harmful practices," such as indoor cooking in "native huts" that led to suffocation; swaddling babies in goatskins that "almost suffocate them"; and feeding them "unsuitable" milk from "native cows."[54]

Not all delegates laid the blame for infant mortality at the feet of African mothers. For esteemed anthropologist Emil Torday, it was the infamous rubber companies in the Congo that caused infant death by introducing a system of "forced labour" in which "a man is taken from his home, sometimes never to return." This undermined African family structures, and Torday's report for the conference (which he did not deliver in person, having died a few weeks before it took place) asked how, "deprived of a husband's strong arm, and overworked, can women bear children and rear them?"[55] Other Conference delegates (including John Harris, president of the Anti-Slavery and Aboriginal Protection Society) took up his concerns. A report presented at the conference by Charles Roden Buxton similarly denounced the use of migratory male labor to staff mines in Nyasaland, and spoke both of the burden this placed upon mothers and the potentially fatal effects for children.[56] For Buxton, it was possible to distinguish between the kind of profit-driven exploitative capitalism of mining companies, and the form of ethical, international trade he envisaged. In his writings, Charles Buxton was (unsuccessfully) seeking to uncouple colonial capitalism from colonial development: he saw the former as unethical profiteering and the latter in service of a greater, internationalist good. However, Buxton remained stuck in the paper-thin space between his two ideas: Africa needed industrialization and trade in order to "develop," but industrialization and trade led to exploitation that undermined the development process.[57]

Save the Children and the majority of its conference delegates were also confounded by this tension. On the one hand, they believed that modernization and industrialization were desirable and enhanced the value of African children to the wider world, making it their duty to "save African children" from their "ignorant" mothers. On the other, they feared that industrialization and modernization could be damaging if introduced too quickly or intensively. African children needed protection simultaneously both *for* and *from* growing business interests on the continent. This was the very dilemma that Charles Buxton had seen in Lugard's proclamation of a "Dual Mandate": was it possible to fulfill the "trust" of stewarding African natural resources and labor for the good of the wider world via industrialization, while also protecting indigenous communities? This dilemma was not the only one facing the conference organizers. De Bunsen, Fuller, and Lewis Golden were also keen to preserve the relationships they had built with the British Colonial Office and influential figures such as Lord Lugard.[58] Any proposed solutions, therefore, should not alienate their new alliances. Rather than proposing any substantive change to colonial policies, the solutions suggested by conference delegates lay entirely in curbing the abusive practices of colonial businesses (none of which were represented at the conference). Instead of advocating welfare interventions by the colonial state, missionaries and humanitarians were urged to "educate" African mothers.[59]

What the conference provided, then, was not a manifesto for a new form of international humanitarian intervention in Africa, but an endorsement of British colonialism by British humanitarians. British conference delegates contended that this independence was far off and that European rule would continue for the foreseeable future. Speaking about the needs of children was a way to speak about the future development of Africa, casting the "progress" of Africa as gradual. According to Noel Buxton, "The quickest and surest way to progress [is to] cure the ills that children suffer and in a generation you have solved all the problems concerning adults. . . . This is at once the line of least resistance and the quickest method of obtaining betterment and reform."[60] In this way, childhood provided a metaphor for the entire continent as immature, in need of oversight and education from its European elders.[61]

ANTI-COLONIALISM AND THE AFRICAN CHILD

The interwar years saw not only increased international organization and coordination of imperial power through the League of Nations, but also increased international organization and coordination of anti-colonial movements. In 1927 the first meeting of the League Against Imperialism convened in Brussels, bringing together nationalists from Africa, Asia, and South America and supporters from Europe and North America. Though organized by the Comintern, a Soviet-directed body that aimed to bring about world Communism, the League Against Imperialism drew participants from across the left, including delegates from the Independent Labour Party.[62] The name implied a critique of the League of Nations and its vision of internationalism that perpetuated colonial rule via the mandates system.[63] The League Against Imperialism played an important role in connecting African, Caribbean, and African American anti-imperialists, and led to the formation of a working party, the Negro Commission, which passed a resolution demanding "complete freedom of the peoples of Africa and of African Origin," "complete equality between the Negro race and all other races," and "control of the land and governments of Africa by the Africans."[64] The conference spawned several new international anti-colonial organizations, and provided one of the first meeting spaces for an African cosmopolitan anti-colonial elite that increasingly resided in the capital cities of interwar Europe.[65]

Delegates at the Save the Children conference were no doubt keenly aware of this growing organized critique of colonialism in Africa. Labour Party delegates had colleagues who had attended the first meeting of the League Against Imperialism, and the Colonial Office had long debated strategies for engaging with (or avoiding) anti-colonial crusaders such as Kenyatta, who now resided in London. A number of the African delegates of Save the Children were representing organizations that had grown out of the League Against Imperialism, such as James Ford, representing the International Trade Union Council of Negro Workers. Save the Children organizers, however, did their best to ensure that anti-imperial sentiments went unexpressed. Focusing on the future potential of children was a means of avoiding discussions about the present political demands of adults. Indeed, when anti-colonial principles and movements were spoken of, they were characterized as illegitimate and inherently violent. The Catholic missionary and delegate Father Joyeaux warned against adults having "recourse to doctrines of anarchy and revolution" and feared they "would listen to the promises of agitators, who would play on their wounded pride." He saw better living conditions in Africa as a necessary prophylactic against anti-colonial politics.[66] African adults were repeatedly infantilized in these, incapable of forming rational political perspectives. One delegate stated, "We must not put into brains lacking proper preparation a mine which may one day explode, and which we cannot prevent exploding."[67] Anti-colonial sentiments were interpreted as proof of the need for continued "guidance" from European powers, rather than legitimate political grievances.

However, though hoping to avoid discussions of political questions, conference organizers had been keen to include some African delegates to show the modern, collaborative nature of the event. The prohibitive cost of travel to the conference effectively excluded all but the most elite Africans, and those who attended from nearby European cities cobbled together funds for transport and registration from sponsoring organizations that saw the conference as an opportunity to lobby for the anti-colonial cause. The two hundred delegates included five Africans, one West Indian, and one African American. For this self-proclaimed lobby of "Negro-delegates" the conference was a maddening experience, as their attempts to bring politics back into the discussion of African childhood were repeatedly shut down.[68] A discussion of education took place on the third day of the conference and anti-colonial delegates vocalized their dissent. Gladys Casely Hayford (daughter of prominent feminist anti-colonial educator Adelaide Casely Hayford) spoke on behalf of her mother: Adelaide had been unable to raise enough money to pay for passage to Geneva. Gladys Casely Hayford questioned the conference's adherence to the principles of trusteeship. If colonial powers were "developing" Africans for eventual self-rule, why were they not educating African children?[69] Influenced by an emerging strand of cultural relativism in anthropological thought (typified in the work of Hungarian anthropologist, Franz Boas), when white missionaries spoke about educating African children, they emphasized the need to preserve "tribal customs" and endow African children with manual skills that would suit them for the industrial economy. They should be "first rate Africans, rather than second rate Europeans."[70]

Gladys Casely Hayford countered that it was possible for African children to have pride in their heritage without limiting their education to vernacular languages and manual trades. To have any value, education had to encourage independence and leadership, not just colonial subject-hood and workmanship.[71] Gold Coast delegate J. W. de Graft Johnson followed Casely Hayford, adding that the missionaries in attendance "have not educated a single one of our children."[72] African American Communist James Ford, whose conference attendance was being funded by Comintern, connected this critique to the wider capitalist character of European colonialism. He argued that the new interest in African children was due to the growth of industries on the continent, which needed obedient, strong workers. The "chief pride" of European educators, he stated, was to "furnish white contractors with a staff of fit workmen."[73] At this point, Noel Buxton interjected, "reminding" the "African delegates inclined to criticize European efforts" that "there would be no schools in Africa were it not for the missionaries."[74] Thus, Buxton designated all the conference's Black delegates "African" (Ford was African American), drawing upon racist stereotypes of "angry Black men" to dismiss their critiques.

The conference also refused to engage explicitly with race, as European delegates made vague statements about the intrinsic difference between Europeans and Africans and simultaneous noncommittal declarations of racial equality. According to Charles Roden Buxton, who had recently published *The Race Question in Africa*, African people, though more "childlike and primitive" would, in time, be "as capable" as their European counterparts. In his view, there was no essential racial difference and so the question of race was simply outdated. Charles Roden Buxton lamented that "race consciousness" was growing among the "world's backwards peoples," fearing that its only consequence would be to cause "serious problems to the governing authorities" and might result in "violent uprisings."[75] In spite of Charles Roden Buxton's objections, various speakers at the conference had promoted the view that racial differences *did* exist: African children had fundamentally different capabilities, and would fulfill a role in the international community different from their European counterparts. Recognizing this, James Ford tried to secure an acknowledgment of the equality of Europeans and Africans and the existence of racism. On the last day of the conference, he raised the Scottsboro Eight, a group of teenage boys on trial for their lives for the alleged rape of a white woman in the American South. The Scottsboro Eight had become an international symbol of racial inequality and had united the European left and anti-colonial organizations worldwide with civil rights movements in the United States.[76] This case, Ford argued, showed what imperialism did to children. The "rights of the child" could not be realized until the rights of African people worldwide were realized.[77] Ford began his speech as follows:

> You have done everything to keep us from speaking. . . . You claim to be saving the Children of Africa. But, if we examine the board of patrons and organizers of the Conference, we find them to be the same people who are associated with plundering and exploiting the African colonies; they are members of the highest nobility, high colonial officers, industrialists, "labour leaders" of the 2nd international and "labour" minsters, bishops, generals, and diplomats. [From the floor below, Lord Noel Buxton shouted at him to halt, but Ford continued] You explain that the time has come to Save the Children of Africa, but this is a hypocritical gesture invented because you fear that the African population that produces huge profits may die out and endanger the income of the imperialist coupon-clippers. . . . It is imperialist barbarism in the colonies, and in particular Africa, that is the immediate cause of the terrible death rate among [African] children.[78]

At this point, a white male missionary dragged Ford roughly off the stage and Lord Noel Buxton explained to the delegates that the conference "had not been convened to discuss political questions, but to study how the African children could be helped under the general conditions existing."[79]

When other delegates such as Mitra Sinanan from the West Indian League of Coloured People and Nigerian trade unionist Israel Ransome Kuti suggested that imperial rule might be the cause of, rather than the solution to, "the misery and poverty that existed in Africa," they too were reminded forcefully of the "non-political nature" of "the African Child."[80] From the outset of the conference, while appreciating the legitimacy that the presence of the "African delegates" conferred on the gathering, European delegates had listened to dissenting opinions without truly hearing them. These voices were then discredited by all possible means and expunged from the conference's vast official records and publications.

Having been physically prevented from delivering his speech at the conference, James Ford penned an "Exposé of the Save the Children Conference on the African Child," which he immediately submitted for publication in the Comintern-sponsored international newspaper *The Negro Worker*. It also appeared as a separate pamphlet titled "Imperialism Destroys the People of Africa," and in the new journal of the organization that he represented, the International Trade Union Council of Negro Workers, which was also financed by the Comintern.[81] In these essays, he referred to organizers of the Fund as "Slave Drivers" (a powerful slight, given how far the identity of the Buxton family rested on its abolitionist ancestry). He emphasized the connection between concern for African children and desires to enhance the productivity of colonial economies. Though Ford regarded his work as an "exposé," conference organizers were frank about their unsentimental, economic approach to African Children. They would not, however, have recognized themselves in his critique. Charles Buxton, in the tradition of Lord Lugard and the leading thinkers on "ethical imperialism," had strenuously prized apart two visions of imperial capitalism. Theirs was one of trusteeship and development, totally separable from the capitalism of "exploitation" and profiteering Ford described. Ford drew no such distinctions: for him trusteeship and humanitarianism all amounted to capitalist imperialism. They were a cause of, rather than solution to, African children's suffering.

Ford's various writings about the Conference (published far more rapidly than the official accounts, which are preserved only in the archives of the League of Nations and the SCIU) circulated throughout the alternative international sphere. Networks created and solidified by the League Against Imperialism reached across eastern and western Europe, as well as Africa, Asia, and South America. Ford's pamphlet has been preserved in collections in Moscow, Harlem, Johannesburg, and beyond.[82] Its argument connected the conference to a wider critique of the rhetoric of trusteeship to justify imperialism. It also prefigured a genre of aid critique associated with a much later period of decolonization and Cold War polarization.

Ford was not the only Black delegate for whom the conference was formative. Israel Ransome Kuti founded the Nigerian Union of Teachers just three days after the conference. As well as lobbying for better pay and conditions for African teachers, the foremost aim of the Union was to secure education for independence across Nigeria and oppose limited, colonial manual and vernacular training.[83] Gladys Casely Hayford was also driven by the attitudes she encountered at the conference to become involved in anti-colonial politics and teaching, leaving her life as a cabaret dancer in Europe and joining her mother at her girls' school in Sierra Leone to write acclaimed poetry that urged cultural pride and colonial resistance.[84] Future Kenyan president Johnstone (later Jomo) Kenyatta also went on to write about the Save the Children Conference on the African Child in his 1938 examination of Kikuyu culture, *Facing Mount Kenya*. He described the shortsightedness of European humanitarian interventions, and their failure to understand and respect local custom.[85]

In the interwar period, international institutions legitimized colonialism in an era when its legal, economic, and moral basis was increasingly challenged.[86] Save the Children's Conference on the African Child certainly functioned in this way. At the same time, the conference provided an incubator for both critiques of colonialism and the role of humanitarianism and education in legitimating and upholding it. While the Buxtons had sought to show that, ultimately, British imperialism was humanitarian, for James Ford and other Black delegates at the conference, humanitarianism was imperialism.

HUMANITARIANISM, COLONIAL REVISIONISM, AND THE "ETHIOPIAN CRISIS"

Another outcome of Save the Children's conference on Africa was the formation of the Child Protection Committee headed by Victoria de Bunsen. Based in London, it continued the work that the conference had begun, examining the welfare of children in British colonies, though it proposed no concrete action and had no funding. As a lobbying body, while it debated issues from child marriage to clitoridectomy, the committee was hamstrung by its desire to criticize neither the Colonial Office nor colonial rule.[87] The Fund's first and only interwar intervention in Africa came in 1935, when fascist Italy invaded Ethiopia. In his satirical novel *Scoop*, Evelyn Waugh referred to the conflict as the "microcosm of a world drama."[88] It showcased the dangers posed by fascist states and the frailty of the international order, and it called into question the legitimacy of colonial rule. Before the Italian invasion, Ethiopia had been one of two independent states in Africa and a member of the League of Nations. As such, it should have been protected under Article Ten of the Covenant of the League of Nations, which guaranteed assistance to member states encountering external aggression. Instead, the weak international response highlighted the growing threat of fascism, and the demise of the League of Nations. It was the beginning of the end of the vision of international order that Save the Children had been founded to promote.

Ethiopia's position within the international order had always been contested. In 1923, Ethiopia's emperor, Haile Selassie, had requested membership of the League of Nations. Ethiopia, however, had a system of domestic slavery, which Lord Lugard claimed to be evidence that it had not reached the same standards of civilization as European members of the League. He proposed that Ethiopia should be admitted to the League but placed under supervision similar to mandatory rule by a council of European powers (a model very similar to Charles Buxton's vision of "world responsibility"). French delegates, however, seeing Lugard's suggestion as an attempt to gain British control of additional territory in East Africa, supported Ethiopia gaining full membership, supported by other British internationalists such as the ASAPS, which argued that Ethiopian admission to the League would itself hasten the end of slavery.[89] Ethiopia joined the General Assembly of the League of Nations in 1923, as the only independent Black African nation with full-member status. In 1932, Lord Noel Buxton visited Ethiopia on behalf of ASAPS and was convinced by Emperor Haile Selassie's promise that slavery would be abolished within twenty years. For Buxton, Ethiopia's membership in the League was not so much an indication of its civilized status as part of its civilizing process.[90]

Italy had long harbored imperial ambitions in Ethiopia. Ethiopian land separated its existing colonial possessions of Eritrea and Somaliland and Italy had attempted a previous invasion in 1896 to create a unified East African territory. This had failed (a rare defeat of a European power by an African army) and was remembered in Italy as a national humiliation. Italian imperial sensitivities were exacerbated when, in 1920, Italy was the only Allied power not apportioned new territories to administer under the mandates system. In 1922, Benito Mussolini seized power in Italy, instituting a cult of militarism and nationalism.[91] The invasion of Ethiopia in 1935 was a way to showcase Italian might. In order to present the Ethiopian invasion in internationally acceptable terms, Italy exploited the international ambivalence about Ethiopia's domestic trade in slaves. Couching the invasion in the language of trusteeship, Mussolini promised that Italy would "crush slavery in a barbaric country."[92] The invasion was thus presented as an act of humanitarianism, rather than unprompted aggression.

When Italian troops marched over the Ethiopian boarder at 5 a.m. on 3 October 1935, the international outcry was immediate. Emerging antifascist movements and existing anti-colonial lobbies protested outside Italian embassies from Paris to New York. In Soho, the windows of Italian shops and restaurants were smashed.[93] The invasion made headlines day after day and Lewis Golden saw an opportunity for the Fund to both take action on African soil and attract fresh public support for the Fund via the familiar rhetoric of horror and atrocity. Within a week of the invasion, the SCF appointed its first "field worker" in Africa, Fritzi Small. Small was a career aid worker who had started working for the International Red Cross in her native Hungary in 1919 at the age of seventeen. She had spent the 1920s and early 1930s employed by the SCIU, coordinating nursery school work in the Balkan states.[94] On her appointment, Golden instructed her to "give us some really awful stories." Save the Children would, in return, provide funding for a nursery school for the child victims of war.[95]

As preparations for Small's departure were taking place at Save the Children's Golden Square Office, a mile away at the Farringdon Memorial Hall, members of London's anti-colonial lobby, including several of the Black delegates who had attended the 1931 Conference on the African Child, were organizing a rival aid intervention. Announcing their formation as the International African Friends of Abyssinia, they pledged to raise funds not—as Save the Children was—for Ethiopian children or civilians, but to provide arms for the Ethiopian army and medical assistance to wounded soldiers.[96] Their efforts were supported by London's newly formed "Hands off Abyssinia" committee and an international network of Ethiopian solidarity campaigns and appeals. Speakers in the Farringdon Memorial Hall (including Kenyatta) not only condemned the invasion, but also derided the League of Nations and international organizations for their role in promoting the humanitarian rhetoric being used to justify it. It was not just humanitarian rhetoric, but humanitarian organizations that worked to legitimize the

LIFE SEEMED FAIR IN ABYSSINIA

FIGURE 8. Far away from the front lines, Small was unable to find the "awful stories" Golden had hoped for. "An Abyssinian Girl." *The World's Children* (front cover), November 1935.

invasion. The president of ASAPS, John Harris, had been taken in by Italian antislavery propaganda, and had announced his optimism about an Italian intervention.[97] During the speeches in Farringdon, terms such as *development* or *civilization* were denounced as fig leaves for imperial rule, eliciting cries of "shame" from the crowd.[98]

Neither Save the Children's president Noel Buxton nor Fritzi Small were won over by Italian attempts to court humanitarian opinion. They saw the invasion as unjustifiable and regarded the Fund's planned intervention as an opportunity to express support for Ethiopian independence. Small was a committed pacifist, incensed by Italy's reckless threat to the increasingly precarious peace of the mid-1930s.[99] Small attempted, through child welfare work, to bolster Ethiopian nationhood. During her time in the Balkans, she had argued that "national development" hinged on two things: a healthy child population, and a strong civil society in which the nation's rich cared for its poor. She set about replicating this work in Ethiopia, inviting upper-class members of the Women's Association of the Ethiopian Red Cross to participate in Save the Children–led child welfare projects. Her hope was that when Save the Children's invariably brief funding for Ethiopian work dried up, she would have created lasting childcare structures, staffed by newly trained volunteers.[100]

First, Small wrote to the daughter of Hailie Selassie, inviting her to be an official patron of the Fund's efforts.[101] Next, she went about identifying an area to work in. Keen to avoid Italian troops, she chose a wealthy sub-urb of Addis Ababa, where she founded a feeding center for children whose fathers were serving on the front lines and a nursery school. The children were drawn from elite church schools, the offspring of upper- and middle-class Ethiopians. This suited Small well, as she was more interested in their moth-ers than the children themselves. At the nursery, which mothers attended alongside their children, Small held "baby-washing" demonstrations, "edu-cating" mothers about diapers and vaccinations.[102] Small's assumptions that Ethiopian mothers needed to be taught the most basic forms of care for their children and that Ethiopian civil society was nonexistent, were typical of the attitudes on display at the Conference on the African Child four years ear-lier. Though Small considered Ethiopians (who were mostly Christian and, of course, citizens of an independent African state) more "civilized" than other Africans, she nonetheless assumed that European intervention was necessary to "save" Ethiopian children from the ignorance and indifference of adults, despite the fact that her feeding center was staffed almost entirely by volunteers from the Women's Association of the Ethiopian Red Cross, an organization founded in Ethiopia by Ethiopians. Small praised the work of these middle- and upper-class volunteers, ignoring Golden's warning that "Ethiopians, most likely, have the same capacity for deception as Orientals."[103]

Small demonstrated her commitment to Ethiopian independence at both the feeding center and the nursery, where the Ethiopian national anthem was sung daily, under high-flying Ethiopian flags.[104] This was a gesture of defiance, as in the spring of 1936 Italian troops began to advance on the capital. Small's "political" gestures drew disapproval, especially from the SCF's long-standing ally, the International Committee of the Red Cross (ICRC). With close ties to the governing elite of Switzerland, the ICRC had been nervous about the Italian invasion. While Italian contravention of the Geneva Conventions (which the ICRC was meant to uphold) was clear, ICRC leaders felt they could ill afford to anger the powerful neighbor they shared a border with. Setting a pattern of acquiescence to fascist powers that would continue during the Second World War, the ICRC failed to condemn Italy for its use of mustard gas, and warned Small that she, too, must remain "impartial."[105]

Small's presence in Addis Ababa irritated other members of the city's expatriate community, including a group of British missionaries (several of them cousins of the large Buxton family), who had assumed that they, not an interloping organization, would receive money created by the sudden outpouring of public support for Ethiopia. Most irritated, however, was the British Foreign Office, which regarded the presence of a female aid worker as an "undue liability" at a time of war. Foreign Office officials also objected to a prominent British organization engaging in what appeared pro-independence work in Ethiopia. While the British government condemned Italian aggression, it also feared that actively opposing it would alienate Europe's fascist powers and undermine the increasingly precarious peace of the 1930s. Lewis Golden, driven to despair at Small's adventures in Addis Ababa, warned her sternly to keep her distance from "overtly political" work.[106] She was, he would later remember, a woman of "inflexible determination . . . [with] a complete lack of self-consciousness": perfectly suited to the adventurous life of the traveling relief worker, but not a natural diplomat.[107]

A majority of the British public were in favor of a collective international response to Italian aggression in Ethiopia, and to curbing the aggression of fascist states. The results of the 1934–35 Peace Ballot, a nationwide survey of opinions on international relations organized by the League of Nations Union, confirmed reluctant support for military action.[108] However, the League of Nations did not make good on its promise of collective security, launching an ineffectual campaign of sanctions against Italy. In November 1935, details of a secret agreement between British Foreign Secretary Samuel Hoare and French Prime Minister Pierre Laval, in which Italy would be granted two-thirds of Ethiopian land, were leaked to the press. Public outcry forced the resignation of both men, but the infamous Hoare-Laval Pact expressed the French and British appetite for appeasement. Emboldened, in May 1936, Italy seized Addis Ababa and proclaimed Italian rule over Ethiopia.[109] The SCF ordered Small to leave Ethiopia, which she did reluctantly, leaving the Women's Association enough money to continue the nursery for three months and hoping that they would thereafter raise the necessary funds themselves. Within three weeks, the nursery was turned into a convalescent hospital for Italian soldiers.[110] This angered Small, but her removal was seen by the SCF Council in London as necessary to ensure a *rapprochement* with the Foreign Office. Golden was hailed by the Foreign Office as a "most sensible man," and the SCF's "ill-advised" mission to Ethiopia and wider opposition to the Italian invasion were quickly forgotten.[111]

Conceding Ethiopia to Italy seemed to the leaders of Save the Children a small price to pay for the preservation of peace. By the mid-1930s, Hitler, too, was mounting a campaign for *lebensraum* ("living space") for German settlers in Africa. He found unlikely allies in Noel and Charles Buxton, who imagined Germany would be granted some of its former colonial possessions by the League of Nations, ruling them in line with the principle of trustee-ship, possibly under some form of international oversight.[112] To the Buxtons, this colonial revisionism seemed preferable to war. Moreover they had always been sympathetic to German demands to have the punitive Versailles Treaty reversed and were interested in new visions of colonialism that incorporated wider sections of the European international community.[113] However, while the Buxtons' desire for peace remained unchanged, the international context was changing rapidly around them. In May 1936, Hitler invaded the Rhine-land. Ethiopia was all but forgotten by liberal and left-leaning British opinion and the question of appeasement became all-encompassing. It was not, how-ever, forgotten by the anti-colonial activists who had organized around the invasion; nor was the alliance between humanitarian principles and imperial aggression. It was, after all, Italy's appropriation of the rhetoric of abolition-ism and humanitarianism that gave the invasion credibility and a measure of support from European publics. As members of the International African Friends of Abyssinia had argued, the notion of "civilization" had won out against collective security: Ethiopia, deemed to be a less advanced society, could not access the promises of mutual protection enshrined in the League of Nations covenant. Anti-colonial activists therefore viewed humanitarian-ism as an adversary in the fight to end imperialism.[114]

THE BEGINNING OF THE END OF
IMPERIAL INTERNATIONALISM?

In 1933, British socialist and anti-colonial activist Winifred Holtby wrote a satirical account of British imperialism, *Mandoa Mandoa*. Dedicated to her closest friend and former Save the Children Council member Vera Brittain, the book parodied the exploits of journalists, travel agents, traders and the "International Humanitarian Association." These groups were drawn to a fictional African country (Mandoa) by visions of paradise, a market for European goods, and an opportunity to end slavery. The International Humanitarian Association is portrayed as a collection of naive liberals, desperately seeking a "first-rate scandal so that we can get [our organization] into front page headlines."[115] Its concern about slavery, more darkly, is shown as "imperialism in the sheep's clothing of humanitarianism," which ultimately justified British colonizing impulses.[116] The role of Holtby's fictional International Humanitarian Association in a multifaceted attempt to advance British economic interests in Africa was clear.

For Save the Children, humanitarian concern for Africa was not just a means to justify colonial rule. Rather, Save the Children's proposed interventions were bound up with a broader interwar drive to integrate Africa into the international economy, for the mutual benefit of Africans and the wider international community. In line with Lugard's vision of a "dual mandate," by saving the child of Africa, the Fund aspired to fulfill the civilizing mission of the British Empire and to unlock Africa's natural resources for Europe. At the start of the 1930s, in an increasingly unsteady global economy, Save the Children was not just saving children to save the world: it was, in the minds of its leaders, saving the children of empire in order to save the international order from the rising threats of economic instability. In doing so, the Fund was not proposing that African children and European children were the same. Save the Children leaders' hope for African children was not equality but utility.

The Geneva Conference on the African Child was the high-water mark of Save the Children's imperial internationalism. Their confidence in this vision barely lasted until the end of the summer of 1931. Fund leaders returned from Geneva to find the British government in crisis, an international financial order that was crumbling, and the relentless rise of fascism eroding the international cooperation they had striven to build. However, if the practicalities of international humanitarianism were (as we will see) dented by global economic depression at the start of the 1930s, it was not until the middle of the decade that the effort was forced to confront the practical and ideological challenges that the rise of fascism posed. Ethiopia had not only showcased the limits of the League of Nations and collective security, but also called into question the very self-confidence on which liberal internationalist institutions had been founded. The world was not, it seemed, working its way toward a more peaceful and mutually prosperous future guided by the enlightening influence of European powers. In 1936, Save the Children's monthly magazine explained that now, "barbarism" was not just the backwardness associated with far-flung sections of empire awaiting European civilization.[117] Through the rise of fascism, barbarism had found a modern, powerful form that internationalism seemed unable to defeat.

FOUR

Protecting Children
in a Time of War

IN 1938, the League of Nations Child Welfare Committee met for the first time in the Palais de Nations, a marble-columned building on the banks of Lake Geneva that had been under construction since 1920. The Palais was to be a permanent home for the League of Nations and, to the delight of the Council of the Save the Children Fund, was a mere mile from the headquarters of their International Union. The geopolitical climate had changed radically in the eighteen years it took to construct the Palais. Rather than symbolizing the permanence of the new world order, one Czech journalist lamented that the Palais de Nations would serve as a bright, white beacon, guiding bombs that might soon fall from the sky.[1] Before long, Nazi troops were fanning out across Europe, and League of Nations officials were fleeing Geneva.

Like those officials, the various members of the Save the Children International Union (SCIU) dispersed when the Second World War broke out, but the war did not precipitate the end of the organization.[2] Rather, the various member societies, and especially the British Save the Children Fund (SCF), embraced total war with an enthusiasm that few could have predicted just two decades after the Fund had been formed to promote peace. This was enabled by two shifts in emphasis within the SCF during the 1930s. First, during the Great Depression era, the Fund cultivated ever-closer ties to the British government. When war arrived, it prioritized these ties over international relief in the hope that partnership between the voluntary sector and the state would lay the foundations for a social democratic welfare state in peacetime. Second, the meaning of humanitarian internationalism shifted. In the 1920s, Save the Children leaders had understood humanitarian internationalism as a form of civic diplomacy: humanitarian aid was an active attempt to forge ties between nations and influence international relations. As diplomatic ties between states frayed, instead of seeking *to influence* international relations, the Fund tried to prevent humanitarianism from *being influenced by* international relations. These twin shifts in the Fund's vision of British internationalism enabled Save the Children to outlast the moment that had produced it. They also enabled Save the Children to look away from the suffering of children living under fascist rule before and during the Second World War. The Fund's ever-closer relationship with the British government and its commitment to preserving ties between humanitarians inhibited its action on behalf of Europe's Jewish children and Spanish child refugees.

INTERNATIONAL CRISES, NATIONAL SOLUTIONS

Save the Children's response to the Second World War was shaped by its response to the impact on Britain of worldwide depression. During the Great Depression, the Fund worked alongside the British government in caring for working-class children. This new insider status pulled the Fund away from its internationalist principles. In the 1920s, the Fund's relationship with the Labour Party had served to extend its international outreach, culminating in the Fund's 1931 Conference on the African Child, formally sponsored by the Colonial Office under Labour prime minister Ramsay MacDonald. However, Labour Party delegates at the conference returned to London to find their party in crisis. Since the financial crash of 1929, unemployment in Britain had doubled to 2.5 million: a fifth of the working population.[3] Exports fell, and the Labour government fought over how to cut expenditure. To break the deadlock, Ramsay MacDonald resigned from the party and joined a group of predominantly Conservative ministers to form a new "National Government" to steer Britain through the economic crisis. Fiscally conservative, the National Government cut provision for the unemployed.[4]

British poverty struck a blow to the Fund's confidence in Britain's role as a global leader. In his 1924 *Handbook on Child Welfare and Protection,* Save the Children's press secretary, Edward Fuller, argued that national standards of civilization could be read through the extent of child welfare services. The most advanced nations provided for children through the state; less advanced nations through robust philanthropic endeavor; and "uncivilized" nations were reliant on the interventions of foreign humanitarians.[5] In Britain, Fuller stated, children had been the first beneficiaries of the burgeoning welfare state in the early twentieth century: a period of Liberal welfare reform before the First World War had increased education provision and child protection legislation. Child labor had been abolished; child cruelty legislation had been passed; and, in 1918, an Education Act had promised education for all children between the ages of five and fifteen.[6] Thus, Fuller stated that British children were healthier and better cared for than their counterparts in continental Europe or Africa. This conviction had always led the Fund to spend only token sums in Britain.

The founders of Save the Children had never denied that poverty existed in England. With its Labour and trade union connections, many of the Fund's British interventions in the 1920s had been performances of solidarity with out-of-work or striking miners, whose children were provided with bread and boots. During the 1930s, as the visibility of unemployment grew, journalists flocked to workless towns to report on the nation's poor. Striking a tone reminiscent of Victorian philanthropic "slum-travelers," Save the Children volunteers also wrote articles and gave speeches with titles like "What Is to Be Done about the North?"[7] Britain's "backward" industrial communities were presented as housing a generation of undernourished, unruly children "unable to keep pace with the advances of civilization."[8] Their new concern for these victims of the Great Depression was in the context of a national and global rediscovery of poverty. Middle- and upper-class Britons "rediscovered" British poverty during a decade of hunger marches, factory closures, and desperation.[9] At the same moment, photographers, documentary-makers, and social surveyors commented on domestic poverty, highlighting the living conditions of those in America's "dust bowl," the "poor whites" of South Africa, and the unemployed miners of Germany and France.[10] Save the Children, like governments across the world, imagined that the solution lay in state-led modernization, directed at the poorer classes. This, they imagined, would draw Britain's working-class communities into a reinvigorated economy, continuing the onward march of progress that the Fund had been founded to secure.

Save the Children worked to transform the British poor through interventions directed at the young. While the existence of state education and a variety of medical and nutritional services provided by schools insulated many children from the worst effects of Depression-era poverty, there was only piecemeal provision for children under five.[11] In 1923, Christian socialist Margaret McMillan founded the Nursery Schools Association, a body committed to lobbying for state preschool provision, while providing nursery care for under-fives in working-class communities.[12] Based on a model that McMillan pioneered during the First World War, the Nursery Schools Association opened a series of "outdoor nurseries" funded through cooperation between local charities, Labour Party branches, and trade unions.[13] For McMillan, outdoor nurseries represented a reclaiming of the land by the workers, as well as an opportunity to endow the youngest members of society with the virtues of "industry and co-operation."[14] After McMillan's early death in 1931, her "dear friend" Independent Labour Party activist Katherine Bruce Glasier proposed that SCF found its own McMillan-style outdoor nursery schools.[15]

Nursery schools were presented by Glasier as an economically sound way to bring about change at a moment when donations to Save the Children were in sharp decline. McMillan-style outdoor nursery schools were cheap to build, needing only a small sheltered area and garden space. Conservative MP Nancy Astor offered to pay the salaries of nursery staff employed by Save the Children for the first year if the SCF would agree to nursery schools being run on "McMillan principles."[16] The language of efficiency and economy extended beyond these nursery schools to the children who attended them. Ignoring young children, one volunteer counseled, was "pennywise and pound foolish," for an unhealthy toddler would cost the state in the form of future dole payments. Using a distinctly upper-class metaphor tinged with eugenicist thinking, the volunteer explained Britain would "never breed a winner without feeding her yearlings." At state level, material relief for Britain's poor was being cut, and so childcare was taken on by civil society as a national investment in the workers of tomorrow.[17]

In the tradition of Save the Children projects from central Europe to Ethiopia, the outdoor nurseries that Save the Children established from 1933 onward sought to prepare children's minds and bodies for productive citizenship. The nursery day was designed to shield children from the influence of unemployed fathers. Between the hours of 8:30 a.m. and 4:30 p.m., nursery schools would rescue children from "the atmosphere of the "unemployed" home and . . . the evils of indiscipline and neglect which tend to flourish under adverse economic conditions." In this time, children would be given three meals, and taught "civilized" standards of living and the dignity of work.[18] Both McMillan and Eglantyne Jebb had been influenced by the work of German educational theorist Friedrich Frobel, whose play-based learning trained children in "concentration and arouse[d] . . . an interest in practical life" and "love of work."[19] The SCF nursery schools sought to put Frobelian principles into practice, with activities that taught dexterity and industry, such as clay modeling, weaving, and gardening. Nursery schools also

FIGURE 9. In North Shields in 1937, children were also engaged in building an extension to their own nursery, in line with the Fund's focus on education for practical labor. "Nursery Schools in the Special Areas," *The World's Children*, December 1937.

attempted to engage working-class parents to prevent the "demoralization of idleness." The schools, many of which were built from scratch, relied on the voluntary labor of mothers and fathers who tended the grounds, made curtains, cleaned, and cooked. Fundraising pamphlets explained how the nursery schools "brought some happiness into the drab lives" of unemployed families and transformed working-class communities.[20]

The Fund did not mimic the assertions of Labour Party women's groups and of the McMillan movement that SCF's nursery work had grown out of: that nursery education was a right of the working-class mother. Nursery education was framed by the Fund, almost exclusively, as a means of creating fit, healthy future citizens. In the words of Nazi-sympathizer Nancy Astor, nursery schools would lead to "a better civilization," rather than bettering the lives of present parents. Astor was scathing on the socialist ideals that animated Labour women's calls for nurseries and stated that the desire to create "economic equality" via nursery schools was "impossible." At most, nurseries could create "spiritual equality."[21] For Astor this consisted of manners and morals, making the children of the unemployed working classes more like their perceived social superiors.[22] Nursery schools were a form of class conciliation, rather than working-class or female empowerment. At the same time, while the Save the Children Fund benefitted from the work of the interwar feminist movement, its leaders spoke of women's participation in politics as a means to an end—the betterment of the lives of children—rather than viewing childcare as a means to achieve greater equality for women.

Save the Children's nursery schools program expanded rapidly after 1934 when the National Government passed the Special Areas Act. A feeble version of the American New Deal, the Act was intended to provide short-term economic help to areas of high unemployment in the industrial north of England, southern Scotland, and Wales. The Act provided centralized funding for voluntary organizations that could take over welfare services, ordinarily the preserve of (overburdened and underfunded) local authorities. The Act provided only £2 million initially and a further £4 million in 1937; this was barely enough to scratch the surface of Depression-era need and meant the scheme was reliant on voluntary organizations taking over the running of welfare services and partly funding them.[23] Yet for Save the Children, the Act was not a failure of the government to provide for its citizens, but an opportunity

Save the Children sent out local organizers to "distressed area" communities to drum up enthusiasm for Save the Children–led nurseries.[24] These organizers offered nursery schools to local councils on the condition that SCF nurseries were registered as official providers, thus making them eligible for partial funding via the Special Areas Act. Save the Children paid half of the building and operation costs, with the rest funded by Special Areas funding.[25] Seventeen nursery schools were opened in England and Wales and a further seven in Scotland using this model. This was a significant increase on the number of nursery schools in Britain which, in 1932, numbered only fifty-six.[26] Save the Children's left-leaning Nursery Schools Council firmly believed that welfare, and especially childcare, should be the responsibility of the state. By participating in a mixed economy of welfare, they imagined that the Fund would eventually withdraw "and that the local authorities may, in time, take them over for inclusion in the regular educational machinery."[27] The Fund used this moment of relative weakness on the part of the state in terms of welfare provision to secure new forms of childcare as a function of the state. Through mixed economy provision, they were building the welfare state in the midst of the Great Depression. Voluntarism was a means to a statist end.

Feminist founder-members of Save the Children were able to realize their ambitions by working with and through the government. The late 1920s and early 1930s saw an increase in the trickle of female MPs entering Parliament, such as former suffragist and Save the Children Council member Margaret Bondfield. In their campaigns, these women had drawn a natural connection between getting women into Westminster and expanding child welfare services.[28] The increased influence of Save the Children in Westminster had also come about through the growing power of the Labour Party, which, since the First World War, had established its place as a party of government or the major opposition.[29] Leveraging these connections, outdoor nursery schools were not just intended to bring about the realization of a welfare state but the transformation of the working class.[30]

Although Save the Children's nursery schools neither transformed working-class childhood nor heralded the dawn of universal state provision for the under-fives, they did transform the Fund itself. Before its Emergency Nursery Schools program, the SCF's access to government funding had depended on its relationship with the Labour Party. After the mid-1930s, however, the Fund became a recognized expert on child welfare and was approached to advise government ministries and Parliament, regardless of which party was in power. SCF's 1934 report on the condition of children from unemployed families became the basis for a parliamentary inquiry that resulted in daily milk and food rations for all primary school–aged children in Britain.[31] Caught up in its new domestic role, the Fund neglected the Save the Children International Union in Geneva. In the midst of the Depression, donations to the Fund hit an all-time low in the mid-thirties. Coupled with increased spending on domestic work, this meant that, from 1932, the Fund was officially a debtor to the International Union.[32]

MEANWHILE, IN GENEVA

There were challenges facing the International Union far greater than lack of funding. Far from sparking international coordination (as many international economic experts hoped it might), the Depression catalyzed the rise of far-right nationalist movements across Europe. In the summer of 1933, just after Hitler became chancellor of Germany, the council of the SCF in Britain penned an addendum to the minutes of their council meeting. The Fund was, it noted, "impressed with the danger to world order accruing for industrial and agricultural distress, exaggerated nationalism."[33] The rise of "exaggerated nationalism" in Europe dealt another blow to the Fund's confidence in the inevitable triumph of civilization and internationalism in the wake of the First World War. As we saw in chapter 1, liberal internationalism complemented British nationalism and imperialism. Liberal internationalists imagined that "civilized" (by which they meant ethnically white) nation-states should be self-determining and autonomous and that this would establish the basis for international collaboration. Moreover, such states were conceived of as democratic, which would naturally ensure that the peaceable will of the people guided foreign policy, guarding against conflict in Europe.

The leadership of the SCF in Britain was divided in its response to fascism. Some, most significantly the Fund's president Lord Noel Buxton, seemed cautiously optimistic. First, the efficiency and comprehensiveness of fascist child welfare programs was something other European nations aspired to. Mussolini's Italy and Hitler's Germany pursued pro-natalist policies that placed the production and health of children at the center of society, highlighting their value as future soldiers and the bearers of the purity of the race.[34] State-sponsored welfare initiatives in Germany sought to produce healthy bodies for material, military, and ethnic expansion. Expanded state provision for preschool children and mass organized leisure for older children did not differ much in rhetoric or appearance from Save the Children's own programs, designed to promote productive, healthy children.[35] Nazi welfare policies sat within a new drive toward state welfare and planning, embraced by liberal, fascist, and socialist states alike as a response to the Great Depression.[36] In the United States, President Roosevelt's "New Deal" centralized a host of interventions designed to create healthy workers to underpin economic recovery. As states increasingly intervened in welfare, care for citizens was a cultivation of biopower, to fuel not only economic recovery but, eventually, total war.[37]

However, SCF president Noel Buxton doubted that war was the endgame of Nazi welfare policies, finding a number of overlaps between his own liberal internationalist worldview and the foreign policy agenda of the Nazi Party. In the last chapter, we saw how the Buxton brothers, Noel and Charles, were able to shift the emphasis of their calls for international oversight of imperial territories to support German and Italian calls for colonial territories, hoping to curb the expansionist desires of fascist states and internationalizing imperial oversight so that all major European powers shared the burdens and responsibilities of colonial rule. This also made sense to other British internationalists for whom the greatest failing of the postwar period had always been punitive treatment of Germany. A small number of Independent Labour Party members left to join Oswald Mosley's British Union of Fascists. The Buxtons held fast to their left-liberal political affiliations, but their determination to read fascism as compatible with liberal internationalism caused them to overlook the threat Nazi expansion posed to European stability.[38] Liberal internationalism had always rested on the principle of self-determination, imagining nations as ethnically homogenous entities with borders determined by the communities within them. The Buxtons read German territorial expansion as an overdue reunification of ethnically homogenous Germans, in keeping with the Wilsonian principle of self-determination.[39] Liberal internationalism and Nazism shared enough that, by squinting at both, the Buxtons could regard them as similar.

The 1930s saw a rise of war consciousness in Britain, as a generation who had spent their childhood living in the long shadow cast by the First World War reached adulthood. Books such as Robert Graves's autobiography *Goodbye to All That* became national bestsellers, and "never again" became the rallying cry of a generation.[40] In 1933, members of the Oxford Union voted that they "would not take [up] arms for king and country," and other public declarations of pacifism by Britain's youth followed.[41] The League of Nations reached the apex of its popularity in Britain at the very moment that its international influence was beginning to decline. In 1935 a mass participation "Peace Ballot" organized by the League of Nations Union showed overwhelming public support for collective security, to be achieved via the League of Nations.[42] Meanwhile, reports of concentration camps for political dissidents, anti-Semitism, and the victimization of the clergy began to reach Britain from Germany. While some trade unions, pacifist groups, and clergy in Britain protested these abuses, many in Whitehall dismissed such reports as Communist propaganda.[43] During the mid-1930s, the National Government, now led by Conservative Stanley Baldwin, strove to preserve diplomatic and economic ties with Nazi Germany, while many ordinary British men and women pledged to avoid war.

Germany withdrew from the League of Nations in 1933 but remained inside other internationalist structures. Alongside displays of internationalism such as hosting the 1936 Olympics, the Nazi government encouraged German societies that were members of international organizations to continue their collaborations, in order both to propagandize and to gather information.[44]

In Geneva, the original German affiliate society of the Save the Children International Union was disbanded. Its Jewish leaders went into exile, and the remaining staff were absorbed into a new Nazi-dominated child welfare organization, the Deutsche Zentrale für freie Jugendwohlfahrt (the Independent German Centre for Youth Welfare), which replaced its predecessor at the SCIU.[45] These changes passed without comment at the International Union, where the expertise of the Deutsche Zentrale on matters ranging from the children of the unemployed to organized leisure was celebrated.

The British SCF was aware that child welfare in Nazi Germany was deeply exclusionary. In 1936, all youth groups other than the Nazi Party–sanctioned Hitler Youth and Bund Deutscher Mädel were prohibited, and Jewish children were banned from participation. Many Jewish children or the children of political prisoners were routinely victimized at school or excluded altogether. The economic restrictions placed on Jewish families by the Nuremburg laws plunged Jewish children into poverty. Reports from Germany (relayed in secret by the original, non-Nazi leaders of the Deutsche Zentrale) pointed to the material and psychological toll that exclusion and poverty were having on children.[46] The Nazi state was in violation of the Geneva Declaration of the Rights of the Child, which was prefaced with the command that all children must receive care regardless of race, nationality, or creed. However, the Declaration had no legal basis: though it had been adopted by the League of Nations, it was a set of aspirations rather than obligations. As we saw in the previous chapter, in spite of the universalist framing of the Declaration, its approach to children was both statist and utilitarian: it assumed that states would be the upholders of children's rights in recognition of the benefits that a healthy young population conferred upon the nation. Its authors had never imagined or made provision for a reality in which states did not value (or indeed actively wished to remove) a section of its able-bodied child population, as was now taking place in Nazi Germany.

The International Union had no mechanism to censure a state, or its national affiliate organizations that comprised its membership. The Save the Children movement also had no mechanism for intervening in the lives of children within a state that had not invited it in. The policy of the International Union had always been to seek governmental approval wherever it intended to work.[47] In lieu of direct intervention, the British SCF half-heartedly sought to raise awareness of the living conditions of "non-Aryan" children in Nazi Germany. From 1936, it published occasional articles in *The World's Children* highlighting the exclusion of Jewish children from education, and the poverty of "non-Aryan families."[48] These were met with a swift rebuttal from the Deutsche Zentrale, which threatened to resign from the International Union if "untruths" about Nazi childcare continued to be published.[49] While the British Fund was critical of Nazi policies, other members of the International Union were supportive. The now fascist-dominated Italian society and a number of the Scandinavian societies, themselves supporters of eugenics, publicly admired Nazi child welfare restrictions and racial laws. An ideological rift was opening up at the International Union.[50]

William Mackenzie, the general secretary of the International Union, believed that the threatened resignation of Deutsche Zentrale and its Italian and Scandinavian supporters would spell the end of humanitarian internationalism.[51] As we saw in chapter 1, when the International Union was founded in 1920, it claimed to represent a "true internationalism," superior to that of the League of Nations, which had excluded former enemy states and Soviet Russia. The purpose of the SCIU, according to Eglantyne Jebb, was to model its version of true internationalism for the wider political and diplomatic community.[52] Now, as diplomatic ties between nations frayed, Mackenzie believed that instead of seeking to influence international politics, humanitarians must prevent their work from being influenced by the growing tensions between states. It was more important to Mackenzie that the unity of the humanitarian community should be preserved, rather than any of the liberal internationalist ideas that had led to its formation. While Noel Buxton imagined that fascism and liberal internationalism could coexist, his colleagues from across the International Union were uncoupling humanitarian internationalism from liberal internationalism altogether, ceasing to imagine humanitarianism as a form of civic participation in international relations designed to influence the conduct of states. Instead, the International Union was pursuing a policy of humanitarian unity that operated outside formal international relations, which they hoped could withstand the fragmentation of the liberal international order.

THE PROTECTION OF CHILDREN IN WAR

As war in Europe became more likely, Save the Children had only one prior experience of war to guide their preparations: the 1935–1936 Italian invasion of Ethiopia. When Fritzi Small returned to Geneva from Addis Ababa in 1936, she brought with her firsthand experience of aid work during a conflict and a stark warning about the future of warfare. Laws of war laid out in a 1925 Geneva protocol had been flouted in Ethiopia, with Italy using chemical weapons and targeting civilians with aerial bombing. Small and the SCF general secretary Lewis Golden began work on protecting children in future conflicts. Drawing on Small's experience of the Ethiopian conflict (but without citing her authorship or expertise), Golden wrote a memorandum outlining possible consequences of war for Europe's children. He urged the Fund's council that they must "Save the Children from War. And, if this cannot be done, save them from War's worst effects."[53] To concede that another war was coming and that humanitarian collaboration did not offer hope for peace marked another departure from the Fund's early years.

Trading idealism for realism, Save the Children moved closer to the outlook of the International Committee of the Red Cross (ICRC). Unlike Save the Children, the ICRC had never envisaged a world without war. It had been founded in 1853 to secure the medical aid of soldiers in conflict. Though the Save the Children movement dealt with civilians, it had always drawn on the rhetoric of the ICRC, claiming the essential impartiality of the humanitarian movement. Now, with another war approaching, the ICRC provided a model of how international effort could humanize conflict. In 1929, the ICRC had secured international agreement on the Geneva Conventions, which regulated the treatment of prisoners of war.[54] Inspired, Golden and Small began to devise a similar convention that would protect children.[55]

Golden argued for a distinction between combatants (able-bodied adults capable of providing war services) and noncombatants (children, the elderly and disabled, and able-bodied adults caring for these groups), rather than soldiers and civilians.[56] Noncombatant populations would be protected in "immunized zones" marked by a flag featuring a black circle on a yellow background. By narrowing the definition of noncombatants, he hoped to show that an international agreement on protection for children and a small number of professionally trained carers (more efficient and fewer people than if parents accompanied children) was not intended to prevent or limit war.[57] Golden was unsentimental about preserving the bonds between parents—especially mothers—and children. Although this might seem surprising when read alongside the maternalist attitudes of the wider philanthropic and child welfare community in Britain it mirrored Save the Children's programs elsewhere across Europe. The Fund was bringing the practice of family separation in times of crisis home to the British Isles, as well as standardizing it across all war-affected nations. Golden's plan was to gain simultaneous approval

THIS SIGN MAY SAVE CHILDREN IN TIME OF WAR

The Save the Children Fund has proposed an ' Immunity Symbol ' for the protection of children and other non-combatants in time of war. The device suggested is a black disc on a yellow ground, to be recognised by International Convention and used for the identification of immunised areas and buildings by being exhibited on flags, roofs, etc.

VOLUME XVII
No. 2

NOVEMBER 1936
FOURPENCE

The World's Children

*The Official Organ of the Save the Children Fund
and of the Declaration of. Geneva*

EDITORIAL ADVISORY BOARD OF 'THE WORLD'S CHILDREN'

SIR PHILIP GIBBS, K.B.E.

SIR WILLIAM ROTHENSTEIN
Hon. A.R.C.A.

Dr. R. G. GORDON, M.D., D.Sc.

Dr. MALCOLM SARGENT
Mus.D., A.R.C.O., F.R.C.M.

THE
MARCHIONESS TOWNSHEND

Editor : EDWARD FULLER

THE HON. MRS. ST. AUBYN

MISS ELSIE COHEN

PATRICK BRAYBROOKE

LESLIE PAUL

THE SAVE THE CHILDREN FUND, 20 GORDON SQUARE, LONDON, W.C.I

FIGURE 10. A proposal for children's wartime evacuation homes and their signage, 1936. *The World's Children* (front cover), November 1936.

from the British government, the International Union, and the ICRC, so that other Red Cross and Save the Children branches would lobby their own governments to sign the convention.[58]

For this to succeed, the International Union needed to keep its fascist members onside. This became more difficult when, in the summer of 1936, war broke out in Spain. Spain quickly became a bloody arena for the wider ideological conflicts of the moment: Nationalist forces were supported by the German air force and volunteers from fascist Italy, and the Republican side was backed by Soviet forces and left-wing volunteer International Brigades.[59] Despite fierce public interest in the Spanish Civil War, Lewis Golden and William Mackenzie hesitated to intervene to protect Spanish children, fearing it would tear the International Union apart.[60] The Conservative-dominated National Government and the Labour Party also advocated nonintervention. Protesting at governmental inaction, and in support of the Republican government, British socialists and trade unionists flocked to Spain to fight. In November 1936, pro-Republican activists in the National Joint Committee (NJC) for Spanish Relief raised over £71,042 in donations.[61] In the interwar period, the "Aid Spain" movement was second only to the Russian famine in the breadth and depth of support that it drew from the British public. Throughout 1936 and 1937, collections, concerts, and raffles raised funds from factories in North Yorkshire and village halls in South Wales. Gifts of clothes, bandages and condensed milk were collected at the NJC headquarters.[62] These donations came from the constituencies that Save the Children had always considered its own natural base (the TUC, local Labour Party branches, and members of organizations such as the League of Nations Union), at a moment when the Fund was struggling to make ends meet.

The NJC not only drew left-wing and liberal support away from the SCF, but also patrons and council members. The Secretary of the NJC, Katherine Stuart-Murray, Duchess of Atholl, had previously served on the Fund's nursery schools committee, and her husband was the president of the Scottish branch of the SCF.[63] Another NJC leader, trade unionist Robert Smillie, had been on the Fund's council since 1920. Like many in the British Labour movement, Smillie had family fighting in Spain with the Republican army. His grandson (named after him) joined an Independent Labour Party delegation to the International Brigade and later died in prison in Barcelona. Through the Aid Spain movement, these individuals were able to support the Republican forces in spite of the nonintervention of the British government, and the lack of support from the British Labour Party.[64] Thus, the NJC was a philanthropic protest organization, much as Save the Children itself had been in its early days, designed to critique and overcome the shortcomings of official policy via humanitarian aid.[65]

The partisan nature of the Aid Spain movement made the SCF even more reluctant to intervene in the Spanish Civil War. Given the anti-fascism of many Save the Children left-leaning council members, it seemed impossible to retain the facade of impartiality. Golden was especially wary, given his recent encounters with Small, whose anti-fascism had almost cost the SCF the support of the British Foreign Office in Ethiopia. In September 1936, however, an opportunity for a cost-effective, impartial intervention presented itself to the International Union. When the war broke out, many Spanish children were at "summer colonies," residential camps where working- and middle-class children often spent the school holidays. With the rapid advance of Nationalist troops, many children found themselves on the wrong side of the ever-shifting military frontier. In late August, the SCIU received telegrams from Spanish child welfare organizations, asking them to return these children to their families.[66]

William Mackenzie had been as reluctant as Golden to get involved in Spain, but he decided that the return of children to their parents was "unlikely to draw allegations of partisanship."[67] Importantly, the endeavor did not require a significant financial commitment, as the SCIU was able to rely largely on diplomatic and business contacts. The president of the SCIU, Norwegian Nobel Peace Prize winner Christian Lange, was able to convince a Norwegian shipping company to lend him a cargo ship capable of evacuating 1,500 children and also persuaded the French Navy to escort the ship to the Spanish-French border, from where the children (mostly from pro-Republican families) could safely return to their homes in the north.[68] In the six weeks it took to arrange the evacuation, however, many of the children had already returned to their parents by other means. In the end, only 457 children embarked on the ship. Setting sail on a cold November night, the ship had little in the way of shelter or blankets, so the children were wrapped in bedsheets. When they were reunited with their parents, they looked like "tiny ghosts," cloaked in white.[69]

While the International Union had been attempting to coordinate the return of children from the safety of Geneva, thousands of volunteer relief workers from across Europe were arriving in Spain. Like the volunteers for the International Brigades, many of these relief workers had undertaken the journey due to ideological commitment rather than professional expertise.

Relief efforts were patchy and later satirized in both memoirs and fiction.[70] The SCIU had agreed to partly fund relief efforts undertaken by the British Quakers, whom they felt they could trust to remain impartial.[71] However, as accounts of the unprofessionalism of wartime relief work reached Fritzi Small, now living in Geneva, she persuaded a reluctant Golden that she should undertake an impartial "fact-finding mission" to Spain.[72] The Foreign Office had claimed that a woman posed an "undue liability" in a time of war while Small was in Ethiopia in 1935. A year on, Save the Children deployed Small in a war zone because a woman was seen as somehow less overtly "political" than a male relief worker. Nevertheless, a young, expert woman working alone irritated male medics, missionaries, and relief workers in Spain, just as it had in Ethiopia. When Small attempted to advise on the logistics of relief, she was dismissed and quickly gave up attempting to coordinate the activities of other agencies.[73] Instead, Small decided to test-run the draft Convention for the Protection of Children in Spain. Without informing Golden (who would no doubt have tried to prevent her), she sought an audience with General Franco. Drawing on the draft convention, she planned to argue that both sides should agree on protected neutral zones for children and noncombatant carers so that, rather than refugees having to flee as the front lines of the conflict shifted, they could remain safely in one place.[74] Small never met Franco, but eventually secured an audience with a Nationalist army general, the Comte of Argillo. He raised two objections: that protecting children and their carers implied that other adult civilians and those outside the neutral zones were unimportant; and that he felt the Republican side would not agree to the neutral zones. Small's neutral zones in Spain were written off.[75]

EVACUATING CHILDREN FROM DANGER

Other humanitarian organizations and solidarity networks were undertaking mass evacuations of children out of Spain.[76] France took 78,629 child refugees, many of them unaccompanied, the greatest proportion of the evacuated child population. Soviet Russia provided a home for around 3,300 children from Republican families, and similar numbers were taken by Belgium. A smaller number of children from Nationalist families were evacuated to Nazi Germany. Small was skeptical about these evacuations. Unlike many SCF workers in this period, she felt that children should, if possible, remain with their families, and she observed that many evacuated children were taken without their parents" permission.[77] Golden was also opposed: moving Spanish children to "cold, [P]rotestant England" seemed unduly upsetting and was, he feared, a propaganda stunt for the pro-Republican relief movement. Both Small and Golden were overtaken by events when, in April 1937, Nazi and fascist air forces bombed Guernica. The images of the ensuing suffering in the British press were shocking, showing the destructiveness of new, modern warfare, and the brutality and strength of fascism. Basque victims were met with outpourings of concern, and a renewed call for the mass evacuation of children.[78] Despite considerable opposition from a Conservative pro-Franco lobby, the Home Office bowed to pressure from the NJC to evacuate Basque children to Britain, on two conditions: that there would be no cost to the Treasury for the children's maintenance, and that children from either side of the conflict would be eligible.[79]

To gain cross-party support, the pro-Republican NJC wanted to disassociate itself from the evacuation, and so it set up a new organization: the Basque Children's Committee.[80] The Committee was led almost entirely by NJC stalwarts, including independent MP Eleanor Rathbone and Labour MP Leah Manning.[81] However, to appear impartial, it also invited Conservative figures such as John Macnamara MP, who had previously declared his opposition to the scheme, and Liberal MP Wilfred Roberts. To further bolster the Basque Children's Committee's claim to impartiality, Save the Children was invited to join. Despite his initial skepticism, Golden felt that Save the Children could not refuse to take part in what was fast becoming the largest humanitarian appeal in Britain since the Russian famine.[82] The Basque Children's Committee set out to evacuate equal numbers of children from Republican and Nationalist families. When Leah Manning traveled to Bilbao to select two thousand children for evacuation in May 1937, she met with an overwhelmingly enthusiastic reception. Despite the registration progress being regularly interrupted by air-raids, in just two days over 17,000 children registered for evacuation to Britain, and after hurried consultation the Home Office agreed to take 4,000. On 17 May 1937, 3,889 Basque children, 219 female teachers and 15 priests boarded the ship *Habana* and began their crowded and uncomfortable journey to Southampton.[83] The children were packed in like sardines, in many cases sleeping in corridors, outside on deck and on the floor of the ship's ballroom. Once they arrived in Southampton, a team of medical orderlies screened the children for diseases. Most were taken for "de-lousing"—their heads were shaved and their clothes burned.[84]

Next, they were taken to a camp outside Southampton. On the journey, they saw streets lined with flags and banners for the coronation of King George VI a few days earlier, and some happily believed that these were in celebration of their arrival. The children were presented with coronation memorial mugs, chocolate, and white bread and led to five hundred canvas tents that had been loaned by local scout troops and pitched in a buttercup-filled field.[85] While the Basque Children's Committee reported these charming details in the press, enabling them to raise £17,000 to support the children's first month in the United Kingdom, the reality was much less rosy.[86] Many older boys remembered their instant distrust of the camp authorities (none of whom spoke Spanish) and likened the camp to a prison.[87] Having been malnourished for so long, children hoarded bread under their clothes, for which they were punished; others refused to eat bland English food. There was a typhoid outbreak in the camp, and a girl died from tuberculosis, generating medical bills that almost bankrupted the Committee.[88]

Some older boys pushed into the food queue, returning for fifth servings before younger children had eaten their first.[89] To counter this, children were each presented with a yellow ribbon to exchange for their meal. In response, a group of boys went on hunger strike: yellow was the color of the Nationalist forces. Camp administrators could not understand why these once-hungry boys would not eat (and did not locate Spanish speakers to ask the children).[90] This misunderstanding was typical of the evacuated children's experience.[91] While fundraising propaganda presented the children as the innocent victims of war, grateful and uncorrupted by the political opinions of their communities and families, many of the younger children were traumatized, suffering from nightmares, bedwetting, and becoming hysterical when planes flew above the camp. Violence between the older children, particularly those with opposing political convictions, was regular.[92] When the fall of Bilbao was announced, riots broke out and local police were sent to restore order. A number of the boys were said to be engaged in "homosexual activity."[93] Thus, while the younger camp inhabitants failed to behave like grateful "saved" children, the older inhabitants, holding political convictions and forming sexual relationships, confounded the Basque Children's Committee's image of childhood entirely. Basque children were not just political symbols, but political agents.

The Children's Committee had never intended for Basque children to stay in the Southampton camp for more than a few weeks. However, the Basque Children's Committee agreed with the Home Office that the children should not be cared for in foster families, as they had first proposed, as this might make their eventual deportation more difficult. Instead, the Committee settled the children in groups of between ten and fifty in a hundred foster homes throughout the country.[94] It was hoped that this would lessen the financial burden on the Basque Children's Committee, because once a particular town felt ownership of "their" refugees, they would provide for their care.[95] However, the relationship between children and the communities to which they were sent varied drastically. A refugee colony of young girls on the Isle of Wight proved popular with locals, who contributed to the cost of their care by attending dance performances for a small fee and making regular donations.[96] The Witney Basque Home in Oxfordshire organized cooking rotas to feed the children and weekend trips to the cinema or the countryside. Meanwhile in London, groups of older boys were frequently rejected by foster carers, eventually ending up in a work facility for adult male alcoholics. Five of these "troublesome" boys were moved to a children's colony in France following an incident in which a cook was allegedly threatened with a knife.[97]

Examples of bad behavior were seized upon by the right-leaning British newspapers, such as the *Catholic Herald* and the *Express*, which avidly supported the Nationalist side. The Basque children were termed "red devils," and there were claims that they would break out of the camps and "corrupt" innocent British children. The right-wing press ran regular anti-Basque headlines, stating that charities should be putting "Britons Before Basques!"[98] In June 1937, following complaints in the press about the expense of maintaining the Basque children, the Wilson Repatriation Committee was formed under the leadership of pro-Nationalist Conservative MP Sir Arnold Wilson. The move to send Basque children back to Spain was welcomed by many on the left too, who noted that, while each Spanish child in Britain cost ten shillings to maintain each week, the government provided a mere five shillings additional dole to unemployed men for each child they had.[99]

Amid the bad press, the initial wave of enthusiasm for the Basque Children's Committee waned and donations dried up. The Basque children themselves became increasingly involved in fundraising, with a Basque Children's Choir touring Britain and producing records, but with little success.[100] As finances waned, so did the hospitality of the British government. With the Basque territories now fully under Fascist control, the first children began their voyages back to Bilbao in October 1937.[101] In a number of cases, families could not be located or had died in the conflict. Four hundred ten Basque children remained in Britain in 1945, and many never returned to Spain.[102]

The Basque evacuations were a cautionary tale for Save the Children. Once the initial wave of enthusiasm for Basque evacuations had passed, there was little interest in international issues at the expense of domestic philanthropy. Even in cases where the British public were enthusiastic about providing relief for children overseas, they were reluctant for these same children to be cared for in Britain, later making the Fund wary of bringing child refugees from Hitler's Third Reich onto British soil.

In the autumn of 1936, while the SCF had been tiptoeing around the German society in Geneva and desperately trying to maintain an appearance of impartiality in Spain, Golden had been approached by a retired British army general and evangelical Christian Zionist, Wyndham Deedes. Deedes was planning to remove Jewish children from Nazi Germany, bring them to England and eventually resettle them in Palestine.[103] Much like the Basque Children's Committee, Deedes sought the partnership of the SCF because he believed that the Fund, with its ties to the British government, would lend his scheme the credibility necessary to secure visas for Jewish children. Predictably, Save the Children was reluctant. To avoid infringing the sovereignty of the Nazi state and provoking the Deutsche Zentrale, it had confined its interventions in the lives of German Jewish children to modest funding for refugee relief on the French border.[104] SCF leaders believed that an evacuation scheme that removed children from inside Germany could be seen as an infringement of sovereignty.

Jewish refugees posed an intellectual and practical problem for the leaders of Save the Children. At a conference of the International Union in 1933, the Fund predicted the imminent "liquidation" of the refugee population in Europe, through the resettlement and full assimilation of refugee groups into the cultures and customs of their host nations. As we saw in chapter 2, the Fund sought to place refugee children in what they viewed as "ethnically similar" host nations, and advocated that children forget their own languages, cultures, and parents if it hastened assimilation. However, in the case of Jewish refugees, this model of resettlement-as-assimilation was more contentious. The Fund viewed Jewish people as ethnically distinct from other European populations and saw their cultural assimilation as unlikely. For those who had imagined a liberal international order as one made up of ethnically homogenous nation-states, it had never been clear where the Jewish people, with no state of their own, would fit.[105]

Despite the Fund's reservations, Deedes was persuasive. As a Zionist, his ideal solution to the "Jewish question" (as he called it) was the creation of a Jewish homeland in Palestine, and he thus hoped that Britain would be a temporary home for Jewish children before eventual resettlement. However, Deedes conceded that, in the event that Jewish children from the Third Reich could not be relocated to Palestine, he would make sure to select those most likely to assimilate into British society or Commonwealth nations. He persuaded the SCF to make a donation of only £5 a month to his newly founded Inter-Aid Committee, hoping that the Fund's involvement might ease the process of securing entry visas for German children.[106] Beginning its work at the end of 1936, the Inter-Aid Committee chose children for evacuation based on two criteria: the extent of the threat to children's "mental and moral equilibrium" in Germany, and their ability to assimilate into and contribute to another society.[107] Deedes and Golden believed that such children were those with "Jewish blood" in otherwise "Aryan" families, especially if they were middle class and well educated.[108] Thus, far from questioning Nazi categorizations, Deedes was *using* them to determine the likelihood of children's settlement in Britain, privileging the children deemed the least culturally and ethnically Jewish.

The Inter-Aid Committee thus adopted the selective criteria that Save the Children had put in place across Europe for its own interventions. It imagined middle-class children as more productive, and Christian children as more easily assimilated, relying on Nazi categorizations of children and their families. The Committee also (secretly) gathered information on possible transportees via one of the few remaining non-Nazi members of the Deutsche Zentrale für Freie Jugendwohlfahrt, Dr. Ruth Weiland. Of the first 130 children brought to England by the Inter-Aid Committee, 62 were practicing Jews, and 68 were Protestants with some Jewish ancestry.[109] An appeal made in the *Times* newspaper in October 1936 raised £1,060 for their care.[110] By November 1938 the Inter-Aid committee was responsible for 471 children they had evacuated to Britain.[111] With subsidized schooling, the cost per head was estimated at £29 5s per year, a fraction of which came from the Save the Children. With limits placed on Jewish immigration by the British government (despite widespread knowledge of the treatment of Jews in Germany), a larger number seemed unlikely.[112] After Kristallnacht on 9 November 1938, however, the evacuation of Jewish children from Germany rapidly accelerated. Representatives of the Inter-Aid Committee met Conservative MP Samuel Hoare to discuss waiving standard immigration procedures for children aged under seventeen, and a motion was passed in Parliament on 28 November allowing 15,000 children to enter the country. The Inter-Aid Committee now worked closely with

REFUGEE CHILDREN FROM GERMANY HELPED
BY THE SAVE THE CHILDREN FUND

FIGURE 11. The Fund's brief participation in the Kindertransport was much publicized, both before and after the fact. This image still features prominently on Save the Children's website. Evacuated Children from Germany, Save the Children Photo Collection, Save the Children Archives, Birmingham, UK.

another evacuation group that had emerged from the Jewish community in Britain, the Movement for the Care of Children from Germany.[113] With a constituency of Jewish donors, this movement quickly raised funds where the Inter-Aid Committee had failed. Sensing an opportunity, Deedes proposed that his committee should break with the SCF in favor of affiliation with this wealthier organization.[114] Save the Children did not object, thus ending the Fund's brief, half-hearted participation in the Kindertransport.

The full extent of the horror that Jewish children and their families were facing (and would face in the Holocaust) did not emerge until the latter days of the war. Nonetheless, Save the Children had a detailed picture of the lives of Jewish children in prewar Germany but chose to remain quiet. By 1938, the Fund was working closely with the British government in war preparations for children's evacuations, as well as on their growing nursery school programs. The Fund's council had been hesitant to spend funds and political capital on an unpopular migration scheme, especially after the controversial evacuations of Spanish refugees. Its guiding concern had become its national reputation and cultivating influence on domestic social policy.

Furthermore, in the interwar years, the Save the Children International Union had seen stateless children as an international charge but regarded the welfare of Jewish children as a particularly Jewish responsibility. When working in Eastern Europe, the Fund had often devolved the care of Jewish children to Jewish aid organizations, such as the American Joint Distribution Committee. At the SCIU, the only member body that did not represent a nation-state was the Union Universelle de Juive, a Zionist organization that advocated separate education and leisure for Jewish children in Europe.[115] Many British internationalists had never fitted Europe's Jews into their vision of self-determined, ethnically homogenous nation-states. However, while the limitations of liberal internationalism enabled the Save the Children movement to overlook the plight of European Jews, the British Fund's attempts to maintain ties with the Nazi child welfare organization limited its interest and action in terms of the Kindertransport. Fearful of undermining the precarious unity of the International Union, the Fund steered clear of anything that could be construed as a criticism of Nazi rule. By preserving unity over speaking out against Nazi abuses of children's rights in the immediate term, the leadership of the British SCF perhaps imagined that they might be able to wield more influence, and save more lives, if a war did come. Their optimism turned out to be misplaced.

PREPARING FOR TOTAL WAR

In September 1938, following the annexation of Austria in March 1938, Germany occupied the Sudetenland, an area of Czechoslovakia home to a large German-speaking community. British prime minister Neville Chamberlain met Hitler in Munich and famously declared he had secured "peace in our time" by permitting the occupation. For many Britons, the Munich Agreement marked the moment at which another world war now seemed inevitable. For the leadership of the SCF, however, Chamberlain was demonstrating a bold and commendable commitment to peace. In a poem written for *The World's Children* in October 1938, General Secretary Hubert Digory Watson urged Save the Children donors to increase their contributions to support refugees now fleeing the Sudetenland, as the "price of peace."[116] While the rest of the Fund's council were in denial about the likelihood of war, by 1938 Golden and Small not only were sure that conflict was coming, but also believed that any attempt to secure international protection for children would be hopeless. Golden had also become drastically more pessimistic about the ability of humanitarian organizations to protect the young, predicting that children would be targeted, because their suffering would "weaken the morale of the entire population."[117] This realization represented another major shift. Golden had, like Jebb, previously believed that the symbolic appeal of children would secure international collaboration for their protection even when diplomatic relationships broke down. Now, he predicted that this symbolic power would mean that governments would refuse to agree on any specific terms of an international child protection agreement. Golden cautioned the Fund that, even if there was international will for a Convention for the Protection of Children, it would be almost impossible to secure such an agreement quickly. Issues such as defining what was meant by a "child" and/or a "noncombatant" would take years to resolve, long after war had broken out.[118]

Golden's pessimism was unpopular. The SCF council had not conceded that a war was even likely, and they were certainly not prepared to imagine that if conflict did come, the movement they had been building for twenty years could not ameliorate its impact on the young. Golden resigned in frustration at the end of 1938; in 1939, at the age of thirty-five, Fritzi Small died from a chronic illness.[119] Undeterred, the council of Save the Children dismissed Golden's insights as defeatist and pressed ahead with the proposed convention, which was published in the summer of 1939 with the endorsement of the International Union, but no other supporters. The convention outlined plans for children to be evacuated en masse to special zones of immunity, where they would receive food and medical protection in the event of a blockade and be protected from aerial bombardment or invading armies. It had taken three years to secure an agreement even among the Fund's "friends" at the International Union in Geneva, and it seemed almost certain that there was not enough time left to secure international agreement on the convention via the League of Nations. The ICRC, too, was reluctant to lend its support: echoing Franco's general's dismissive response to Small when she had attempted to set up children's safety zones in Spain, the ICRC feared that separating the young from the rest of the civilian population implied that adult noncombatants were acceptable targets.[120]

Edward Fuller imagined that he might be able to secure recognition of the convention by other means. Following the success of its Emergency Nursery Schools program, the Fund had been invited to sit upon the Andersen Evacuation Committee, convened by the British government in 1936 to plan for evacuation of children in war.[121] The Fund squandered its influence by doggedly promoting its Convention, despite an official lack of enthusiasm. While other delegates were discussing the logistics of mass civilian evacuation, Save the Children presented plans for special children's homes to be marked with a cross symbol visible from the sky, so that enemy bombers knew not to target them.[122] When other members of the evacuation committee pointed out that this symbol could also make it easier to target children (an "x marks the spot"), the Save the Children delegate simply suggested a different symbol.[123] Fuller also began direct communication with the German authorities. In August 1939, he sent a series of letters to the German Embassy in London, proposing neutral zones for children before war broke out. Predictably, the German embassy replied. Two weeks after this telegram arrived, Britain declared war on Germany. Fuller made a final attempt to secure children's immunity zones via the German Red Cross and the Deutsche Zentrale, but the only response he received was a single, two-line telegram from the German Red Cross: "We are unable to sign such an agreement. Germany cannot reveal in advance its war objectives. War today is total warfare," exactly as Golden had predicted.[124]

SAVING CHILDREN ON THE HOME FRONT

Golden did not predict, however, how wholeheartedly Save the Children would throw its weight behind the British war effort. The British Fund, and the other representative societies of belligerent powers, resigned temporarily from the International Union. The years of effort that the SCF had put in trying to preserve its friendly relations with fascist SCIU branches were proved futile overnight. There was no discussion over whether humanitarians—having fought so hard to remain in community with one another despite the growing international tension in the 1930s—might continue to collaborate in wartime. It was taken for granted that national member societies would participate wholeheartedly in their nations' war efforts. Rather, the SCF Council hoped, in resigning at the moment that war began, that a version of the International Union could continue to exist—one comprised solely of neutral powers—and could thus continue to model humanitarian collaboration in a time of war.[125]

Its ties with the International Union severed, the Fund's horizons narrowed during the war as it devoted itself almost entirely to the welfare of

British children. This meant swelling coffers, as for the first time, British children were on the receiving end of donations from Save the Children affiliates in the British dominions. The American Save the Children Fund, founded in 1936, was also an enthusiastic supporter of the British war effort, especially before the United States joined the conflict itself. For the first time since the Russian famine appeal, donations arrived in London faster than they could be spent.[126] It was more than the prospect of financial gain that made an organization founded to secure lasting peace so wholly supportive of the British war effort. Many of the Fund's idealistic founders had drifted away from its leadership in the later 1930s, some because of old age, others because of the pull of other left-leaning organizations such as the NJC. For Noel Buxton, the start of the war—a great disappointment to him politically—coincided with a series of personal crises: his son was killed in a car accident, and his daughter was imprisoned for shoplifting. Devastated and depressed, he withdrew from the day-to-day life of Save the Children.[127] Golden, meanwhile, had been replaced as the Fund's general secretary by Captain George Gracey. Like Golden, Gracey was a career relief worker, who had worked with the Near East Relief Fund in the aftermath of the First World War. Unlike Golden, however, Gracey came to aid work via the army, and was in favor of coordination between humanitarian organizations and the British military, alongside the Fund's already well-established connections with the British state.

The Fund's long-standing partnership with the Board of Education in the provision of nursery school education placed it in prime position for wartime collaboration. The expansion of state welfare during the Second World War—the "warfare state"—depended on the extension of the existing mixed economy of welfare. A host of voluntary organizations from the Women's Institute to St. John's Ambulance offered support to a host of wartime ministries.[128] Save the Children made a convincing case for the importance of nursery care. In regions where mothers were employed in war work, day nurseries were considered part of the war effort.[129] Furthermore, the Fund's Nursery School Committee argued, nursery schools for "nonworking" mothers should also be considered vital, as they raised morale. In many regions, the government had offered mothers of children under five the option of evacuation with their children. The hostels into which they were evacuated (usually hotels in remote areas) were overcrowded, with mothers and children sharing small bedrooms. In these cases, the Nursery School Committee feared that both the emotional development of children and the mental stability of their mothers was at risk. For under-fives evacuated away from their mothers, the Fund noted the considerable additional burden placed on foster parents. Nurseries, based on the emergency Depression-era model, which cared for children from 8:30 a.m. to 4:30 p.m., would relieve the pressure on mothers.[130]

Between 1939 and 1942, Save the Children's provision of day nurseries increased from thirty-six to eighty-seven.[131] For the Fund's council, however, the real excitement lay in residential nurseries. Founded for the care of children whose mothers could not be evacuated with them (often due to war work), or children who had been orphaned in the Blitz, these residential schools most closely resembled the children's immunity zones envisaged before the war. The Fund's leaders had always been enthused by the possibilities of mass childcare.[132] Without the influence of parents, they could raise the ideal citizens of the future, trained in the principles of industry and community.[133] They were also excited by the "scientific" possibilities created by a nationwide network of childcare facilities. After a series of "experiments" involving children across the country, Save the Children's council excitedly reported that while children under three could not fasten buttons, most children over four could be taught to tie shoelaces.[134] The nursery school teachers were convinced that these facilities offered the best possible care for preschool children. The story of Valerie, for example, who entered a residential nursery at age one in 1940 and did not want to return in 1945 to a mother she barely knew, was offered as proof of the happy environment nurseries provided, rather than institutionalization.[135] Save the Children's nurseries were few among a vast national network of childcare institutions founded by religious organizations and child welfare experts during the war.[136] Research efforts at other war nurseries, drawing on new psychoanalytic theories, were gathering evidence that would later challenge the Fund's preference for mass residential facilities.[137] As we'll see in the next chapter, ideas about the nature of the attachment between parents and children, which grew out of studies of children in wartime care facilities, dented the popularity of preschool out-of-home care.

Save the Children's work had always been premised on the idea of children as ambassadors for their nations, winning far-off friends to enhance postwar cooperation. In wartime Britain, children became ambassadors for their class. An editorial in the Fund's monthly magazine hypothesized that encounters with the urban poor would ignite the social conscience of the middle class.[138] The Fund preempted the work of sociologist Richard

FIGURE 12. At a residential wartime nursery in Kent in 1942, funded in part by the Save the Children Fund Honolulu branch, young children watch war planes overhead. Save the Children Photo Collection, Save the Children Archives, Birmingham, UK.

Titmuss, who would later argue that the postwar welfare state was founded in response to the poverty that the rural and suburban middle class encountered by way of their urban, working-class wards.[139] War was providing a blueprint for postwar, expanded state welfare and childcare interventions. With the nutrition of many children enhanced by rationing, new clinics taking care of children's health and mass preschool education (the Fund's special concern) in major towns and cities, many visions of child welfare were being realized.

WAR IN EUROPE

While the Fund was focused on Britain, it hastily withdrew funding and staff from Axis states and occupied territories. Due to Hungary's alliance with Nazi Germany, Jewish Save the Children worker Julia Vajkai was informed by the Council of the British SCF that she was no longer eligible to receive funding for her work school.[140] She was reported to have "disappeared" in

September 1940 and was not heard from again until the end of the war.[141] Likewise, the Fund's monthly donation of £50 to a refugee project in Salonika was halted following the German occupation of Greece.[142] While ceasing its assistance to Nazi-occupied territories, the British Fund was still receiving information about the impact of starvation, especially in blockaded Belgium and Greece from 1940. The neutral members of the International Union were traveling, where possible, to Nazi and Axis territories, and corresponding with relief workers and child welfare experts based there.[143] However, the Fund continued to overlook the suffering of Jewish children across the continent. In 1942, International Union president Gregory Thélin visited Berlin to report on child welfare in Germany, claiming (in the face of published accounts of wartime suffering) that the welfare of children in Berlin seemed generally excellent, mentioning in passing that he had "not come across any Jewish children."[144]

Save the Children was not the only humanitarian organization that failed to speak out against the Holocaust. The ICRC was invited by the Nazi government to visit concentration camps during the war. Reluctant to do so because of the propaganda potential of an endorsement from the ICRC for the conditions of concentration camp life, its leaders were nonetheless persuaded. Despite this, it did not publicly speak out against concentration camp conditions, instead hoping to preserve the relationship with the (now Nazi-dominated) German Red Cross society, which was working in (and therefore tacitly endorsing) camps. The ICRC's interests in wartime were, primarily, access to soldiers in battle, and (as per the 1929 Geneva Conventions) the treatment of prisoners in war. It was, however, the cofounder of the SCIU Suzanne Ferrière who made the most significant challenge to the ICRC's decision not to intervene in the fates of concentration camp victims. Ferrière argued that the ICRC should extend its categorization of prisoners of war to include all imprisoned by the Nazi regime so as to investigate standards in concentration camps more freely. Ferrière did not manage to convince the ICRC of this and had little success in raising the issue of concentration camps at the SCIU. International humanitarianism made no provision for the victims of sovereign states within their borders, nor would it for years to come.[145]

There were practical (as well as ideological and imaginative) constraints that prevented Save the Children from working overseas during the war. In 1942, the SCF joined the new Council of British Societies for Relief Abroad (COBSRA), founded to plan and distribute both state- and privately funded relief in Europe after the war. Its members included many organizations involved in home front relief efforts, including the British Red Cross, St. John's Ambulance, and Save the Children. As a condition of joining COBSRA, the Fund agreed not to provide aid to the occupied territories during the war. In return, after the war, COBSRA membership meant that the Foreign Office would pay 50 percent of Save the Children's overseas operating expenses and grant the Fund special access to newly liberated areas, with military protection if needed.[146] It became apparent, however, that the Foreign Office intended COBSRA to contain rather than enable the relief efforts of aid organizations. Once assured that humanitarians would not venture into occupied territories unchecked, it had little interest in facilitating their work.[147] Assessing their war work in 1945, Save the Children's council concluded that membership in COBSRA had left the Fund "with nothing to do."[148]

The location and nature of the work of COBSRA was, in turn, directed by the United Nations Relief and Rehabilitation Administration (UNRRA). Founded in 1943, UNRRA drew together forty-seven member states, pooling resources and expertise to coordinate relief across Europe and Asia. Governed by a committee of French, British, American, and Soviet officials, UNRRA had a staff of eleven thousand relief workers, and before it was disbanded in 1946, distributed a total of $3.7 billion, providing food, shelter, medical care, and, later, agricultural equipment for displaced persons (DPs) and other victims of the war.[149] In an era of growing warfare states and nascent welfare states across Europe and North America, UNRRA embodied a New Deal penchant for planning, led by efficient, coordinated structures of governmental (and intergovernmental) agencies.[150] As with COBSRA, though on a much wider basis, voluntary organisations became auxiliaries to state and military directives, with little room for independent action.

Not all humanitarian organizations conformed to wartime policies. For many, opposition to blockades of occupied territories was a focal point for dissent. News of life behind the blockade of Nazi-occupied territories, where civilians in Greece and Belgium were living on less than five hundred calories a day, reached the British public. In 1942 the Peace Pledge Union began a campaign against "total war," arguing that supplies must be sent to the "starving innocents" under Nazi occupation.[151] Many of the campaigners had been associated with Save the Children since 1919: Quaker relief worker Edith Pye, who had distributed SCF relief in Austria after the First World War; former council member Vera Brittain; and former patrons Robert Cecil and

Gilbert Murray.[152] Robert Cecil's vocal opposition to the blockade was especially significant, as he had served as minister of blockade during the First World War, and had been a target for Dorothy Buxton's ire. Cecil's support for the Peace Pledge Union showed how far mainstream opinion had shifted between the wars.

On 29 May 1942, the Oxford Famine Relief Committee was formed by several Peace Pledge Union anti-blockade campaigners. Focusing initially on occupied Greece, the Committee claimed that starvation was being used as a weapon against civilians and that the British public had a moral duty to intervene. The Committee's appeals drew particularly on the plight of "innocent children" in Greece, who, they argued, could not be regarded as having any role or stake in the war.[153] They raised over £13,500 for food relief and medical supplies that were sent directly behind the blockade (with the reluctant permission of the War Office), using supply lines established by the Turkish Red Crescent. Throughout the war, the Oxford Famine Relief Committee campaigned for the relaxing of blockades on Belgium and Nazi-occupied central Europe, echoing the arguments of the Fight the Famine Council and the early SCF, and drawing an older, more radical generation of former SCF council members into its ranks. The Committee later became Oxfam, Save the Children's most significant collaborator (and competitor) in the decades to come. It was just one of a host of rapidly founded organizations that, in the Second World War, pledged to feed noncombatants caught behind the blockade, and expressed public disquiet at Allied military policy.[154] In the tradition of Save the Children's early work, humanitarian campaigning had again become a form of political critique at a time when British people had few avenues through which to question the conduct of the war.

In 1944, Dorothy Buxton made her last attempt to engage the council of the SCF in a more radical form of war work. She asked that "the Council would consider very seriously whether the Fund was still justified . . . in drawing a hard and fast line round the sphere of the SCF to avoid touching on what might be considered as a political matter—i.e. pleading even for the slightest relaxation of the Blockade. . . . If the SCF was to remain worthy of its name it should take part in the movement for an immediate relief scheme in Belgium and elsewhere."[155]

Victoria de Bunsen, Dorothy Buxton's sister-in-law, noted that she "spoke for many when she claimed that such an approach would jeopardize the Fund's ability to participate in [the] Council of British Societies for Relief

Abroad."[156] With many of its former supporters now working with Oxfam and Buxton shunned, the Fund had severed its final connections with its radical early membership. It had ceded to Oxfam its original vision of humanitarianism as political protest. In the late 1930s and during the war, the SCF had become a truly "establishment" organization, while newer agencies representing the traditionally left-wing politics and causes drew away the Fund's older members and supporters. Save the Children leaders' determination to preserve humanitarianism as a "nonpolitical" endeavor had led it to work alongside the British government and military in war, while overlooking the plight of the child victims of Nazi oppression.

SAVING CHILDREN FROM THE WORLD

On 15 November 1945, exactly seven months since the first Allied troops entered Berlin, the British government began the mass evacuation of children from the city. With winter drawing in, food shortages, and the threat of typhoid, the British military command feared that children would die, provoking international moral outrage. The British devised a solution based on the evacuation of British children from cities during the war: it would relocate fifty thousand German children away from major cities and into the countryside to wait out the winter with better provisioned rural families. It announced that German children should report for evacuation at schools and train stations, with winter coats and boots and a blank postcard addressed to their families that would be sent with the children's new address on arrival.[157] Many German parents feared that the evacuation was intended as a form of collective punishment. Rumors that the children would be permanently resettled or murdered circulated around the city.[158] Save the Children was called upon to calm these fears and to coordinate the evacuations. The Fund's iconic emblem, a swaddled baby with outstretched arms, was worn on the uniforms of British soldiers tasked with escorting children out of the city.[159]

Save the Children, an organization founded to protest against British militarism and promote a lasting peace and that had proclaimed a vision of child rights encompassing all, regardless of race, nationality, or creed, had looked away from the plight of Jewish children and children in Nazi-occupied territories. In scholarship and public discourse, aid organizations are often presented as facing a clear choice between complicity with or challenge to power.[160] However, Save the Children never made a single choice that led to its failure to challenge either Allied wartime policy or the abuses of the Third Reich. The depression of the 1930s led the Fund into partnership with the government as it took on preschool provision for children, hoping to eventually expand the reach of the state in this area, and the Fund became increasingly financially reliant on state support and therefore increasingly unable to challenge successive British governments at home or overseas. During the Spanish Civil War, a veneer of impartiality gave the Fund access to fascist-controlled territories, and the British SCF had sought to preserve this impartiality—above the liberal democratic ideals of its initial internationalist vision—within its International Union, and so it retained ties to member societies that became dominated by fascists.

Yet, however constrained or contextual their choices, ultimately, Save the Children's Council privileged their relationships with the British government and with fascist child welfare organizations in Europe over their ability to protest against the conduct of the war and the treatment of children in totalitarian states. Save the Children's aspirations for a child-centered postwar welfare state in Britain had shaped and inhibited its thought and action on Jewish children in Europe. As the liberal international order fragmented and fascist regimes rose across Europe, the Fund did not seek to influence international relations with the vision of collaboration that had originally inspired it. Rather, it sought to remain insulated from international political concerns.

FIVE

Hearts and Minds
Humanitarianism

IN 1953, Save the Children's press secretary, Edward Fuller, was on a mission: he needed to find a new role for Save the Children in the changed landscape of postwar humanitarianism. Now the longest-standing member of the Save the Children Council, he imagined that the Fund's future role might lie in its history, and specifically the 1924 Declaration of the Rights of the Child. In 1948, the United Nations General Assembly had adopted the Universal Declaration of Human Rights. Widespread popular support for human rights, he hoped, might reignite interest in children's rights and restore Save the Children to its rightful position as the organization that had "given child rights to the world." However, after attending the meetings of a number of London-based human rights lobbying groups in 1948, he concluded that human rights were unlikely to catch on and would remain a marginal concern for "feminists and minorities, especially Jews."[1]

Fuller's forays into the new world of human rights were part of a series of attempts by Save the Children to design a new role for itself in a world where states were playing an increasing part in international relief. With the disbanding of the League of Nations in 1946, Save the Children had lost its position of influence in Geneva, and in the aftermath of the Second World War British humanitarian efforts remained dwarfed by those of the United States. It was in this context that Save the Children shifted the geography of its work, moving from Europe into the British Empire. It did so at a moment of anti-colonial struggle that heralded the empire's end. During the 1950s, Save the Children worked alongside the Colonial Office, not only to restore its own prominence but also, more significantly, to use humanitarian intervention to maintain British imperial power. Opening a series of "reformatories" across the empire, Save the Children drew upon new psychiatric and psychoanalytic knowledge in a bid to win the hearts and minds of disaffected teenage boys and turn them into loyal colonial subjects.

The 1950s has been passed over in many of the existing histories of humanitarian aid, which leap from European postwar reconstruction into the postcolonial aid of the 1960s. The rare histories that do address the 1950s deal primarily with American-led humanitarian interventions in the "hot" sites of the Cold War, especially North Korea. Like most major aid agencies at the time, Save the Children's work encompassed both European reconstruction and war relief work in North Korea. In these activities, the work of the British Save the Children Fund was forged within the strictures of a burgeoning American-led international aid sector. This chapter deals with the Fund's forgotten work in the British Empire during the 1950s, where it was able to work autonomously and where we can more clearly see how its leaders sought to forge a distinctly British mode of humanitarian internationalism for the postwar world. Following Save the Children's work in Malaya, Somaliland, and Kenya, this chapter reveals how an organization founded to promote child welfare became involved in the punishment and imprisonment of children during the decolonization struggles of the postwar period. It casts light upon the wider entanglement of humanitarian organizations in colonial violence. Save the Children approached colonial emergencies as opportunities to create the disciplined, loyal subjects of a British Empire fit for a modern era. In the 1950s, Fund leaders did not imagine the end of empire, but hoped for a new beginning for British world leadership.

LOSING A ROLE, FINDING AN EMPIRE

Nineteen-eighteen saw long delays in food relief; vast, uncoordinated, and often deadly population movements; and a slow response to epidemics across Europe. The loss of life during the First World War was far outstripped by lives lost from the disease and hunger that followed in its wake. In 1919, SCF founder Dorothy Buxton argued that there would be no lasting peace without immediate postwar relief, and Save the Children had been founded to protest punitive postwar sanctions that were hampering reconstruction.[2] By 1939, international opinion accorded with Dorothy Buxton's arguments from twenty years earlier. Economists, diplomats, and politicians agreed that the failure to plan for post-1918 relief and reconstruction had facilitated the rise of fascism and led, ultimately, to the Second World War. A fresh global conflict represented a failure, but also another opportunity to create a stable, prosperous, and peaceful Europe.[3] Relief and reconstruction were central to Allied military policy, expressed most obviously by the formation of the United Nations Relief and Rehabilitation Administration (UNRRA) in 1943. However, as former Save the Children relief worker Francesca Wilson observed, this widespread acceptance of the ideas of Save the Children's founders had practical drawbacks. Planning for reconstruction at an intergovernmental level meant that voluntary societies had "less scope" for independent action as their activities were now subject to the direction of the UNRRA.[4] Did the Fund still have a role in postwar Europe?

The expansion of the welfare state in Britain also led members of the Save the Children council (many of whom had spent their lives campaigning for the expansion of children's services) to doubt their role in Britain. The Council feared that donations would further decline as the public saw children's needs being met by new state services at home, and by UNRRA- and US-funded reconstruction projects overseas.[5] By the end of the 1940s, Fund income, which had spiked during the war, dropped back to Depression-era levels.[6] Previously well-funded wartime projects began literally falling apart: in 1949, a young boy was killed in a Save the Children afterschool club in London when an iron railing fell on him, and in 1950, the Fund's chairman Captain Louis Green was seriously injured when the roof of the head offices in Bloomsbury collapsed.[7]

Save the Children feared not only the material consequences of state coordination of welfare and relief, but its wider, international implications. Edward Fuller viewed UNRRA as a smokescreen for an American takeover of international relief and was keen to disentangle the SCF from the competitive sphere of emergency relief and postwar reconstruction, believing the Fund would be able to carve out a more distinct role for itself in "long-term child welfare" within the newly founded United Nations.[8] Save the Children had been at the center of the League of Nations Child Welfare Committee and so, Fuller reasoned, it should expect to enjoy a similar status within the UN. When the League of Nations formally disbanded in 1946, many of its subsidiary bodies were transferred wholesale into the UN. While their titles and acronyms often changed, in many cases their personnel, structure, and ideological underpinnings remained.[9] Fuller hoped that the League of Nations Child Welfare Committee would be reborn as a United Nations Child Welfare Committee, securing the Fund's role—and by extension Britain's role—at the head of the international child welfare movement. When UNRRA was disbanded in

1946; however, a new organization, the International Children's Emergency Fund (ICEF), was established under the auspices of the United Nations (in 1953, it became UNICEF, as it is known today).[10]

The displacement of the League's European-led child welfare body by UNICEF, which was largely funded and dominated by the American government, was part of a wider shift from the Geneva-based, European-led League of Nations internationalism of the interwar era to the New York–based, American-led UN internationalism of the postwar period. The League's Child Welfare Committee had been dominated by the British Save the Children Fund. In contrast, UNICEF drew both its leadership and the bulk of its funding from the United States. American child welfare experts and internationalists, including Eleanor Roosevelt, argued that by circumventing European child welfare agencies they were avoiding "political" entanglements. They hoped that a new organization—free of the resentments and infighting to which the League of Nations Child Welfare Committee had been prone— would generate fresh enthusiasm, making child welfare "truly international."[11]

As the SCF was failing to embed itself in the new world of the UN in New York, its international connections in Geneva were also fragmenting. In 1946, the Save the Children International Union had merged with a Belgium-based child welfare association to become the International Union for Child Welfare (IUCW). This merger was intended to consolidate the Europe-based child welfare movement and offer an alternative to the US-dominated UNICEF, but in fact American donations to the IUCW rapidly declined, as the American SCF saw little need for an international child welfare society in addition to UNICEF.[12] The British Fund quickly grew disillusioned with the IUCW, claiming that it was "declining in influence" and "failing to occupy the role that it should within international relations."[13] The Fund also complained that the IUCW was "too European," and resented direction from its now predominantly Swiss and Belgian leadership about where and how the British Fund should work.

In its work across Europe in the aftermath of the Second World War, the British Fund worked in partnership with IUCW affiliate societies in nations such as Italy, France, and Greece. Their work here mimicked interwar interventions on the continent and in Britain: sending malnourished children to sanatoria, setting up clinics to advise mothers of baby care, and founding outdoor nurseries. Often, the Fund depended on UNRRA for the food and medical supplies their projects distributed, and it complained bitterly about an excess of "red tape" preventing rapid action. In one instance in France in

1946, UNRRA gave the Fund a consignment of powdered milk for pregnant mothers. By the time it had been cleared for distribution, the women had all given birth and were no longer eligible recipients. In displaced persons camps, the Fund was subject not only to the UNRRA regulations but also the overlapping authorities of the camps themselves and (often) the military. One British relief worker remarked to a group of soldiers in a DP camp, "Why don't you go and fight someone [rather than] meddle with peaceable human beings?"[14] Due to these frustrations, from the late 1940s, the Fund sought new spaces in which to provide autonomous, distinctly British aid. The Fund's interest in humanitarian internationalism ended when British claims to lead the international movement were no longer credible; it then began to reorient itself toward the empire.

Building on the relationships that the Fund had forged in Britain with the Departments of Health and Education, the Fund began to seek out new partnerships with the Colonial Office. In part, it was the changing composition of the Fund's leadership that shifted the geographies of its work. Before and during the Second World War, many of the Fund's old guard departed: some as they aged, others in protest at the Fund's decision to uphold the Allied blockade through its membership of government-sponsored Council of British Societies for Relief Abroad, and in a few cases defecting to Oxfam.[15] The Fund's new leaders came from the military, the intelligence services, and the Colonial Office. They displaced those with experience of Edwardian philanthropy; aid work; and, in many cases, feminist movements and the Labour Party. In 1948, Brigadier Tony Boyce, a military intelligence officer who had served in India, the Middle East and China, replaced George Gracey, a career relief worker, as general secretary. The Fund's president, Lord Noel Buxton, a Labour politician from a family of abolitionists and humanitarians, was replaced in 1949 by Lady Edwina Mountbatten, the last viscountess of India. Lady Alexandra Metcalfe (daughter of another former viceroy of India, Lord Curzon) joined the Fund as chair of the Foreign Relief Committee in 1952. This new leadership brought the Fund closer to both the military and the governors of the British Empire. Without nostalgia for the Fund's early days, Boyce and Mountbatten argued that the Fund should cut its ties to Geneva altogether, ceding "international" issues to UNICEF and "the Americans," and focusing on a more "natural" sphere of influence in the empire.[16]

Boyce argued that by shifting its focus from postwar Europe to the empire, the Fund could enjoy relative autonomy and carve out a distinctive field of expertise, away from continental Europe's rivalries and American control. Its long-standing relationship with the government and deepening ties to the Colonial Office, coupled with the relative lack of international aid organizations working outside Europe, meant that Save the Children could have the "inside track" on imperial child welfare.[17] In 1962 US secretary of state Dean Acheson famously claimed that the British had "lost an empire, but not yet found a role."[18] For Save the Children in the preceding decade, the opposite was true: the empire was a space in which the Fund could retreat from the complexities and competition of American-led international aid, playing a more insular, imperial role.

The Fund's turn to empire took place at a moment when empire itself was being reimagined, with an increased focus on welfare and social development. Imperialism had always been about profit, but its ideological justification had been bound up with discourses of civilization and progress. In 1929, the first Colonial Welfare Act had been married with the ideological and economic underpinnings of empire, seeking to enhance industrialization and profit through increased attention to social care.[19] The Second World War deepened and extended the British government's commitment to colonial welfare to win the wartime loyalty of colonial subjects. Further Colonial Welfare and Development Acts in 1940 and 1945 heralded the arrival of the "welfarist" era of late imperialism.[20] Under the postwar Labour government of Clement Attlee, the Colonial Office, led by Arthur Creech Jones, was influenced by the same brand of Fabian "ethical" colonialism that had animated Save the Children's interest in Africa in the 1930s. For Creech Jones, advances in welfare and education were necessary for economic development, especially in an era of industrialization and "detribalization." In both the colonies and Britain, the government envisaged economic productivity and social welfare as intimately bound together.[21]

Attention to colonial welfare had an international logic as well as internal imperial justification. In the wake of the Atlantic Charter and a global war apparently waged to free the world from tyranny, British colonialism drew scrutiny from American allies and the international community.[22] The welfare colonialism of the 1940s and 1950s was part of a wider rebranding project, seeking to fit imperialism into the norms of the post-1945 international order.[23] In an era of rising Cold War tension, the value of the empire increasingly lay in its ability to limit the influence of the USSR in Africa and Asia. Demonstrating the "benefits" of British rule in the shape of social reform and welfare was an attempt to counter anti-colonial resistance inspired by Communist ideals. Increased resources to do so were allocated by both the British

Colonial Office and the US government, which viewed British imperialism as a bulwark against communism.[24] Colonial welfare reform was a bid to win the hearts and minds of colonized people in an era when alternatives to colonialism were increasingly visible.[25]

Despite the economic and strategic importance of colonial development, postwar British politicians were reluctant to devote resources beyond Britain at a moment of welfare-state expansion and postwar debt. The empire had always been intended to pay, rather than be paid for.[26] Partnership with humanitarian organizations was an efficient cost-saving mechanism. It demonstrated colonial concern for welfare and development while freeing up limited resources to focus elsewhere.[27] However, Save the Children was not just enabling welfare interventions on the cheap; it was also participating in an empire-wide expansion of colonial policing. The work of Save the Children was directed at projects intended to stymie anti-colonial resistance among a newly identified problem population: the youth. In the 1940s and 1950s, imperial child welfare work became a tool for colonial social control.

CHANGING CHILDREN IN A CHANGING WORLD

When Save the Children offered its services to the Colonial Office, it was seeking not just new places to work in, but a new type of child to work with. After the Second World War, the Fund became caught up in an international moral panic centered on juvenile delinquency. Juvenile delinquency was not a new concept in the 1940s but dated back to the rise of industrial capitalism. In the Victorian era, youth crime not only stoked fears that working-class youths would be unable to participate in industrial economic life but was also signaled the ill effects of industrial capitalism on the British population, with young offenders imagined as mentally and physically degenerated by the conditions of urban life.[28] Now, in the aftermath of the Second World War, fresh concerns about the impact of the war on children sparked moral panic. As prosecutions for youth crime spiked worldwide, a host of child welfare experts, among them associates of Save the Children, argued that both the war and the totalitarian regimes that preceded it had damaged older children. According to child welfare experts, war had brought about a broad cultural shift in which qualities usually unsuited to "civilized life," such as pugnaciousness and anger, had been venerated. It was hypothesized that young men, attracted to the military culture, had been drawn to warlike behavior even though they had not been in service. Meanwhile, it was claimed that young women, without the "stabilizing influence" of their fathers, and often exposed to nonfamilial military men, had become "promiscuous." Experts argued that this pugnaciousness and promiscuity had been compounded by better nutrition and welfare provision, causing children to reach physical maturity at a younger age, something that these adolescents were not emotionally ready for.[29]

This postwar panic about the moral lives of adolescents was underpinned by advances in psychiatry. In the late 1930s, a new generation of psychoanalysts such as Anna Freud and John Bowlby posited that children's "attachment" to their parents, particularly their mothers, was the foremost predictor of healthy, mentally stable adult life. In this context, the mass evacuation, orphaning, and abandonment of children during the Second World War seemed to be the harbingers of continent-wide social dislocation. A series of psychological studies carried out on children who had been evacuated or lost parents during the war argued that the "best interests" of children lay in lasting relationships with their biological families and, where this was not possible, in consistent care from an individual or small group of primary carers with whom they could form a lasting emotional bond.[30]

These arguments were a decisive departure from interwar humanitarian interventions, which had focused on the bodies of children, rather than their minds. In the early twentieth century, children had been viewed, first and foremost, as a biological resource for nation-states: girls and boys were the mothers and soldiers of the future. The major innovation of Save the Children had been to present the biological health of children not purely as a national concern, but as an international good: children were both potential soldiers and potential workers whose labor would create mutual prosperity and thus international stability. When the Fund had spoken of children's minds, it had done so either in terms of education (a precursor to productive economic citizenship) or in vague, spiritual terms. Children were emotive objects, not emotional subjects. Their significance was in wider national and international societies, rather than within the structure of their families or communities. Now, psychoanalytic theory proposed a new precursor to good citizenship: emotional security. Even well-educated, healthy children could become a detriment (or even danger) to society if deprived of affection and attachment in early life.[31]

The power of adolescents had been illustrated on a global scale in the 1930s and 1940s. Fascist movements showcased the weaponization of adolescence as they built militarily trained, ideologically compliant mass youth movements.

The susceptibility of young people to fascism was explained by humanitarian organizations and governments alike as a consequence of the physical deprivation that many had suffered in the aftermath of the First World War: as the American National Planning Association argued, "the starving children of 1919 are the stormtroopers of today."[32] Yet susceptibility to fascism was also imagined to derive from emotional deprivation. Proponents of "attachment theory" claimed that children who had grown up without stable authority figures were susceptible to the promises of totalitarian leaders, who filled an emotional void left by absent parents. Familial love was thus essential to the development of a "democratic personality": a stable, discerning temperament needed for participation in the liberal political order.[33] In the emerging Cold War context, with the rise of Communist youth movements across Eastern Europe and in colonial states, questions about emotional security, family life, and citizenship became bound up in a worldwide ideological struggle.[34] If deprivation and lack of parental attachment in the aftermath of the First World War had created a generation of children who later fought for totalitarian fascist regimes in the Second, the children of Europe might grow up to fight for totalitarian communism in a generation's time.[35] The stability of Europe—and the wider world—was therefore contingent on the emotional and physical well-being of the young. Mass family tracing and repatriation programs took place across the war-ravaged continent, as children and parents who had become separated were matched and moved vast distances by UNRRA and the American Red Cross for reunification.[36]

New ideas about children's emotional security and the centrality of families had an immediate impact on government policy in Britain. The 1948 Children's Act established adoption and fostering, rather than institutional care, as preferable for children without families of their own.[37] In Britain, as in other expanding European welfare states, postwar welfare and employment policies conspired to push women back into their homes to raise the next generation of well-adjusted, emotionally attached children. Where states themselves were not leading the drive for the creation of nuclear families, humanitarian organizations took up the slack. American aid organizations and philanthropic foundations sought to "reconstruct" Europe and "modernize" societies in northeast Asia and Latin America via the promotion and preservation of nuclear family units. During the Cold War, organizations such as the American Red Cross and Plan International sought to prevent a new generation becoming juvenile delinquents and to ward off totalitarianism via the creation of emotionally robust citizens.[38]

Save the Children relief workers recognized children's desire for family life. One recalled how, at an "orphanage" for children who had become separated from their families in France, children would decorate their lockers with magazine cuttings of mothers, fathers, babies, and dogs to "pretend we have a real family of our own."[39] Yet the Fund did not participate in reunification efforts: the new drive to raise children within families posed a challenge to Save the Children's methods. As we have seen, the Fund's largest-scale and often most popular projects centered on creating children-only spaces such as orphanages. This was sometimes described in terms of efficiency (it was easier to concentrate aid on children if they were separate from the rest of the population), but it was also an ideological preference. Pessimistic about the ability of adults to overcome wartime trauma and fearful of the moral threat posed by "idleness," the Fund viewed itself as saving children not only from violence and poverty, but also from the influence of their families and communities. Children offered what felt like a less ethically and politically complex mode of intervention. While the Fund never renounced its past child-removal practices, from 1945 its language began to shift. Its publications highlighted the importance of parental affection and discipline, and its relief workers in Europe were involved in large-scale child-reunification programs organized by UNRRA. After 1945, the international humanitarian community saw families, rather than children, as the root of reconstruction.[40]

However, while the Fund accepted the importance of families for children's emotional stability after the Second World War, it did not alter its methods. It continued to privilege forms of education and provision that removed children from communities and families by shifting its focus to the so-called "maladjusted child" or "juvenile delinquent": children whose families were deemed too dysfunctional to provide the authority and emotional attachment difficult children needed.[41] The Fund's work with young lawbreakers began in Germany in 1945 when it was invited by the occupying British authorities to intercept "young smugglers" crossing the borders from the American to the British sectors, carrying items to sell on the black market. Once the youths (usually between the ages of ten and sixteen) had been intercepted by Save the Children relief workers waiting at the border, they were searched (coffee beans—the items of choice—were often found in the soles of shoes or even in children's ears) and taken to children's homes. If their parents could be located, they were prosecuted, but the children remained in care.[42] The same was true in Italy, where the Save the Children Fund (in a rare instance of work with adolescent girls) attempted to "reclaim" "children who had become prostitutes" for occupying American forces during the war, removing them from their communities to attend countryside schools (where the girls themselves trained in child welfare work).[43] Preventing a child from entering a "life of crime" warranted removing a child from their parents, many of whom Save the Children argued (as they had in 1918) were too psychologically damaged to raise children.[44] Now, though, child removal would only be justified when it was clear that a child had become "criminal" or "maladjusted."[45]

The Fund's twin shifts in interest (from infants to adolescents, and from "normal" to "maladjusted" children) cast it as a modern and progressive competitor to the host of child-focused humanitarian organizations that emerged after 1945.[46] In reality, the Fund had been behind the curve in its thinking on both teenagers and delinquency: as we saw in chapter 4, its leaders remained interested during the Second World War in late nineteenth-century educational philanthropy, such as the work of German educational theorist Frobel, and were unaware of the advances taking place in psychoanalysis. At the end of the war, the Fund's insularity and traditionalism meant that it had been left behind. In a bid to place itself at the center of the discourse on juvenile delinquency the British SCF and IUCW hosted a series of international conferences on the "delinquent," "maladjusted" child throughout the 1950s. They brought together child welfare experts, psychiatrists, and humanitarians to compare "best practice" from boarding schools, prisons, Borstals, and reformatories that housed "juvenile delinquents" away from their families across Europe and the US.[47] These conferences showcased the work of local European organizations under the bambino banner of the international Save the Children movement, and the SCF hoped to show that it still had a credible claim to be "leading" postwar work in juvenile delinquency, even as its underfunded programs were becoming ever more limited.

Comparing institutions founded for so-called juvenile delinquents across Europe, the SCF and the IUCW conferences defined a set of scenarios in which children should be removed from their families, and guidelines around how schools and reformatories could best mimic the authority and emotional security provided by a functional family.[48] These guidelines advocated that if parents and siblings would undermine the progress that a child had made away from a life of crime or delinquency, contact should be severed while the child was "reformed." Educators could act as proxy parents, and fellow pupils or inmates as siblings. Juvenile reformatories should be subdivided into smaller groups ("houses"), with measures of authority given to children dependent on their age and time spent in the reformatory, under the direct authority of a housemaster or mistress. These houses within reformatories would create loyalty, emotional connection, and a structure that mimicked the nuclear family in its absence. Reformatories would also provide training in manual labor and craftsmanship, to enable inmates to become productive citizens.[49] These "innovations" in the care of adolescents were not new at all, but directly reproduced the structure of British public schools. Housemasters, prefects, and houses would have looked familiar to the vast majority of Save the Children's upper-class council. The Fund's success in the postwar years did not lie in its innovation or adoption of new child-rearing methods, but its ability to repackage and rebrand its existing work and prejudices in line with the concerns of the era.[50]

Following its work with adolescents on the European continent and the British Empire, the Fund opened its first residential center for adolescents in Britain in 1950, a seaside home in Essex named Hill House. Hill House was intended to rehabilitate psychologically damaged children and "delinquents" from war-torn central Europe, who came from "fractured families," or whose relatives had experienced psychological trauma during the war or in concentration camps.[51] In these cases, it was reasoned, the care provided at Hill House by a male warden and a female matron would mimic a stable nuclear family life. The children could behave as "children again," through playing in wild orchards, sea-swimming, and craft activities.[52] "Bad behavior" such as fighting and aggression, which children had learned in their unstable childhoods and from war-scarred parents, were to be eradicated through disciplinary measures ranging from "gentle words" to "caning."[53]

Having proclaimed its special interest and expertise in delinquent children, Save the Children staff in Britain were remarkably reluctant to work with criminal—or even mildly disruptive—young people. Despite their academic understanding of the psychological effects of war and its connections to criminality, most relief workers were unable to think of children as anything other than innately innocent. Even at Hill House, staff were more interested in children as symbolic "emissaries of peace" than as war-damaged individuals. Bridget Stevenson, one of Save the Children's longest-standing relief workers, selected the first children to visit Hill House from a displaced persons camp in Uelzen in Germany in June 1950. She chose well-behaved, bright children with "some personal tragedy" who would be "the first German children that many English people will have seen since the war." She was aghast that on arrival at Hill House, the children all "made wooden guns and wooden knives, and cheerfully sold these to the local village children for vast sums of pennies, expended later on ice cream." Her "carefully chosen," "peace-ful" children had "armed everyone in sight." (Reflecting on this incident later, she concluded that her "fears were unfounded. This was not the start of the Third World War . . . but the real beginning of NATO!")[54]

Hill House continued to host "well-behaved" children and adolescents from displaced persons camps in Germany until 1956.[55] Yet framing Hill House as a rehabilitation program for potential criminals allowed the Fund to portray its work as modern and innovative, while retaining its old family separation practices almost unaltered. Though its postwar programs were couched in the language of psychological rehabilitation, they in fact mim-icked the Fund's work from almost thirty years earlier when, in the aftermath of the First World War, they had removed German and Austrian children from parents to send them to sanatoria or far-away boarding schools, privileg-ing the importance of fresh air and rural living above family life. At a moment of mass family reunification programs across Europe, when states and the international aid community alike celebrated the sanctity of the family and its centrality to healthy nationhood, the practices of Save the Children remained largely unchanged.[56]

"A MALAYAN EXPERIMENT
IN TRAINING IN CITIZENSHIP"

The lines of influence in the increasingly global work of Save the Children were tangled. It was not the case that work in Europe provided the model for work in the empire: in the postwar periods European and colonial projects were forged in tandem, and the empire often provided a site of experimenta-tion for practices that came back to Britain's shores. This was the case for Hill House, which was modeled on a project begun in Malaya two years earlier: the Serendah Boys School. Like Hill House, Serendah promised to provide care for war-damaged youths and juvenile delinquents. Serendah was, in turn, influenced by youth rehabilitation schemes that had been piloted in central Europe in the immediate aftermath of war, both in reformatories and displaced persons camps. In both, "rehabilitation" encompassed not only psychological rehabilitation from the horrors of war or involvement with criminality, but also training in new trades to produce self-sufficient citizens of the future. Rehabilitation could be achieved through labor, creat-ing the capacity for economic self-sufficiency following a period in which an individual had been reliant on governing authorities or aid organizations for their material needs.[57] In this tradition, Serendah also provided a form of "rehabilitation" by using "educational facilities and training in certain trades so that they could become useful citizens."[58]

Through Serendah, the Fund was not just seeking to rehabilitate children, but to strengthen the British Empire in the aftermath of the war. Between 1941 and 1945, Malaya—formerly a collection of British protectorates—had been under Japanese occupation. During the occupation, an estimated one hundred thousand Malayans were killed, forty thousand people were displaced, and malnutrition and disease were endemic.[59] Recognizing the scale of the crisis, the Military Administration appealed to British humanitarian organizations for staff to be relocated to Malaya.[60] Enthusiastic about expansion into the empire, Save the Children's new general secretary, Tony Boyce, agreed that the "problem of unaccompanied and destitute children in Malaya was as pressing as [that] in mainland Europe." Boyce argued that the foremost concern of the Colonial Office should be adolescent boys, many of whom had left for the capital city seeking work or had otherwise been separated from their parents. As in Europe, young men were blamed for a rapid rise in youth crime, as some stole and looted to support themselves.[61] They were also, Boyce feared, being lured into Communist and anti-colonial youth leagues. Just as the stability of Europe was contingent on the emotional well-being of European youth, Boyce claimed that in Malaya humanitarian interventions in the lives of adolescent boys was vital for "the stabilisation of Malaya and the re-establishment of British rule."[62]

Serendah was a former hospital, donated to the Fund by the British High Commissioner for Malaya, and the day-to-day expenses of the school were also covered by the Colonial Office via its Juvenile Delinquency Fund, an empire-wide fund established in 1946 to deal with the "rising problem" of youth crime.[63] None of the school's first intake of fifty-two boys, mostly homeless children aged ten to sixteen, had been convicted of any crimes, and the school was, in the words of one of its nurses, Jane Bibby, "more of a boarding school than a reformatory."[64] Bibby, like most of the school's staff, had relocated from displaced persons camps in Europe. She was delighted to be working in the calm, constructive environment of a school, which gave her "far more pleasure" than the often chaotic relief missions in continental Europe. In Europe she had been answerable to the multilayered authorities of the displaced persons camps, but in Malaya, the SCF could operate autonomously. No longer working alongside other relief organizations,

FIGURE 13. The Boys at Serendah, c. 1958. The traditions of the scouting movement are reflected in the boys' uniforms. Here, the bambino logo has been rendered to suggest an older boy wearing a cloth around his waist, rather than a swaddled baby. Save the Children Photo Collection, Save the Children Archives, Birmingham, UK.

the SCF staff in Malaya concentrated their energies on a single, flagship project.[65]

The school sought to teach poor and working-class Malayan boys elite British values.[66] In the tradition of British public schools, girls were excluded. The boys in Serendah were organized into four boarding houses, named after "pillars" of the British Empire: Mountbatten, Milner, Gent, and Blake. They played rugby and cricket and sang British songs such as "Jerusalem" and "It's a Long Way to Tipperary."[67] The "backbone" of the school was a system of prefects, in which each house appointed senior representatives to instill discipline in their juniors through punishments (caning) and rewards (small sums of cash).[68] Alongside "British values," the school also claimed to teach "self-sufficiency." Every boy in the school was engaged in vocational training in farming, sewing, or cobbling. This set them up for employment and, crucially, helped to fund the school. Between 1948 and 1957, the boys raised over £500 each year through selling garden produce and making furniture. The colonial government also regularly purchased handmade Union Jacks made by the boys. "Self-help was impressed on the boys upon entering the home," explained Lieutenant Colonel Frank Adams, the school's headmaster from 1950 onward. "Every boy was told that he must do something to help the home if he expected help from others."[69]

The emphasis on "self-help" at Serendah also reflected the ethos of the British colonial government. Despite the rise of a new welfare colonialism in the postwar period, the colonial government in Malaya constantly claimed that it must not do "too much" lest Malayans become "dependent" on British aid.[70] To avoid this, the colonial government laid out a vision of "self-help" in welfare, achieved through the partnership of Malayan elites and colonial authorities. To this end, Red Cross representative and soon-to-be Save the Children president Lady Edwina Mountbatten had founded the Welfare Council for Malaya in September 1945. Welfare Council funds would then be "matched" by the colonial government in order to "foster voluntary action" and promote "self-help" over dependence, on a national scale.[71] This was the global heritage of Victorian liberalism, as the ideals of the Charity Organisation Society were rehashed in postwar colonial welfare policy. While the Charity Organisation Society had sought to inculcate self-sufficiency in individuals, now the same impulse was transposed onto entire populations. With scant regard for long-standing indigenous traditions of voluntary service and charity, Lady Mountbatten's Welfare Council claimed, patronizingly, to be "teaching" Malayans to "take responsibility for the welfare of their own people."[72] The Welfare Council presented welfare as the remit of civil society, rather than the state, and sought to build and strengthen civic life as a corollary to participatory politics after independence.

In postwar Malaya, the discourse of "self-help" had an anti-Communist inflection. The Fund's work in Malaya was taking place against the backdrop of the struggle between the Communist insurgents of the Malayan National Liberation Army (MNLA) and the British colonial state. In 1948 the British High Commission declared a state of "emergency," which lasted until 1960.[73] British counterinsurgency was brutal and repressive. In an attempt to gain a tactical advantage, the British military aimed to cut off supplies and support for the MNLA by local communities. Tens of thousands of rural peasants were rounded up and forcibly settled in "New Villages": compounds surrounded by wire fences to prevent their inhabitants from contacting anti-colonial fighters. When suspected fighters were captured, they were interned and, in some cases, tortured.[74]

Alongside the cruelty of the military war effort, the British colonial government ran a multifaceted "hearts and minds" campaign. Announced in 1952 by General Gerald Templar, the British high commissioner for Malaya, this campaign drew on postwar denazification efforts in postwar Germany.[75] It proposed a psychological approach, seeking to draw support for British rule through propaganda on the one hand and, on the other, the "benevolent" provision of welfare services and material goods. As in postwar Germany, humanitarian organizations shored up the British hearts and minds campaign in Malaya through their attempts to enhance the well-being of populations and thus win their support for British rule.[76]

It was not just Save the Children but also its old competitor and collaborator, the British Red Cross, that had entered the country in 1948 seeking fresh autonomy and opportunity in the British Empire.[77] The British Red Cross undertook sanitary and health education campaigns in the "new villages," where starvation and disease were endemic. The Red Cross denied that the causes of starvation and disease lay in mass forced resettlement, focusing their interventions on changing the behavior of villagers through mothercraft and dental hygiene lessons.[78] It presented suffering as a product of "appalling ignorance" on the part of the local population, with wartime aid and education as the solution.[79] The British Red Cross weaponized education. A multitude of youth groups were founded to promote British values, democratic citizenship and, by implication, anti-Communist principles.[80] The British Red Cross established Junior Red Cross brigades, focused on health, hygiene, social responsibility, and British culture, with young delegates playing brass instruments, parading, and learning football and badminton.[81]

Save the Children also weaponized education. While the British Red Cross focused on "ordinary school children," Save the Children's Serendah devoted its energies to destitute and vagrant boys, seen as especially susceptible to the Communist ideology of the MNLA. In 1950, the British government increased its spending on juvenile delinquency in Malaya, reasoning that combatting youth crime would lessen youth involvement with the MNLA. The Serendah school received a portion of this grant and was praise as an organization that would keep young men away from criminality as well as Communist ideas and organizations.[82] Like the British Red Cross, Save the Children participated in a colonial mixed economy of welfare and discipline and repression. In wars of counterinsurgency, international humanitarian organizations colluded with the colonial government in the repression and subjugation of colonized peoples.

Save the Children of course claimed that its work in Malaya was "entirely non-political." In reports, Save the Children staff stubbornly avoided referring directly to guerrilla warfare and counterinsurgency, some of which was

FIGURE 14. A publicity postcard generated for the Serendah school, which shows its spacious campus and floral borders. Save the Children Photo Collection, Save the Children Archives, Birmingham, UK.

taking place a few miles from the school.[83] Despite its reluctance, the Fund was forced to confront the war on 12 December 1948, when a rubber plantation ten miles from Serendah was invaded by British troops, who shot and killed twenty-four Malayan villagers while in search of guerrilla fighters. In the unrest that followed, Serendah became a target for MNLA insurgents. On the night of 15 December a group of "Communist guerrillas" entered the school compound. Hammering on the door of the Serendah's first principal, Alan Blake, they threated to burn the school down. When Blake came to the door, the guerrillas followed him into the house, where he was shot and killed; the men then set his house alight and fled.[84]

Blake's murder ignited international sympathy. *The Spectator* magazine established a fund to replace the pupils" Christmas gifts, which were lost in the arson attack.[85] Yet, after the shock at Blake's murder had passed, the school was described by the Fund as a "haven" in the midst of Malaya's "troubles."[86] Even at the height of the emergency, the school hosted prominent visitors. Violet Attlee, the prime minister's wife and Save the Children patron, remarked on visiting the school, "I knew it would be good, but I didn't know it would be this good." Nannette Boyce, the oldest daughter of Save the Children general secretary Tony Boyce, praised an institution that combined the best of an English public school with practical training in a beautiful setting. Above the school flew the Union Jack, the Fund's bambino logo, and the Selangor state flag (all hand-sewn by Serendah boys). Classrooms were well equipped and surrounded by "colorful flower borders" ("always an attraction to Asians," remarked Nannette Boyce). The boys were "well cared for" and the atmosphere "collegiate" and "homely."[87]

The successes of old boys were well publicized, and the school's second headmaster Colonel Frank Adams claimed that Serendah graduates were so in demand that there was a waiting list of local businesses seeking boys as apprentices.[88] One high-flier joined the Malay Regiment at the age of eighteen and eventually trained at Sandhurst.[89] Old boys were regular visitors at the school, and many of the school's new admissions were brought to Serendah by friends or relatives. In a period of frustration for Save the Children, Serendah was seen as a success. It was a flagship initiative that the Fund tried (and failed) to replicate elsewhere in the empire. Between the school's own revenue-generating activities and support from the local community and the colonial government, it was also an "efficient enterprise." Claiming just 7 percent of the annual budget between 1946 and 1956, Serendah was a bargain for Save the Children in terms of what the Fund gained in morale, publicity, and prestige. Despite this, when Malaya gained independence in 1957, the Fund relinquished Serendah to Malayan educational authorities, due to concerns about staff safety without the protection of the colonial government. Just as independence was presented as the culmination of Britain's tutelage in government, giving up Serendah was packaged as a measure of the school's success and evidence of the SCF having taught the "Malayan people to care for their own children."[90]

JUVENILE DELINQUENCY IN BRITISH SOMALILAND

The Colonial Office Juvenile Delinquency Fund that Save the Children had benefitted from in Malaya also provided a gateway into Somaliland. In 1949, the Fund was invited to care for "vagrant and delinquent" boys in the capital Hargeisa by its reformist governor, Gerald Reece.[91] Reece had taken on the governorship of British Somaliland six months earlier and identified juvenile delinquency as a central problem. He was not merely importing postwar European moral panic into an African context: juvenile delinquency had been a growing concern in British East and West Africa in the interwar period, as urban industrialization led increasing numbers of young men to move to cities, only to be faced with high unemployment. As "vagrancy" and petty crime in colonial cities from Nairobi to Lagos rose, the Colonial Office set up a Juvenile Delinquency Commission in 1937. Renamed the Youth and Juvenile Welfare Committee after the Second World War, it began distributing grants to projects—such as those run by Save the Children—across the empire to stem a feared rising tide of youth crime.[92]

In Somaliland, as in Malaya, the "problem" of juvenile delinquency was bound up with anti-colonial youth resistance.[93] The chief opposition to British rule across Somaliland was the Somali Youth League. Founded as a "self-help" organization, it drew together the new, urbanized Somali middle classes. It sought the unification and eventual decolonization of Somali territories and promoted the education and professional advancement of its members.[94] Gerald Reece hoped that, through vocational training for uneducated urban Somalis, he could create a working class loyal to British rule, countering the threat posed by the politicized, educated Somali Youth League, while also reducing youth crime.[95]

Enlisting humanitarian organizations to care for suspected young offenders channeled new "expertise" from Europe into the colonial context and lent often regressive youth crime regimes the legitimacy of humanitarian operations. By inviting the SCF into Somaliland, Reece was both showcasing the benevolent, progressive nature of British rule in the territory and outsourcing the problem of youth crime to a non-state body. His invitation came at a moment when, as we have seen, Save the Children's income was rapidly declining. Recognizing that in order to continue overseas work, it would need to draw increasingly on state partnerships and governmental budgets, the Fund enthusiastically accepted.[96] In Somaliland, Save the Children became, in effect, a government contractor, drawing funds from the empire-wide Juvenile Delinquency Fund and receiving direction from Reece on where and how to undertake its work.

In April 1951, Save the Children representative John Watling left for Hargeisa to begin a school for vagrant boys. The son of a Yorkshire shopkeeper, Watling was typical of a new postwar generation of relief workers: lower-middle-class war veterans with little prior knowledge of child welfare but passionate for travel. What Watling lacked in experience he made up in enthusiasm, but with little direction from the Fund's council and no contacts

in Hargeisa, he found his first year "very uphill."[97] The school was dilapidated, and the boys, who had been "rounded up" from the city streets by the
colonial police slept under canvas.[98] The school was nothing like Serendah or
the juvenile reformatories across Europe from which Save the Children drew
inspiration. In Hargeisa, the Fund failed to implement the IUCW recommendations on youth reformatories as laid out in the series of conferences
on juvenile delinquency that had influenced the organization of Serendah.
Rather than smaller, family-style groups like the Serendah "house" system,
the limited staff in Hargeisa required a more authoritarian hierarchy.[99] There
were no prefects, and everyone answered directly to Watling. At Serendah,
in line with the approach to "juvenile rehabilitation" pioneered in postwar
Europe, boys were allowed a measure of freedom, leaving and returning to
the school at will. In Hargeisa, the boys were effectively imprisoned. Those
who "escaped" were returned by police, and the Fund regularly petitioned
the colonial administration for financial support to build a more secure compound in which boys could be "detained."[100]

Hargeisa most closely resembled Serendah in its work program. The boys
were trained in cobbling by local tradesmen, and they partly financed the
school through sandal production. Education in skilled, artisanal crafts was
central to Governor Reece's plan to create a stable new working class to
counteract the anti-colonial radicalism of the educated middle classes, but
this vision did not match reality. Despite the sandal workshop's financial
success, headmaster Watling doubted it was achieving its paramount aim:
reforming the characters of the Hargeisa boys. He reported that his attempts
to instill a work ethic among the boys were largely fruitless, complaining
that "they will work hard under supervision but will not do it voluntarily,
although they know that the work they do is in their interest."[101] He felt there
was a pervasive attitude of "entitlement" and reported an incident in which
schoolboys had been given surplus boots by the master of a local Scout troop.
One eleven-year-old was presented with two size-seven boots that did not
match. The boy, "quite unknown to anyone in the camp . . . approached the
captain quartermaster of the Scouts and *demanded* that he should be given a
proper pair of boots in exchange to those he had." Meanwhile, "other boys to
whom boots had been issued immediately took them to the township, sold
them, and then asked for more."[102]

Watling's outrage at the boys' sense of "entitlement" did not recognize
the unpaid work that these young men were undertaking. The boy who
demanded his own pair of matching boots worked six days a week making

sandals for other people. Unlike his contemporaries at Serendah, he did not receive regular bonus pay, Christmas presents, a school uniform, or a holistic education. The school's failure to teach literacy was a conscious anti-delinquency policy adopted by several colonial administrations across Africa. "Training with a literary bias" was seen as the reason that so many young men were "coming to regard their natural environments as inferior," leaving their rural homes and coming to cities, failing to find work, and turning to crime. Care for juvenile delinquents was intended to reverse this trend by offering practical professions rather than educational opportunities and subsequent unmet aspirations.[103] Days at the Hargeisa home, therefore, consisted almost entirely of sandal making or the maintenance of the grounds and farm. A "chosen few" were sent to do groundwork at a local expatriate golf course, for which they received no payment.[104] In 1956, after repeated escape attempts, a group of ten boys went on strike, refusing to work until they received weekly bonuses. Watling reluctantly gave in when he realized that paying professional sandal makers would have been far more expensive than providing minimal compensation to his unpaid charges.[105]

The Fund did not see the difference in the boys' behavior in Malaya and Somaliland as connected to contrast between the treatment they received in the flower-lined flagship project in Malaya and the dilapidated, high-walled camp in Somaliland. Instead, the Fund blamed cultural differences. Drawing on colonial stereotypes of Africans as unsuited to Western, capitalist economies, Watling described the boys as "workshy." He reminded the Fund's council that they must not "expect too much of the boys who know nothing of civilization or western ideas and regard begging for a living as a normal means of livelihood." He believed that his boys only had experience of "raiding of water holes, and the carrying off of women," and it would take a long time for them to adjust to "modern life."[106] Watling's views echoed the Colonial Office's early interwar discussions of juvenile delinquency. Rather than regarding the increasing levels of youth crime in major colonial cities as due to rapid industrialization, urbanization, and unemployment as a result of the worldwide economic depression, the Colonial Office sought essentialist racial explanations. Youth crime, experts claimed, was due to a particularly African inability to adjust to the breakdown of "traditional" society and tribal discipline. Influenced by the British Eugenics Society, patrons of the empire's first juvenile reformatory (founded in Nairobi in 1907) regarded juvenile delinquency as a racial failure to adapt to modernity, rather than a symptom of the colonial economy failing to provide security for African youth.[107]

As an organization, Save the Children considered itself "progressive" on "the question of race."[108] In the postwar period, it regularly claimed that "all children were alike in character" if not color, rejecting ideas about inborn "violence" or criminality in the children of Commonwealth migrants.[109] In postwar Britain, the Fund worked to create "racial harmony" through a set of playschools that brought working-class white and black children into contact in British cities (named "domino clubs" or "rainbow clubs").[110] However, despite its work against "racialism" in Britain, in Africa, Save the Children leaned on thinly disguised racist tropes to explain the "criminality" of African boys. According to Watling, "tribal life" had left African youth with little understanding of industry, labor, and urban living. It was, he imagined, the role of Save the Children to "help" African young men through a transition that was both personal and epochal: the coming of age of themselves and their nations.[111]

By working to "reform" juvenile delinquents in Hargeisa, the SCF was, again, part of a colonial mixed economy of discipline. In Hargeisa, it sought to create a stable, loyal colonial working class. After the Second World War, the Fund publicized its "new" attitudes on youth and delinquency, but its practices in Somalia drew heavily on its long tradition of using labor to inculcate discipline in impoverished communities, offering it as a universal solution for any marginalized group. This had been the case in refugee resettlement schemes in interwar Greece and Macedonia, and for "orphan" children across central, eastern, and southern interwar Europe. Labor had always been central to the creation of "stability" and discipline, whether in the form of continued colonial control or interwar European economic prosperity. The Fund's use of labor in this way was never more obvious than in the Kenyan war of independence.

COLONIAL COLLUSION: "SAVING" MAU MAU CHILDREN

In Malaya and Somaliland, Save the Children had participated in projects designed to further the wider aims of the colonial state via the creation of loyal, young colonial subjects. In Kenya, rather than undertaking preventative work with young men they imagined might become criminals, the Fund became embroiled in explicitly punitive work. The Fund's work in Kenya took place during a "state of emergency," one of the most violent episodes in the decolonization of the British Empire. In the 1950s, Mau Mau guerrillas engaged in what was effectively a civil war aimed at ending British rule in Kenya.[112] In 1952, the colonial government embarked upon a program of incarceration and rehabilitation to "cleanse" suspected Mau Mau of their anti-colonial beliefs. It is only recently that the full scale of state-sponsored violence during the Kenyan Emergency has come to light. Oral testimonies and the recovery of documents hidden by the British Foreign and Common- wealth Office have revealed a "pipeline" system: a process through which Mau Mau insurgents were imprisoned and psychologically and physically tor- tured, with the aim of remaking them as obedient British subjects.[113] Colonial officials at every level were implicated in this process, as were humanitarian organizations. During the Kenyan Emergency, Save the Children became an architect of a system for the punishment and reeducation of children and young men involved in anti-colonial activism.

Tony Boyce touched down in Nairobi in 1954 on a flight from Somaliland, where he had been inspecting the Save the Children work school in Hargeisa. Just as in Somaliland the stability of British rule rested on the prevention of youth radicalism, in Kenya Boyce believed that the anti–Mau Mau campaign hinged upon the successful rehabilitation of children, the Kenyan colonial subjects of the future.[114] He proposed an "Operation Anvil for children." The Operation Anvil launched by the British army involved the imprisonment and "screening" of Kikuyu men and women to ascertain whether they were Mau Mau rebels. Boyce suggested that Save the Children should "round up" children in Nairobi aged ten to seventeen and place them in compulsory "res- idential schools," similar to the school in Hargeisa. These children would be "rehabilitated" and "re-educated to support the colonial cause."[115] Alongside these schools, Boyce suggested a network of kindergartens, where children of suspected Mau Mau rebels would be given "milk and medical care," to "soften" their mothers' attitudes to British rule.[116]

Boyce received a warm welcome from the colonial government in Kenya, which also viewed the unrest in Kenya as a crisis of youth. Resistance to Brit- ish rule had centered on land disputes. The vast farms owned by white settlers led to severe land shortages for Africans. Young Kikuyu were unable to attain the resources needed to begin new family units and become economically independent from their elders, and they felt this land shortage most acutely. In frustration, many young men left the reserves designated by the colonial state as Kikuyu farmland and headed to the city.[117] Rapid urbanization and stringent vagrancy laws had led to rising prosecution rates of young men.[118] Colonial officials regarded rising prosecution rates in cities as evidence of the influence of the Mau Mau movement in urban youths, who they claimed were a "soft target" for anti-colonial propaganda.[119] Children as young as four were alleged to be acting as runners for messages and supplies passed between Mau Mau insurgents in Nairobi and the surrounding countryside.[120]

Boyce's proposed "Operation Anvil for children," was rejected by the colonial secretary Alan Lennox-Boyd, on the grounds that forcibly rounding up Kenyan women and children for screening and imprisonment would lead to an international outcry.[121] However, Boyce found a powerful ally in Thomas Askwith, the colonial commissioner for community development in Kenya and a key architect of the adult rehabilitation scheme. Askwith, the former principal of a development training academy founded and funded by the colonial state, favored a liberal, "gentle" approach to rehabilitation. The Kikuyu, he believed, were caught between tradition and modernity. Askwith viewed the emergency as a generational conflict produced by the psychological effects of missionary education and urbanization.[122] Drawing upon the work of psychiatrists and ethnographers such as Louis Leakey and J. C. Carothers, Askwith argued that "tribal discipline has disappeared" due to the fact that young men were more educated than their elders.[123] Mau Mau, Askwith believed, was a symptom of the "disintegration" of a "whole generation" psychologically damaged by the absence of elder authority.[124] For Askwith, Mau Mau illustrated the psychological distress of troubled youths, rather than legitimate political grievance. Askwith believed that the remedies aid organizations had employed for juvenile delinquents in a European context could be reconfigured for the Kenyan Emergency and accepted Save the Children's offer of expertise in this endeavor.[125]

There were few institutions to deal with the youngest suspected Mau Mau. The Child Protection (Emergency Regulation) Act of 1954 decreed that unaccompanied minors in Nairobi should be sent to reserves or missionary orphanages.[126] However, the chaos of mass incarcerations and the overburdening of Nairobi municipal courts meant that many children and teenagers spent months in transit camps designed for "screening" adults.[127] Children as young as seven were beaten by prison guards, often going days without food, shelter, clothes, or blankets.[128] Living in such conditions and close to suspected adult Mau Mau, it seemed to Boyce inevitable that these boys would be "contaminated" by Mau Mau ideas.[129]

Within the colonial administration there was confusion about the age at which youths ceased to be covered by the 1954 Child Protection Act and became legally adult.[130] Consequently, the problem of juvenile delinquency was passed around a number of departments, all reluctant to accept responsibility.[131] Partnership with Save the Children offered a solution to the problem of youth in the emergency.[132] As in Somaliland and Malaya, humanitarian assistance provided the government with a form of "expertise" that allowed them to recast the meaning both of colonial government and the struggle against it. Whereas Askwith regarded the Mau Mau movement as symptomatic of a rupture in Kenyan society, Boyce linked it to an international "crisis of adolescence." Citing the work of Save the Children in postwar Europe, Malaya, and Somaliland, Boyce argued that this "crisis" was a consequence of upheaval as societies struggled to adapt to a changing world after the Second World War.[133] In this imagining of the postwar world, the "rehabilitation" schemes of the colonial government in Kenya became progressive rather than repressive, helping Kikuyu youths to adjust to postwar modernity with humanitarian experts and European scientific knowledge.[134]

The colonial government gave the SCF two assignments. First, they would found and administer a camp for three hundred accompanied minors and juvenile delinquents called Ujana Park.[135] Second, they would provide a small amount of funding and staff for a parallel project spearheaded by Askwith: Wamumu Approved School, home to over eighteen hundred boys.[136] Both the camp and the school were prisons in all but name. However, the stated aims of Wamumu and Ujana Park were "liberal rehabilitation rather than punishment."[137] Both institutions were based on experimental juvenile reformatories across Europe, and the traditions of the British public school system. Inmates were referred to as pupils, and their days were filled with physical labor, practical lessons and vigorous sport designed to prepare them for productive adulthood. By learning trades such as cobbling, carpentry, and mechanics, young men were given "pathways to manhood" that did not depend upon land. At the same time, they were encouraged to experience the end of their adolescence "uncorrupted" by Mau Mau ideology.[138] Football and gymnastics enabled the boys to "blow off steam," while learning "co-operation and team-work," which both Boyce and Askwith regarded as hallmarks of colonial masculinity. The camp and school also drew upon the "principles of Outward Bound and the Scouting Movement," seeking to create the "Kenyan men of the future": loyal colonial subjects and productive workers.[139]

What evidence remains of day-to-day life at Wamumu and Ujana Park paints a less grim picture than life in the adult internment camps, and though wire fences and watchmen were present at both camps, Save the Children staff imagined that many boys remained through choice.[140] When, in May 1955, the motorcar of Colonel Turner, the principal of Ujana Park, broke down a

FIGURE 15. "Wamumu boys" make a human pyramid, with the Union Jack held at the top. The A-frame huts in which they slept are pictured in the background, c. 1956. British Empire Collection of Photographs, INF 10/159/14, UK National Archives.

short distance outside the gates, "tens of boys swarmed through" a large hole in the camp's fence to offer their assistance. This suggested to Turner that the boys could have escaped at any point, but chose not to.[141] Similar inferences were made when two escapees from Wamumu returned to the camp after a number of hours, realizing that the environment beyond its wire fences was worse than the discipline and regimentation inside.[142] Yet, though both the British government and the SCF sought to deny it, the camps met minor infractions with harsh discipline, such as beatings or solitary confinement, and the harshest punishments were for those who attempted escape.[143]

The extent, or indeed existence, of children's resistance to Save the Children's Emergency rehabilitation schemes is not clear in the existing archives. However, in the archival trail left by the British Red Cross—the other major aid organization operating alongside the colonial government at the time—attempts to undermine so-called humanitarian interventions are clear.[144] In Kenya, as in Malaya, the colonial government conducted mass forced resettlement of noncombatants, in order to prevent them supporting fighters. Tens of thousands were removed to "new villages" with limited food and endemic disease.[145] By 1954, almost one in five infants died from malnutrition. The British Red Cross, drawing funding from UNICEF, distributed condensed milk and soup and began a series of "mothercraft" programs, focused on skills such as knitting, baby-washing, and baking. They were frequently disappointed by the lack of enthusiasm (or indeed, resistance) of Kenyan women, who failed to attend and, on occasion, threw stones at Red Cross vehicles.[146] One woman trying to care for her starving child while her husband was imprisoned by the British poured condensed milk from the Red Cross onto the ground.[147] The entanglement of aid organizations with the colonial government and its violent repression of resistance was clear to the recipients of aid.

The work of humanitarian organizations in Kenya was an attempt to make up for the shortfalls in welfare planning by caring for resettled noncombatants, or policing vagrant and criminal young men. The presence of humanitarian organizations also functioned as a mechanism for deflecting critiques of colonial policy. The Kenyan Emergency was a period in which many members of the British public began to reevaluate their perceptions of the empire as benevolent and progressive.[148] Questions were raised in the press and in Parliament about British conduct during the rebellion, often centered on the plight of women and children, and could be addressed by citing the "excellent work" of Save the Children, the British Red Cross and various missionary societies.[149] Save the Children and the British Red Cross issued regular ringing endorsements of the colonial government that had (they claimed) ensured that the "emergency has not been allowed to interfere with the long-term welfare of these people."[150] The humanitarian organizations attributed high child mortality rates and the spread of disease to the "ignorance" of Kenyan mothers, and claimed that the emergency resettlement had simply provided an opportunity to make "far seeing reforms" that would tackle preexisting problems in Kenyan society.[151]

Humanitarian attention on Kenya also provided a compelling narrative of the Kenyan Emergency for the British and international public. When Save the Children launched its Kenyan appeal in 1955, it raised more money than in any year since the Russian famine appeal in 1921.[152] Donations to the Red Cross similarly spiked. The Kenya appeals of these organizations gave the British public a means of engaging with the Kenyan Emergency while ignoring its broader political context. Both the British Red Cross and Save the Children used images of children presented as "victims of Mau Mau" almost exclusively in their appeals. Mau Mau, in turn, became a force that victimized both Black Kenyans and white settlers.[153] Public giving to the Kenya Emergency appeals did not simply express support for the colonial government, but also compassion for the Kenyan people. Through the interventions of British-based international humanitarian organizations, the good of the empire and the good of humanity were aligned in the eyes of the British public, and the brutality of colonial violence was obscured. Humanitarian organizations cast Kenya as a site of benevolent intervention, rather than political struggle.

The work of Save the Children in Kenya contributed to a wider reframing of Mau Mau resistance as psychosis generated by a "tribal" society as it attempted to come to terms with modernity.[154] Kenyan youth, caught in the transition from childhood to adulthood, served as a metaphor for Kenyan society itself. Working with the internationally renowned SCF, the colonial government framed its reforms as progressive and compassionate. Humanitarian intervention lent legitimacy to the incarceration of teenage boys and the wider campaign against the Mau Mau. In Kenya, Save the Children effectively worked as an auxiliary to the colonial counterinsurgency by importing new child welfare expertise developed in wartime Europe and adapting it to fit racist colonial norms. Save the Children lent credence to the myth that rehabilitation in Kenya was a progressive program enacted by a liberal empire to modernize its subjects, rather than a ruthless attempt to suppress anti-colonial resistance by any means necessary. In Kenya, humanitarianism's collusion enabled colonial brutality.

EMBEDDING EMPIRE'S AFTERLIVES IN INTERNATIONAL AID

The forgetting of the 1950s in the histories of British oversees aid is, no doubt, due to the design of humanitarian organizations themselves. Though it is impossible to know when this process took place, archival silences appear to have been deliberately curated to coincide with colonial emergencies. In the official archives of Save the Children, the paper trail goes cold for almost the entire decade, before well-populated folders reemerge for the "development decade" of the 1960s. Details of SCF's projects at Serendah, Wamumu, and the Hargeisa school were gathered from the Colonial Office papers and the Kenyan National Archives. They were also found in the archives of the International Union of Child Welfare (no friend to the British SCF in the 1950s) and the archives of other humanitarian organizations, themselves often restricted, redacted, or only recently released. Save the Children, it seems, did not question its actions or alliances during the wars of decolonization, but quickly forgot (and wanted others to forget) them afterward.[155]

Though passed over in official accounts of Save the Children, the 1950s was a pivotal decade for the Fund. Fearing that it was being squeezed out of an increasingly US-dominated international relief movement, the SCF "rediscovered" the British Empire. Searching for a new role, and influenced by ideas about family life, parental attachment, and emotional stability, the Fund increasingly focused its attention on adolescents rather than children. Wayward youths, who had turned to juvenile delinquency in the absence of stable parental authority were a metaphor for the unruly British Empire, not yet ready for independence from its parental power. Save the Children, in its attempts to introduce stability and authority to the youth of the empire was, at the same time, seeking to shore up the benevolent, parental leadership of Britain. These new directions were not as different from the Fund's interwar work as they appeared. They continued to fit children for citizenship (or colonial subjecthood) through work and imagine the types of labor different children would undertake as being contingent on their race and class. In the 1950s, though the founders dream of lasting peace had failed in the Second World War, the Fund continued to pursue its own form of utopianism: a world order guided by benevolent British imperial leadership.

This dream was also set to fail. As we see in the next chapter, humanitarian interventions in Asia and Africa outlived the empire that they had been marshaled to protect.[156] Empire found an afterlife in humanitarian organizations, too. In 1960, Save the Children unanimously appointed the former secretary of state for the colonies, Alan Lennox-Boyd, as its president. The appointment of someone who had conspired to cover up torture and prison massacres during the Kenyan Emergency was a celebration and confirmation of the close ties that the SCF had forged with the Colonial Office during the rebellions.[157] At the height of colonial violence, and under the auspices of international aid organizations, individuals and ideals from the late colonial period became embedded in an international humanitarian movement, and would remain there for decades to come.

SIX

War, Development, and Decolonization

IN OCTOBER 1972, Tim Mayhew penned a hasty letter to Save the Children headquarters in London. He had been described in a recent Save the Children newsletter as a "former colonial official," a title he feared would only serve to "inflame local sensitivities." While this was an accurate description of his position in Uganda, where he had remained after the end of British rule in 1962 to establish a child welfare program, he was keen to elide its implications. "Colonialism is an even dirtier word than imperialism in these parts of the world," Mayhew explained. He had no desire to leave his post (Kampala was "much safer at the moment" than his native Belfast) and so the Fund needed to be careful to obscure his, and its own, ties with the former British Empire. "Things are tough as they are," he added, "and they should not be made tougher."[1]

In the early years of the 1960s, the British Empire disintegrated at a speed few had predicted. As this happened, Save the Children, which had worked closely with colonial governments in its projects across Asia and Africa, expanded. Former colonial officials such as Tim Mayhew were hired by the Fund to stay on in decolonized states to create new "development" projects after empire's end. Save the Children was not alone in this expansion: in the 1960s a host of experts, missionaries, humanitarians, and enthusiastic young volunteers flocked to newly independent states, where they sought to "develop" economies and societies.[2] Yet the story of international aid in the 1960s is not just one of colonial continuities. During the decade, Save the Children became an incubator for critiques of international aid and development that would profoundly reshape the sector. A new generation of staff who hailed from and worked in the Global South challenged embedded hierarchies and began a patchy and uneven process of decolonization from within the organization. Save the Children was being changed from without too, by an emerging aid and development sector with roots quite different from those of Save the Children.

For the rest of Britain's rapidly expanding international aid sector, developmentalism represented a new form of utopianism. It promised to raise living standards across the world where formal colonialism had failed. While embedding old hierarchies, development seemed to offer collaboration with postcolonial regimes and their poorest citizens, presenting a participatory solution to global poverty that could be realized within a fast-approaching future. However, for Save the Children, the end of the British Empire marked the death of their particular utopia. After a brief and halfhearted embrace of development, by the end of the decade the Fund shifted its focus to a more hierarchical model of emergency relief. As the world order that Save the Children had sought to build receded, and new humanitarian and political regimes emerged, the Fund embraced a mode of operation based on an ongoing state of crisis.

THE END OF EMPIRE AND THE EMERGENCE OF AN "AID AND DEVELOPMENT SECTOR"

For Britons watching the nightly news throughout the late 1950s and 1960s, flag ceremonies became a regular sight.[3] Ghana swapped its Union Jack for a red, green, and gold banner on 6 March 1957. In the ten years that followed, twenty more colonial territories would lower the British flag and raise their own. In these ceremonies, independence was presented as the culmination of British rule, rather than a rejection of it. So-called "young nations" had "grown up" and were ready for the responsibilities of self-governance, assured of the ongoing "help" and "guidance" of Britain via the Commonwealth.[4] Postcolonial states greeted British offers of guidance and Commonwealth friendship with varying levels of suspicion and enthusiasm. British people at home, meanwhile, took readily to this new language of international duty and friendship.[5] Many expressed their belief in Britain's global role and responsibilities through their growing support of humanitarian organizations such as Save the Children.[6]

Save the Children only spoke of decolonization euphemistically. Its sterile council minutes noted "political changes" and "new contexts," and the need to preserve "continuity" in existing relationships.[7] The Fund did this with surprising ease. Just as the SCF had been welcome to provide welfare on the cheap to overstretched colonial governments seeking to broadcast their benevolent intentions, so too was it welcomed by postcolonial governments in their attempts to roll out viable social and welfare programs with limited resources.[8] The relationship between the Fund and postcolonial governments was often formalized through the appointment of new elites to symbolic roles. In Uganda and Somalia, post-independence presidents became official patrons of national Save the Children societies.[9] In Kenya, a boys' school funded by the SCF (which drew staff both from Wamumu Approved School and Ujana Park) was officially patronized by Kenyan government minister Tom Mboya. The school was also regularly visited and praised by President Jomo Kenyatta, a former critic of the Fund's 1931 Conference on the African Child. Like many postcolonial leaders once critical of the imperial attitudes of British humanitarians, Kenyatta now recognized the usefulness of their international development funding and expertise.[10]

Despite the Fund's attempt to embrace new postcolonial elites overseas, the British Empire lived on in the Fund's leadership in London. The Fund's president from 1960 to 1970 was Alan Lennox-Boyd, former Conservative secretary of state for the colonies. Its director general (a new title for the general secretary), Colin Thornley, had worked in the colonial service in East Africa, as private secretary to Lennox-Boyd, and as governor of British Honduras. The Fund's chairman during the 1960s, Edward Windley, had served as the minister for African affairs in the Kenyan colonial government during the Mau Mau emergency. Many SCF leaders had been staunch opponents of nationalist movements and of independence during their time in the colonial service and strongly believed that, in the absence of formal structures of empire, Britain would still need to "take responsibility" for its former colonial territories.[11] These ex-colonial administrators were as worried about the changing status of their organization in Britain as they were about the changing position of Britain in the world. After the Second World War, Save the Children had already seen its position diminished by the rise of UNICEF. During the 1950s, its two major competitors, Oxfam and Christian Aid, began to consolidate their positions in Britain. The rise of these British organizations signaled the emergence of a new humanitarian regime arising globally in the context of decolonization. Many of what later became major aid and development organizations of the 1960s were founded in the context of the Second World War but quickly adapted to the conditions of decolonization, seeking new forms of post-imperial partnership with emerging independent governments and the "development" of economies and democracies along Western lines.

Founded in 1942 to protest the Allied blockade of Nazi territories, Oxfam spent the postwar period mostly engaged in relief and reconstruction projects in Europe. In 1961, the *Daily Mirror* published a headline story on child victims of a famine in the South Kasai region of Congo, following the country's independence from Belgium, a military coup, and the assassination of its president, Patrice Lumumba.[12] The famine seemed to Oxfam's business-minded Chairman Lesley Kirkley an opportune moment to expand Oxfam's work to a new continent. He seized upon the *Mirror's* coverage, mailing copies of its front page to five hundred thousand donors. Oxfam quickly raised £100,000, its most successful appeal to date. According to Oxfam's official historian, it was the images of starving African children that Oxfam began to circulate during the South Kasai famine that determined its direction for years to come. Oxfam leaders argued that the famine in South Kasai was not a "one off," but an example of the precarious food supply for Africans across the continent.[13] From 1961, Oxfam reoriented the bulk of its funds to new African and Asian agricultural modernization projects.[14] Unlike Save the Children, Oxfam's leaders took an overtly political line on the structural causes of the hunger they fought. Hunger was presented as a symptom of the exploitation of underdeveloped economies by the West.[15] In addition to supporting small-scale "development" projects across Asia and Africa, Oxfam sought to educate its supporters on the causes of poverty and inequality, hoping to create a public lobby that would encourage government intervention in terms of international development.[16] Like Dorothy Buxton in Save the Children's early years, Oxfam's Lesley Kirkley saw humanitarian action as a form of political education.

Christian Aid was founded in 1942, as the humanitarian arm of the British Council of Churches. Its first projects had been in Europe, where it worked to meet the needs of displaced persons and refugees from 1945 onward.[17] While citing biblical inspiration to alleviate suffering, Christian Aid was not evangelical: its aim was relief, rather than proselytization. Against the backdrop of British secularization and the liberalization of Anglican theology, Christian Aid expanded as traditional missionaries societies fell out of vogue.[18] Like both Save the Children and Oxfam, Christian Aid's first intervention in Africa came during a crisis of decolonization: it funded the work of missionary societies in the relief of forcibly resettled women and children in Emergency-era Kenya.[19] Like Oxfam, Christian Aid enthusiastically embraced new ideas about development, and especially agricultural modernization. It divided its funding between Eastern Europe, Africa, and Southeast Asia.[20] By 1964, Christian Aid's income was three times what it had been in 1959, and the majority of this was spent within the British Empire and Commonwealth, where Christian Aid often worked with well-established British missionary schools, hospitals, and churches.[21]

Save the Children regarded Oxfam and Christian Aid as competitors.[22] Yet, rather than being in direct competition, it was often the case that different organizations appealed to different donors. Where Save the Children had always drawn support from nonconformist congregations, Christian Aid's donors were primarily within the Anglican Communion.[23] Oxfam secured donations from Britain's (broadly grammar school–educated or university-attending) youth, as well as left-wing individuals and organizations such as the Fabian Society. Save the Children, meanwhile, had firmly established itself as the aid organization of the establishment. By 1959 it had secured the patronage of the Queen (a long-cherished ambition), and in 1970 her teenage daughter Princess Anne became the Fund's president (a position she holds to this day).[24] In spite, or perhaps because, of its establishment connections, Save the Children drew far broader support from the working classes than any other major humanitarian organization in postwar Britain. By the end of the 1950s, 40 percent of SCF's income came from its Penny-a-Week scheme, which was supported by the Trades Union Congress and drawn from the weekly wages of workers in factories, mines, docks, and offices across the UK.[25] By 1964, rather than having suffered from "competition," donations to Christian Aid, Oxfam, and the SCF had all risen overall. The three agencies between them were raising (in today's terms) £100 million each year.[26] With financial clout and a widespread following, Oxfam, Save the Children, and Christian Aid were emerging as the leaders of what was becoming known as the "aid sector."[27]

This new sector benefitted from (and helped to create) a massive upsurge in popular support for international development: a vision of the eradication of poverty worldwide through the rapid "modernization" of colonial and postcolonial industries, agriculture, and economies. This idea, of course, predated the 1960s. Development had long been part of the vocabulary of imperialism as a way of describing the benefits of modernity and prosperity that the civilizing process of colonial rule promised to confer. The 1929 and 1940 Colonial Development and Welfare Acts had focused on large-scale agricultural and industrial modernization, in an attempt to uplift living conditions across the empire and make the empire more profitable for Britain.[28] The developmentalism of late British imperialism shared much with "modernization theory," which had emerged from American universities in the 1950s. Early US-led modernization initiatives first took place in Asia in the context of Cold War competition, as a means of modeling nations in the image of Western capitalist economies.[29] They involved large-scale industrialization projects, designed to stimulate developing economies, in the hope that this would be felt by all levels of society.

By the beginning of the 1960s, disillusionment with the modernization dogma had begun to mount, and a fresh wave of thinkers and volunteers (often young, left-wing university graduates from Britain, the United States, or Western Europe) took on small-scale, local development projects, setting out to "develop" a group of farms or villages in Asia, Africa, or South America. They hoped that these projects could be scaled up later, rather than waiting for the positive effects of large-scale interventions to filter down.[30] Development, then, could mean many things to many people. It could be a celebration, or critique, of the methods and experts involved in massive modernization projects; and it could encompass grand designs for dams and factories, or small community irrigation or vaccination projects. With such fluidity and flexibility, development ideology drew widespread support.[31]

Development was fixed as an international priority when, in 1960, the United Nations launched its Freedom From Hunger Campaign, a decade-long, global attempt to eradicate undernourishment through both large-scale agricultural projects and small-scale community interventions and public education.[32] The Campaign followed the success of the United Nations' World Refugee Year (1959), and like its predecessor was intended to draw the public into lobbying governments to "speed up" the current "unsatisfactory rate" of progress in tackling global hunger. Alongside governmental efforts, the campaign would also draw funds from international and local civil society networks, including aid organizations, churches, and schools.[33] Freedom From Hunger involved one hundred countries as donors and recipients.[34] Nowhere was it as popular as in Britain, where Freedom From Hunger, as Anna Bocking-Welch argues, was presented as a "seamless and satisfying alternative to the imperial burden."[35] The British government founded and funded a British Freedom From Hunger Campaign, and politicians, clergymen and Prince Philip described how the British would "lead" the initiative and "set an example" to the rest of the world.[36] For some, it was a direct continuation of the imagined traditions of empire. In the House of Lords, the Bishop of

Coventry argued that Freedom From Hunger could be "one of our finest hours, if, having trained many countries for self-government and freedom we teach them, and other nations, industrial self-development."[37] This recasting of old imperial duties in new international terms was, of course, a project that Save the Children had been engaged in since the end of the First World War.

The British Empire lived on in the geographies of aid. British Freedom From Hunger funding ended up almost exclusively in nations of the current and former British Empire.[38] This was understood both as a way of preserving Commonwealth ties, and as the best use of the local knowledge of the former colonial officials hired by British aid organizations.[39] However, while the Commonwealth had a near monopoly on British aid, British aid did not have a monopoly within Commonwealth states. As a report by the newly founded Overseas Development Institute noted in 1965, while the majority of British donations ended up in the Commonwealth, 80 percent of all aid and development funds in Commonwealth states came from the United States, as it sought to prevent the spread of Communist ideals and alliances.[40] The new international development regime was, primarily, an American-led response to Cold War divisions. Freedom From Hunger, by contrast, was presented to the British public as a continuation of imperial duties and a form of world leadership in the postcolonial period.

Save the Children was initially reluctant to be involved in the Freedom From Hunger Campaign. It would impose restrictions and regulations on the Fund, meaning that projects would have to focus on nutrition and whole communities, including adults. This would disrupt the Fund's existing modes of intervention, which tended to focus on child education (via boarding schools or work training schemes) or on infant health (usually via hospital wards and nurseries). SCF leaders also feared the "political" nature of Freedom From Hunger: it was not simply about the transfer of expertise; rather, it involved wide-ranging programs that would address structural global inequality and the role of the West in creating it. It might, Fund leaders feared, attract student activists, as well as left-wing campaigners associated with movements such as the Campaign for Nuclear Disarmament.[41] In the end, however, the financial benefits outweighed the feared reputational cost. By participating, Save the Children received money from the Freedom From Hunger central fund, filled by the mass enthusiasm of the British public, who raised money through cake sales, jumble sales, sponsored walks, and church collections. This was distributed to existing aid organizations for Freedom From Hunger–approved projects.[42] Additional financial backing came via a

UN Central Fund and the British government. With this money, Save the Children was able to begin new projects in Uganda, Tanzania, the Caribbean, and Nigeria and to extend its existing work in Kenya.

The centralized administration of the Freedom From Hunger Campaign forced the organizations of the emerging British aid sector into closer collaboration, as did the creation by the incoming Labour government of a new Overseas Development Ministry (ODM) in 1964. The ODM would, in the first instance, reallocate the Colonial Development and Welfare budget to territories now outside the empire, most of them newly independent Commonwealth states.[43] This was met with disapproval by many within the Colonial Office, who saw it as another attack on their position.[44] Its first minister, Barbara Castle, worked to enhance the legitimacy of the new ministry by emphasizing its ethical appeal. She sought close partnerships with the nongovernmental aid and development sector in the belief that it would further enhance the new ministry if aid organizations were seen to both petition for and endorse government development work.[45] Castle also had a close connection with Oxfam, as her brother Jimmy Betts was Oxfam's first overseas field director. Through Oxfam, Castle sought to organize a central committee comprised of major aid organizations, which would simplify communications and consultation with the ODM. Launched in 1965, the Voluntary Committee on Overseas Aid and Development (VCOAD) brought together Oxfam, Christian Aid, War on Want, Tearfund, and the Catholic Fund for Overseas Development to coordinate their own work and lobby for government support.[46]

In the twentieth century, aid organizations in Britain often gained their proximity to power via the Labour Party. War on Want, the aid sector's most radical voice, had been established in the early 1950s by a group of anti-war and anti-colonial activists and politicians, including Harold Wilson, who became prime minister in 1964.[47] Oxfam shared many leaders and supporters with the Labour Party through organizations such as the Fabian Society. The Labour Party had provided Save the Children's connection to government in the 1930s too. However, in the course of its wartime work, the Fund had eschewed direct ties with the party in favor of less obviously partisan connections with government departments, in particular the Ministry of Education and the Colonial Office. These connections to the apparatus of state, rather than to a single political party, had enabled Save the Children to weather changes in government while retaining access. The Fund was, therefore, reluctant to join with Oxfam and War on Want in VCOAD, which in its early days appeared to be a purely left-wing, Labour Party initiative.[48] In the end, though, the fear of appearing "aloof" or "out of touch" to its donors prompted Save the Children (reluctantly) to participate.[49] However, as a member it acted as a brake on the more explicitly political and radical activities of its fellow aid organizations. By threatening to resign from VCOAD, the Fund repeatedly halted initiatives challenging the political causes of "underdevelopment" and dismissed other agencies' desires to highlight the causes of poverty as "naïve" and "counterproductive" attacks on the government.[50] Far from its roots in left-wing protest, Save the Children had now become explicitly anti-radical.

While Save the Children certainly slowed the "politicization" of the aid and development sector in Britain, the existence of this sector changed Save the Children. At the beginning of the 1960s, Save the Children displayed a rare lack of enthusiasm for development work. The implied critique of colonial governments and global inequalities seemed "political" to the Fund. While SCF had always participated in what it had termed "reconstructive" or "rehabilitative" work, it had preferred to focus on children themselves, ignoring the wider structural conditions of the communities it worked within and thus sidestepping questions about present-day change. Had it not been for the financial and reputational incentive provided by Freedom From Hunger, it is likely that SCF would not have altered its methods at all. However, in the end, Freedom From Hunger and the discourse of development more widely would both alter and expand the work of Save the Children, despite its leaders' ambivalence.

NEW COUNTRIES FOR OLD MEN

Save the Children's leaders in London, and its representatives on the ground, were not unique in their positions, as former colonial administrators became aid and international development workers. During the 1960s, over a third of United Nations development officials were recruited from European colonial powers.[51] Indeed, for Oxfam, the sudden availability of ex-colonial "experts" with local connections was a direct cause of their expansion into Africa: when again would Oxfam find such a well-trained, ready-made staff?[52] The postwar British Empire, with its increased emphasis on welfare and development, had been the ideal training ground. In the 1950s, colonial governments had instigated a host of new development programs in agriculture, forestry, and industry. After independence, the experts who had staffed them were useful not only to international development organizations, but to newly independent governments. Despite drives to "Africanize" or "indigenize" government and business in newly independent states, former Colonial Office employees often possessed expertise that the meager educational opportunities afforded to colonized peoples in empire had prevented them from attaining.[53]

Historians and international development scholars have shown how former colonial experts embedded old imperial attitudes and assumptions in the heart of postcolonial planning and development.[54] Yet for many of those who stayed on, decolonization marked, if not a clear break from old ideas, then at least a shift.[55] One Oxfam worker described the "Oxfam type": usually young (having worked in the empire after 1945), with technical expertise in forestry or agriculture (rather than former administrators or governors), and driven by the ideal of "service." Jimmy Betts, for example, saw his duties as an Oxfam field director, in part, as an atonement for the shortcomings of empire. For him, it was the duty of British experts to continue to strive for the "development" in Africa that the empire had failed to realize.[56] This separation from old imperial attitudes and lifestyles was central to the construction of a post-imperial development profession. Oxfam staff agonized over both their field offices and their own personal appearance, taking care that neither should appear too luxurious (a reminder of colonial officialdom) or shabby (disrespectful to the local elites they encountered).[57]

British development workers were not just former employees of the Colonial Office. Since the interwar years, British missionaries too had focused increasingly on the welfare of local populations, and they had often raised funds for medical and educational initiatives rather than for purposes of direct proselytization. Now, with donations from the British public to missionary bodies declining further in the increasingly secular 1960s, many missionaries found a fresh source of income in international development organizations. Christian Aid in particular ran many of its projects in Africa and Asia in collaboration with existing missionary hospitals and community development projects.[58] Again, this did not represent a straightforward colonial continuity. The missionary relationship with empire had always been ambiguous. Spreading Christianity had been an early justification for imperial expansion, and by promoting British cultural practices and education, missionaries had attempted to mold colonized peoples in the image of the colonizer. However, as at Save the Children's 1931 Conference on the African Child, missionaries had often been critical of the way that imperial capitalism or the lack of colonial welfare programs had worsened, or failed to better, the living standards of their congregations.[59]

The upper echelons of Save the Children's 1960s staff were different from either the "Oxfam types" or the missionary partners of Christian Aid. They were often older, having come of age in the interwar empire, before Britain's last-ditch attempts at development and partial democratization. Instead of bringing technical, environmental, or agricultural expertise, Save the Children's highest-ranking staff had backgrounds in colonial governance or policing. They transplanted the assumptions of colonial lawmaking and discipline into humanitarian work, casting new colonial governments and local populations alike as incapable, "lazy," "ignorant, or "corrupt."[60] Save the Children's senior staff had none of the lifestyle angst that plagued Oxfam workers. Tim Mayhew, Save the Children's chief administrator in Uganda, not only thought that Kampala was safer than Belfast, but warmer, cheaper and "more fun." Mayhew, who had been posted in Kenya and Nigeria as a district officer before moving to Uganda in 1960, had no desire to return to a "small house in a grey country" that he had left in 1938.[61] John Birch, Save the Children's administrator in Nigeria, felt the same. A regular at the Lagos Polo Club since moving to Nigeria as an undersecretary in the colonial government in 1950, he had no interest in leaving his friends or his lifestyle.[62] Humanitarian work was a means of continuing not only the principles but also the perks of colonial life.

Enthusiastic participation in expatriate life placed Save the Children staff close to business elites. While Oxfam and (to a degree) Christian Aid were atoning for the damage done by imperial capitalism, Save the Children saw opportunities for donations. Its flagship Kenyan school, Starehe, was partly funded by British Petroleum.[63] In Nigeria, the Fund received regular donations from a British timber company, and in Uganda from a British soap manufacturer.[64] Save the Children staff, while they recognized that empire was a "sensitive" issue, never questioned or renounced old colonial practices. They were not atoning for the shortcomings of empire, but "continuing" British duties. Instead of fully embracing development, they found ways to tweak the Fund's existing practices to make them appear new. They added "kitchen gardens" to boarding schools or introduced the education of mothers, in both cases to meet Freedom From Hunger stipulations. Save the Children's reluctance to embrace change became self-reinforcing. More "traditionally minded" staff left the "critical" and "political" Oxfam for the Fund.[65] Save the Children became an establishment enclave in a fast-changing aid sector.

All British humanitarian organizations had imperial continuities, but there were different forms and degrees. Save the Children's particular form of continuity—one built on ties to empire's aristocratic leadership and the institutions of colonial policing and punishment—made it especially hard for the Fund to adapt to the new post-imperial world. Changes to the organization and its mode of operation, therefore, were made not by its leaders but by a new generation of staff, mostly women who came from and worked in newly decolonized states. This generation of development workers has been overlooked by the existing literature, which fixates on the figure of the white, ex-colonial male expert. Through two case studies of Save the Children's rural development programs in Nigeria and the Caribbean (selected for the richness of the existing archives), this chapter now spotlights Black women workers, restoring them to the central position they occupied in the forging of new forms of development in the 1960s and beyond.

DEVELOPMENT, WELFARE, AND SOCIAL WORK IN THE CARIBBEAN

Initially, Save the Children's Freedom From Hunger work in the Caribbean followed the format of its previous colonial interventions. In 1958, in a final bid to control decolonization in its Caribbean colonies, the British government launched a short-lived West Indies Federation. Its governor, Lord Hailes, sought to highlight the benevolent nature of British rule, announcing fresh interventions in welfare and development. His wife, Lady Diana Hailes, commissioned the SCF to investigate and report on child mortality on the islands, which she estimated at 30 percent of children under five. Following this invitation, in 1960, Monica Green, a British social worker hired by Save the Children, made her first visit to Jamaica and its neighboring British-controlled islands. Unusually for a senior Save the Children staff member, Green had spent her life so far working in institutions of the British welfare state, rather than the British Empire. She proposed two solutions to the problems she saw on the islands. First, voluntary organizations should mitigate the under-production of food in the Caribbean (where agriculture was increasingly geared toward the export banana and sugar markets), by distributing cheap modern proteins, such as a powdered soy product called prolo produced in Wales. Secondly, they should educate mothers about childcare and nutrition. Ignoring the wider economic problems on the islands, Save the

Children blamed maternal ignorance and indifference for high rates of child malnutrition and mortality.[66] Green believed that what was needed was a network of social workers and education programs that would closely resemble similar state-funded schemes in slums in Britain.[67]

On her first visit to the Trenchtown neighborhood of Kingston in 1960, Green was surprised to find that the local population "distrusted whites." It was only the presence of her "coloured" host that enabled her to converse with mothers.[68] At a time when Caribbean islands were moving toward decolonization and the British were "especially disliked," Green concluded that any social work program in the Caribbean could only be effective if run by local staff.[69] The expansion of social work training in the United Kingdom, alongside increasing numbers of Commonwealth students who had traveled to Britain to study in the 1950s and 1960s, meant Green had little trouble finding staff with local connections who were trained in British methods.[70] Her first full-time appointee, Peggy Antrobus, was born in Trinidad, and studied economics at the University of Bristol before enrolling in a new "social work" diploma at the University of Birmingham.[71] She had spent two years learning a variety of new social scientific approaches to poverty and child welfare: psychology, sociology, child development and theories about the importance of the family.[72] Her practical training had taken place in the slums of Birmingham: Winson Green, Balsall Heath, and Aston. She returned to Jamaica in 1958, where her father was a wealthy car salesman, and married her high school boyfriend Kenneth Antrobus, who had trained in Britain as a pediatrician.[73] Together, they embodied the image of model Commonwealth citizens. They had attended university in Britain and then taken their knowledge "home," rather than remaining in a country that was increasingly hostile to the Commonwealth citizens it had welcomed in the aftermath of the Second World War.[74]

The practices of professional social work that Peggy Antrobus brought to Jamaica were by no means new. Though embellished with social scientific theories, the casework model of social work Antrobus practiced remained true to its origins in the Charity Organisation Society at the end of the nineteenth century. It was the same social work tradition that had influenced Jebb and the early staff of the SCF. It individualized the causes of poverty, taking each "case" as a problem to be solved through changing personal attitudes. The architects of the British welfare state had worked to enshrine the importance of individual responsibility. Meager unemployment benefits afforded by the postwar welfare state were intended to encourage people back into work, ensuring that state provision would not result in "dependency."[75] With

FIGURE 16. Peggy Antrobus visits a mother in the Windward Islands, 1964. Save the Children Annual Report (back cover), 1964.

emphasis on individual responsibility, and an army of new social workers to enforce this at the family level, the British welfare state had always been as much about creating self-reliant individuals as it had been about remolding society at large.[76]

Peggy Antrobus began her work in the Caribbean for Save the Children in 1962, focusing on the especially poor Windward Islands. The Windward Islands were British dependencies, and their economy rested almost entirely on exporting bananas. There was, Monica Green noted, a high proportion of single parent families: many men were leaving the islands altogether to look for work, as banana export companies preferred to employ female pickers on lower wages.[77] At the same time, there were few medical staff and social workers on the islands: many went to Britain for training, but few returned. Antrobus's work was based around home visits, in which she inspected the living conditions of children and "educated" their mothers.[78] In what Antrobus described as a "typical case," a mother worked all day, and so her baby was left with a neighbor who was afraid to have him play with her own young children, lest he get hurt and the mother blame her. The baby sat tied to a chair all day and was underweight. Antrobus provided the protein formula prolo for the child to increase its weight, while the neighbor was encouraged to let the baby play with her own children. The mother was invited to a series of mothercraft classes run by the Fund, where she was taught how to bathe, clothe, and feed her child.[79] These classes reproduced almost unaltered the work carried out by Fritzi Small in Addis Ababa in 1935, based on the assumptions that "non-European" mothers were "ignorant" and that motherhood itself had a universal and cross-cultural form. Basic training in child-rearing would spark an "instinctive" love for children, which, due to her own incompetence and fear, the mother had not allowed herself to feel.[80]

Despite the high hopes of Antrobus and her team, mothercraft classes were patchily attended, as many mothers on the island worked six days a week. In the half-empty classes, Antrobus and her colleagues sought to inspire "good motherhood" through a competitive culture. One week there would be a prize for the mother who could construct the best baby garment from a used flour sack; the next, the best soft toy from straw and rags. The largest prizes (usually samples of powdered milk, which the Fund never connected to diminishing rates of breastfeeding) were reserved for the mothers of the heaviest babies.[81] From 1966, islands across the Caribbean held Save the Children Baby Shows, where commemorative shields and hampers donated by local businesses were awarded to the plumpest, "glossiest," healthiest-looking children.[82] The Fund seldom mentioned fathers, save to comment that many had left the islands to look for better paid work and that many working mothers were unmarried or separated. Where fathers were present, no attempts were made to engage them in childcare, reflecting the gendered assumptions in the academic literature on attachment, which held mothers entirely responsible for children's mental and physical health.[83]

These approaches individualized the causes of poverty, presenting maternal ignorance as the greatest threat to the young, and maternal education as the solution. However, maternal education could not solve the basic problem that many young children were, of necessity, left unattended during working hours. Despite the social and economic differences between the Caribbean and 1960s Britain, Save the Children's interventions in the Caribbean were based on the same logic as childcare in the British welfare state. They fused Edwardian ideas about poverty and ignorance with new postwar social scientific discourses of maternal attachment. If maternal attachment was the primary path to healthy adulthood, then working mothers were a threat to their children and to society.[84] Unlike in Britain, where postwar employment legislation and family allowances pushed women out of paid work and back into their homes, there was no alternative for many of the women in the Windward Islands. Save the Children, like the British state and an army of social work experts in the postwar period, prized the nuclear family over other forms of kinship structure. In its absence, the Fund sought to provide the next best thing: daytime nurseries in which children could be cared for by affectionate child welfare experts and returned to their mothers after work. From 1964, it opened a network of children's day centers across the islands, with newly trained Caribbean social workers arriving from British universities to run them, such as Millicent Iton, who had trained at Cardiff University and brought ideas with her about the importance of play-based education, and how to create attachment between nursery nurses and their charges that would make up for the "developmental disadvantage" of having working mothers. These nursery schools, of course, did not solve any of the wider issues facing mothers in the Windward Islands: food scarcity, low wages, male unemployment, and uninvolved fathers.[85]

Both Peggy Antrobus and her husband Kenneth were interested in the long-term effects of children's lack of attachment, as theorized in the psychoanalytic approaches that now underpinned the study of child welfare in British universities. In babies, this was thought to be expressed through listlessness and withdrawal, and in older children through juvenile delinquency. On his ward rounds, Kenneth, like early trailblazers in British pediatrics, produced detailed notes of the mental and physical state of his patients. Babies such as "Earl, with a detachment as aristocratic as his name" were diagnosed with attachment disorders and malnutrition.[86] Peggy began a program for what she termed "pre-delinquent children." Like parallel programs in Britain, Peggy Antrobus's program identified children from "problem families" whose upbringing and neglect seemed to be leading them on a "path to criminality."[87]

Full of praise for the professionalism and "community insight" of Peggy and Kenneth Antrobus, Save the Children used Freedom From Hunger

FIGURE 17. Monica Green (front center) and her team, c. 1967. Kenneth Antrobus is pictured in the second row, far right, wearing glasses. Caribbean, Images, A191, Save the Children Archives, Birmingham, UK.

funding to pilot a social work course at the new University of the West Indies.[88] From 1965, with a syllabus that closely resembled what Peggy Antrobus had studied at the University of Birmingham, Caribbean students learned psychology, nutrition, child development, and sociology, completing their practical training in Trenchtown rather than in British slums. Across different Caribbean islands, less formal training schemes were also implemented, in which British-trained nurses and social workers were "shadowed" by secondary school graduates who could then practice alone. These locally trained social workers were employed variously by Save the Children and local government welfare services. At the level of agricultural and industrial planning, development innovations continued to be dominated by white, male, and often former colonial "experts," but at the local level, communities in the Caribbean were creating and sustaining local expertise.

These new experts were by no means egalitarian in their outlook. True to the British casework model it had grown out of, social work in the Caribbean imported a pathology of the working class from postwar Britain.[89] In the face of deeply rooted structural problems, these efforts focused on the perceived shortcomings of individual mothers. Yet social workers such as Peggy Antrobus found their practice limited without the wider supporting apparatus of the British welfare state. She could not refer families for medical or maternity care or rely on free school meals or social housing. She began to advance wider, structural critiques of poverty on the Islands, centered on social and economic underdevelopment rather than maternal ignorance. Writing in 1970, Antrobus explained that working with mothers had not only ignited her sympathy but, ultimately, fostered a critique of the forms of development through maternal education that the Fund was promoting.[90]

In her later post as Advisor on Women's Affairs to the Government of Jamaica in the 1970s and in her activism and scholarship in the 1980s, Peggy Antrobus emphasized that development could not be achieved through individual educational and nutritional programs without economic reform. Caribbean mothers could not make up for the failures of a low-wage economy that necessitated long working hours and mass migration.[91] Save the Children's 1960s Caribbean programs, Antrobus recalled, "did not reach out into other areas of the lives of the women with whom I worked, and to that extent failed beyond saving the lives of severely malnourished children."[92] While the Fund did little to challenge the structural conditions for mothers and children in the Caribbean, its employment of a new generation of experts was a slow incubator for critiques of its own work. Following the devaluation of the pound in 1967 and the end of Freedom From Hunger in 1970, which led the Fund to scale back its overseas commitments, SCF work in the Caribbean was taken over by a local committee comprised of newly trained Caribbean social workers. Save the Children itself was being partially and unevenly decolonized, albeit at a slower pace than the world in which it operated.

NEW EXPERTS IN NIGERIA

By the early 1960s, the process of "indigenization" was well underway in Save the Children's Asian and African programs, although this was not always welcomed by its expatriate British staff. In the Caribbean, Save the Children's employment of local staff had been a matter of economy and practicality. This cost-saving incentive also led to the hiring of local staff elsewhere: at the end of the 1950s, John Watling had left the Somali boys home in Hargeisa, to be replaced by a "most trustworthy" Somali man, Abdi Said, who had relaxed the harsh discipline at the school and brought his young grandsons to live there as pupils. There were also political pushes for a move toward local staff. In Nigeria, the postcolonial government, in power since independence in 1960, had made the presence of international aid organizations in the country dependent on their employing at least 50 percent Nigerian staff. As had been the case for Save the Children in the Caribbean, many of these new "local" staff had undergone training in Britain before returning "home" to take up their posts. Thus, aid and development organizations were not simply vehicles through which former colonial officials continued to exert influence and pursue neocolonial agendas: they also ultimately provided spaces for new experts to disrupt old power dynamics and seek to transfer (and adapt) knowledge gained in the emerging British welfare state into local communities.

In Nigeria, Save the Children hired middle-class Nigerian women trained at British nursing schools. Twenty-five-year-old Nigerian nurse Remi Domingo had spent seven years in education in London before she began work for Save the Children in the western Nigerian town of Ilesa in 1965. Domingo had grown up in a middle-class suburb of Lagos, where there were "schools and roads and hospitals." She was shocked by the condition of the roads between Lagos and Ilesa ("even worse than the M1!") and by the poverty she encountered when she arrived.[93] Domingo was part of a team of British and Nigerian nurses, overseen by two former colonial officials, Colonel John Hawkins and John Birch. Enthusiastic recipients of Freedom From Hunger funding, both Hawkins and Birch believed that the region had good land and that the cause of child malnutrition in Ilesa was "ignorance" on the part of mothers.[94]

Save the Children chose Ilesa as a base for its West African program due to the presence of the Wesleyan Guild Hospital, a widely known and respected missionary hospital established in the mid-1930s. Working in partnership with preexisting missionary- and state-funded pediatric clinics, Save the Children leaders believed that they could quickly establish an example of "what could be achieved in Africa, if money were well spent."[95] The Fund was far from the only Western aid organization operating in Ilesa. By the mid-1960s the Wesleyan Guild hospital could boast the support of Save the Children,

Oxfam, UNICEF, the World Health Organization, and various British and American missionary organizations. These overlapping interventions were typical of 1960s development work, where large international aid organizations tended to latch onto small projects that had already proven successful in a bid to expand their global reach without risk. In line with development thought in the era, organizations believed such projects could be scaled up and would therefore benefit whole countries, not just small communities.[96]

Small-scale projects also chimed with the marketing logic of aid organizations. Just as schemes like SCF's child sponsorship programs had enhanced donations since the 1920s by confronting Western publics with the more relatable and "fixable" poverty of a single child, in the 1960s schemes such as town twinning and donation drives focused on single villages, hospitals, or agricultural projects, reigniting public passion for humanitarianism. In this way, aid organizations made development "knowable" to the British public.[97] The concentration of donations in single locales meant the impact of nongovernment aid and development initiatives was patchy and uneven, while the success stories coming from well-funded individual projects made development appear far-reaching and successful to the British public. In the case of Ilesa, several British organizations that claimed to be "developing Nigeria" were concentrated in this single locale, all dutifully trying to avoid overlap and duplication, but all reluctant to risk relocation. Save the Children devoted itself to a clinic for under-fives, founded by a missionary doctor, and focused on malnutrition. While extreme cases were admitted to the hospital, for the most part the program was run by health visitors and nurses like Remi Domingo, who traveled between eighteen villages in white Land Rovers, instructing mothers on breastfeeding and weaning and following the progress of children via the casework method.

Known locally as the "car ladies," Domingo and her coworkers were (according to John Birch) able to establish a rapport with local mothers.[98] The relationship between Domingo and Hawkins was, however, more complex. Domingo, who had been away from her family in Lagos for seven years during her training, had a stream of visitors in Ilesa. Apparently irritated by the disruption, Colonel Hawkins implemented a rule that no more than one additional family member at a time could stay in Domingo's bungalow on the Save the Children compound, despite Domingo paying rent out of her wages.[99] Hawkins, Domingo responded, did not understand Nigeria and its customs: Nigerians expected to be able to stay in the homes of their families, and if Domingo could not allow her family to do so, she would become

FIGURE 18. A Save the Children Health Visitor in Ilesa, 1967. Save the Children Annual Report, 1967 (back cover). The health visitor is unnamed.

isolated. Domingo shared her grievances with another Nigerian Save the Children employee, Mrs. Ossai. They found that as "local" staff, they were being paid less than their British counterparts, and less than nurses doing similar jobs employed by the local government.[100] Writing to Hawkins's supervisor in London, the two women warned that "Nigeria does not tolerate racial discrimination" and that "if this got to a nauseating point" they would alert Ilesa's local governor.[101] After making their own complaints directly to London, they rallied the rest of the Nigerian workers on the Save the Children compound, demanding a pay raise for all, stating, "We Nigerians are very poor and have large families to look after." They also demanded maternity leave for female staff, stating that "Nigerians cannot live without having children."[102]

Birch realized that an allegation of racism would be disastrous. Writing, "One knows how sensitive newly independent peoples are," he imagined that the Fund might lose permission to work in Nigeria if it was seen to be discriminating against Nigerian staff.[103] However, Birch could not convince Hawkins to change his behavior, who insisted that the problem lay with Domingo: "[She] behaves as though she is the only person on the team and always has a complaint." He resented having to employ Nigerian staff at all, claiming that Domingo and Mrs. Ossai were too "easy going and undisciplined [in their] attitude to work."[104] Hawkins's dismissal of Domingo as lazy and insubordinate was heavy with the racist stereotyping of the colonial period and echoed similar coded allegations about the "lack of initiative," "untrustworthiness," or "low standards of personal cleanliness" made by British Save the Children staff against their new African coworkers across the continent.[105] In their fight against these attitudes, Nigerian staff at Save the Children were engaged in a battle about the nature of expertise in postcolonial states.

Domingo and Ossai pointed out that it was they, not British expat staff, who were leading Save the Children's work on the ground in Ilesa. The British nurses they worked alongside knew little of local culture and nothing of local foodstuffs. Many of the British medical students at the local hospital "had never seen inside a Nigerian house, Nigerian food, or a cooking pot."[106] Their suggestions of how to help malnourished children were meaningless until they could be "educated" in local customs and culture, a job that Domingo, Ossai, and six other Save the Children Nigerian nurses took on, allowing medical students and expat staff of other aid organizations to accompany them on their visits.[107] Somewhat reluctantly, Birch recognized that, where European staff were often greeted with mistrust and suspicion, advice from Domingo was heeded and celebrated.[108]

Hawkins, who tended to stay in his bungalow in the hospital compound, had little control over the work Domingo and Ossai were doing in Ilesa. Increasingly, they ignored his suggestions, particularly his insistence that Save the Children should found an orphanage. There was, Domingo argued, a cultural problem with orphanages in Nigeria. "Orphans" were not a recognized category, because motherless children were usually cared for by neighbors and relatives.[109] While maternal deaths, especially in childbirth, were common, Domingo was almost always able to secure care for motherless children with neighbors and relatives. Instead, she proposed an educational program to deal with the more common problem of child malnutrition by focusing on when and how to wean children, and demonstrating how to run a small cottage garden to grow protein-rich foods for young children.[110] This educational center, which was eligible for Freedom From Hunger funding because of its agricultural focus, opened in 1967.[111] In the Caribbean, SCF staff with a background in social work worked to introduce Western cultural norms, especially those relating to the bonds of attachment between mother and child. In Nigeria, SCF staff with a background in nursing worked as translators between two different cultures. While they sought to import scientific knowledge about the nature of and need for protein, they also consulted local mothers on available foodstuffs and cooking practices before making nutritional recommendations. Nigerian nurses supplanted former colonial experts not just because of their connections with, and willingness to listen to, local mothers, but because of their relationship with local elites.[112] In 1966, Remi Domingo became the third wife of a local chief, granting her even greater status in Ilesa. Her connections with the wealthy elites and business community also gave her access to local funding.[113] As the Freedom From Hunger Campaign wound up at the end of the 1960s, an increasing proportion of the income of Save the Children in Nigeria was coming from local radio appeals and business donations, rather than UK donors.[114]

Postcolonial development projects, such as the Wesleyan Guild Hospital, served as a laboratory for technologies and techniques of child-rearing that would travel back to Britain. In 1962, a controversial experiment on Nigerian children at the hospital was the first successful trial of the measles vaccination, which would be rolled out by the National Health Service for all British preschoolers in 1963.[115] Through international networks, Save the Children's local innovations were also transferred to other postcolonial contexts. A move on the part of Nigerian nurses to limit the use of powdered baby milk (which, they noted, decreased breastfeeding, and was often mixed with dirty water), influenced the later work of Monica Green when she left the Caribbean for new Save the Children projects in Uganda.[116] Concerned that the introduction of milk powder and prolo in the Caribbean had created dependency on foreign aid, Green looked to the Nigerian staff and their promotion of breastfeeding to stop what she termed "milk begging" (i.e., asking aid organizations for powdered milk) in Uganda.[117]

While postcolonial development projects prolonged the presence of colonial "experts" in Africa and the Caribbean, they also provided space for horizontal and multidirectional flows of knowledge. Yet, these flows were mediated through other white Westerners, who often passed the innovations of local staff off as their own. The contributions of an early generation of local staff working in international development projects was undervalued in the 1960s and has also been overlooked in recent literature on development, which has focused almost exclusively on ex-colonial male expertise and privileged narratives of colonial continuity over those of postcolonial change.[118]

SAVING BIAFRAN BABIES

While Save the Children had been consolidating its development work in the quiet leafy town of Ilesa, six years of political turbulence in the Nigerian capital of Lagos had culminated in two military coups in January and July of 1966. Following these, the Igbo people, an ethnic group that originated in the east of Nigeria, were targeted in bloody reprisal massacres. One hundred and fifty thousand died and one and a half million fled east. On 30 May 1967, fearing for the safety of its people and resenting the political dominance of Northern Nigeria, the government of the eastern territory seceded, declaring itself the independent Republic of Biafra. The Nigerian government responded with an economic blockade of the newly proclaimed state and, on 6 July, the Nigerian Federal Army marched onto Biafran soil. This marked the outbreak of a war that would drag on for two and a half years before Biafra was finally defeated. This early invasion captured Biafra's trading ports, leaving it sealed off from imports of arms and, crucially, food.[119]

Initially, the Biafran conflict barely featured in Save the Children's dispatches from Nigeria, or in the British press. This changed on 12 June 1968, when the *Sun* ran a three-page spread featuring images of starving children in the secessionist state.[120] Following these reports, John Birch rushed east from Ilesa to provide Save the Children with its own accounts of the famine. Flying on a Nigerian Federal Army plane into Biafra, he encountered "a hell of torment, humiliation, hunger and death."[121] Birch's report declared that "if rice and beans did not arrive in the next few days, the people would become food for vultures, or fill the shallow graves already prepared for them." It was reprinted in the *Times, Guardian*, and *Daily Express*. It appeared alongside reports from a host of Western journalists who had, by the beginning of July

1968, rendered "Biafra" synonymous with crisis. Biafra was, as the *Sun* put it, "The Land of No Hope," where "Children Wait to Die."[122] Over the next two years, it would become the subject of the largest humanitarian relief operation since the Second World War.

Setting aside a fifth of its annual budget for Biafra at the start of July 1968, Save the Children claimed it was "mortgaging its future" on the crisis, committing funds to Biafra they were not sure could be raised.[123] This was an exaggeration. By the time Save the Children committed resources, a groundswell of public concern for the Biafra crisis was evident, and relief organizations were vying to get boots on the ground first. Save the Children, due to its existing work in Nigeria (and thus government connections) and its close relationship with the International Committee of the Red Cross (ICRC) and the British government, was in prime position. Its first relief teams had salaries (and, crucially, life insurance) paid by Save the Children, vehicles, and medical supplies.[124] Yet these SCF teams worked under the auspices of the ICRC: they wore the iconic red cross on their lapels and were subject to the terms that the ICRC had established with the Nigerian government.

The policy of the ICRC was to respect the sovereignty of the states in which it intervened. As few in the international community recognized Biafra's claim to independence, the ICRC negotiated the terms of relief solely with the Nigerian federal government, which had spent the 1960s seeking to limit the post-independence role of European development workers. The Nigerian federal government was naturally suspicious of a massive intervention by international aid organizations, fearing a "Trojan horse" for old, imperial power relations to be reinscribed on the newly independent state.[125] They reluctantly granted access to aid organizations on the condition that relief would be confined to the area of Biafra that had been "liberated" by the Nigerian Federal Army. The ICRC's (and therefore SCF's) agreement to these terms was controversial.[126] The growing famine in Biafra was created by the federal blockade: starvation was a weapon of war and, by working within the rules set by the government, the ICRC could only feed those fleeing the conflict (or away from its shifting front lines), rather than those behind the blockade.

The way in which humanitarian organizations have positioned themselves relative to blockades has been a defining feature of the politics of aid in the twentieth century. Save the Children was founded in protest against the continued allied blockade after the First World War and its failure to breach the allied blockade of Nazi territories in World War Two had cemented its new role as a conservative, establishment organization. This separated Save the Children from new, left-leaning organizations like Oxfam, which delivered food behind the front lines to civilians in Nazi-occupied Europe.[127] The blockade of Biafra led to the birth of a new generation of humanitarian organizations, which, like Oxfam in the Second World War, would defy the conventions of international diplomacy and the wishes of governments to deliver aid behind the blockade.[128] Organizations founded at the time of, or as a direct result of, the conflict—most famously Médecins Sans Frontières—denounced the "impartiality" of the ICRC. These "New Left" aid workers proclaimed the birth of a new humanitarianism, which would privilege responding to victims over impartiality.[129] Biafra not only led to the founding of new humanitarian initiatives, but also further politicized some existing agencies. In Britain, organizations like Oxfam and War On Want explicitly sided with Biafra in their appeals, denouncing the cruelty of the man-made famine.[130] New-left humanitarian actors blurred the sharply drawn boundaries between humanitarianism and politics, merging aid with both tacit and overt support for the Biafran side. Humanitarian night flights, organized by a global collection of churches, often carried arms as well as food, and the delivery of food to the blockaded Biafrans allowed the beleaguered side to fight on.[131]

Biafra was a catalyst for change across the aid sector, but not for Save the Children. Instead, the Fund's relief efforts in Biafra heralded a return to far older working patterns. Although Save the Children (through the ICRC) was subject to the terms set by the federal government of Nigeria, it saw the emergency as an opportunity to sidestep the government-imposed "Nigerianization" of its workforce. The Fund used the urgency of the crisis to push for visas for a fresh crop of British expatriates who, Birch believed, would be "easier to control" than local staff.[132] On 25 June 1968, just after reports of the Biafran famine had hit British headlines, the Fund advertised in national papers for individuals "interested in doing a humanitarian service of the highest order and who are prepared to rough it in a hot tropical climate for a period of four to six months."[133] Many of SCF's new, young staff had ties with the former British Empire, as the children of missionaries or of colonial officials. Yet they described their reasons for traveling to Nigeria in very different ways. Alison Begbie, a nurse and the daughter of missionaries based in Tanzania, didn't want to go to Biafra, but felt called by God to do so. Another, John Goodger, had come to "forget I have a wife."[134] Described despairingly by the ICRC as "little more than sixth formers," this enthusiastic and adventurous generation of relief workers was not as easy to control as Birch had imagined.[135]

FIGURE 19. New staff orientation in London, July 1968. BU/PH/BOX 12, Save the Children Archives, Birmingham, UK.

Divided into six teams, and placed along the frontlines of the conflict, answerable to overlapping but often absent authorities in John Birch and the ICRC, Save the Children's young relief workers were often able to carve out largely autonomous operations, especially in the early days of the conflict. There was also time for distractions. In some teams, harrowing days gave way to hedonistic evenings where young relief teams decompressed with partying and sex, which the older generation could do little to discourage.[136] Indeed, in the case of young men, local "girlfriends" were encouraged with a nod and a wink from Birch and his cohort.[137] However, the sexual morality of white female relief workers was rigidly policed and used as a reason to prevent young European relief teams from mixing freely with Nigerian staff. Though reliant on locals for much of the day-to-day labor in relief centers (cleaning, cooking, and crowd control), Save the Children was keen that its relief workers, especially women, should live away from Nigerian men, invoking classically colonial, racialized discourses of sexual danger to segregate British and Nigerian staff.[138]

Save the Children's reluctance to rely on Nigerian staff was also due to a belief that they would be "too emotional" about the conflict.[139] The Fund recycled old colonial discourses around white rationality and native emotionalism, further embellished with ideas that the Biafran conflict was an "ancient" and "tribal" war that could not be approached impartially by Nigerians. Impartiality—a core principle of some humanitarianism that the SCF had adopted from the ICRC and that played a part in popularizing—was presented as a "civilized" and necessarily European virtue. Yet the Fund remained heavily reliant on Nigerian staff throughout the war. Unlike in Ilesa, Nigerian staff were not given formal contracts with the Fund but were employed at the discretion of local relief workers, with casual weekly pay. In many cases, local people volunteered to care for Biafran refugees arriving in their towns. Missionary and government hospitals offered their premises and their staff, unpaid, to European relief efforts. European relief teams were also joined by Nigerians from elsewhere in the country, including a number of university students from Ibadan.[140]

The ad hoc employment conditions of Nigerian staff expressed the undervaluing of their vital local and linguistic knowledge. One Nigerian nurse, Tunde Folarin, complained of being spoken to by an SCF doctor "like a master speaking to a servant . . . which I am not."[141] Informal employment conditions also meant the line between staff and beneficiary was blurred. In a set of feeding centers run by journalist-turned-relief-worker Jack Lundin in Calabar, staff included two Nigerian university students from Ibadan, a Swiss ICRC employee, and a number of Nigerian children and mothers, retained at a "pocket money" rate of five shillings per week. The children, who ranged in age from twelve to eighteen, were not in school, which closed during the fighting. The youngest, Affiong, kept paraffin lamps lit during the night, and older boys Imoh and Paul, both aged fifteen, acted as intermediaries and translators for Lundin.[142] With supplies drawn from Save the Children, the ICRC, and local donations, Lundin and his young staff mixed and distributed a "high protein diet drink" (with a recipe from a WHO doctor) of milk powder, sugar and red palm oil to over six hundred children.[143] Whether Nigerian staff were formally or informally employed, the Fund was always reliant on local efforts.

Nigerian staff never featured in reports from the front lines of the relief effort, where humanitarian publicity focused solely on the heroism of white British relief workers, using their experiences as a vector through which to draw the sympathy and donations of other Britons. Save the Children, which had failed to attract the 'youth' following of rival organizations such

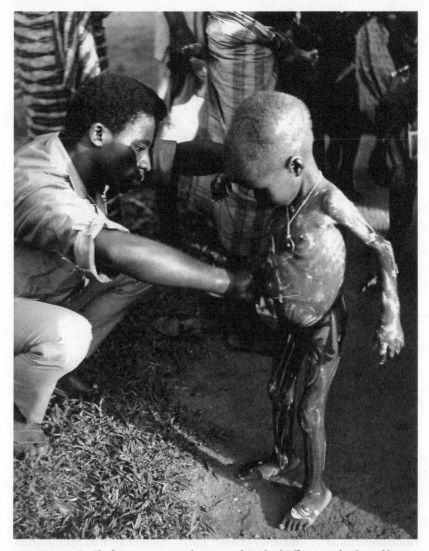

FIGURE 20. An Ibadan university student, named Raphael Effiong, applies benzyl benzoate, a treatment for scabies, to a malnourished child at a Save the Children clinic in Abak, 1968. Jack Lundin personal collection, Western Cape, South Africa. Photo by Jack Lundin.

as Oxfam, now used young relief workers to market its work. Mini-skirted young nurses became the public faces of a Biafra campaign led by ageing former-military officials.

The mishaps and misadventures of Save the Children's young staff were kept out of the public eye (save for one "regrettable" incident when the

FIGURE 21. Publicity shot, Save the Children gains new nurses, July 1968. BU/PH/ BOX 12, Save the Children Archives, Birmingham, UK.

twenty-four-year-old SCF employed nurse Sally Goatcher drove into Biaf-ran territory and was briefly captured, captivating the British press until her safe return after three uneventful days playing travel scrabble in an empty prison).[144] Save the Children's reputation had been founded on its clinical professionalism. Relief efforts were meant to function like a "well-oiled machine" with a clear "chain of command." Reports written for public circu-lation underlined the efficiency of relief and its simplicity: child malnutrition and kwashiorkor could be solved with intensive feeding, vitamin K injections and (as ever) the education of mothers. Even when the crisis was at its peak, the Fund emphasized mother-focused "education," again directing attention away from the wider political causes of child starvation.[145]

The Biafran famine not only allowed Save the Children to return to earlier staffing practices, but also to earlier forms of communication. In its postwar work in Asia and Africa, the Fund had avoided harrowing images of child suffering—the types of images that, after the First World War and during the Russian famine, had ensured its popular appeal.[146] The use of such images was regarded as an implicit critique of the colonial and postcolonial host governments of SCF projects, and resulted in complaints to the publicity department. During the Biafran famine, however, the Fund returned to images of emaciated children, isolated from parents and community members, stomachs swollen by kwashiorkor. International aid organizations, politicians and broadcasters fixed on child suffering as an emblem of the wider destruction wrought by the conflict. In the 1960s, children retained the emotional appeal they had been endowed with by the Victorian "child-saving" movement: in 1968, the highest grossing film in Britain was the musical *Oliver!*, a celebration of the pathos of children (and, specifically, a hungry child asking for food). A focus on children, regarded as nonpolitical subjects, allowed aid organizations to sidestep the complex and complicated politics of the war. Images of African children also appealed to a deep-seated paternalism, an impulse upon which the aid industry rested. Western donors were cast as parents to young and backward nations, again symbolized by the figure of the hungry child.[147]

This now well-established genre of humanitarian imagery was endowed with a new potency by the technological advances of the 1960s. The portability of the new 35 mm video camera allowed journalists to film behind the blockade. Biafran children suffering were encountered in moving pictures, rather than static photographs. After the First World War, photographs were regarded as more real and truthful than paintings, drawings, and words.[148] The Fund had emphasized the truth-telling capabilities of the camera during its Russian famine appeal: "Having now seen their suffering, how could we not act?"[149] Now, it was the moving image that brought an augmented sense of reality to a new crisis. In the era of mass television ownership, images of far-off suffering entered people's living rooms. The images, in which Biafran children (and sometimes their mothers) were broadly represented as stoic, resigned, and passive, were designed to provoke the emotional response of the viewer, rather than the subjectivity of the children.[150] Children were, as ever, emotive but not emotional.

The shared meanings associated with images of child suffering (images billed by the humanitarian community as profoundly nonpolitical) made them a powerful form of political shorthand. The beleaguered Biafran side had realized quickly that support for their fledgling nation could be prompted by sympathy for its starving child victims of the blockade. A Swiss public relations firm, Mark Press, was hired to denounce the barbarity of the federal Nigerian side, and to declare the legitimacy of the Biafran nation, a marginalized people

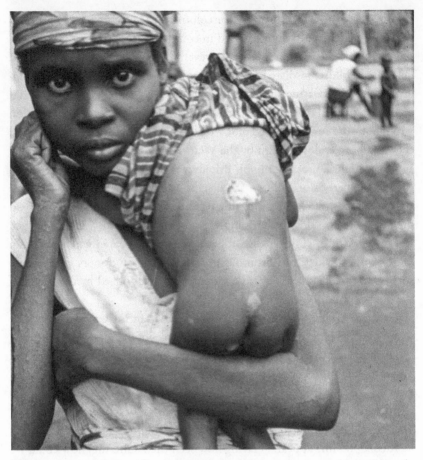

FIGURE 22. A mother with her malnourished baby, whose face is not shown. She or the photographer have exposed the baby's back to show a skin sore, characteristic of kwashiorkor, and the extent of the baby's emaciation. 1968. BU/PH/BOX 135, Save the Children Archives, Birmingham, UK.

under siege, via the promotion and distribution of images of children suffering.[151] It has since been argued that aid organizations ultimately prolonged the conflict by supporting Biafra through night flights. Save the Children was not involved in these efforts, but nonetheless it prolonged the conflict in a less direct way, by creating the very genre of images that endowed the Biafran campaign with support and legitimacy.[152] Save the Children had, in effect, conducted fifty years of market research for the Biafran side.

Photos of starving "Biafran babies" had their intended effect in Britain. During the summer of 1968, a summer that saw student protests, the early days of the Northern Irish troubles and major developments in the Vietnam war, the British public remained captivated by the Biafran relief effort.[153] With an enthusiasm for a single crisis not seen since the Russian famine of 1921, schoolchildren, churchgoers, university students and community groups across the country held bake sales, fetes, sponsored walks, and concerts, or (like my mother for the Belfast branch of the Save the Children Club) collected items such as used stamps and wool for resale. The BBC's flagship children's television program *Blue Peter* made Biafra the object of its annual Christmas appeal.[154] For many, Biafra became not just a site of humanitarian sympathy, but of political protest against the British government. Harold Wilson's Labour government was a staunch supporter of Nigerian unity and, thus, the federal government side. The ongoing unity of Nigeria was not only regarded as a mark of the success of Britain's colonial project (which seemed to be splintering just eight years after independence) but also had important economic implications. The Biafran enclave was the site of Nigeria's oil reserves, on which British buyers depended. With a background in international development and anti-colonial solidarity movements, Harold Wilson was personally conflicted. Despite his reservations, he continued to authorize the supply of British arms to the federal Nigerian side, even as protests mounted in press, public and in parliament. In the House of Commons in June 1968, Wilson was accused by both by the Conservative opposition and the left wing of his party of complicity in the killings: "The fighting in Nigeria may be thousands of miles away," but "so long as we are sending arms we are partly responsible for the bloodshed."[155]

Wilson addressed critiques of British support for Nigeria by underlining the government's humanitarian concern for the people of Biafra.[156] At the same time as supplying weapons, the British government committed £5 million to relief. Much of this was channeled through British aid organizations. Save the Children, a long-standing partner of the British government, had an especially important role. It received almost £300,000 from the government, as well as mutually beneficial publicity when it was named in press releases and parliamentary debates as a vital part of Britain's response to humanitarian crises. In the summer of 1968, Wilson appointed an independent relief commission into the war, led by an explorer-turned-aid-worker (in the model of the Russian famine's Frijdof Nansen), the mountaineer Lord John Hunt. Hunt was joined by members of the aid sector, including Save the Children's director general, Colin Thornley. The commission praised the role of British aid organizations and of the British government in providing relief, without reference to the government's role in fueling the conflict.[157] Humanitarian aid, then, had a dual purpose in Biafra: as a critique of government, or (when endorsed by the government) as a means of diverting criticism about the role of the British state in the conflict.

Biafra is remembered as the birthplace of a "new" humanitarianism, as a new generation of aid workers questioned the impartiality of ICRC, and took an explicitly political stance, standing in solidarity with the Biafran side.[158] Yet, in terms of the history of Save the Children, we see Biafra not as a moment of new beginnings but the denouement of an aid movement that had been fifty years in the making. Humanitarian images framed the crisis. The rapid and professional delivery of aid enabled the Biafran side to fight on. A partnership forged between aid organizations and the government (a model of partnership invented by Save the Children) gave the British government the political capital it needed to credibly continue its support for the federal Nigerian side. Aid profoundly altered not just the representation, but also the reality, of the conflict. This was as true at the level of individual Biafran children as it was at the level of international politics. Images that emphasized the plight of suffering children engendered a response that involved separating them from their families and communities. Under public pressure, Save the Children participated in the evacuation of five thousand Biafran children to "orphanages" in Gabon and the Ivory Coast.[159] Despite a repatriation process in 1970, many families were never reunited. As in the interwar years, the Fund's interventions created the isolated, metaphorically orphaned children that their appeals represented.

The removal of children from the conflict symbolized the Fund's return to an earlier ideological position. Since the 1930s, the Fund had renounced its founding belief that by saving children, it could save the world. In an era of global instability and conflict, it had sought only to save children *from* the world. During its brief stint in "development" work in the 1960s, the Fund had embodied some of the utopianism associated with the wider development movement. Through intervention in the lives of children and their families, it had pointed to a future of independence and self-sufficiency for postcolonial peoples. However, with programs led by disillusioned former colonial officials, the SCF leadership's belief in the utopia of the development era had always been paper-thin. Biafra offered the Fund a return to older methods of relief and a retreat from an idealism it had never fully embraced. Biafra came to symbolize a wider "failure" within the postcolonial project. It was the first in a series of postcolonial emergencies that would allow the Fund to reorient its work, focusing on short, crisis-based interventions rather than long-term development projects.[160] This was an early moment in what would become the permanent crisis-mode that has characterized humanitarianism in the latter twentieth century.[161] For Save the Children, humanitarianism was—once again—no longer a utopian attempt to build a better future, but an ongoing response to the failures of the present.

THE DECLINE OF DEVELOPMENTALISM
AND THE END OF AN ERA

In 1969, to celebrate the Fund's fiftieth anniversary, the SCF council commissioned socialist filmmaker Ken Loach to make a documentary about the Fund. This surprising choice was made after Loach's 1966 film *Cathy Come Home* was aired on BBC television and resulted in a surge of donations to the homelessness charity Shelter. The Fund gave Loach free access to its projects in Kenya and in Britain. Fund leaders hoped that Loach would create a similar narrative to that of SCF promotional materials, capturing the irresistible pathos and vulnerability of children, and the acts of salvation performed by the Fund's staff. He did not. Instead, Loach's ninety-minute film showcased the class prejudice of Save the Children staff in a children's holiday home in Essex, as the competence of working-class parents and the manners of their children were denigrated: working-class children were washed with "coal in the bath" and "just born lazy," these staff claimed. This was juxtaposed with scenes of young boys at the SCF-funded Starehe school in Kenya, banned from speaking their local languages and brought up reading British books, singing British songs, and marching in a brass band. In both Britain and Kenya, Loach's film seemed to argue, children were being taken from their home cultures and communities and brought up according to imposed and inappropriate upper-class British values. In the second part of his film, Loach turned to the problem of poverty more generally, denouncing Save the Children as "stretcher-bearers" of the capitalist world order, who "help bandage the wounds" and "divert our attention from the real cause of racialism, poverty and hunger whether in Birmingham, Liverpool or Kenya."[162]

The SCF rejected the film as "highly derogatory" and a "political tract." After a bitter legal battle, Save the Children banned it from private and public view. It could not, however, silence other critiques of the aid sector. In 1968, twenty-five "young and disillusioned" staff of Oxfam, Christian

Aid, the Overseas Development Institute, and Youth Against Hunger met in a country house in Haslemere, Surrey, where they wrote the widely circulated "Haslemere Declaration," arguing that poverty in the Third World was caused by exploitation, and that Western aid was at best an inadequate form of conscience-salving and at worst another form of exploitation. Charity, they claimed, was "the equivalent of tossing sixpence in a beggar's cap: money given by those who have no intention of changing the system that produces beggars, and no understanding that they are part of it."[163] One of the Declaration's authors, Teresa Hayter, later wrote *Aid as Imperialism*, arguing that humanitarianism was little more than a Western attempt to control the economies and foreign policies of postcolonial states.[164]

At the same time, a growing critique of aid was coming from scholars in postcolonial societies. Dependency theory which had grown out of Latin American economic institutes in the 1950s, gained widespread traction within postcolonial universities and elites. Its proponents argued that, rather than development being a mutual and global process, the vested interest of the West (the core) was to draw resources away from Asia, Africa, and Latin America (the periphery). Developing the economies of these nations, either through Western humanitarian or state-led efforts, was merely an attempt to entrench the existing exploitative economic relationships.[165] The initial shared confidence in the capacity of "development" to solve inequality had not only been eroded but turned on its head. Echoing James Ford's arguments at the Conference on the African Child almost forty years earlier, these critiques posited organizations like Save the Children as a cause of, not a solution to, poverty.

Save the Children sidestepped these growing critiques as they withdrew from the development model. Biafra had given the Fund a new, highly successful model of intervention that both increased its donations and deepened its ties to the British state. It would, thereafter, focus primarily on emergency responses, freeing it of some of the ethical and political controversies associated with development and giving it more operational autonomy "in the field."[166] In 1970 and 1971 successive floods and war in East Pakistan (later Bangladesh) provided a fresh emergency to which to respond. During the rest of the decade, the Fund mounted mass relief missions to Nicaragua (earthquake), the Sahel and Ethiopia (drought), Honduras (hurricane), Lebanon (civil war), and India (another earthquake). Finally, in 1983 it undertook its largest relief mission since Biafra, during the drought and famine in Ethiopia.

At its fiftieth anniversary in 1969, Save the Children had reached the end point of an ideological shift that had been underway since the late 1930s. Save the Children was not the only humanitarian organization, in Britain or internationally, to jettison development work in favor of emergency relief, but for the Fund this shift was the end of a long trajectory. When total war had broken out in Europe in 1939, the Fund had put its internationalist dreams to one side, privileging its position of influence in Whitehall over peace building. In the 1950s its utopianism had been briefly reinvigorated by the belief that it could preserve a vision of a world on the path to civilization and progress by protecting the British Empire. The postcolonial era, and the problems the Fund encountered in its development programs, dented this optimism. Despite the partial decolonization of the organization on the ground, attempts by new staff to reorient the Fund's work toward community development work were only partially successful. The Fund's leaders in London could not wholeheartedly champion development work when they did not believe the world was on a path toward progress and mutual prosperity. Ideas about post-imperial decline in Britain had seeped into the humanitarian mentality. By the 1970s, the Fund no longer imagined that saving children would save, or even change, the world. Instead, it saw crisis as a permanent state that it could save children *from* but could not alter in any meaningful sense. The mirage of a liberal international order in which Britain and its empire led the way to global prosperity, security, and civilization had finally vanished.

Conclusion

ONE HUNDRED YEARS OF SAVING CHILDREN

IN APRIL 2019 a conference convened to mark the centenary of Save the Children. It took place in Holborn, London, just down the road from Save the Children's first shabby, one-room office where Dorothy Buxton had furiously scrawled appeals for "former enemy children." One hundred years later, Save the Children has become a global organization, comprising twenty-nine national member organizations working in 120 countries. Save the Children's UK branch has an annual income of £300 million. It now employs over a thousand staff and is based at a corporate office space in the City of London. Over its first century, Save the Children has moved from a fringe protest movement to one of the world's largest and most influential humanitarian organizations. This book has told the story of the first fifty years of that transformation. It ends in the 1970s for reasons that are both practical and intellectual: it is in the early 1970s that Save the Children's archival trail goes cold. Telephones had replaced telegrams as the main method of communication and—until very recently—documents that were produced after 1972 were hidden from the public view by an organization that feared the reputational damage its past might do.[1] The 1970s, I have argued, also marked an end point for a vision of humanitarian internationalism that had grown from the First World War and was deeply dependent on British imperialism. With empire formally ended, the British humanitarian movement became ever more shaped by the expanding American aid sector and the Cold War considerations that guided it. The illusion of British global leadership had become impossible to sustain.

The story of the wider international aid movement after 1970 is being told in an emerging scholarship on nongovernmental organizations, popular diplomacy, capitalism, migration, and global governance.[2] Humanitarian organizations are beginning to participate in the telling of their own histories.[3] Save the Children's Centenary Conference represented an attempt, driven from within the organization, to grapple with the complicated history of aid to better understand its troubled present and contested future. The organizing committee of the centenary conference—of which I was a member—gathered testimony from those who had seen and shaped Save the Children's more recent half century, from the end of the 1960s to the present day. In a series of witness panels, the conference drew upon the living institutional memory of Save the Children staff and their collaborators in other humanitarian organizations, in government, and on the ground in disaster-affected communities. The panels recalled the era of emergency response in the aftermath of decolonization, moving from Biafra in 1967–70 to Bangladesh from 1971 onward; the rapid growth of Save the Children as it responded to the Ethiopian famine and civil war in Sudan 1980s; a dawning awareness of the limits of humanitarian relief during genocides in Bosnia and Rwanda in the 1990s; and the embroilment of humanitarian organizations in foreign policy, from the Iraq War in 2003 to the present day.

The conference took place after five difficult years for Save the Children UK. The close relationship between the charity's leaders and the British government, and the advocacy of then CEO Justin Forsyth for military intervention in Syria, as well as the organization presenting an award to former UK prime minister Tony Blair in 2014, had angered a younger generation of staff.[4] Revelations about sexual harassment during the course of the 2016 #MeToo movement had led to senior resignations, including Forsyth's, and funding for the organization from the British government (accounting for about a third of annual income) was paused.[5] In this context, there was an appetite for greater transparency and open critique: an opportunity for frank conversations about the future and a demythologized version of the past. After two days of witness panels, recalling interventions from Biafra in the 1960s to the Ebola epidemic in 2014, optimism was in short supply.[6] In the final panel of the conference, former director of emergency relief Lewis Sida said, of the recent history of Save the Children, "This is a time of development failure and protracted crises: most places we are working in today, we were working in fifteen years ago. . . . We're often providing substitute service provision in long-term, broken places. I'm not particularly optimistic about these places: they will continue to be the badlands, and they're where we as humanitarians will continue to find ourselves."[7]

The aid sector seemed to have hit an impasse. Save the Children's founders had believed that by saving children, they would save the world. They had imagined that children's education and nutrition held the key to international peace and prosperity. Fifty years later, abandoning this utopia, a new leadership had thought they could save children from a disordered world by specializing in rapid crisis response. This approach too seemed not to have worked.

POLITICS, AID, AND THE STATE

Though the situation that Sida described seems far removed from the utopian vision of Save the Children's founders, it would not have surprised Dorothy Buxton. Buxton had never imagined that humanitarianism, on its own, would be enough to bring about a better world; rather, humanitarianism was a gateway to forms of political action that would. Save the Children had been founded to inspire people to mount a socialist critique of the inequalities of the liberal internationalist order that had emerged from the First World War. It was Buxton's sister, Eglantyne Jebb, who offered humanitarianism on its own terms as a pathway to a better world. Under her leadership, the Save the Children Fund sought to nourish and educate children, believing that healthy children's minds and bodies would be the basis of mutual peace and prosperity. Unlike Buxton, Jebb did not believe that humanitarians needed to critique or change the existing political order. Rather, they should lead by example, inspiring states to advance child welfare programs and international collaboration.

Jebb believed that the humanitarian ends of Save the Children were above politics, and that they could be attained within the liberal internationalist order that already existed. In the interwar era, Save the Children imagined colonial capitalism as a means for Europe to enhance its prosperity and share its "civilization" with the wider world. Between the wars, Save the Children tasked itself with humanizing British imperial rule and bestowing the benefits of its expertise in foreign relations on a wider, international community via the League of Nations Child Welfare Committee. After the war, the organization sought to modernize British imperialism through the deployment of internationally garnered humanitarian expertise. In the 1950s and 1960s, Save the Children's humanitarianism became a form of conservatism, as the organization sought to protect a version of liberal and imperial international order that was rapidly slipping away.

What happens to a movement when the ideals that it was marshaled to protect begin to disappear? As the British Empire disintegrated, Save the Children's leadership ceased to imagine a prosperous future for the world. Their beliefs about the function of humanitarianism started to shift: it would no longer be a midwife to a better world order, but stretcher-bearer for the casualties of ongoing global disorder. In the three decades following the Fund's intervention in Biafra, the director general position was occupied by retired colonial servicemen and army and air force generals. With expertise in rapid mobilization, off-road transportation, and mass feeding, Save the Children was equipped for rapid responses to the successive crises its leaders imagined would follow in the wake of decolonization. Embracing disaster, rather than development, Save the Children's path diverged from the other major aid organizations that had emerged from Britain and its empire, such as Oxfam and Christian Aid. Where these organizations focused on local "grass-roots" solutions to hunger and poverty, Save the Children used its operational capacity and military experience to respond to complex emergencies. It no longer sought to save children in order to save the world, but rather to save children from a world that was already broken.

For Save the Children, ongoing survival was not just about playing to its operational strengths, but also cultivating its partnership with the British government. It was Save the Children that, in 1921, established a model for a century of state-funded humanitarian aid, acting as a contractor in the delivery of official British aid during the Russian famine. In its first fifty years, the Fund became a ready collaborator with the British military in war, and a partner in the growing development and education work of the Colonial Office. This partnership conferred status and resources on Save the Children, even if it occasionally came at the cost of constraining its action when aid stood in opposition to the British government's economic or diplomatic objectives. For Save the Children's early leadership, these instances were matters of pragmatism rather than a fundamental threat to principles: imagining British power as the basis of a peaceful and prosperous world order, humanitarians and the British state sought the same ends.

However, this cooperation had a cost. Over the course of the last century, Save the Children had entrenched the modern British state's self-fashioning as a humanitarian actor. British imperialism had been cast as inherently humanitarian and, with the collusion of humanitarian agencies, its postcolonial foreign policy would be presented this way too. It was this image that enabled the so-called "humanitarian wars" of the 1990s and the invasion of

Iraq in 2003. In these wars, aid agencies followed on the heels of Western armies, funded by Western states, to heal the casualties their invasions had created.[8] A dawning discomfort with state collaboration, described by Save the Children staff at the centenary conference, came at a moment when aid organizations were more dependent on state funding than ever before. In the years since the Iraq invasion, the global humanitarian sector has quadrupled in size, becoming a $29 billion-per-year industry. Around half of this figure relates to the funding given by (primarily Western) states to so-called "nongovernmental" aid agencies (both directly and via supranational bodies such as the UN and the EU).[9] It is in this period too that humanitarian organizations have increasingly become, as Lewis Sida described at the centenary conference, service providers in "failed" states in the Global South.[10] What the world is left with, then, is aid organizations acting as intermediaries for Western states financing the functions of Southern, often formerly colonized, nations, almost half a century after the era of decolonization.[11]

Scholars have been writing about the neocolonial nature of international aid since the 1960s. They have shown how aid organizations became vehicles for state power, as well as Western cultural hegemony.[12] By tracing the longer history of the modern international aid movement, we have seen that state-led and popular humanitarianism were forged in tandem, shared the same ideological ends, and were performed by the same actors. If crises are endemic and development stagnant, then this is a consequence of the same imperial and capitalist principles that animated the humanitarian movement in the first place. Speaking at the Save the Children Centenary Conference, Sida, admittedly pessimistic about the effectiveness of the humanitarian enterprise, located hope within the humanitarian ethic itself: "What Save the Children has been good at is keeping the flame of hope alive: believing that a better world is possible and that it is worth fighting for."[13] For the founders of Save the Children, humanitarianism was a means to create a new world order. Now that this utopian vision has failed to materialize, humanitarianism—and its bearing of hope in a broken world—has become an end in itself.

LIBERALISM AND CHILDREN'S RIGHTS

During the 2019 centenary year, Save the Children's introduction of the Declaration of the Rights of the Child in 1924 was commemorated as one of the organization's primary contributions to the modern humanitarian movement. Since Jebb walked down from a mountaintop near Geneva holding the 1924 Declaration, the meaning of children's rights has changed, with their contours shifting alongside popular understandings of liberalism. When the Declaration of the Rights of the Child was first authored in the early 1920s, it drew upon a Victorian liberal collectivist tradition. Children were valued not as individuals but because of the contribution they would make to wider society. This contribution was imagined in biopolitical terms: healthy children would become the workers of the future. Child rights, though described as universal, were imagined to apply to healthy children only. The first Declaration of the Rights of the Child did not assume that every child would be equal, nor have the same value. Save the Children drew upon eugenics and colonial racial "science" to determine the relative value of children. The League of Nations Child Welfare Committee, tasked with implementing the Declaration, imagined that nation-states or colonial powers would be the foremost protectors of children's rights. The Declaration of the Rights of the Child provided no ideological or practical challenge to the major abusers of children's rights in this era: colonialism and fascism.

After the Second World War, although the United Nations adopted the League of Nations Child Rights declaration, Save the Children itself moved away from a rights-based discourse, ceding this ground to UNICEF.[14] Save the Children did not rediscover child rights as a framing device for its work until decades later. The early 1990s saw a shift in Save the Children's leadership (toward career voluntary sector workers and away from former military personnel) at the same time that disillusionment was growing within the organization about the long-term impact of disaster relief.[15] In 1989, the United Nations reworked and relaunched the Declaration of the Rights of the Child and, from the 1990s, Save the Children once again styled itself as a "child rights organization." In the 1990s, child rights provided a point for Save the Children, an organization focused primarily on emergency aid, to reenter long-term development work.[16] This reentry took place, not coincidentally, at the moment when "development" was shifting away from economic justice and community-based programs and toward the rights of women and children—and in doing so becoming ostensibly less "political."

The contemporary UN Convention on the Rights of the Child—the version of child rights that Save the Children now strives to realize—is an expression of liberal individualism. It enshrines children's right to the "development of [their] personality," "freedom of expression," and "individual life in society."[17] Whereas, at the start of the twentieth century, children's rights were vested in their position vis-à-vis the community, today children's rights are understood to exist independently from the society they inhabit. At the same time, the 1989 Declaration locates the child within the family, as the "natural environment for . . . growth and well-being." This shift began in the aftermath of the Second World War, as psychoanalysis posited the stability of the nuclear family as central to the emotional health of children and, in turn, the future of (capitalist) democracy. Save the Children began its first family reunification program in the aftermath of the Biafra war in 1970. The largest such program since the Second World War, it marked a belated change in direction for the Fund, which had been reluctant to end its practice of separating children from their families for purposes of education and relief. The Biafran war marked the moment, too, when the Fund parted with its iconic bambino logo, replacing it with the bold, modern "Charlie" logo. In doing so, it removed the icon of an orphan that had been central to its work and its public image for the first half century.

In the mid-1990s, following the mass refugee crisis and family separations generated by the Rwandan genocide, family reunification became a central aspect of Save the Children's work. In major disasters of the twenty-first century, such as the 2010 Haitian earthquake, Save the Children became an expert on and advocate for preserving families, halting the attempts at international adoption made by a host of ad hoc aid agencies. This work located Save the Children's concern for the right of children to family life alongside its traditional strength in disaster relief.[18] More recently, Save the Children UK has lobbied against family separation through legal channels. In 2018, Save the Children sponsored a major legal inquiry into the protection of children in conflict that, like Save the Children's 1938 report on the protection of children in war, advocated the removal of children from conflict zones.[19] In 1938 Save the Children had argued that children should be placed in designated zones and cared for by professionals. In 2018, recognizing the difficulty of re-creating familial environments and the trauma of separation, Save the Children now lobbied for adult civilians in conflict zones to be afforded enhanced protection alongside the children in their care.

Upholding the right of children to family life, Save the Children also advocates safe passage and settlement rights to be granted to the parents of children who have sought asylum abroad, and for children whose parents have found new national homes. In contrast to its successes in family reunification in the Global South, Save the Children has had little success in altering restrictive immigration policies in either Britain or the United States.[20] Nonetheless, attempts to do so are revealing about the changing position of children in the humanitarian imagination. In the 1920s iteration of children's rights, the young claimed their entitlements in relation to their adult selves. In the contemporary iteration of children's rights, it is adults who make claims on sympathy, asylum, and protection through their relationship to children. In neither guise has the language of child rights brought us any closer to a world in which people are valued on their own terms, in the present, as people.[21]

HUMANITARIAN INTERNATIONALISM
IN BRITAIN TODAY

When I carried my oxygen mask down a disused munitions mine to look at Save the Children's archives for the first time, the New Labour government was in its last weeks of power. Its thirteen-year rule had been characterized by an "ethical foreign policy" that echoed many of the tenets of earlier liberal internationalism. This included the rapid expansion of state aid, and the waging of so-called "humanitarian wars."[22] Ten years since my first visit to the archives, as I type these concluding thoughts, a Conservative government has just abolished the Department for International Development. The consensus around international aid, the only budget to have been ring-fenced by successive Conservative-led austerity administrations after 2010, seems to have vanished. Under a government that was elected on a platform of nationalism, border control, and xenophobia, Britain has withdrawn from the European Union. At Save the Children's Centenary Conference in 2019, which took place just after the first missed deadline for Britain's withdrawal from the European Union, delegates wondered if we were witnessing the end of Britain's internationalist century, which had begun in 1920 with entry into the League of Nations.

While humanitarian organizations now lament the end of an era of liberal internationalist consensus, their ideals have done little to challenge the rise of right-wing nationalism.[23] Humanitarianism has always been a highly constrained form of internationalism. It is one that promotes compassion at a distance; it breaks down entirely when those in need of aid approach Britain's borders. By externalizing need, humanitarianism has failed to challenge a century of British reluctance or refusal to welcome refugees. Humanitarianism is also a deeply hierarchical form of internationalism. It places Western states as leaders of—rather than collaborators with—nations overseas. Over the past hundred years, it has been a tool for successive British governments to affirm Britain's "global leadership" in the face of its diminishing economic and geopolitical significance. This nostalgia for "global leadership" (a euphemism for imperialism) remains a fundamental aspect of right-wing nationalism in Britain.

Humanitarianism has often been a means of reimagining the imperial past. Save the Children was engaged in this rewriting of imperial history from its earliest days: its 1931 Conference on the African Child celebrated the centenary of the abolition of slavery in the British Empire and a hundred years of imperial benevolence that followed in its wake. While sentimentalizing some aspects of the imperial past, Save the Children, as we have seen, has also worked to distance itself from histories of colonial violence, expunging these from its archives. The 2019 centenary conference represented a growing desire to grapple with Save the Children's imperial origins, but it was itself constrained by the contingencies of both the colonial past and present-day international relationships. Delegates shifted uncomfortably in their seats when I spoke about Save the Children's 1931 African Child conference, which had just seven African delegates: the audience assembled in 2019 did not look so different. We, the organizers, had failed to locate staff members from the Global South who had worked in the successive crises addressed in the conference's witness panels. Many of the conference delegates traveling from Africa or the Middle East had had their visas delayed or denied by the British Foreign Office.[24] The conference, like the contemporary aid movement, reproduced colonial knowledge and power structures.

Can humanitarianism be uncoupled from the imperialism that birthed it? A new movement to decolonize international aid seeks ways to incorporate local traditions of care into humanitarian emergency responses, to vest decision-making in affected communities and to divest aid financed by Western donors of imposed Western cultural norms.[25] For many humanitarians committed to this decolonization process, history also has an important role to play in recovering alternative origin stories and visions for the contemporary humanitarian movement. In 2019, Save the Children launched its first-ever training course on the history of international aid. While the online course charted the well-known origins story of humanitarianism in the British Empire and the International Red Cross movement, it also explored "southern humanitarianisms."[26] There is vital historical work to be done understanding how humanitarian agencies spoke to or co-opted other traditions of care. There is also important work to be done in terms of understanding how humanitarianism was interpreted, interrupted, challenged, or adapted by local staff and recipients, work that is made challenging by our existing archives, and will remain so for as long as we fail to gather testimony from the vast but forgotten Southern staff of the international aid movement.

There is also a danger that when we search for the global origins of a Western vision of universalism, we are naturalizing it. Rather than seeking multiple origin stories for the particular vision of humanitarianism that has spawned a $29 billion global aid industry, dominated by organizations like Save the Children, historians need to understand both Western and Southern cultures of mutual aid, philanthropy, and solidarity on their own terms. "Humanitarianism" may not be the best framework for so doing.[27] Accepting the specificity of humanitarianism as an ethic for international action that grew out of nineteenth- and twentieth-century Western liberalism might also help us move away from overblown claims about its significance. While the interventions of aid agencies were undoubtedly important, even lifesaving, for many recipients of aid, how far have these interventions actually transformed the governance, economies, and environments of postcolonial states? Whether or not these questions get answered is not for scholars of modern British history to decide. Insisting on using humanitarian interactions as a way to access the historical experiences of the marginalized is its own form of Western narcissism.

The contemporary international humanitarian movement emerged from a particular late-imperial liberal moment. It was as significant for the exploitative forms of governance it legitimated as the version of liberal universalism it ostensibly promoted. If the contemporary humanitarian movement seeks a better world, it needs to own its history and lend its reputation and resources to radical forms of global solidarity that challenge—rather than uphold—global inequality. The aid industry cannot forge a new future until it reckons with its past.

NOTES

INTRODUCTION

1. Nigeria: Biafra War and Relief Needs, House of Lords Debate, 12 December 1969, volume 298 cc 670–98; Memo: T. Bambury 12 November 1969, Nigeria Relief Medical Teams, FCO 65/403. For wider recent literature on humanitarian aid in Biafra, see McNeill, "Frontiers of Need"; Herteen, *The Biafran War and Postcolonial Humanitarianism*; Ignatus, *Britain's Injurious Peace Games in the Nigerian Civil War*.

2. Barnett, *Empire of Humanity*; Davey, *Idealism beyond Borders*.

3. Watenpaugh, *Bread from Stone*; Irwin, *Making the World Safe*; Sasson, "From Empire to Humanity."

4. On interwar humanitarianism and imperialism, see Baughan, "'Every Citizen of Empire Implored to Save the Children!'"; Sasson, "From Empire to Humanity."

5. Recent works on British humanitarianism, which have mostly focused on the postwar period onward, include Bocking-Welch, *British Civic Society at the End of Empire*; and Hilton, "Charity and the End of Empire. On the origins of state-funded international development, see Riley, "The Winds of Change."

6. Here, I follow Foucauldian examinations of the disciplinary functions of Western states, and postcolonial critiques of imperial education and labor discipline. On the former, see Foucault, *Foucault on Governmentality and Liberalism*; Rose, *The Psychological Complex*; and Vernon, *Hunger*. On the latter, see Fanon, *The Wretched of the Earth*; and Alatas, *The Myth of the Lazy Native*. I also draw on the approaches of recent examinations of aid and governmentality such as Scott-Smith, "Control and Biopower in Contemporary Humanitarian Aid"; and Duffield, "The Liberal Way of Development."

7. Haskell, "Capitalism and the Origins of the Humanitarian Sensibility"; Skinner and Lester, "Humanitarianism and Empire"; Brown, *Moral Capital*. See also Baughan et al., "Humanitarianism and History: A Conversation."

8. Other nations, of course, had their own justificatory imperial benevolence myths. See Jerónimo, *The "Civilising Mission" of Portuguese Colonialism*; Conklin, *A Mission to Civilize*; Daughton, *An Empire Divided*.

9. Grant, *A Civilised Savagery*; Everill, "Bridgeheads of Empire?"; Porter, "Trusteeship, Anti-Slavery, and Humanitarianism"; Elbourne, *Blood Ground*.

10. Forsythe, *The Humanitarians*; Moorehead, *Dunant's Dream*; Hermann, *L'humanitaire en questions*.

11. Crowdy, "The League of Nations."

12. On the recent rise of scholarship on the League, see Pedersen, "Back to the League of Nations." On subsidiary bodies and humanitarian work at the League, see Clavin, *Securing the World Economy*; Pedersen, *The Guardians*; Watenpaugh, "The League of Nations' Rescue of Armenian Genocide Survivors"; Boroway, *Coming to Terms with World Health*.

13. Clavin, *Securing the World Economy*.

14. Pedersen, *The Guardians*; Mazower, *Governing the World*; Jackson and O'Malley, "Introduction: Rocking on Its Hinges?"

15. Pedersen, *The Guardians*; Mazower, *Governing the World*; Jackson and O'Malley, "Introduction: Rocking on Its Hinges?

16. Riley, "The Winds of Change"; Lewis, "The British Empire in World History."

17. Hilton, "International Aid and Development NGOs in Britain"; Bocking-Welch, "Imperial Legacies and Internationalist Discourses"; Cooper and Packard, "Introduction," in *International Development and the Social Sciences*.

18. Macekura, and Manela, "Introduction," in *The Development Century*; Engerman, *Staging Growth*; Immerwahr, *Thinking Small*.

19. Hilton, "International Aid and Development NGOs in Britain"; Bocking-Welch, "Imperial Legacies"; Cooper and Packard, "Introduction," in *International Development and the Social Sciences*.

20. Rose, *The Psychological Complex*, 38–61.

21. Harris, "Political Thought and the Welfare State, 1870–1940"; Dean, *The Constitution of Poverty*.

22. Lowe, *The Welfare State in Britain since 1945*.

23. Pedersen, *Family, Dependence, and the Origins of the Welfare State*; Riley, *War in the Nursery*; Thane, "Visions of Gender in the Making of the British Welfare State"; Lewis, "Gender and the Development of Welfare Regimes"; Dale and Foster, *Feminists and State Welfare*.

24. Dwork, *War Is Good for Babies*.

25. Freeden, *Liberal Languages*, 60–77.

26. Poovey, *Making a Social Body*, 55–56. These fears of "degeneration" were further compounded by racist responses to immigration across the late nineteenth and twentieth centuries. See Ittmann, *A Problem of Great Importance*.

27. Davin, "Imperialism and Motherhood"; Bock and Thane, *Maternity and Gender Policies*.

28. Dwork, *War Is Good for Babies*.

29. Discipline and welfare were two sides of the same coin. See Vernon, *Hunger*.

30. Riley, *War in the Nursery*, 22–24.

31. Vernon, "The Ethics of Hunger and the Assembly of Society."

32. Todd, *The People*, 216–35.

33. Koven, "Remembering and Dismemberment."

34. Fieldston, *Raising the World*.

35. Bailkin, *The Afterlife of Empire*.

36. Allman, "Making Mothers."

37. A debate about how "modern" childhood has been ongoing since the publication of Ariès, *Centuries of Childhood*. See also Thane, "Childhood in History"; Thomas, "Children in Early Modern England."

38. Steedman, *Strange Dislocations*; Zelizer, *Pricing the Priceless Child*; Todd and Hendrick, *Children, Childhood and English Society*.

39. Baughan, "Anglo-American Diplomacy and International Adoption"; Tusan, "'Crimes against Humanity.'" On imperial parallels, see Boucher, *Empire's Children*.

40. Zahra, *The Lost Children*; Zahra, "'A Human Treasure'"; Shapira, *The War Inside*.

41. Fieldston, *Raising the World*.

42. Crane, *Child Protection in England*.

43. McCarthy, *Double Lives*, 244–52; King, *Family Men*.

44. Rose, *Mothers*.

45. Davin, "Imperialism and Motherhood"; Lewis, *The Politics of Motherhood*.

46. Starkey, "The Feckless Mother."

47. Ram and Jolly, "Introduction," in *Maternities and Modernities*; Rich, *Of Woman Born*, 84–109. On the role of race in the blaming of mothers, see Davis, *Women, Race and Class*, 3–29.

48. Rose, *Mothers*; Allman, "Making Mothers."

49. Wells, *Childhood in Global Perspective*; Pupavac, "Misanthropy without Border."

50. Freeman, *Children's Rights*; Wells, "Child Saving or Child Rights?"

51. Fassin, *Humanitarian Reason*, 161–80.

52. Recent accounts have tended to discuss how humanitarianism became embedded in contemporary politics without discussing the politics of humanitarianism itself, e.g., Fassin, *Humanitarian Reason*. Scholars of humanitarian law have been more attuned to the shifting meanings and politics of humanitarianism, e.g., Orford, *Reading Humanitarian Intervention*.

53. On internationalism and liberalism see Bell, *The Idea of Greater Britain*; Pitts, *A Turn to Empire*. On its humanitarian iteration, see Gill, *Calculating Compassion*, 20–23.

54. They did, however, view work and markets as intrinsically good, as described by Weber, *The Protestant Ethic and the Spirit of Capitalism*.

55. Porter, *Religion versus Empire?*

56. On the modern construction of children as inherently valuable, see Steedman, *Strange Dislocations*; Zelizer, *Pricing the Priceless Child*; Todd and Hendrick, *Children, Childhood and English Society*. This is not to say, of course, that conceptions of the value of children and their value did not exist before the modern era.

See Thomas, "Children in Early Modern England"; Roper, "'Evil Imaginings and Fantasies.'"

57. On the universalization of children, see Burman, *Deconstructing Social Psychology*; and Steedman, *Strange Dislocations*; on the unifying position of children in postwar British politics, Thomson, *Lost Freedom*.

58. Gleason, "Avoiding the Agency Trap"; Hendrick, "The Child as a Social Actor in Historical Sources."

59. Purvis, "Gendering the Historiography of the Suffragette Movement in Edwardian Britain." For an account of the position of female aid workers more recently, see Read, "Embodying Difference."

60. Kuhlman, *Reconstructing Patriarchy after the Great War*.

61. The hypermasculine culture of aid work, especially at Save the Children, has been a recent subject of debate in the #aidtoo movement. See Shaista Aziz and Alexia Pepper de Caires, "Time for Accountability in Aid NGOs Such as Save the Children," *Third Sector*, March 2019, https://www.thirdsector.co.uk/shaista-aziz-alexia-pepper-de-caires-time-accountability-aid-ngos-save-children/management/article/1675978, accessed 20 April 2020.

62. On our relative lack of accounts of women's international politics, see James and Sluga, "Introduction: The Long International History of Women and Diplomacy."

63. Up-to-date information on British government support for international aid and development projects can be found at: https://devtracker.dfid.gov.uk/sector/18/projects.

64. Baughan and Fiori, "Towards A New Politics of Humanitarian Solidarity." In recognition of the entwined nature of state and non-state humanitarian interventions, this book avoids using the term *nongovernmental organization* or its acronym NGO, which has become a shorthand for a variety of humanitarian institutions.

65. Loss, "Missionaries, the Monarchy, and the Emergence of Anglican Pluralism"; Marshall, "The Conference on the African Child of 1931"; Bocking-Welch, *British Civic Society at the End of Empire*, 154–81.

66. Ferguson, *The Anti-politics Machine*.

67. Hayter, *Aid as Imperialism*; Haslemere Declaration Group, *The Haslemere Declaration*.

68. In the twenty-first century, aid organizations have increasingly taken on functions traditionally associated with democratically elected governments in the Global South, making their "nonpolitical" stance ever more vital. Mann, *From Empires to NGOs in the West African Sahel*.

69. For classic accounts of Save the Children, see Freeman, *If Any Man Build*; Fuller, *The Rights of the Child*; on the early years and Eglantyne Jebb, see Mulley, *The Woman Who Saved the Children*; Mahood, *Feminism and Voluntary Action*.

70. There were around seven hundred local branches in the interwar period. This figure declined to about three hundred in the 1940s and 1950s, and rose again to around six hundred in the 1960s. Branches were evenly distributed between north and south, urban and rural, and the four nations of the United Kingdom. "Annual Report," various, held at Save the Children HQ, London.

71. E. Jebb, *The History and Aims of the Save the Children Fund*, September 1922, EJ270, SCA.

72. Fiori et al., *The Echo Chamber*.

73. On Near East Relief see Watenpaugh, *Bread from Stone*; Tusan, *Smyrna's Ashes*; on Oxfam in the 1960s see Black, *A Cause for Our Times*.

74. Penny A Week Newssheet, No.1, December 1948, Save the Children Archive.

75. *The Record of the Save the Children Fund*, April 1920, BL.

76. Public participation in cultures of decolonization and liberal internationalism, which I deal with to an extent in this book, are examined brilliantly in McCarthy, *The British People and the League of Nations*; Bailkin, *Afterlife of Empire*; Bocking-Welch, *British Civic Society at the End of Empire*.

77. I attempt to read humanitarian archives "against the grain," as histories of the subaltern in the colonial archive have. See Spivak, "The Rani of Sirmur"; Stoler, *Along the Archival Grain*.

78. E. Jebb, Historical Notes on the Russian Famine, EJ203, SCA.

79. Kennedy and Barton, "Debating the 'Global History of Britain'"; Sasson et al., "Britain and the World"

80. Hall, *Civilising Subjects*; Bell, *The Idea of Greater Britain*. On the latter, see Bailkin, *Afterlife of Empire*; Bailkin, *Unsettled*; and Bocking-Welch, *British Civic Society at the End of Empire*.

81. For example, Magee and Thompson, *Empire and Globalisation*; Ballantyne and Burton, *Empires and the Reach of the Global*.

82. For a recent example of an international history told multi-locally, see Pedersen, *The Guardians*. As an examination of the forging of British lives across the globe, see Ogborn, *Global Lives*.

CHAPTER 1. BRITISH INTERNATIONALISMS AND HUMANITARIANISM

1. "For German Babies," *Daily Herald*, 18 January 1919.

2. "Report and Subscription List of German Babies' Teats Fund," FEWVRC/ MISSIONS/10/2/3/1, Friends' House Library (FHL), London.

3. Maltz, *British Aestheticism and The Urban Working Classes*, 33. Eglantyne Louisa's Jebb maiden name was also Jebb, though she was not a blood relation of her husband.

4. Prochaska, *Women and Philanthropy in Nineteenth-Century England*.

5. Harris, "Political Thought and the Welfare State."

6. On the Jebb family, see Mahood, *Feminism and Voluntary Action*.

7. Sylvest, *British Liberal Internationalism*; Palen, *The "Conspiracy" of Free Trade*; Trentmann, *Free Trade Nation*.

8. Mahood, *Feminism and Voluntary Action*, 27.

9. Bell, *The Idea of Greater Britain*, 118; Jebb, "Imperial Organisation."

10. Markwell, *John Maynard Keynes and International Relations*.

11. Mosa Anderson, "Dorothy Buxton, Draft Biography," c. 1935, Buxton Family Papers (BFP), Dorset, 10–14.

12. Woolf, Diary XXII, 5 October 1933, 4:253.

13. de Bunsen, *Charles Roden Buxton*.

14. Buxton and Buxton, *The World after the War*, 60–65.

15. Anderson, "Dorothy Buxton, Draft Biography," 10–14.

16. Pugh, "Pacifism and Politics in Britain"; Ceadal, *Semi-detached Idealists*.

17. Swanwick, *Builders of Peace*; Trevelyan, *The Union of Democratic Control*.

18. Bullock, *Under Siege*; Howell, *MacDonald's Party*.

19. Mosa Anderson, "*The Cambridge Magazine*, 1915–1920," c. 1923, BFP; Anderson and Florence, *C. K. Ogden*, 25.

20. For example, Marion Ellis, Maude Royden, and Kate Courtney. These women also shared close ties with the Union of Democratic Control (UDC) via Helena Swanwick, Barbara Ayrton Gould, and (again) Dorothy Buxton.

21. Blackwell, *No Peace without Freedom*, 19–34; Liddington, *The Road to Greenham Common*, 12–18.

22. Sluga, "Women, Feminisms and Twentieth-Century Internationalism," 63–68.

23. O'Cohrs, *The Unfinished Peace after World War I*.

24. Grieves, *Sir Eric Geddes*, 72.

25. "Hang the Kaiser," *Daily Mail*, 2 December 1918.

26. On the perceived "brutalization" of the public after the war, see Lawrence, "Forging a Peaceable Kingdom."

27. WILPF Executive Committee Minutes, 10 January 1919, WILPF 5/1, LSE.

28. MacMillan, *Paris 1919*.

29. "Fight the Famine," *Daily Herald*, 30 April 1919; Stop the Murders," *Daily Herald*, 8 March 1919; "The Infamy of the Blockade," "Raise the Blockade," *The Nation*, 8 March 1919, "The Guilt of the Famine," 22 March 1919.

30. Fight the Famine Council, April 1919, Buxton Papers 3/1, LSE.

31. Ibid.

32. "Fight the Famine," *The Times*, 6 June 1919.

33. "Fight the Famine," *Daily Herald*, 30 April 1919; Stop the Murders," *Daily Herald*, 8 March 1919.

34. Fight the Famine Council, April 1919.

35. Markell, *John Maynard Keynes and International Relations*, 65–90

36. Fundraising letter, Fight the Famine Council, March 1919; WILPF Executive Committee Minutes, 20 March 1919,WILPF 5/1, LSE.

37. WILPF leaflet 1919, Buxton Papers, 3/3 LSE. I have taken the decision here not to reproduce images of starving children. This leaflet can be found easily using a Google image search. The use of photographic technology to relay the suffering of children echoed campaigning tactics that had been used by many WILPF members in their campaign against the Boer War concentration camps; Kate Courtney, Diary, 3 March 1900, Courtney Papers, 8, LSE. See also Clavin, "The Austrian Hunger Crisis and the Genesis of International Organization after the First World War."

38. FFC Leaflet, Buxton Papers, 3/1 LSE; Buxton and Buxton, *After the War*, 60–65.

39. Zelizer, *Pricing the Priceless Child*. See also, on the "humanitarian discovery of hunger," Vernon, *Hunger*, 17–40.

40. WILPF Executive Committee Meeting, 12 May 1919, WIPF 5/1, LSE.

41. D. Buxton, circular on behalf of the FFC, 10 May 1919, Buxton Family Papers, Dorset.

42. "Fight the Famine," *Times*, 19 May 1919; WILPF Executive Committee Minutes, 1 July 1919, LSE.

43. Thompson, "'Pictorial Lies'?"

44. Dorothy Buxton, draft leaflet for schoolchildren, July 1919, EJ279, SCA; Buxton and Buxton, *After the War*, 8.

45. Dorothy Buxton, circular on behalf of the FFC, 10 May 1919, Buxton Family Papers, Dorset.

46. R. Gordon Millennium to D. Buxton, 11 December 1919, EJ279, SCA; Famine Information Bureau, various letters, 1919, Buxton 3/3, LSE.

47. E. Fuller to D. Buxton, 23 February 1953, BFP.

48. E. Jebb to D. Buxton, 1 September 1919, BFP; E. Fuller to D. Buxton, 23 February 1953, Buxton Family Papers, Dorset.

49. Buxton and Buxton, *After the War*, 44.

50. Ibid., 40–45.

51. D. Buxton, July 1919, and circular re: hunger strike against blockade of Germany, EJ 72, SCA.

52. Jebb, *Cambridge*; Harris, "Political Thought."

53. Moore, "Social Work and Social Welfare; Lewis, *The Voluntary Sector, the State and Social Work in Britain*.

54. Mahood, *Feminism and Voluntary Action*, 121–41.

55. On Jebb's life before the Save the Children Fund, see Mahood, *Feminism and Voluntary Action*; Mulley, *The Woman Who Saved the Children*.

56. The World's Children, July 1923; Notes on the principles of relief and where grants are made to, 1922, EJ270, SCA. On the heritage of the British social work tradition in international aid, see Colpus, *Female Philanthropy in the Interwar World*.

57. Notes on the principles of relief and where grants are made to, 1922, EJ270, SCA.

58. Mahood, *The Woman Who Saved the Children*, 179.

59. F. Haughton October 1919 to Dorothy Buxton, Jebb Family Papers, LSE.

60. Notes on the principles of relief and where grants are made to, 1922, EJ270, SCA.

61. Ibid.

62. *The Glasgow Bulletin*, cited in Sellick, "Responding to Children Effected by Armed Conflict."

63. Bennett, *British Foreign Policy during the Curzon Period, 1919–24*, 57; Clavin, "The Austrian Hunger Crisis."

64. Committee minutes, British board of the Austrian Home for British Children, 3 March 1922, EJ36, SCA; D. Buxton, Report from Vienna Visit December 1920, Austria Helps Herself, EJ37, SCA.

65. On the origins of international adoption and child sponsorship from this moment, see Baughan, "Anglo-American Diplomacy and International Adoption."

66. Buxton and Buxton, *The White Flame*.

67. List of children sponsored through the Jugend Fursorge, EJ53, SCA; Mr Levin to Mr Watson, 18 January 1924, EJ53, SCA.

68. December 1920, SCF allocations department to Mary Houghton, EJ46, SCA. See also Baughan, "Anglo-American Diplomacy and International Adoption" on the role of race, class, and gender in the selection of children.

69. SCF allocations department to Mary Houghton, 16 May 1922, EJ46, SCA.

70. Mary Houghton to Ethel Sidgwick, 8 June 1922, EJ46, SCA.

71. Ibid.

72. Miss Sidgwick's notes: Survey of SCF work by country, 1919–22 and account of SCF work in Austria, 1922, EJ271, SCA.

73. Notes on the principles of relief and where grants are made to, 1922, EJ270, SCA.

74. Dr Macfie to Mr Keeling, 23 April 1922, EJ36, SCA.

75. Frank Hodges to Eglantyne Jebb, 29 August 1922, EJ47, SCA.

76. Fight the Famine, Pamphlet, Buxton Papers, 3/1, LSE.

77. *Ruhr Bulletin*, various copies, Buxton papers 4/4, LSE; James, "State, Industry and Depression in Weimar Germany."

78. Fifty percent of German children were "physically and mentally stunted" by malnutrition. Report of the Mosley Commission, December 1923, EJ125, SC. In the *Ruhr Bulletin*, Oswald Mosley (working alongside Dorothy Buxton's husband) argued that the Ruhr invasion foreshadowed a return to the elitist "secret diplomacy" that had caused the Great War. Members of the Fight the Famine Council sought to "awaken public opinion" about the occupation of the Ruhr.

79. Report of the Mosley Commission, December 1923, EJ125; Report on the Activities of the Mosley Committee, 4 September 1924, EJ129, SCA; Correspondence of Cynthia Mosely with O. Mosley, January 1924, Mosely papers, XOMN/A/2, University of Birmingham.

80. The emergence of a "new international" community in Geneva is examined in Clavin, *Securing the World Economy*; Sluga, *Internationalism in the Age of Nationalism*, 56–65. See also Memorandum on the Objects of the Central Save the Children Union at Geneva, 1920, 92.3.2 AUIPE.

81. Minutes of the Meeting of the Council of the LRCS, 1920, Opening session, 2 March 1919, Box A0800.1 Reports, Federation of Red Cross Societies Archives (FRSA), Geneva. Henderson to Morris, 11 April 1921, Folder 8, "Cannes Conference," Box A0806, FRSA. It had briefly appeared that the LCRS would lend its endorsement to the SCIU, but it reneged in favor of promoting its own child welfare work, Jebb to S. Ferriere, marked "extremely confidential," 22 June 1921, 92.33.56, AIUPE.

82. Note received from Miss Klereck of the Swedish Committee, 16 December 1920, EJ113, SCA.

83. Herren, "Gender and International Relations through the Lens of the League of Nations (1919–1945)"; Beers, "Advocating for a Feminist Internationalism between the Wars."

84. Save the Children Fund, F/Delta 225/1, Dossiers Duchêne, Bibliothèque Documentation Internationale Contemporaine (BDIC), Paris; Rapport de l'exercice du CFSE en 1920 par Gabrielle Duchêne, F/Delta 227/1, Dossiers Duchêne, BDIC.

85. "Origins," Department of Publicity and Publication, March 1920, 4, Box 1, League of Red Cross Archives, Geneva; *Revue International de la Croix Rouge*, 15 February 1921. In this way, the Fund's work followed David Mitrany's theory of "functionalist internationalism": the belief that, when nations cooperated on bureaucratic or technical problems, they would be more likely to find agreement on more controversial, diplomatic matters. Mitrany, *A Working Peace System*. See also Pedersen, *The Guardians*, 9.

86. Memorandum on the relationship between the British SCF and the Union Internationale de Secours aux Enfants, 1920, 93.2.26, AUIPE.

87. Ibid.

88. Ibid.

89. Memorandum on the Objects of the Central Save the Children Union at Geneva, 1920, 92.3.2 AUIPE.

90. Seventeenth Report of the Emery and War Victims Relief Committee of the Society of Friends, 1 April 1920 to 31 March 1921, FHL.

91. Memorandum concernant l'UISE, c. 1930, 3, AUIPE.

92. IWRF First Appeal, March 1920, Beveridge 7/90, LSE; "What Is the Imperial War Relief Fund?" Appeal Leaflet, DF1004/746, Natural History Museum Archives. For a full discussion of the relationship between the British humanitarian movement and efforts in the British dominions, see Baughan, "The Imperial War Relief Fund and the All British Appeal."

93. Memorandum on the relationship between the British SCF and the Union Internationale de Secours aux Enfants, 1920, 93.2.26, AUIPE. This was a common trope in British internationalist and humanitarian discourse. See Baughan, *Every Citizen*.

94. Memorandum on the Objects of the Central Save the Children Union at Geneva, 1920, 92.3.2 AUIPE.

95. Fisher, *The Famine in Soviet Russia, 1919–1923*, 20–34.

96. Hands off Russia Leaflet 1921, BL. On the British left and Soviet Russia see Wright, *Iron Curtain*, 131–91; Ward, *The Red Flag and the Union Jack*, 126–60; Howell, *MacDonald's Party*, 112–18.

97. D. Buxton, various correspondences with E. D. Morel and Hands off Russia Committee, Buxton Papers 3/3, LSE; De Bunsen, *Charles Roden Buxton*,77.

98. Relief was also provided by a joint commission between the ICRC and the League of Red Cross Societies led by Fritdojf Nansen, the League of Nations High Commissioner for the Russian Famine.

99. D. Buxton, personal annotations c. 1921, Dorothy Frances Buxton papers (DBP), SCA.

100. "Save the Children Fund," *Daily Express*, 6 March 1922.

101. "Ought We to Do It?," *Our Own Gazette*, May 1922, 15.

102. "Russia's Hungry Children, *The Record of the Save the Children Fund*, December 1921; E. Jebb to R. E. Blumenfeld, 14 February 1922, EJ197, SCA.

103. D. Buxton, speech notes for the Hornsey Women's Labour Club, Autumn 1921 DBP, SCA.

104. D. Buxton, speech notes for various meetings, c.1921 DB, SCA; E. Jebb to D. Buxton, 4 September 1921, Buxton Family Papers, Dorset; D. Buxton, draft letter to the Manchester Guardian, 1921, DBP, SCA; D. Buxton, correspondence with E. D. Morel and Hands off Russia Committee, Buxton papers, LSE.

105. D. Buxton, speech notes for the Hornsey Women's Labour Club, Autumn 1921 DBP, SCA.

106. Mosa Anderson papers, SCA; D. Buxton, draft speech, 1921 to Horsley Labour Women's Group DB, SCA; D. Buxton, draft letter to *Manchester Guardian*, November 1921, DB, SCA.

107. EB interview with Ben Buxton, family historian and grandson of Dorothy Buxton, 5 October 2010, Dorset.

108. "Save the Children of Russia," *The Record*, September 1921.

109. L. Webster, Report on SCF famine relief, August 1923, EJ203, SCA.

110. On the emergence of child nutritional studies after World War One see Wagner, *Clemens von Pirquet*, 150; Weindling, "The Role of International Organisations in Setting Nutritional Standards in the 1920s and 1930s"; Rooke and Snell, "'Uncramping Child Life.'"

111. Lord Weardale to E. Frick, 8 December 1921, 92.18.1, AIUPE.

112. On this culture, see Patenaude, *The Big Show in Bololand*.

113. Buxton, *The White Flame*, 47; Lord Weardale to E. Frick, 8 December 1921, 92.18.1, AIUPE.

114. E. Fuller to "Savinifana" (the telegram address of the SCF), telegram, EJ203, SCA.

115. Gorvin to L. Webster, Moscow, 5 January1922, 92.31.5, AIUPE.

116. G. Vanchetz of the CISR to S. Ferriere, 22 September 1922, 92.31.5, AIUPE.

117. "The SCF conveys a message of thanks to the UISE," 2 February 1922, 92.31.5, AIUPE; E. Jebb, notes on famine relief efforts, May 1922 UISE 92.33.56, AIUPE.

118. The division of responsibility between European and American agencies had been meticulously negotiated. Resolutions were passed at the conference held on Russian Relief in Geneva, 15–16 August 1921, EJ265, SCA. See also Irwin, *Making the World Safe*, 141–66.

119. Irwin, *Making the World Safe*, 141–66; Patenaude, *The Big Show in Bololand*.

120. E. Jebb, notes on a meeting held between the SCF, GB, RC, and the IWRF, 14 July 1921, UISE, 92.33.56, AIUPE; C. Quinn, ARA note on the activities of the Save the Children Fund in Russia 11 March 1922, ARA Europe, box 87, file 1, HIA.

121. S. Ferrière to E. Jebb, 27 October 1919, 92.33.56, AIUPE; E. Jebb to SF, 3 May 1921 marked "private, the future of the union" 92.33.56, AIUPE.

122. First Meeting of the Societies Comprising the ABA for Germany, December 1923, EJ131, SCA.

123. Ibid.

124. Baughan, "The Imperial War Relief Fund and the All British Appeal.

125. Editorial, *Daily Express*, 24 November 1921; "Clever and Humorous Pictures by C. de Candole," c. 1925," EJ 299, SCA.

126. *The Record*, April 1920.

127. E. Jebb, Historical Notes on the Russian Famine, 1923, EJ203, SCA.

128. "Seeing Is Believing," *The Record*, January 1922.

129. On the use of film in this era by humanitarian organizations, see Tusan, "Genocide, Famine and Refugees on Film."

130. L. Weber-Bauler, *Feuilles de Propagande*, March 1920, UISE, 92.2.6, AUIPE.

131. Rapport de Mlle. Ferrière sur son voyage en Russie, R1754 47/25194/21268, LNA.

132. Ibid.

133. Famine Photo cards, 92.21.7, AUIPE; on this phenomenon in the Victorian era see Koven, *Slumming*, 88–93; Fehrenbach, "Children and Other Civilians," 177. On more recent NGO appeals, see Briggs, "Mother, Child, Race, Nation"; Wells, "Child Saving or Child Rights."

134. "Co-operation, True and False," *The Record*, October 1921; "Russian Famine," *Manchester Guardian*, 19 September 1921.

135. Save the Children Fund appeals: *Times*, 26 August, 9 September 1921; *Manchester Guardian*, 13 April 1922.

136. Abolitionist narratives often emphasized the pain of enslaved mothers and the separation of families; see Spillers, "Mama's Baby, Papa's Maybe."

137. "Real Life in Russia," *The Record*, December 1921.

138. "Russia," *The Record*, 15 December 1922.

139. "Russia," *The Record*, 15 November 1921.

140. Kelleher, *The Feminization of Famine.*

141. Gavitt "Charity and State Building in Cinquecento Florence."

142. Buekens and Humblet, "A 15th Century 'Bambino.'"

143. "Operation Stork" HQ Military Government Hannover Region, 31 January 1946, FO 1010/96, British National Archives (BNA).

144. Irwin, *Making the World Safe*, 141–66; Tusan, "Genocide, Famine and Refugees on Film."

145. "Russia," *The Record*, November 1921.

146. Instructions les délègués du Comité International de la Croix-Rouge concernant les renseignements utiles à la propagande de l'Union Internationale de Secours aux Enfants, 1921, 92.2,71, AUIPE

147. Fehrenbach, "Children and Other Civilians."

148. SCF Executive Council, 19 August 1921, SCA.

149. Meeting of the SCF, British Red Cross and the Imperial War Relief Fund, 14 July 1921, 92.33.56, AUIPE.

150. Editorial, *Headway, The Monthly Journal of the League of Nations Union*, May 1923.

151. Mandler, *The English National Character*.

152. Kent, "The Politics of Sexual Difference"; Light, *Forever England*.

153. McCarthy, "The League of Nations, Public Ritual and National Identity in Britain, c. 1919–56"; Trentmann, "After the Nation-State."

154. Yearwood, *Guarantee of Peace*.

155. Monie, *Toc-H Under Weigh*; McCarthy, "Parties, Voluntary Associations, and Democratic Politics in Interwar Britain."

156. McCarthy, *The British People and the League of Nations*.

157. WILPF Executive Committee Minutes, 6 December 1919, WILPF 5/1, LSE.

158. L. Weber-Bauler, *Feuilles de Propagande*, March 1920, UISE, 92.2.6, AUIPE.

159. "The Most Terrible Devastation," *Observer*, 28 August 1921; "In a Russian Graveyard," *Lancashire Evening Post*, 11 November 1921; "Russian Famine," *Yorkshire Post*; "Two Million Lives Hang in the Balance," *Observer*, 19 March 1922.

160. Kelly, *British Humanitarian Activity in Russia, 1890–1923*.

161. Ibid.

162. House of Commons Debate, 17 March 1922, volume 151, columns 2545–626.

163. To the Chancellor of the Exchequer (undated c. November 1921), T161/164 15175/1, NA; G. Barton to Montgomery, 16 December 1921, T161/164 15175/1, TNA.

164. L. B. Golden to E. Clouzot, 8 March 1921, 92.31.4, AUIPE.

165. *Economic Conditions in Central Europe*, a report presented to HM Government by William Goode, 1920; Bowden and Higgins, "British Industry in the Interwar Years."

166. "The Save the Children Fund and the Daily Express," *The Record*, 1 October 1921.

167. Editorial, *Daily Express*, 6 December 1921.

168. "Cheap Publicity," *The Record*, 15 November 1921.

169. E. Jebb to R. E. Blumenfeld, 14 February 1922, EJ197, SCA.

170. Ibid.

171. "Russia," *The Record*, 1 November 1921; *The Record*, 15 November 1921; *The Record*, 1 January 1922.

172. E. Jebb, Historical Notes on the Russian Famine, 1923, EJ203, SCA.

CHAPTER 2. THE GENEVA DECLARATION OF THE RIGHTS
OF THE CHILD AND STATELESS CHILDREN

1. Fuller, *The Rights of the Child*, 35.

2. "Constantinople," *Bulletin of the Save the Children International Union*, January 1924; B SCIU, November 1924, 591, LC. On the question of refugees and

human rights, see Arendt, *The Origins of Totalitarianism*; Oman, "Hannah Arendt's 'Right to Have Rights.'"

3. E. Jebb, "The World Policy of the Save the Children Fund," *The World's Children*, May 1934. Written in 1928, this was reprinted after Jebb's death in 1934.

4. "A Retrospect and Appeal," *The World's Children*, Third Quarter, 1922. On the refugee crisis in the interwar Near East, see Gatrell and Zhvanko, *Europe on the Move*; Watenpaugh, *Bread from Stones*; Tusan, *Smyrna's Ashes*; Frank and Reinisch, "Introduction: Refugees and the Nation-State in Europe, 1919–59."

5. "A Retrospect and Appeal," *The World's Children*, Third Quarter, 1922.

6. Skran, *Refugees in Interwar Europe*; Marrus, *The Unwanted*; Siegelberg, *Statelessness*.

7. Sallinen, "Intergovernmental Advocates of Refugees"; Tusan, *Smyrna's Ashes*,164–70.

8. Long, "Early Repatriation Policy."

9. M. Maundsly to D. Buxton, 20 February 1920, EJ203, SCA. On Russian exiled voluntary organizations see Gleason, "The All-Russian Union of Towns."

10. D. Buxton, various correspondence with E. D. Morel and Hands off Russia Committee, Buxton Papers 3/3, LSE.

11. Weardale claimed that "the true way to fight Bolshevism is through a policy of friendliness to the Russian people as a whole." He hoped that the people of Russia would form a government "free of the impossible vices of Bolshevism. . . . The Jewish riff-raff in Russia, and indeed over the whole world, are the instigators of the Bolshevist Movement." Weardale/Butler correspondence, c. 1921 (undated), Special Collections, SCA.

12. "Real Life in Russia," *The World's Children*, November 1921.

13. Minutes of Conference on the plight of Russian refugee children held in London, 17–18 March 1921, with the ICRC, the ARA and the ARC, SCF and SCIU, EJ205, SCA; copy of a letter from Gustav Ador to the president of the LON, 20 February 1921, EJ205, SCA; L. Golden to J. E. Drummond1925, 92.33.39, AUIPE.

14. Proceedings of the Conference on Russian Refugees convened by the League of Nations, comprising delegates from interested member states, the ICRC, SCIU and LRCS, Geneva, 22–24 August 1921, R1721/ 13562, LNA.

15. E. Jebb to D. Buxton, 1 June 1920, Jebb family papers (JFP), Shropshire.

16. Proceedings of the Conference on Russian Refugees, Geneva, 22–24 August 1921, R1721/ 13562, LNA.

17. Ibid.

18. "America Aids Constantinople," *Baltimore Sun*, 12 June 1921; "Notes from the Foreign Lands," *The Record*, October 1920.

19. "The situation of Russian refugee children at the end of the 1920s—various subsidized organisations report to the SCF," 92.31.14, AUIPE.

20. Miss Houghton's Correspondence & Reports: 19 January 1921 to 16 October 1922, EJ32, SCA.

21. E. Jebb, "The problem of Russian children in Constantinople," c. November 1921, EJ138, SCA.

22. Ibid.

23. Boucher, *Empire's Children*; Swain, "Child Rescue."

24. "News from the Relief Areas," *The World's Children*, April 1921.

25. Observations by the High Commissioner for the Relief of Russian Refugees and the International Russian Relief Committee on the Letter from the Minister of Foreign Affairs of the Czecho-Slovak republic, C114/ M68 1922, LOC.

26. Ibid.; Les réfugiés russes en Tchécoslovaquie: Rapport du Dr. Girsa sur la situation de réfugiés russes et les mesures prises en leur faveur, 1921, R1724/45/16011/13955, LNA.

27. Mackenzie to Gehri, 4 December 1921, 92.31.4, AUIPE.

28. Ibid. These children were originally intended to be part of an internal mass relocation scheme, moving from the famine-stricken Saratov province to elsewhere in Russia, but hungry children were rejected by many cities. Czechoslovakia was a last resort. Ball, *And Now My Soul Is Hardened*, 71–79.

29. "News from Relief Areas," *The World's Children*, March 1922.

30. "News from the Relief Areas," *The World's Children*, November 1921.

31. Jebb, "The World Policy of the Save the Children Fund."

32. Chinyaeva, *Russians outside Russia*, 20–24; The All-Russian Union of Zemstvos, Russian Refugee Children in Europe, 1927, 92.31.4, AUIPE.

33. The SCF framed its work in a number of Balkan and Baltic states as "nation-building." Lady Muriel Paget's Mission to Czechoslovakia: Accounts, 19 November 1919–12 November 1921, EJ91, SCA; Tributes to SCF from Jan Masaryk, Czech Ambassador, c. 1922, EJ283, SCA. On the connection between children and nation building see also Zahra, *Kidnapped Souls*.

34. Conférence des organisations volontaires pour les réfugiés russes, 24 Novembre 1921, file 87, box 6, "SDN," ACICR.

35. M. Gehri to F. Nansen, 25 October 1925, R1719/17080, LNA. On refugee children from Saratov see also file R1719/17823, LNA.

36. T. Whittemore to the Boston Committee for Russian Refugees, 20 December 1921, Box 23, Bakhmeteff Archive, Columbia University Special Collections (CUSC); Minutes of a meeting between the SCF, All British Appeal, American Red Cross and Russian Relief Association, 16 December 1921, Box 23, Bakhmeteff Archive, CUSC.

37. Petruševa, "Le soutien du zemgor aux écoles de la diaspora"; Nicolas, "Le CICR au secours des réfugiés russes 1919–1939"; White, "The Struggle against Denationalisation in Europe."

38. L. Brunel to de Feldmann, 24 February 1922, SCIU, file "Réfugiés Bulgarie," box 3, ACICR.

39. Efron, *No Love without Poetry*, 145.

40. Svedeniya o deyatel'nosti Predstavitel'stva Vserossiiskago Soyuza Gorodov v Korolevstve SHS v dele pomoshci russkim detyam No. 15427, 30 October 1920 (Hoover, Collections, Paleologue 005/10.), HIA. See also Miroslav, "Accelerated Maturity."

41. Russian Zemstvos and Towns Relief Committee, *The Children of Russian Refugees in Western Europe* (Paris: Russian Zemstvos, 1921); White, "The Struggle against Denationalisation."

42. Svedeniya o deyatel'nosti Predstavitel'stva Vserossiiskago Soyuza. See also Miroslav, "Accelerated Maturity."

43. Aleksandr Dehterev, S det'mi emigracii 1920–1930 gody (Shumen. 1931), in Miroslav, "Accelerated Maturity." On Russian émigrés in Czechoslovakia, see Chinyaeva, *Russians outside Russia.*

44. Miroslav, "Accelerated Maturity."

45. Constantinople," *Bulletin of the Save the Children International Union,* January 1924.

46. H. Campain to Maundsly, 2 November 1922, EJ142, SCA; SCF to Baker, 20 January 1923, R1764/26559, LNA; L. B. Golden to W. Kennedy, 21 March 1924; E. Cluzot and C. F. de Geer to the Balfour, 2 December 1924, 92.33.29, AUIPE; SCF Report on the problem of Russian children in Constantinople, addressed to LNHRC, 31 January 1924, EJ138, SCA.

47. SCF Report on the problem of Russian children in Constantinople. For similar schemes established by the Young Women's Christian Association, see "Russian Women in Constantinople," 1922, R1738/17871 and R1738/2286, LNA.

48. Advertisements: *Manchester Guardian,* 3 July 1925; *Christian Science Monitor,* 8 June 1925.

49. Maltz, *British Aestheticism and the Urban Working Classes.*

50. SCF Report on the problem of Russian children in Constantinople, addressed to LNHRC, 31 March 1924, EJ138, SCA.

51. Ibid.

52. "Salonika," *Boston Daily Globe,* 14 January 1923.

53. SCF Executive Council, London, June 1922, SCA.

54. Fielden to Baker, 2 December 1922, R1764/ 24954, LNA.

55. Simpson, "The Work of the Greek Refugee Settlement Commission"; League of Nations, *The Settlement of Bulgarian Refugees: Scheme for an International Loan* (Geneva, 1926), LNA.

56. Proctor to Johnson, 12 April 1924, R1764/26559, LNA.

57. Ibid. Echoing these concerns, see Report by Nansen of the Western Thrace Refugee Settlement to the Council of the League of Nations, 19 April 1923, R1762/4954, LNA; Childs to Johnson, 4 April 1924 R1764/28828, LNA; Report sent to Mr Johnson, 3 December 1923, R1764/32571, LNA.

58. Proctor to Baker, relaying conversations with Alden, 20 January 1923 R1764/26559, LNA; Alden to Nansen, 30 August 1923, R1764/26559, LNA; Telegram to Nansen, signed by L.B. Golden, 31 March 1924, 92.31.4, AUIPE.

59. Proctor to Baker, relaying conversations with Alden, 20 January 1923, R1764/26559; Alden to Nansen, 30 August 1923, R1764/26559, LNA; Alden et al., "Unemployment,"; "Interview with Percy Alden on the Condition of Greek Refugees," *Daily Chronicle,* 19 February 1925.

60. Readman, "The Place of the Past in English Culture c.1890–1914."

61. Joffe, "Vocational Training of Jews in Europe"; Noria, "Two Years with Displaced Persons," US Zone, 1948, Folder 31, Margaret Eleanor Fait Papers, 1945–1946, Hoover Institute Library, Stanford, CA.

62. The Save the Children Fund in Bulgaria, June 1925; Notes on Atolovo, *The World's Children*, April 1927.

63. SCF Executive Council, September 1920, SCA; "A Straight Talk on an Urgent Matter," IWRF leaflet, Beveridge papers, 7/90, LSE.

64. E. Jebb, Report for the SCIU on the first meeting of the League of Nations Committee for Child Welfare, 1925, R3.3, AIUPE.

65. Ibid.

66. *The Friend*, 4 April 1930, A. Ruth Fry Papers, box I, Swathmore College Peace Collection.

67. Minutes of the First Assembly of the League of Nations; Minutes of the Executive Council of SCIU, 8 December 1920, AUIPE.

68. *Bulletin de l'Union International de Secours aux Enfants*, 10 June 1921, AUIPE.

69. Minutes of the Executive Committee of the SCIU, 25 November 1920, AUIPE.

70. Jane Addams, President of WILPF, Conference on the International Aspects of Child Welfare Work, "Child Welfare etc., to June 30th, 1924," 1919–1946, S/152/7, LNA.

71. Minutes of the Executive Committee of the SCIU, 25 November 1920, AUIPE.

72. Miss Courtney, "Child Welfare etc.," 30 June 1924, S152/7, LNA; Marshall, "The Construction of the Child as an Object of International Relations"

73. Buxton and Buxton, *The White Flame*, 6; Mahood, *Feminism and Voluntary Action*, 194.

74. Geneva Declaration of the Rights of the Child, Adopted 26 September 1924, League of Nations (accessed at UN Documents Gathering a body of global agreements, http://www.un-documents.net/gdrc1924.htm, 6 May 2020).

75. Draft of the Children's Charter produced by the International Council of Women, 1922, EJ285, SCA.

76. E. Jebb to S. Ferrière, 2 February 1924, 92.33.57, AUIPE.

77. Cabanes, *The Great War and the Origins of Humanitarianism, 1918–1924*; Marshall, "The Construction of the Child"; Metzger, "Towards an International Human Rights Regime during the Inter-War Years."

78. "A Great British Philanthropy," *The World's Children*, April 1923; The Declaration of Geneva, *The World's Children*, July 1923.

79. SCIU executive council, 1 March 1923, AUIPE.

80. Ibid.

81. *Bulletin de l'Union Internationale de Secours aux Enfance*, 1.2, May 1923; *Bulletin*, 1.5 January 1924; *Bulletin*, 2.3, January 1925. All accessed at the Library of Congress (LOC).

82. Magna Carta translates as "big charter," though to Jebb it seems to have figured as a declaration of rights rather than, in fact, a charter.

83. Freeden, *Liberal Languages*.

84. *Bulletin de l'Union Internationale de Secours aux Enfance*, 2.10. May 1925.

85. E. Jebb, "Notes on the declaration," c. 1924, Jebb Family Papers, Shropshire.

86. "International Work for Children," *The World's Children*, November 1926.

87. J. E. Vajkai to E. Jebb, 22 October 1924, EJ269, SCA.

88. *Salvage in Austria*, Save the Children Fund Film, 1922, British Film Institute Archives, London.

89. M. E. Durham to L. Golden, 25 May 1920, EJ220, SCA.

90. Blacker, "Maternity and Child Welfare Work and the Population Problem."

91. E. Jebb, "Notes on the Geneva Declaration as Applicable to England," EJ259, SCA.

92. Ibid.

93. A Child's Rights, *The World's Children*, October 1923, "The Rights of the Child," Child Rights in Britain, *The Word's Children*, September 1925. For discussions at the Child Welfare Council see "Training and Treatment of Mentally Deficient Children," Discussions at the Third Session of the Child Welfare Committee, May 1927, R700/59164/50610, LNA; "Treatment and Training of the Feeble Minded Child," Liaison Sub-committee, Advisory Commission for the Protection and Welfare of Young People, August 1926, R700/52130/50610, LNA.

94. Denise Riley articulates this distinction between biological and social citizenship in *War in the Nursery*, 1–5.

95. E. Jebb, "Save the Child, A Posthumous Essay," 92.33.59, AUIPE.

96. Fuller, *The International Year Book of Child Care and Protection*, 12.

97. Ibid., 1–15.

98. Ibid., 12.

99. *Bulletin de l'Union Internationale de Secours aux Enfance*, 5.13, July 1924.

100. Susan Pedersen terms this "remarkable humanitarian entrepreneurialism" in "Back to the League of Nations."

101. Report of the fifth child welfare committee to the sixth assembly, 22 September 1925, R 682/ 46230, LNA.

102. Resolutions adopted by the Council regarding the constitution of the advisory committee of the Traffic of Women and the Protection of Children, R680/30401, LNA; Report of the fifth child welfare committee to the sixth assembly, 22 September 1925, R682/ 46230, LNA.

103. L. B. Golden to the Secretary General of the League of Nations, 17 May 1921, 92.33.39, AUIPE.

104. Thirteenth Session of the Council of the League of Nations, Minutes of the Eighth Meeting, 30 September 1924, R1763/39533, LNA; Nansen to Goulkevitch, 9 April 1924, SCIU 92.31.4, AUIPE; Nansen Memorandum, 22 August 1924 C 45/38178/12319, LNA.

105. F. Nansen, Report to the Assembly of the League of Nations, 17 November 1922, R1672/247722, LNA.

106. Ibid.

107. Meeting between the ICRC and LNHCR, 26 February 1923, R1672/247722, LNA.

108. Rev. H. Harcourt of the Near East Relief Fund, "Report on Work with Armenian Children," *The World's Children*, January 1924. This was remarkably similar to Turkish genocide/assimilation strategies for dealing with Armenian women: see Watenpaugh, "The League of Nations' Rescue of Armenian Genocide Survivors."

109. J. Mackenzie, Recommendations, 1 May 1925, R3.7, AIUPE. See also E. Jebb, "What the League of Nations Can Do for Children," *The World's Children*, June 1927; E. Jebb, "The League and the Child," *The World's Children*, June 1925.

110. Convention International concernent le repatriasment de mineurs abandonnés et delinquents, 17 September 1923, R360/30929, LNA.

111. Child Welfare Committee, minutes of the Second Session, 25 April 1926 R681/50519, LNA; E. Jebb, Report for the SCUI on the first meeting of the League of Nations Committee for Child Welfare, 1925, R3.3, AIUPE; Private Memo, 6 May 1925, R3.7, AIUPE.

112. Legal Subcommittee of the Child Welfare Committee, Draft international convention of the assistance or repatriation of foreign children, June 1926, R694/52256, LNA.

113. Ibid.

114. Memorandum concerning the assistance and repatriation of foreign children who are abandoned, neglected or delinquent, June 1926, R694/50490, LNA

115. Convention International concernent le repatriasment de mineurs abandonnés et delinquents, 17 September 1923, R360/30929, LNA.

116. Ibid.

117. Discussions regarding the repatriation of abandoned, neglected or delinquent children of foreign nationality, Minutes of the Second Session of League of Nations Child Welfare Committee, June 1925, R682/50519, LNA; Memorandum concerning assistance or repatriation of children who are abandoned, neglected or delinquent, 1926, R964/50490, LNA; Legal subcommittee of the Child Welfare Committee: draft of the international convention for the repatriation or assistance of foreign children, June 1926, R694/52256, LNA; Discussions at the Fifth Session of the Child Welfare Committee, 19 April 1929, subcommittee on Child Refugees regarding Child Assistance or Repatriation Convention, R3093/11457, LNA; Memorandum of the General Secretary of the League of Nations, 30 July 1930, R3094/13608, LNA.

118. Memorandum concerning the assistance and repatriation of foreign children who are abandoned, neglected or delinquent, June 1926, R694/50490, LNA.

119. On children and the flexibility of nationality, see Zahra, *Kidnapped Souls*.

120. Sous-comité pour l'*étude de la condition des enfants réfugiés, 8 Octobre 1929,* AUIPE. They clashed with Russian refugee organizations in this respect. See News of the Russian Zemztovs and Towns Committee, 1927, R1720/18837, LNA.

121. Mme Jecoline, "Committee for the Relief and Education of Russian Children," May 1925, Box 23, Bakhmeteff Archive, CUSC.

122. Boucher, *Empire's Children*.

123. Zahra, *Lost Children*.

124. The position of children without or with different or disputed nationality, appendix A R694/52256, LNA.

125. Child Welfare Committee, minutes of the Second Session, 25 April 1926 R681/50519, LNA.

126. "What the League of Nations Can Do for Children, *The World's Children*, June 1927.

127. Legal Subcommittee of the Child Welfare Committee: Draft of the international convention for the repatriation or assistance of foreign children, June 1926, R694/ 52256, LNA; Discussions at the Fifth Session of the Child Welfare Committee, 19 April 1929, Subcommittee on Child Refugees regarding Child Assistance or Repatriation Convention, R3093/11457, LNA; Memorandum of the General Secretary of the League of Nations, 30 July 1930, R3094/13608, LNA.

128. Report on the work of the Seventh Session of the Child Welfare Committee, 14–30 April 1931, R3905/14608, LNA.

129. Arendt, *The Origins of Totalitarianism*.

CHAPTER 3. EMPIRE, HUMANITARIANISM, AND THE AFRICAN CHILD

1. Participants at the Conference on the African Child during a social occasion at Le Reposoir, Archives de l'Union Internationale de Protection de l'Enfance, Archives d'État de Geneve, 92.4.11

2. Sharp, *The African Child*, 3.

3. Manela, *The Wilsonian Moment*.

4. Hobson, *Imperialism: A study*. On how far Hobson can be considered "anti-colonial," see Cleays, *Imperial Sceptics*, 236–71.

5. Grant, "Christian Critics of Empire: Missionaries, lantern lectures, and the Congo reform campaign in Britain"; Krebs, "The Last of the Gentleman's Wars."

6. Porter, *Missionaries versus Empire*, 1–14; Grant, *A Civilised Savagery*; Everill, "Bridgeheads of Empire?"

7. On Fabianism and imperialism, see Riley, "Monstrous Predatory Vampires and Beneficent Fairy-Godmothers, 83–88; Hinden, "Economic Plans and Problems in the British Colonies"; Schneider, "Fabians and the Utilitarian Idea of Empire."

8. de Bunsen, *Charles Roden Buxton*.

9. Covenant of the League of Nations, Article 22.

10. On the Mandates Commission, see Pedersen, *The Guardians*; Callahan, *A Sacred Trust*; Callahan, *Mandates and Empire*; Pedersen, "The Meaning of the Mandates System"; Wheatley, "Mandatory Interpretation."

11. Pedersen, *The Guardians*, 4–13.

12. Buxton, *The Race Problem in Africa*, 45–58.

13. Buxton, *The Race Problem*, 1–10; see also Kelemen, "Modernising Colonialism," 227–28.

14. Lugard, *The Dual Mandate in British Tropical Africa*.

15. Pedersen, *The Guardians*, 108–12.

16. Howe, "Labour and International Affairs."

17. *The World's Children*, March 1935.

18. Charles Roden Buxton, *Secret Diplomacy*, Union of Democratic Control Series, No. 3, (London 1917); Ballinger to C. Roden Buxton, on the UDC, the Buxtons and Empire, 9 July 1930, D2.I.4.8, Ballinger Papers, UCT. See also John Harris, "The Mandatory System after Five Years Working," Reel 16, the Antislavery International Microfilm Collection, Part 2.

19. Buxton, *The Race Problem*, 45–58.

20. Forclaz, *Humanitarian Imperialism*, 50–55.

21. Pedersen, "The Maternalist Moment in the British Colonial Policy"; Pedersen, "National Bodies, Unspeakable Acts."

22. Pedersen, "National Bodies, Unspeakable Acts."

23. Fuller, "L'enfance non-européene," 1928, M.8.1; AUIPE. On the relative stability at the end of the 1920s, see O'Cohrs, *The Unfinished Peace after World War I*, 287–96.

24. "Em" to Mabel Few, 21 December 1928, general collection (uncataloged), SCA.

25. de Bunsen, *The Soul of a Turk*.

26. "The African Child," *The World's Children*, March 1931.

27. W. MacKenzie to Victoria de Bunsen, 1 November 1930, Interim report on the steps taken and the arrangements in connection with the international Conference on African Children, 92.19.25, AUIPE.

28. Notes on the conclusions of the Conference—undated, 92.4.11, AUIPE. The SCF shared this view with the ILO. See Mgr. De Guébriant, Supérieur Missions étrangères de Paris, and H. A. Grimshaw of the ILO, referenced in pamphlet L'enfance non-européenne, 1928, 12–13, 25–26, M.8.1., AUPIE.

29. The literature on missionaries and empire is vast. See for example Porter, *Missionaries versus Empire*, 1–14; Grant, *Civilised Savagery*; Everill, "Bridgeheads of Empire?"

30. Sharp, *The African Child*, 52.

31. Resolutions 23 and 24, in the Lambeth Conference resolutions from 1930, Anglican Consultative Council, 2005, accessed on 1 January 2019 at https://www.anglicancommunion.org/media/127734/1930.pdf.

32. Loss, "The Institutional Afterlife of Christian England."

33. For various examples, see *The World's Children*, October 1928, November 1929, April 1930, September 1930, March 1931, July 1932, January 1934.

34. Notes on the conclusions of the Conference—undated general correspondence re non-European children, 92.4.11, AUIPE.

35. Ibid.

36. Diaries of Sir Albert Ruskin Cook (1870–1951), 22 May 1931, Box 4, Contemporary Medical Archive Center, Wellcome Institute, London.

37. Introductory Speech, Proceedings of the International Conference on the African Child, 22–25 June 1931 (hereafter: Proceedings), 1, 92.4.9, AUIPE.

38. Cox, "From Empire of Christ to the Third World."

39. Introductory Speeches, 22 June 1931, Proceedings.

40. Notes on the conclusions of the Conference, undated general correspondence re non-European children, 92.4.11, AUIPE.

41. Draft of a speech approved by Drummond, 22 June 1931, 94.4.9, AUIPE.

42. Sharp, The African Child, 98–107.

43. Interim report on the steps taken and the arrangements in connection with the international Conference on Africa Children, 92.19.25, AUIPE.

44. Sharp, The African Child, 5.

45. Fuller, The International Handbook of Child Care and Protection, 32.

46. Sharp, The African Child, 14.

47. Ibid., v–vi.

48. Correspondence with Lord Passfield, June 1931, 94.4.9, AUIPE. Kelemen, "Planning for Africa."

49. Fourth Session, the general conditions of work for children and adolescents and the protection of children at work, 24 June 1931, Proceedings. See also Ame et al., Children's Rights in Ghana, 23.

50. Sharp, The African Child, 56.

51. Dominque Marshall examines the position of missionaries at the 1931 conference in "Children's Rights in Imperial Political Cultures."

52. Second Session, Still Birth and Infant Mortality, 22 June 1931, Proceedings.

53. Dr. Mary Blacklock, report on Afrique Occidentale/West Africa 14-16, 94.2.10, AUIPE.

54. Dora Earthy, Third Session, stillbirth and infant mortality from the social and economic point of view, 23 June 1931.

55. E. Torday, Annex 1, Proceedings.

56. Third Session, still birth and infant mortality from the social and economic point of view, 23 June 1931, Proceedings.

57. Sixth Session, Examination of conclusions, 25 June 1931, Proceedings.

58. L. B. Golden to F. Small, undated letter c. 1936, 92.19.12, AUIPE.

59. V. de Bunsen to F. Small, 20 May 1932, Victoria de Bunsen Correspondence. On colonial perceptions of African motherhood, see Allman, "Making Mothers"; Gaitskell, "'Getting Close to the Hearts of Mothers'"; Kanogo, "Mission Impact on Women in Colonial Kenya."

60. Lord Noel Buxton, Introduction, 22 June 1931, Proceedings.

61. See also George, Making Modern Girls.

62. Petersson, Willi Munzenberg, The League Against Imperialism, and the Comintern, 1925–1933 1:198–260; Hakim Adi, Pan-Africanism and Communism, 87–123.

63. Prashad, The Darker Nations, 21.

64. Adi, *Pan Africanism and Communism*, 38.

65. Matera, *Black London*; Goebel, *Anti-imperial Metropolis*, 116–48.

66. Father Joyeaux, Rapporteur for North Africa, Proceedings.

67. Father Guilicher, delegate for West Africa, Third Session, still birth and infant mortality form the social and economic point of view, 22 June 1931, Proceedings.

68. James W. Ford, "Imperialism Destroys the People of Africa," pamphlet, Harlem Section of the American Communist Party, Museum of African American History and Culture, Washington, DC.

69. Sharp, *The African Child*, 60; Cromwell, *An African Victorian Feminist*, 102–3.

70. H. Junod, opening remarks, Fourth Session, Education and the Preparation of Children for Life, 24 June 1931, Proceedings; Mandler, *Return from the Natives*, 4–10.

71. Sharp, *The African Child*, 9.

72. Sharp, 60. De Graft Johnson critiqued missionary educational practices in *Towards Nationhood in West Africa*, 42–50.

73. Fourth Session, the general conditions of work for children and adolescents and the protection of children at work, 24 June 1931, Proceedings.

74. Notes on the conclusions of the Conference—undated general correspondence re non-European children, 92.4.11, AUIPE.

75. Buxton, *The Race Problem*, 50.

76. Pennybacker, *From Scottsboro to Munich*, 20–37.

77. Ford, "Imperialism Destroys the People of Africa," 456

78. James W. Ford, "The Truth about the African Child," Material for the National Convention of the Communist Party of the United States of America, April 2–4, 1934.

79. Lucie Schmidt, "Note sur la conference internationale pour l'enfance Africaine, typed document, 2 July 1931, 2, 13, D600/406/9/2, Archives of the International Labour Office (AILO).

80. M. Sinanan, League of Coloured Peoples, British West Indies, Third Session, 23 June 1931, Proceedings.

81. Ford, "Imperialism Destroys the People of Africa."

82. Ibid.; Ford, "The Truth about the African Child.

83. Smyke, *Nigeria Union of Teachers*, xiv, 28–39. Israel Ransome Kuti was the father of afrobeat musician Fela Kuti, born in 1938.

84. Hunter, *An African Treasure*.

85. Kenyatta, *Facing Mount Kenya*, 126–27.

86. Most significantly, Pedersen, *The Guardians*, 394–407.

87. Fonds Commémoratif Eglantyne Jebb pour la protection de l'Enfance d'orgine non-européenne, de règlement et by-laws, c. 1930, 92.4.14, AUIPE. See also Child Protection Committee minutes, 10 August 1934, SCA; Child Protection Committee Minutes, 13 July 1937.

88. Waugh, *Scoop*, 14.

89. Forclaz, *Humanitarian Imperialism*, 139–45.

90. Buxton, *Slavery in Abyssinia: Address Given at Chatham House*; Buxton, "Slavery in Abyssinia," 698–709.

91. Burgwyn, *Italian Foreign Policy in the Interwar Period, 1918–1940*.

92. *Daily Mail*, August 26, 1935.

93. Forclaz, *Humanitarian Imperialism*, 176. On British reactions see McCarthy, *The British People and the League of Nations*, 212–42.

94. "Death of Mrs Lothian Small," *The World's Children*, December 1939.

95. L. B. Golden to F. Small, 19 February 1936, Small Correspondence (1935–36), uncataloged, AUIPE.

96. Padmore, *Pan-Africanism or Communism*, 145.

97. See Forclaz, *Humanitarian Imperialism*, 174.

98. An appeal for funding support from the International African Friends of Ethiopia, 1935; Trades Union Congress, MSS.292/963/2, University of Warwick; "African's Pride in Abyssinia," *Manchester Guardian*, 29 July 1935.

99. Rapport présenté en amharique à l'impératrice de l'Ethiopie par Mme Small délégué du UISE (traduction), Novembre 1935, 92.65.1, AUIPE.

100. Ibid.

101. Ibid.

102. Ibid. See also L. B. Golden to F. Small, 4 February 1936; Allman, "Making Mothers; Gaitskell, "Getting Close to the Hearts of Mothers."

103. L. B. Golden to F. Small, 92.65.1, AUIPE.

104. Ibid. See also Rapport présenté en amharique à l'impératrice de l'Ethiopie par Mme Small délégué du UISE (traduction), Novembre 1935, 92.65.1, AUIPE.

105. Rapports des délégués, No. 1, 14 November 1935, S. Brown to CICR, 92.65.1, AUIPE. On the use of gas, see Baudendistel, *Between Bombs and Good Intentions*, 56; Sbacchi, "Poison Gas and Atrocities in the Italo-Ethiopian War (1935–1936)."

106. L. B. Golden to F. Small, 4 February 1936.

107. "Death of Mrs Lothian Small," *The World's Children*, December 1939.

108. The survey had 11.6 million respondents, 38 percent of the adult population. McCarthy, *The British People and the League of Nations*.

109. Allain, "Slavery and the League of Nations."

110. UISE procès-verbal Comité executif, 1934–1937, 21 November 1935.

111. Internal memo 3 October 1936 on a meeting with Golden, 14 November 1935, CO 535/110/5, NA.

112. On colonial revisionism, see Pedersen, *Guardians*, 335–36.

113. N. Buxton, "What Norman Angell Forgets," typescript article for contemporary review about Germany's colonial claims, 2/6, ff. 88–91, 193, 5 February 1938, Rhodes House Library; Callahan, *A Sacred Trust*, 124; Pedersen, *Guardians*, 335–36.

114. Hogsbjerg, "C. L. R. James and Italy's Conquest of Abyssinia."

115. Winifred Holtby, *Mandoa Mandoa* (London, 1934), 121.

116. Brown, "Satire of Imperialism."

117. "Civilisation: Barbarism," *The World's Children*, January 1936.

1. Habe, *Tödlicher Friede*.

2. Clavin, *Securing the World Economy*, 267–95.

3. Ridell, *Labour in Crisis*.

4. Williamson, *National Crisis and National Government*.

5. Fuller, *An International Handbook on Child Welfare and Protection*.

6. "Great Britain and the Declaration of Geneva," *The World's Children*, April 1925.

7. "When Father Has No Work, *The World's Children*, November 1933; "The Health of an Elementary School Class," *The World's Children*, February 1934; "How Can You Change the North," *The World's Children*, July 1936.

8. "Our Greatest National Asset, Save the Children Nursery School Committee" (London, 1940), Bodleian Library, Oxford.

9. Vernon, *Hunger*, 118–34

10. See for example Gelderblom and Kok, *Urbanisation: South Africa's Challenge*, 1:i–iii; Gordon, "Dorothea Lange: The Photographer as Agricultural Sociologist,"

11. On improvements to provision before the 1930s, see Lewis, *The Politics of Motherhood*.

12. "Origins of the Nursery School Committee," 1943, SCF/A1221 (M8/3); SCA.

13. Beatrice Green, "Care for the Toddlers," *Labour Woman*, January 1927; Elizabeth Andrews, "The Need for a National Campaign for Nursery Schools," *Labour Woman*, January 1928; BACE 24/3, LSE.

14. Steedman. *Childhood, Culture, and Class in Britain*.

15. "Origins of the Nursery School Committee," 1943. M8/3, SCA.

16. For a detailed study of Save the Children's nurseries in the 1930s, see Gill and Leeworthy, "Moral Minefields.

17. "How Nursery Schools Save Child Life," *The World's Children*, July 1938.

18. Save the Children Fund, *Unemployment and the Child: An Enquiry* (London, 1933), 23.

19. E. Jebb, "The World Policy of the Save the Children Fund," *The World's Children*, May 1934. Written in 1928, this was reprinted after Jebb's death. Similar ideals underpinned other late nineteenth-century European educational traditions, in particular those of Maria Montessori. See also "Nursery Schools in the Special Areas," *The World's Children*, December 1937.

20. Our Greatest National Asset.

21. "Opening of a Nursey in Brynmawr," *Merthyr Express*, 19 May 1934, quoted in Gill and Leeworthy, "Moral Minefields, 225.

22. Ibid.

23. Ibid.

24. Ibid.

25. Ibid.

26. Historic notes on Nursery schools, 1943, M/8/1/1, SCA.

27. Lloyd, "'Emergency Nursery Schools.'"

28. Bondfield, *A Life's Work*; Abrams, *Freedom's Cause*, 223; Beers, *Red Ellen*, 133–64; Pedersen, *Eleanor Rathbone and the Politics of Conscience*, 219–40.

29. Worley, *Labour Inside the Gate*.

30. "Opening of a Nursey in Brynmawr."

31. This was suspended during the war, but later enshrined, again in part due to the lobbying of Save the Children, in the 1944 Education Act. On school meals and milk, see Vernon, "The Ethics of Hunger and the Assembly of Society."

32. April 1933, Accounts of the Save the Children Fund 1930–1940, Save the Children Head Offices, London.

33. SCF Executive Council, Thursday, 16 November, 1933.

34. On the place of children in European fascist societies, see Pine, *Education in Nazi Germany*; Weindling, "Fascism and Population in Comparative European Perspective"; Nash, "Pronatalism and Motherhood in Franco's Spain"; Bock, "Antinatalism, Maternity and Paternity in National Socialist Racism"; Hoffmann, "Mothers in the Motherland"; de Grazia, *How Fascism Ruled Women: Italy, 1922–1945*, 41–76, 116–65.

35. H. Watson to the General Secretary of the Duestche Zentrale, 17 March 1938, 92.19.2, AUIPE.

36. Aly, *Hitler's Beneficiaries*.

37. Aly, *Hitler's Beneficiaries*.

38. Pugh, *Hurrah for the Blackshirts!*.

39. Ceadel, *Semi-detached Idealists*; Mazower, "Minorities and the League of Nations in Interwar Europe."

40. Graves, *Good-Bye to All That*.

41. Ceadel, "The King and Country Debate, 1933."

42. McCarthy, *The British People and the League of Nations*.

43. Copsley, "'Every Time They Made a Communist, They Made a Fascist.'"

44. Herren, "Fascist Internationalism."

45. SCF Executive Council, 18 January 1945; Friedländer's dismissal from the Deutsche Zentrale für freie Jugendwohlfahrt,1933, Walter A. Friedländer Papers,4/1, 2.2, University of Albany; "Kinderhilfe, Internationale Vereinigung für, 1920–1938, Germany Deutsche Kongress-Zentrale records, Hoover Archives, Stanford, CA.

46. SCF Executive Council, 17 October 1935,

47. Memorandum on the Objects of the Central Save the Children Union at Geneva, 1920, 92.3.2 AUIPE.

48. The Save the Children Fund accepted Nazi categorizations and reproduced them in their publications. "The Modern Ishmael: The Tragedy of the Non-Aryan Child in Germany," *The World's Children*, November 1936.

49. Watson to the General Secretary of the Duestche Zentrale, 17 March 1938, 92.19.2, AUIPE.

50. SCF Executive Council, 3 October 1939.

51. Ibid.

52. Memorandum on the relationship between the SCF and the International Union, 1922, 92.3.26, AUIPE.

53. Note by the General Secretary, 27 February 1936, Children and War, miscellaneous notes, M13/14 SCA.

54. Alexander, "A Short History of International Humanitarian Law."

55. Golden drew especially of the ideas of a French military medic named Georges Saint-Paul, who had proposed special civilian zones, which he termed "Les Lieux de Genève." L. Golden, Les Lieux de Geneva, (Very Confidential), 23 June 1936, M13/14, SCA.

56. Ibid.

57. Special Meeting held at 20 Gordon Square, 19 March 1936, Strictly Confidential, M13/14 SCA.

58. If War Comes, Important Proposal at Red Cross Conference, Safety of Non-participants," 13 October 1936, M13/14, SCA; "Children in a Time of War, An Immunity Scheme," The World's Children, March 1938.

59. Steiner, Triumph of the Dark, 181.

60. Lord Noel-Buxton, president of the Save the Children Fund, "Neutrality of the Save the Children Fund," from an article in The British Weekly, reprinted in The World's Children, January 1937.

61. Buchanan, Britain and the Spanish Civil War, 93–120.

62. Bailkin, Unsettled, 16–21, 153, 167–70.

63. Stewart-Murray, Searchlight on Spain (Middlesex, 1938).

64. Buchanan, The Spanish Civil War and the British Labour Movement, 137; Pedersen, Eleanor Rathbone, 188.

65. Holloway, "Britain's Political Humanitarians."

66. Guerre Civil Espagnole: Demande d'aide à L'UISE (SCIU) de la Fédération des Sociétés des Amis de l'Ecole pour l'évacuation des colonies des enfants, 92.16, AUIPE. SCIU Executive Committee minutes, 21 September 1936.

67. SCIU Executive Committee minutes, 21 September 1936, annex, No. 9, Intervention en Espagne, 2, AUIPE.

68. "Fleeing Spain," The World's Children, November 1936.

69. Ibid.

70. Mitford, The Pursuit of Love; Orwell, Homage to Catalonia.

71. FSC Committee on Spain, minutes, 16 November 1936, no. 46, Friends House London.

72. Notes, rapports et voyages en Europe nationaliste et gouvernemental de Mme Frédérique Small et de Mlle Miette Pictet, Octobre 1936–Décembre 1937, 92.16.6, AUIPE.

73. A. Jacobs to Mackenzie and Small, 7 and 12 December 1936, FHL; A. Jacob to Small, 12 December 1936, FHL.

74. F. Small, "Mission en Espagne—Suite de journal," 27 November 1936, 92.16.6, AUIPE.

75. Ibid.

76. SCIU Executive Committee, minutes, 10 March 1937, AUIPE; Correspondence between M. Huici and Dr. Pictet, 10 February 1937, in Mme Small's report, 2 February 1937, 92.16.6, AUIPE.

77. Executive Committee minutes, 10 March 1937; "Intervention de l'UISE (SCIU) en Espagne," AUIPE.

78. Minutes of the NJC, 22 March 1937, quoted in Legarreta, *The Guernica Generation*, 101.

79. "Basque Children: A History of Case," 6 May 1937, TUC collection (TUC) 292/946/37/1, WUSC.

80. Memorandum, W. Citrine on Behalf of the Trade Union Congress, 4–6 May 1937 TUC/292/946/16a/39, WUSC.

81. "Basque Children: A History of Case."

82. Minutes of a Special meeting of the Executive Council to discuss proposed evacuation of children from Bilbao, 10 May 1937, M1/9, SCA.

83. "Basque Children: A History of Case."

84. Williams, "The Arrival of the Basque Children at the Port of Southampton." On children in the Basque camps, see Bailkin *Unsettled*, 16–21, 135, 153, 167–70.

85. Bulletin no. 11, National Joint Committee for Spanish Relief, TUC/292/946/39/1, WUSC.

86. Bulletin no. 7, National Joint Committee for Spanish Relief, TUC/292/946/39/99, WUSC.

87. Minutes of Executive Committee Meeting, Basque Children's Committee, 20 July 1937, TUC/292/946/39/67, WUSC.

88. Bulletin no. 8, National Joint Committee for Spanish Relief, TUC/292/946/39/1, WUSC.

89. Minutes of Executive Committee Meeting, Basque Children's Committee, 20 July 1937, TUC/292/946/39/67, WUSC.

90. Cloud, *The Basque Children in England*, 33–35.

91. Bailkin, *Unsettled*, 73–75.

92. Ibid., 40–43; Minutes of Executive Committee Meeting, Basque Children's Committee, 20 July 1937, TUC/292/946/39/67, WUSC.

93. Minutes of Executive Committee Meeting, Basque Children's Committee, 11 October 1937, TUC/292/946/2/110; Bulletin no. 8, National Joint Committee for Spanish Relief, TUC/292/946/39/1, WUSC.

94. W. Citrine, Memorandum on Behalf of the Trade Union Congress, 4–6 May 1937 TUC/292/946/16a/39, WUSC.

95. Bulletin no. 11, National Joint Committee for Spanish Relief, TUC/292/946/39/1, WUSC.

96. Interviews conducted with former inhabitants of Weston Manor, 1937–38, cited in Legarreta, *The Basque Children*, 113–14.

97. Minutes of the Basque Children's Committee 5 July 1937, 21 August 1937, cited in Legarreta, *The Basque Children*, 123–25.

98. *Catholic Herald*, 15 October 1937; Bulletin no. 11, National Joint Committee for Spanish Relief, March 1938, TUC/292/946/39/1, WUSC.

99. *Catholic Herald*, 15 October 1937

100. Bulletin no. 11, National Joint Committee for Spanish Relief, March 1938, TUC/292/946/39/1, WUSC.

101. Minutes of Executive Committee Meeting, Basque Children's Committee, 11 October 1937, 292/946/2/110, WUSC.

102. Legarreta, *The Basque Children*, 134.

103. Elath et al., *Memories of Sir Wyndham Deedes*, 68–70.

104. "France," *The World's Children*, October 1935

105. Hacohen, "Dilemmas of Cosmopolitanism"; Abramsky, "Lucien Wolf's Efforts for the Jewish Communities in Central and Eastern Europe."

106. The First Annual Report of the Inter-Aid Committee for Children from Germany, 27 April 1936–31 August 1937, M14/23, SCA.

107. Ibid.

108. Ibid.

109. Special Meeting held at 20 Gordon Square, 19 March 1936, Strictly Confidential, M13/14 SCA.

110. Fast, *Children's Exodus*.

111. Baumel-Schawrtz, *Never Look Back*, 37.

112. Bailkin, *Unsettled*, 17, 45. On the longer history of Jewish migration and British antisemitism, see Feldman, *Englishmen and Jews Social Relations and Political Culture, 1840–1914*.

113. Fast, *Children's Exodus*; Baumel-Schawrtz, *Never Look Back*, 37.

114. W. Deedes to M. Watson, 11 January 1939, 92.19.25, AUIPE.

115. SCF Executive Council, 26 October 1936, SCA.

116. "The Price of Peace," *The World's Children*, November 1938.

117. L. B. Golden, Children and War (Confidential), 28th February 1938, M13/14, SCA.

118. Ibid.

119. Early death from chronic illness, or housebound middle age, after a decade of humanitarian work overseas, were common patterns in the lives of early female aid workers. Countless examples populate Oldfield, *Women Humanitarians*.

120. Save the Children International Union, Protection of Children in Times of Armed Conflict, General Council Meeting, 6 June 1939, M14/13, M14/14, SCA.

121. Ibid.; Allen, *Britain under Bombs*.

122. *The World's Children*, March 1936.

123. SCF Executive Council, 6 June 1939, "Protection of Children in Time of War," EJ112, SCA.

124. *Times*, 29 November 1939.

125. SCF Executive Council, 18 January 1945.

126. April 1937, Accounts of the Save the Children Fund 1930–1940, Save the Children Head Offices, London.

127. SCF Executive Council, 2 October 1941.

128. Beveridge and Wells, *The Evidence for Voluntary Action*.

129. "Protection of Children in Time of Armed Conflict," Discussion at the General Council, June 1939, M14/14, SCA.

130. Memorandum drafted in accordance with minute number N206, for the Ministry of Health and Board of Education, SCA/ MA/2.

131. On wartime increases in preschool provision more widely, see Davis, *Preschool Childcare in England, 1939–2010*.

132. "Children in a Time of War, An Immunity Scheme," *The World's Children*, March 1938; "War Nurseries," *The World's Children*, Winter 1941–42.

133. "War Nurseries," *The World's Children*, Summer 1942.

134. "Study of Child Development," War Nurseries (undated), Residential nurseries in Scotland in 1941 and 1942 SC/MA/1-3.

135. "Residential Nurseries," *The World's Children*, Summer 1945.

136. Different forms of childcare for evacuees are discussed in Isaacs, *The Cambridge Evacuation Survey*, and Johnson, *The Evacuees*.

137. For example, see Freud, "Special Experiences of Young Children, Particularly in Times of Social Disturbance"; Burlingham and Freud, *Young Children in War-Time in a Residential War Nursery*.

138. *The World's Children*, Winter 1941–42; The literature on evacuation is vast. For useful overviews, see Welshmann, "Evacuation and Social Policy during the Second World War; MacNicol, "The Effect of the Evacuation of School Children on Official Attitudes to State Intervention."

139. Titmuss, *Problems of Social Policy*, 103, 507–8. Titmuss's claim has been widely rejected in recent literature. See Lowe, "The Second World War, Consensus and the Foundation of the Welfare State."

140. Mme. Vajkai, 1940 XIVe Rapport concernant les infants réfugiés polonaise, Budapest, 21 September 1940 discussed at council meeting 20 July 1939, SCA.

141. Ibid.

142. SCF Executive Council, 24 April 1941, SCA.

143. Summary of M. Thélin's report on his journey in unoccupied France, 18–30 May 1942, M14/13, M 14/14 SCA; *Children in Bondage: A Survey of Child Life in the Occupied Countries of Europe and in Finland, Conducted by the Save the Children Fund* (London, 1942).

144. Extraordinary meeting of the council on the occasion of the visit of Dr. George Thélin, 25 January 1945; see also Gollancz, *Leaving Them to Their Fate*.

145. Steinacher, *Humanitarians at War*, 44–47.

146. Leith-Ross, "Opening Lecture."

147. Ibid.

148. SCF Executive Council, 19 April 1945.

149. Fox, "The Origins of UNRRA"; Salvatici, "'Help the People to Help Themselves.'"

150. Reinisch, "Internationalism in Relief; Reinisch, "'Auntie UNRRA' at the Crossroads."

151. Black, *A Cause for Our Times*, 9.

152. National Famine Relief Council formed 29 May 1942: Oxford Committee for Famine Relief Minute Book 942, Bodleian Library, Oxford.

153. Ibid.

154. On the wider humanitarian critique of war policy via anti-blockade campaigning, see Vernon, *Hunger*, 18, 150; Gollancz, *Leaving Them to Their Fate*.

155. SCF Executive Council, 20 January 1944, SCA.

156. Ibid.

157. "Operation Stork" HQ Military Government Hannover Region, 31 January 1946, FO 1010/96, BNA.

158. "Operation Stork," *The Argus*, 15 November 1945; Marshall, "German Attitudes to British Military Government 1945–47."

159. Aktion Storch, 21 October 1945, FO 1012/62, BNA.

160. For example, see Steinacher, *Humanitarians at War*; Klose, *Human Rights in the Shadow of Colonial Violence*.

CHAPTER 5. HEARTS AND MINDS HUMANITARIANISM

1. General Council of the IUCW Fourth session, 31 March–2 April 1948, AP 92.1.32, AUIPE.

2. She was, as we saw in chapter 1, not alone in this contention. See William Goode, "Economic Conditions in Central Europe, a report presented to HM Government by William Goode," 1920; "Relief for Europe," National Planning Association, 1–3.

3. "Relief for Europe," National Planning Association, Washington, DC, 1942, 1–9; European Regional Organization, "International Mutual Aid: The Task of UNRRA," *The World Today*, 2.1 (January 1946): 35–44.

4. Wilson, *In the Margins of Chaos*, 293.

5. SCF Annual Report 1950–51; SCF Executive Council, 17 January 1952.

6. Income of the Save the Children Fund, 1920–1946, Accounts of the Save the Children Fund, Save the Children Head Quarters, London.

7. SCF Executive Committee minutes, 20 January 1949; 19 July 1956.

8. Co-operation with UNICEF, AP 92.12.13, AUIPE.

9. Clavin, *Securing the World Economy*, 341–59.

10. John J. Charnow, International Children's Emergency Fund, Department of State publication 2787, United Nations Information Series 15, Library of Congress, 1–6; Morris, *Origins of UNICEF, 1946–1953*.

11. Morris, *Origins of UNICEF*, 11–30.

12. "Report on the American Review of the IUCW," 21 April 1945, AP 92.12.13, AUIPE.

13. Co-operation with UNICEF; Boyce to Eleanor Roosevelt 13 April 1953, AP 92.12.13, AUIPE.

14. She added that the "army should "stick with something [it] understood, rather than encroaching on the autonomy of humanitarian organizations." Wilson, *Aftermath*, 19.

15. National Famine Relief Council formed 29 May 1942: Oxford Committee for Famine Relief Minute Book, 942, Bodleian Library, Oxford.

16. SCF Executive Council, 10 October 1958.

17. Ibid.

18. Brinkley, "Dean Acheson and the 'Special Relationship.'"

19. Cooper, *Africa since 1940*, 20–37.

20. Riley, "The Winds of Change Are Blowing Economically.

21. Riley, "Monstrous Predatory Vampires and Beneficent Fairy-Godmothers."

22. Louis, *Imperialism at Bay*.

23. Lewis, "The British Empire in World History"; Darwin, *Britain and Decolonization*, 141–46, 244–46.

24. Louis and Robinson, "The Imperialism of Decolonisation"; Westad, *The Global Cold War*.

25. Lewis, "The British Empire in World History," 24–32.

26. Riley, "Monstrous Predatory Vampires."

27. Draft Speech for Mr. Airey Neave at the Annual Meeting of the Save the Children Fund (1954), CO 859/658, BNA.

28. King, "The Rise of Juvenile Delinquency in England, 1780–1840; Shore, *Artful Dodgers*.

29. European Committee on Crime Problems, *Juvenile Delinquency in Post-war Europe*, 6; Lunden, *War and Delinquency*; Fishman, *The Battle for Children*, 1–3; Shapira, *The War Inside*.

30. International Union for Child Welfare, third section of the executive committee, 11–12 September 1947, Geneva AP 92.1.32, AEG. See also Shapira, *The War Inside*.

31. Shapira, *The War Inside*; Commission consultative de l'enfance délinquante et socialement inadaptée, 21e session du commité executive, Mars 23–26 1955, AP 92.3.156, AUIPE.

32. National Planning Association, *Relief for Europe*, 3.

33. Bailkin, *The Afterlife of Empire*, 23–54.

34. On this global "crisis of youth," see Fowler, *Youth Culture in Modern Britain, c. 1920–c. 1970*; Jobs, *Riding the New Wave*; Fishman, *The Battle for Children*.

35. Macardle, *Children of Europe*; Zahra, *The Lost Children*, 88–117.

36. Zahra, *The Lost Children*, 67–88; Pettiss and Taylor, *After the Shooting Stopped*, 5–6.

37. Crane, *Child Protection in England, 1960–2000*, 14–15.

38. Zahra, "'A Human Treasure'"; Fieldston, *Raising the World*, 78–107.

39. Freeman, *If Any Man Build*, 66.

40. Zahra, *The Lost Children*.

41. International Union for Child Welfare, third session of the executive committee, Paris 11 September 1947, 92.1.32; Rapport, Commission consultative de l'enfance délinquante et socialement inadaptée, 1954, 92.3.156, AUIPE.

42. Freeman, *If Any Man Build*, 63.

43. SCF Executive Council, 19 April 1945.

44. SCF Executive Council, 21 April 1955.

45. Rapport, Commission consultative de l'enfance délinquante et socialement inadaptée, 1954, 92.3.156, AUIPE.

46. Report presented by the International Union of Child Welfare to the First Congress of the UN for the Prevention of Crime and the Treatment of Offenders, Geneva, May 1955, AUIPE 92.1.34.

47. Commission consultative de l'enfance delinquante et socialment inadaptee devenu le groupe consultif de UIPE pour le problems sociuax de l'enfance et de la jeunesse, rapports, 1947–1958, 92.3.167, AUIPE.

48. First Congress of the United Nations for the Prevention of Crime and Treatment of Offenders, statement by the International Union of child welfare on the prevention of delinquency, May 1955, 14–18, 92.3.156.

49. Ibid.

50. On the evolution of the British public school, see Joyce, *The State of Freedom*.

51. Report in the month of March 1952, Save the Children in Uelzen Camp, Bridget Stevenson, SC-BC-1-4, SCA.

52. Report of the study group on Hill House, November 1950, A-2-1-3, SCA.

53. Charlotte Schornak, A Holiday in England, March 1952, SC-BC-1-4.

54. Report of the study group on Hill House, November 1950, A-2-1-3, SCA

55. Ibid.

56. Zahra, *The Lost Children*.

57. Baughan, "Rehabilitating an Empire."

58. Minutes of the Second Meeting of the Provisional Board of Management for the Serendah Boys Home, 31 August 1950, CO 859/229/1, BNA.

59. Harper, *The End of Empire*.

60. *British Association of Malaya*, "Dealing with Juvenile Delinquency."

61. Ibid.

62. SCF Annual Report, 1951–1952.

63. Fourchard, "Lagos and the Invention of Juvenile Delinquency in Nigeria, 1920–60."

64. Minutes of the Second Meeting of the Provisional Board of Management for the Serendah Boys Home, 31 August 1950, CO 859/229/1.

65. "Dealing with Juvenile Delinquency."

66. Minutes of the Second Meeting of the Provisional Board of Management for the Serendah Boys Home, 31 August 1950, CO 859/229/1, BNA.

67. "Serendah Boys' Home," *Sunday Tribune*, 13 November 1949.

68. "Serendah Boys' Home," Account by Nanette Boyce, *The World's Children*, January 1950; Report from Malaya by Lt. Col. Frank Adams, December 1951, CO 859/229/2, BNA.

69. Report from Malaya by Lt. Col. Frank Adams, January 1952, CO 859/229/1, BNA.

70. Harper, *The End of Empire*, 57–64

71. Aspalter, *Social Work in East Asia*, 107.

72. Harper, *The End of Empire*, 66.

73. On comparative counterinsurgencies in the British Empire, see Wagner, "Savage Warfare"; Shipway, *Decolonization and Its Impact*, 140–72; Bayly and Harper, *Forgotten Wars*; Burleigh, *Small Wars, Far Away Places*. For a comparative study of humanitarian responses, see Klose, *Human Rights in the Shadow of Colonial Violence*.

74. Harper, *The End of Empire*.

75. Dixon, "'Hearts and Minds'?"

76. On denazification through welfare interventions, see Reinisch, *The Perils of Peace*.

77. Reports of the British Red Cross Society Overseas Branches for the year 1950, RCC/1/31/2, Confidential Report no. 7, 18 January 1950, British Red Cross Archives (BRCA), London.

78. Reports for 1954, Mambang Diawan Report, Miss Nares to Miss Sacker, 29 June 1954, RCC/1/31/2, BRCA.

79. Diary of visit to Overseas Branches, Extract, 16 August 1951, RCC/1/31/2, BRCA.

80. Harper, *The End of Empire*, 68.

81. Reports for 1951, First Annual Report of the Selangor Branch, November 1951, RCC/1/31/6, BRCA.

82. Colonial Development and Welfare Scheme No. D.1407, 10th January 1951, CO 717/195/11, BNA.

83. SCF Annual Report, 1948–1949, Save the Children HQ, London.

84. Ibid.

85. "Murder of Headteacher at Malaya School," *The Spectator*, 11 March 1949.

86. "Serendah Boys" Home," Account by Nanette Boyce, *The World's Children*, January 1950.

87. Ibid.

88. Adams, "A Malayan Experiment,"

89. "Serendah Boys" Home," *Sunday Tribune*, 13 November 1949; SCF annual report, 1951–1952.

90. Adams, "A Malayan Experiment."

91. SCF Executive Council, 21 July 1949.

92. Campbell, "Juvenile Delinquency in Colonial Kenya, 1900–1939."

93. Stewart, *The First Victory*.

94. Barnes, "The Somali Youth League."

95. On the gendering of colonial juvenile delinquency, see Bell, "'A Most Horrifying Maturity in Crime'; George, *Making Modern Girls*.

96. Brigadier Boyce to Miss Darlow, 21 June 1949, CO 859/229/1, BNA.

97. E. M. Hall to M. M. Pender, 26 June 1956, CO 859/659, BNA.

98. SCF Annual Report, 1951–1952.

99. Commission consultative de l'enfance délinquante et socialement inadaptée devenu le groupe consultatif de UIPE pour les problèmes sociaux de l'enfance et de la jeunesse, rapports, 1947–1958, 92.3.167, AUIPE.

100. Report from British Somaliland from John Watling, October 1953, CO 859/658, BNA.

101. Report from British Somaliland from John Watling, February 1952, CO 859/229/2, BNA.

102. Ibid., emphasis in the original.

103. Juvenile Offenders, Report of the Penal sub-committee, comments of the colonial governments, Gold Coast, CO 859/73/15.

104. Foreign Relief and Rehabilitation Committee, Summary of the Report on work in Somaliland, June 1956, CO 859/659, BNA.

105. SCF Foreign Relief and Rehabilitation Committee, July, August, and September, 1956, from Mr. Abdi Said, Acting Superintendent, CO 859/659, BNA.

106. Report from British Somaliland from John Watling, February 1952, CO 859/229/2, BNA.

107. Campbell, "Juvenile Delinquency in Colonial Kenya," 129–51.

108. SCF Annual Report 1957–8, Save the Children Headquarters, London.

109. On race, ideas about crime, and policing in postwar Britain, see Panayi, "Middlesbrough 1961"; Peplow, *Race and Riots in Thatcher's Britain*.

110. SCF Annual Report 1957–58. On ideas about race, difference, and integration in wartime and postwar Britain, see Webster, "The Empire Comes Home"; Schofield, *Enoch Powell and the Making of Postcolonial Britain*.

111. Report from British Somaliland from John Watling, October 1953, CO 859/658, BNA; Boyce to Lennox-Boyd, 27 September 1954, CO 859/658, BNA. These views were shared by the British colonial administration, see Ocobock, *An Uncertain Age*; Linstrum, *Ruling Minds*; Tilley, *Africa as a Living Laboratory*.

112. On the Kenyan Emergency as a civil war, see Branch, *Defeating Mau Mau*.

113. Elkins, *Imperial Reckoning*; Anderson, *Histories of the Hanged*; Branch, *Defeating Mau Mau*; Bennett, *Fighting the Mau Mau*.

114. Boyce to Lennox-Boyd, 27 September 1954, CO 859/658, BNA.

115. Confidential memorandum by the Minister for African affairs, 29 September 1954, FCO 141/6131, BNA.

116. Boyce to Lennox-Boyd, 27 September 1954, CO 859/658, BNA.

117. Notes on a meeting held in the secretary of state's room at 4.30 p.m. on 17 November 1954 (with Brigadier Boyce, SCF), CO 859/660, British National Archives (BNA); Bell, "'A Most Horrifying Maturity in Crime,'" 480–81.

118. Burton and Ocobock, "The "Travelling Native."

119. Secretary of state for Kenya (UK) to Evelyn Baring, 23 August 1956, BZ/8, KNA; Lonsdale, "The Moral Economy of Mau Mau."

120. *Daily Telegraph*, 30 September 1954, quoted in Kanogo, *Squatters and the Roots of Mau Mau, 1905–1963*, 147.

121. Notes on a meeting held in the secretary of state's room at 4.30 p.m. on 17 November 1954 (with Brigadier Boyce, SCF), CO 859/660, BNA.

122. Ocobock, *An Uncertain Age*, 191–225.

123. "Youth Training," 7 November 1954, FCO 141/6269, BNA; see also Askwith, *From Mau Mau to Harambee*, 103–6; Leakey, *Mau Mau and the Kikuyu*; Carothers, *The Psychology of Mau Mau*.

124. "Youth Training," 7 November 1954, FCO 141/6269, BNA.

125. See also Linstrum, *Ruling Minds*, 155–88.

126. Colony and Protectorate of Kenya Government Notice No. 16, Emergency (Welfare of Children) Regulations, 1954, in *The Kenya Gazette*, 8 March 1955, 188.

127. Boyce from J. R. Gregory, Save the Children Kenya, 6 December 1954, CO 859/658, BNA.

128. "Account of Juveniles in Latanga Camp," Eileen Fletcher to Miss Shepherd, 23 December 1954, Archives and Special Collection, School of Oriental and African Studies (SOAS), Conference of British Missionary Society Papers (CBMS) 278; Fletcher, *Truth about Kenya*.

129. Boyce to Lennox-Boyd, 27 September 1954, CO 859/658, BNA.

130. Memorandum on Youth Crime, 14 January 1957, AB/2/66, KNA.

131. Thomas Askwith to Secretary for Local Government Health and Housing, 9 January 1956, MCO/LIA 89/2, KNA; "Vagrant Juveniles," Memorandum by the War Council, 7 June 1957, CO/822/1804, BNA; "Juvenile Reception Centres," 17 October 1957, AB/2/74, KNA.

132. Lewis, *Empire State-Building*, 144.

133. Commission consultative de l'enfance délinquante et socialement inadaptée, 21e Session du Comité executive, 23–26 Mars 1955, AP 92.3.156, L'Archives d'état de Genève (AEG); C. S. Owen, Rehabilitation of Youth, 23 April 1956, BZ/8/13, KNA.

134. E. D. Emley, Memorandum on Juveniles, 18 November 1955, AB/2/60, KNA. See also Pringle, "Humanitarianism, Race, and Denial."

135. "Ujana Park," *The Sunday Post*, 6 November 1955.

136. "Boys" Training," *East African Standard*, 14 September 1955.

137. Wamumu Approved School and Youth Camp, Annual Report for 1956, VQ/21/3, KNA; Rehabilitation of Youth, 1956, VQ/21/3, KNA. See also Ocobock, *An Uncertain Age*.

138. Wamumu Approved School and Youth Camp, Annual Report for 1956, VQ/21/3, KNA; Rehabilitation of Youth, 1956, VQ/21/3, KNA.

139. Rev. H. D. Hooper, "We're the Wamumu Boys," December 1956 CMBS 279, School of Oriental and African Studies, London (SOAS); *The East African Standard*, 19 January 1956, LOC. Alec Dixon (future founder of VSO) was invited to pilot Outward Bound principles at Youth Detention Camps in 1954, FCO 141/6269, BNA.

140. Telegram from the secretary of state for the colonies to the officer administering the government of Kenya, 10 May 1957, CO 822/1239, BNA; see also White, "Separating the Men from the Boys."

141. Telegram from the secretary of state for the colonies to the officer administering the government of Kenya, 10 May 1957, CO 822/1239, BNA.

142. G. Gardener, Escape from Wamumu, 28 September 1955, AB/1/116, KNA.

143. Notes for responses to parliamentary questions, June 1955, CO 822/1239, BNA.

144. The provincial commissioner Central Province requests the assistance of Red Cross Women, 10 February 1955, RCC/1/12/1/37, BRCA.

145. Report on the Status of Mau Mau Women, 1954, CO 859/658, BNA.

146. Report for August to February, 1955–56, Gichugu Division, Embu—Moyra Keating, MOH/12/117, KNA.

147. "Ill Fed Children a Big Problem in Kikuyuland," *East African Standard*, 19 November 1955.

148. Lewis, "Daddy Wouldn't Buy Me a Mau Mau."

149. For example, House of Commons Debate, 8 December 1954, Hansard vol. 535 cc. 944–46; Secretary of state for the colonies, Preparation for parliamentary questions, 20 March 1957, CO 822/1239, BNA.

150. Draft speech for Mr. Airey Neave at the Annual Meeting of the Save the Children Fund (1954), CO 859/658, BNA.

151. See for example *The World's Children*, October–November 1954, LOC; Draft speech for Mr. Airey Neave at the Annual Meeting of the Save the Children Fund (1954), CO 859/658, BNA.

152. Bulletin of the Save the Children International Union, October–December 1955, LOC.

153. "The Youngest Victims of Mau Mau," *The World's Children*, October/November 1954.

154. Kennedy, "Constructing the Colonial Myth of Mau Mau," 243; Lonsdale, "Mau Maus of the Mind."

155. On the silences in the (post) imperial archives, see Bailkin, "Where Did the Empire Go?"

156. Cooper and Packard, *International Development and the Social Sciences*; Hodge, *Triumph of the Expert*; Mitchell, *Rule of Experts*.

157. Andy McSmith, "Cabinet 'Hushed Up' Torture of Mau Mau Rebels," *Independent*, 7 April 2011.

CHAPTER 6. WAR, DEVELOPMENT,
AND DECOLONIZATION

1. Tim Mayhew to Colin Thornily, 27 October 1972, A80, Save the Children Archives (SCA).

2. Beinart, Brown, and Gilfoyle, "Experts and Expertise in Colonial Africa Reconsidered; Mitchell, *Rule of Experts*; Hodge, *Triumph of the Expert*; Hodge, "British Colonial Expertise"; Tilley, *Africa as a Living Laboratory*; Cooper and Packard, "Introduction" in *International Development and the Social Sciences*, 1–41; Hilton et al., *The Politics of Expertise*.

3. Seventy percent of Britons owned television sets in 1960, and this figure would continue to rise throughout the decade. Williams, *Entertaining the Nation*, 14; Donnelly, *Sixties Britain*, 77.

4. Barring, "Introduction: Independence Day Ceremonials in Historical Perspective." On ceremony, see also Mar, "Introduction," in *Decolonisation and the Pacific*, 1–21.

5. On cultures of decolonization in Britain, see Craggs and Wintle, *Cultures of Decolonisation*; MacKenzie, "The Persistence of Empire in Metropolitan Culture."

6. Bocking-Welch, *British Civic Society at the End of Empire*.

7. SCF Executive Council, 16 January 1956; SCF Executive Council 15 April 1963.

8. Hilton, "Charity and the End of Empire, 510; Rossi, *From Slavery to Aid*; Li, *The Will to Improve*.

9. Save the Children Fund (Uganda) Annual Report 1967–1968, A80, SCA.

10. As we saw in chapter 3, Kenyatta had been at loggerheads with the Fund thirty years earlier over the issue of clitoredectomy. On Kenyatta's relationship with the Fund in the 1960s, see Hilton, "Charity, Decolonization and Development."

11. Aide Memoire (confidential) by Colin Thornberry director general of the SCF, FO 371/190407, BNA.

12. "The Heartbreak of the Congo," *Daily Mirror*, 6 January 1961, 1.

13. Black, *A Cause for Our Times*, 74–75.

14. For an example of such projects see "Oxfam in Bihar Villages: An Experiment in Development. Report from January 1968 to July 1969," Folder 1, DON/2/1, OXFAM.

15. Harrison, "Oxfam and the Rise of Development Education."

16. Milford, *The Oxfam Story* (Oxford, 1964).

17. Lacey, *Christian Aid*; Bocking-Welch, *British Civic Society*, 154–81.

18. Cox, "From the Empire of Christ to the Third World." Missionaries remained, nonetheless, an important of the international development scene. See Manji and O'Coill, "The Missionary Position."

19. Christian Council of Kenya, Committee on Rehabilitation, 6 September 1955, Council of British Missionary Societies (CMBS), 279, SOAS. Christian Aid was known as the Inter-Church Aid and Refugee Service until it changed its name in 1964.

20. "The Tractors for the Hungry Scheme," 1963, C.A.F.1.2B, SOAS archives.

21. Bocking-Welch, *British Civic Society*, 154–81.

22. Memo, W. N. Hibbert, 2 February 1968, A0072, SCA; Colin Thorney SCF to Nicolas Stacey, Oxfam, 7 January 1969, A0072, SCA; SCF Executive Council, 16 July 1964.

23. Bocking-Welch, *British Civic Society*.

24. Save the Children Fund Annual Report, 1970.

25. Save the Children Fund Annual Report, 30th Year, 1948–1949; SCF Executive Council, 15 July 1965.

26. In 2019, this figure is close to £500 million.

27. Hilton, "Charity and the End of Empire," 494. By 1960 the term *aid sector* appeared regularly in publications and committee minutes across all three organizations and peaked in usage in the late 1960s.

28. Riley, "Monstrous Predatory Vampires"; Hodge, *Triumph of the Expert*.

29. Rist, *The History of Development*; Nunan, *Humanitarian Invasion*, 46–118.

30. Immerwahr, *Thinking Small*, 1–15.

31. Development, of course, had multiple meanings, not only in the West but in "developing" countries themselves. Lal, "Self-Reliance and the State"; Moskowitz, "'Are You Planting Trees or Are You Planting People?'"; Aerni-Flessner, *Dreams for Lesotho*.

32. UN Development Decade, "World Campaign against Hunger, Disease and Ignorance," 23 June 1964, FO 371/178233, BNA; "What Every Non-governmental Organization Should Know about Freedom From Hunger Campaign," Freedom From Hunger Campaign (FFHC), May 1960, CA/I/3/3, SOAS.

33. "What Every Non-governmental Organization Should Know about Freedom From Hunger Campaign," Freedom From Hunger Campaign (FFHC), May 1960, CA/I/3/3, SOAS.

34. Food and Agriculture Organization (FAO) Director General, "Report on Progress of the Freedom From Hunger Campaign," 30 September 1962, MAF 252/241, TN; FFHC, The First Five Years: Freedom From Hunger, 1960–65 (committee report, 1965), COM/3/1/5; OXFAM, Bodleian Library, Oxford.

35. Bocking-Welch, *British Civic Society*, 134; Bocking-Welch, "Imperial Legacies"; Vernon, *Hunger*, 272.

36. Duke of Edinburgh, Service Overseas by Volunteers, 1966, CA/I/3/2, SOAS.

37. Points from Parliament, *Daily Mail*, 5 March 1963.

38. Hilton, "Charity and the End of Empire."

39. Bocking-Welch, "Imperial Legacies."

40. Williams, *Aid in the Commonwealth Overseas Development Institute*; Tomlinson, "The Commonwealth, the Balance of Payments and the Politics of International Poverty.

41. Memo: Fast/Vigil to be organized in Trafalgar Square by Youth Against Hunger, 13 December 1966; see also Memo: Youth Against Hunger, the politics of aid, 1965, CA2/I/18/3, SOAS.

42. Hilton, "Charity and the End of Empire"; FFHC, "List of Approved Projects," 1 December 1962, OD 11/71, BNA.

43. On the history of the ODM, see Clarke, "A Technocratic Imperial State?"; Riley, "The Winds of Change Are Blowing Economically."

44. Ireton, *Britain's International Development Policies*. The Colonial Office ceased operations in 1966, merging with the Commonwealth Relations Office to become the Commonwealth Office. In 1968 the Commonwealth Office in turn merged with the Foreign Office, to form the Foreign and Commonwealth Office.

45. Ministry of Overseas Development, "Aid Policy," 16 November 1964, Overseas Development Papers: OD 15/15, BNA.

46. Meeting at Oxfam's Headquarters on 1 September 1965, A0072, SCA; Parliamentary Secretary for Overseas Development to Colin Thornily, 6 March 1965, A0206; Arthur Rucker, Proposal for an Overseas Aid Council, May 1967; and VCOAD, Minutes of Special Meeting, 10 May 1967, OD 25/207, BNA.

47. Luetchford and Burns, *Waging the War on Want*, 12–20.

48. Meeting at Oxfam's Headquarters on 1 September 1965, A72, SCA.

49. SCF Council, 21 January 1965, SCF Executive Council, 15 December 1964, SCA.

50. SCF Executive Council, 19 November 1968; SCF, 24 July 1969, SCA.

51. Muschik, "The Art of Chameleon Politics."

52. Black, *A Cause for Our Times*, 74–75; Hilton, "Charity and the End of Empire," 498.

53. On the "indigenization" of expertise, see Schauer, *Wildlife between Empire and Nation*, 1–16

54. Burton and Jennings, "Introduction: The Emperor's New Clothes?, Hodge, *British Colonial Expertise*; Cooper, "Introduction."

55. Muschik, "The Art of Chameleon Politics."

56. Jennings, "'Almost an Oxfam in Itself.'"

57. Duffield, *Development, Security and Unending War*, 60–63; Jones, *Two Ears of Corn*.

58. Manji and Coill, *The Missionary Position*, 567–83.

59. Porter, *Missionaries versus Empire*, 1–14; 316–30.

60. The SCF Report on Visit to Uganda, 1–23 April 1970 by LT Col J. V. Hawkins, Director of Overseas Relief and Welfare.

61. Tim Mayhew to Colin Thornily, 27 October 1972, A80, Save the Children Archives (SCA).

62. Jack Lundin, interview, January 1969, Jack Lundin Papers (JLP), Western Cape.

63. J. G. Francis to James Gichuru, minister for finance, 11 July 1963: KNA, A2G1/7/82.

64. Save the Children Fund (Uganda) Annual Report 1967–1968, SCF A80; Reduction of the Work Overseas, A Reassessment, March 1967, A206, SCA.

65. John Brimacombe to Colin Thornely, 10 October 1965, A72, SCA.

66. On the history of Caribbean child welfare, see Fox, *Freedom and Welfare in the Caribbean*; on Caribbean economies, see Brereton, "Independence and the Persistence of Colonialism in the Caribbean"; on European ideas about motherhood and Caribbean women, see Brereton "European Stereotypes in the Position of Women in the Caribbean."

67. Green, "The Save the Children Fund in the West Indies."

68. Monica Green to London, 5 June 1961, A91, SCA; Miss Green to London, 29 March 1961, A91, SCA.

69. Monica Green, Report from Jamaica, Summer 1962, A91, SCA.
70. Bailkin, *The Afterlife of Empire*, 95–131.
71. Rowley and Antrobus, "Feminist Visions for Women in a New Era"; Colin Thornley to Edward Ford, Buckingham Palace, 12 January 1965, A81, SCA.
72. Syllabi (various), Graduate Diploma in Social Work, University of Birmingham 1959–1962, 5/V, Cadbury Library, Birmingham.
73. Antrobus, *The Global Women's Movement*.
74. Bailkin, *Afterlives*, 56–94.
75. Beveridge, *Full Employment in a Free Society*; George, *Social Security: Beveridge and After*, 99–114.
76. Todd, "Family, Welfare and Social Work in Post-war England."
77. Monica Green, St Vincent–West Indies Freedom From Hunger Report for December 1963; Save the Children, The Windward Islands (1961–1969), A91, SCA; Brereton, Independence and the Persistence of Colonialism"; Mawby, *Ordering Independence*.
78. Monica Green, The Save the Children Fund in the West Indies.
79. Casework Reports, "Jonas," February 1966, A82, Save the Children Archives, Birmingham, SCA.
80. Monica Green, St Vincent–West Indies Freedom From Hunger Report for December 1963; Save the Children, The Windward Islands (1961–1969), A0911, SCA. On colonial attitudes toward mothers see Allman, "Making Mothers"; Akujobi, "Motherhood in African Literature and Culture."
81. This was a tradition that dated back to eugenic movements in early twentieth century Britain and North America and had spread throughout the British Empire. On breastfeeding, see Sasson, "Milking the Third World?"
82. Monica Green, Report from the Caribbean, Summer 1966, B82, SCA.
83. It also reflected the distribution of labor within the Antrobus marriage, in which Kenneth, despite his pediatric expertise, left the care of their adopted son solely to Peggy. See Rowley and Antrobus, "Feminist Visions."
84. On ideas about working mothers in Britain, see McCarthy, "Social Science and Married Women's Employment."
85. Millicent Iton, Report, February 1965, A81, SCA.
86. V. K. Antrobus, Pediatric Report, June 1966, A81, SCA.
87. Peggy Antrobus, Pre-delinquent Children, 1965, A191, SCA.
88. Beryl Rose to IB Hurgon, 28 December 1970; Beryl Rose to Eileen Watson 4 December 1970, A191, SCA.
89. Todd, "Family, Welfare and Social Work," 387.
90. Rowley and Antrobus, "Feminist Visions."
91. Antrobus, "Women and Children's Well-Being in the Age of Globalization."
92. Antrobus, "Women and Children's Well-Being," 56.
93. Report by Remi Domingo, November 1965, A163, SCA.
94. "Western Nigeria," November 1965, by Captain L. M. Brown, A163, SCA; "Nigerian Challenge," Col. Hawkins, The World's Children, December 1964.
95. "Western Nigeria," November 1965, by Captain L. M. Brown, A163, SCA.

96. Immerwahr, *Thinking Small*.

97. Such was the popularity of the hospital at Ilesa that, in July 1968, a rally and walk in Newcastle to raise money for an Oxfam Freedom From Hunger project descended into chaos when twelve thousand people, rather than the expected six thousand, attended. A nineteen-year-old woman died in the crush, and the Margret Hurford wing of the hospital in Ilesa was named after her. Pearson, *Front Line Hospital*, 46.

98. John Birch to Eileen Watson 9 October 1967, A163 SCA.

99. Major Owen Weeks to Miss Watson, 24 July 1965, A163, SCA.

100. Mrs Watson to Keith Dowling, 3 March 1967, A163, SCA.

101. Ossai to Hawkins, 22 March 1966, A163, SCA.

102. The local staff of the SCF, Ilesato Lt. Cl. Hawkins, January 1966, A163, SCA.

103. Keith Downing to Mrs Watson at London Office (exact date missing) 1966, A163, SCA.

104. Dowling to Watson, 23 February 1966, A163, SCA.

105. The SCF Report on Visit to Uganda, 1–23 April 1970 by LT Col J. V. Hawkins, Director of Overseas Relief and Welfare, SCF A80. In this report, Hawkins relays the comments of other white British Save the Children staff about their African counterparts.

106. Pearson, *Front Line Hospital*.

107. Mrs Ossai to Hawkins, 22 March 1966, A163, SCA.

108. John Birch to Eileen Watson, 9 October 1967, A163, SCA.

109. Quarterly report July to September 1969, by Mrs Remi Agunlejika. This argument was made by another African social worker, Ruth Semba, in the *Uganda Quarterly Report* July–October 1972, Miss Monica Green, A80, SCA.

110. Quarterly report July to September 1969, by Mrs Remi Agunlejika, A163, SCA.

111. Report from Nigeria (Ilesa) By Lt. A. Irvine Neave, "Nigeria Revisited," A163 SCA.

112. For a rich portrait of life in and around Ilesa, and the relationships between elites and the wider community see Trager, *Yoruba Hometowns*; on elite African womanhood, see Ejikeme, "From Traders to Teachers."

113. Record of discussion held between director for overseas relief and Captain L. Brown, 11 January 1966, A163, SCA.

114. Reduction of the Work Overseas, a Reassessment, March 1967, A206 SCA.

115. Pearson, *Front-Line Hospital*, 59–60; Hartfield and Morely, "Efficacy of Measles Vaccine."

116. The SCF Report on Visit to Uganda, 1–23 April 1970 by LT Col J. V. Hawkins, Director of Overseas Relief and Welfare, A080, SCA; Mwanamugimu Nutrition Unit, Save the Children Uganda, Report October–December 1969, A0080, SCA.

117. On breastfeeding and formula milk in colonial and postcolonial Africa, see Hunt, "'Le Bebe en Brousse'"; Sasson, "Milking the Third World?"

118. See notes 2 and 54.

119. There has recently been a surge in historical interest in the humanitarian interventions during the Biafran conflict. See McNeil, "Frontiers of Need"; Heerten, *The Biafran War and Postcolonial Humanitarianism*; O'Sullivan, "Humanitarian Encounters"; Desgrandchamps, "Revenir sur le mythe fondateur de Médecins Sans Frontières." For popular accounts of Biafra and the war, see Achebe, *There Was a Country*; Forsyth, *The Making of an African Legend*.

120. "The Land of No Hope," *Sun*, 12 June 1968.

121. John Hunt and Colin Thornily, "A Second Reconnaissance," in Frederick Tomlinson, ed., *Operation Biafra: An Account of the Save the Children Fund and Other Organisations' Emergency Work in Nigeria, April 1968 to 1971*, SCA. Birch had made an earlier visit east in April 1968, though this did not prompt much in the way of a response from the SCF.

122. "The Land of No Hope," *Sun*, 12 June 1968.

123. Tomlinson, ed., *Operation Biafra*, SCA.

124. SCF/ICRC agreement, 6 July 1968, A163, SCA.

125. "Rebels and Humanitarianism," *New Nigerian*, July 1968, FCO 65/288, BNA.

126. For a detailed examination of the changing nature of ICRC relief and its relationship with the Nigerian federal government throughout the crisis, see Desgrandchamps, "'Organising the Unpredictable'"; Forsythe, *The Humanitarians*, 201–41.

127. O'Sullivan, "Humanitarian Encounters."

128. A number of studies of the ICRC have claimed that Biafra was a sharp break in the contemporary aid movement. For examples, see Bornet, *Entre les lignes ennemies*; Forsythe, *The Humanitarians*, 62; Moorehead, *Dunant's Dream*, 614–15.

129. This mythology is complicated by Desgrandchamps, "Revenir sur le mythe fondateur de Médecins Sans Frontières," and Davey, *Idealism beyond Borders*.

130. O'Sullivan, "Humanitarian Encounters."

131. Koren, *Far Away in the Sky*.

132. Birch to his Excellency Mt B.A.T. Balewa, the deputy high commissioner for Nigeria, 5 July 1968, A164, SCA.

133. SCF press release, 25 June 1968, A164, SCA. This appeal chimed with the ethos of Voluntary Service Overseas, a British government-led scheme intended to deploy British young people in development programs across the Commonwealth to build international connections and individual character. See Bailkin, *Afterlife*, 23–54.

134. Richard Autouy to Hawkins, 16 December 1968, A164, SCA; Press release, "More Nurses for SCF Nigeria," 27 August 1968, A164, SCA.

135. "Devon Drivers Volunteer for Nigeria," press release, 29 July 1968, A164; 25 July 1968 to Hawkins from John Hickey, A164, SCA; "High Praise for SCF Work in Nigeria/Biafra," press release, 1 May 1969, A164, SCA.

136. For discussion of youth cultures of development work in the 1960s, see Geidel, *Peace Corps Fantasies*, 1–13, 71–110.

137. Richard Autouy to Hawkins, 16 December 1968, A164.

138. Sally Goatcher, "An Introduction to the Save the Children Fund Team in Nigeria," 4 February 1969; Reynolds, "From a Woman's Point of View," in Tomlinson, (ed.), *Operation Biafra: An Account of the Save the Children Fund and Other Organisations' Emergency Work in Nigeria, April 1968 to 1971*, SCA.

139. Tunde Foliran to Dr. Hickney, 7 September 1968, JLC.

140. Confidential, Jack Lundin to John Birch, 14 November 1968, Jack Lundin personal collections (JLC), Western Cape, South Africa.

141. Tunde Foliran to Dr. Hickney, 7 September 1968, JLC.

142. Confidential, Jack Lundin to John Birch, 14 November 1968, JLC; "From Fleet Street Gossip Column to the Front Line of the Biafran Civil War," *Press Gazette*, 1 April 2014.

143. John Birch to Jack Lundin, 20 October 1968, Jack Lundin personal collections (JLC), Western Cape, SA; Oscar Bjorn Jensen, team leader of Swedish SCF-team to the chief of Federal Immigration Office, 22 January 1969, JLC.

144. D. H. Doble to West African Department FCO, 31 May 1969, A164, SCA.

145. Noel Moynihan, "The Moynihan Team, Its Work and Its Problems," in Tomlinson, *Operation Nigeria*.

146. See S. R. Dawson to W. N. Hibbert, 20 December 1965; W. N. Hibbert to S. R. Dawson, 3 January 1966, A079.

147. See chapter 3. See also Allimadi, *The Hearts of Darkness*; Wells, "The Melodrama of Being a Child."

148. Herteen, *The Biafran War*, 118.

149. See chapter 1. See also Fehrenbach, "Children and Other Civilians"; Heerten, "'A' as in Auschwitz, 'B' as in Biafra"; Doron, "Marketing Genocide."

150. Herteen, *The Biafran War*, 107–39.

151. Doron, "Marketing Genocide."

152. Herteen, *The Biafran War*, 107–39.

153. On the turbulent 1960s, see De Groot, *The Sixties Unplugged*; Fink, Gassert, and Junker, *1968: World Transformed*; Horn, *The Spirit of '68*.

154. Christmas Appeal, *Blue Peter Annual*, vol. 4 (London, 1968).

155. Conservative MP John Tilney, The House of Commons, 12 June 1968, columns 248–49.

156. Young, *The Labour Governments 1964–1970*, 2:193–296; Herteen, *The Biafran War*, 115–20; see also Uche, "Oil, British Interests and the Nigerian Civil War."

157. Hunt et al., *Nigeria: The Problem of Relief*; "Nigeria and Biafra Relief," House of Lords Debate, 31 July 1968, columns 313–20.

158. See note 149.

159. "5,000 Children Evacuated from Biafra in Civil War Will Be Repatriated from Gabon and Ivory Coast," *New York Times*, 11 October 1970. The International Union of the Save the Children Fund worked alongside the Nigerian government in the repatriation of these children in 1970–71.

160. This was also the case for the International Committee of the Red Cross, who, after Biafra, shifted their focus to preparedness for postcolonial emergencies, which it imagined would be plentiful.

161. Duffield, "Complex Emergencies and the Crisis of Developmentalism."

162. Transcript of Save the Children Fund Film, A43, SCA. On this episode, see also Hilton, "Ken Loach and the Save the Children Film."

163. The Haslemere Declaration. The Haslemere Committee, UK, Oxford, 1968.

164. Hayter, *Aid as Imperialism*; Haslemere Declaration Group, *The Haslemere Declaration*; Simon M. Stevens, "Humanitarian Critique, Anti-Imperialism, and the Anti-Corporate Turn in Anti-Apartheid Activism in Britain," paper presented at the European University Institute, Florence, November 2015.

165. Palma, "Dependency." On African theorists, see Emeh, "Dependency Theory and Africa's Underdevelopment."

166. Memorandum by the Council of Save the Children on the policy for work overseas, 1969, A206, SCA.

CONCLUSION

1. After negotiations between archivists and the Save the Children legal team, documents are now being released up until 2003. See https://www.birmingham.ac.uk/facilities/cadbury/membership/avonpapers.aspx.

2. Tehila Sasson, *We Are the World: Humanitarian Ethics, Global Markets and Everyday Life* (forthcoming 2021); Davey, *Idealism beyond Borders*.

3. The most striking example of this is MSF's Centre de Réflexion sur l'Action et les Savoirs Humanitaires. See also Davey, Borton, and Foley, *A History of the Humanitarian System*; Fiori et al., *The Echo Chamber*.

4. Justin Forsyth, "We Must Not Turn Our Backs on Syria," *Daily Telegraph*, 31 August 2013; Plenary session, Save the Children Centenary Conference, 2019.

5. These allegations were addressed eventually in Susan Shale, *The Independent View of Workplace Culture at Save the Children UK, Final Report*, October 2018 https://www.savethechildren.org.uk/content/dam/gb/reports/independent-review-of-workplace-culture-at-save-the-children-uk.pdf, accessed 20 June 2020.

6. A conference report, as well as video recordings of six witness panels and historical discussions of Save the Children, is accessible online at https://www.savethechildren.org.uk/conference100; see also Mike Aaronson, "100 Years of Save the Children UK: What Have We Learned?," *Open Democracy*, June 2019, /https://www.opendemocracy.net/en/transformation/100-years-save-children-uk-what-have-we-learned/ accessed 20 June 2020.

7. Plenary session, Save the Children Centenary Conference 2019.

8. Fassin, *Humanitarian Reason*, 223–43; Panel 6, "Iraq to Yemen: The Present Century," especially the comments of Gareth Owen.

9. *Global Humanitarian Assistance Report, 2019*, https://www.alnap.org/help-library/global-humanitarian-assistance-report-2019, accessed 26 June 2020

10. Panel 6, "Iraq to Yemen: The Present Century."

11. Mann, *From Empires to NGOs in the West African Sahel*.

12. Krassowski, *The Aid Relationship*; Hayter, *Aid as Imperialism*; Myrdal, *Asian Drama*. More recently see Unger, "Postwar European Development Aid"; Sabaratnam, *Decolonising Intervention*.

13. Plenary Session, Save the Children Centenary Conference.

14. Wells, "Child Saving or Child Rights."

15. Children's Rights workshop session, Save the Children Centenary Conference.

16. Ibid.

17. The United Nation Convention on the Rights of the Child, November 1989, at https://www.unicef.org.uk/what-we-do/un-convention-child-rights/.

18. *A Practice Handbook: For Family Tracing and Reunification in Emergencies*, Save the Children Resource Centre (2018), accessed online, https://resourcecentre .savethechildren.net/library/practice-handbook-family-tracing-and-reunification -emergencies.

19. Fatima, *Protecting Children in Armed Conflict*.

20. MPs Reject Dubs Amendment—Save the Children Response, 23 January 2020, https://www.savethechildren.org.uk/news/media-centre/press-releases/mp -reject-dubs-amendment-save-the-children-response.

21. My thinking has been influenced by Lewis, *Full Surrogacy Now*.

22. Riley, "The Winds of Change Are Blowing Economically."

23. Rutazibwa, "What's There to Mourn?"

24. This was covered in "'Prejudiced' Home Office Refusing Visas to African Researchers," *The Guardian*, 8 June 2019, https://www.theguardian.com/politics /2019/jun/08/home-office-racist-refusing-research-visas-africans.

25. Rutazibwa, "On Babies and Bathwater." See also "Aid Reimagined," https:// medium.com/@aidreimagined, accessed 20 June 2020.

26. I contributed to this online course, which was made available to Save the Children staff globally via an online learning platform.

27. Hilton et al., "Humanitarianism and History."

BIBLIOGRAPHY

ARCHIVES

Antislavery International Microfilm Collection
Archives de l'Union Internationale de Protection de l'Enfance (AUIPE), Archives
　d'État de Genève
Archives du Comité international de la Croix-Rouge (ACICR)
Archives of the International Labour Office (AILO)
A. Ruth Fry Papers, Swathmore College Peace Collection
Ballinger Papers, University of Cape Town
Bibliothèque Documentation Internationale Contemporaine (BDIC), Paris
British Film Institute Archives, London
British National Archives, Kew (BNA)
British Red Cross Archives (BRCA)
Buxton family Papers, Dorset (BFP)
Columbia University Special Collections (CUSC)
Federation of Red Cross Societies Archives (FRSA)
Friends' House Library, London (FHL)
Hoover Institute Archives, Stanford, CA (HIA)
Jack Lundin personal collections, Western Cape, South Africa (JLP)
Jebb family papers, Shropshire (JFP)
Kenyan National Archives (KNA)
League of Nations Archive (LNA)
Library of Congress (LOC)
London School of Economics (LSE)
Medical Archive Centre, Wellcome Institute, London
Museum of African American History and Culture, Washington, DC
Natural History Museum Archives
Oxfam archives, Bodleian Library, Oxford
Rhodes House Library
Save the Children Archive, Cadbury Library, Birmingham (SCA)

School of African and Oriental Studies (SOAS)
Trades Union Congress, University of Warwick (TUC)
Walter A. Friedländer Papers, University of Albany

NEWSPAPERS AND PERIODICALS

The Argus
Boston Daily Globe
Bulletin de l'Union Internationale de Secours aux Enfance
Contemporary Review
Daily Chronicle
Daily Express
Daily Herald
Daily Mail
The Friend
Headway, The Monthly Journal of the League of Nations Union
The Independent
Labour Woman
Lancashire Evening Post
Manchester Guardian
The Nation
The New Nigerian
The Observer
Opportunity: Journal of Negro Life
Our Own Gazette
Revue International de la Croix Rouge
The Times
The World Today
The Yorkshire Post

WORKS CITED

Abrams, Fran. *Freedom's Cause: Lives of the Suffragettes*. London: Profile Books, 2003.
Abramsky, Chimen. "Lucien Wolf's Efforts for the Jewish Communities in Central and Eastern Europe." *Jewish Historical Studies* 29 (1982): 281–95.
Achebe, Chinua. *There Was a Country: A Personal History of Biafra*. London: Penguin, 2013.
Adams, Frank. "A Malayan Experiment in Training for Citizenship." *Journal of the Association of British Malaya* (February–June 1953).
Adi, Hakim. *Pan-Africanism and Communism: The Communist International, Africa and the Diaspora, 1919–1939*. Trenton, NJ: Africa World Press, 2013.

Aerni-Flessner, John. *Dreams for Lesotho: Independence, Foreign Assistance, and Development.* Notre Dame, IN: Notre Dame University Press, 2018.

Akujobi, Remi. "Motherhood in African Literature and Culture." *Comparative Literature and Culture* 13.1 (2011): 2–7.

Alatas, Syed Hussein. *The Myth of the Lazy Native.* London: Taylor & Francis Ltd, 2010.

Alden, P., et al. "Unemployment." In *Labour and Industry: A Series of Lectures,* 27–58. Manchester: Manchester University Press, 1920.

Alexander, Amanda. "A Short History of International Humanitarian Law." *European Journal of International Law* 26.1 (2015): 109–38.

Allain, J. "Slavery and the League of Nations: Ethiopia as a Civilised Nation." *Journal of the History of International Law,* 8 (2006): 213–44.

Allimadi, Milton. *The Hearts of Darkness: How White Writers Created the Racist Image of Africa.* New York: Oxford, 2002.

Allman, Jean. "Making Mothers: Missionaries, Medical Officers and Women's Work in Colonial Asante, 1924–1945." *History Workshop Journal,* 38 (1994): 25–48.

Aly, Götz. *Hitler's Beneficiaries: Plunder, Racial War, and the Nazi Welfare State.* London: Verso, 2008.

Ame, Robert Kwame, DeBrenna LaFa Agbényiga, and Nana Araba Apt. *Children's Rights in Ghana: Reality or Rhetoric?* Lanham: Lexington Books, 2011.

Anderson, David. *Histories of the Hanged: The Dirty War in Kenya and End of Empire.* New York: Oxford University Press, 2005.

Anderson, J. R. L., and P. Sergeant Florence, *C. K. Ogden: A Collective Memoir.* London: Allen and Unwin, 1977.

Antrobus, Peggy. "Women and Children's Well-Being in the Age of Globalization: A Focus on St Vincent and the Grenadines and Small Island Developing States." *Development* 44.2 (2001): 53–57.

———. *The Global Women's Movement: Origins, Issues and Strategies.* London: Zed Books, 2004.

Arendt, Hannah. *The Origins of Totalitarianism.* New York: Oxford, 1951.

Ariès, Phillippe. *Centuries of Childhood: A Social History of Family Life.* Trans. Robert Baldick. New York: Random House, 1965.

Askwith, Thomas. *From Mau Mau to Harambee: Memoirs and Memoranda of Colonial Kenya.* Cambridge: Cambridge University Press, 1995.

Aspalter, Christian. *Social Work in East Asia.* Basingstoke, UK: Palgrave, 2008.

Bailkin, Jordanna. *The Afterlife of Empire.* Berkeley: University of California Press, 2012.

———. "Where Did the Empire Go? Archives and Decolonization in Britain." *American Historical Review* 120.3 (2015): 884–99.

———. *Unsettled: Refugee Camps and the Making of Multicultural Britain.* Oxford: Oxford University Press, 2018.

Ball, Alan M. *And Now My Soul Is Hardened: Abandoned Children in Soviet Russia, 1918–1930.* Berkeley: University of California Press, 1994.

Ballantyne, Tony, and Antoinette Burton. *Empires and the Reach of the Global, 1870–1945.* Cambridge, MA: Harvard University Press, 2014.

Barnes, Cedric. "The Somali Youth League, Ethiopian Somalis and the Greater Somalia Idea, c. 1946–48." *Journal of Eastern African Studies* 1.2 (2007): 277–91.

Barnett, Michael. *Empire of Humanity: A History of Humanitarianism.* Ithaca, NY: Cornell, 2011.

Barring, Terry. "Introduction: Independence Day Ceremonials in Historical Perspective." In Robert Holland, Susan Williams, and Terry Barringer (eds.), *The Iconography of Independence: "Freedoms at Midnight."* London: Routledge, 2013.

Baudendistel, Rainer. *Between Bombs and Good Intentions: The International Committee of the Red Cross (ICRC) and the Italo-Ethiopian War, 1935–1936.* New York: Berghahn Books, 2006.

Baughan, Emily. "The Imperial War Relief Fund and the All British Appeal: Commonwealth, Conflict and Conservatism within the British Humanitarian Movement, 1920–1925." *Journal of Imperial and Commonwealth History* 40.5 (2012): 845–61.

———. "'Every Citizen of Empire Implored to Save the Children!' Empire, Internationalism and the Save the Children Fund in Inter-war Britain." *Historical Research* 86.231 (2013): 116–37.

———. "Anglo-American Diplomacy and International Adoption, c. 1918–1925." *Past & Present* 239.1 (May 2018): 181–217.

———. "Rehabilitating an Empire: Humanitarian Collusion with the Colonial State during the Kenyan Emergency, ca. 1954–1960." *Journal of British Studies* 59.1 (2020): 57–79.

Baughan, Emily, Eleanor Davey, Bronwen Everill, Matthew Hilton, Kevin O'Sullivan, and Tehila Sasson. "Humanitarianism and History: A Conversation." *Past & Present* 241.1 (2018). Online edition.

Baughan, Emily, and Juliano Fiori. "Towards a New Politics of Humanitarian Solidarity: Assessing the Contemporary Import of Dorothy Buxton's Vision for Save the Children." *Disasters, Special Edition: Academic Histories for a Practitioner Audience* 39.2 (2015): 129–45.

Baumel-Schawrtz, Judith Tydor. *Never Look Back: The Jewish Refugee Children in Britain, 1938–1945.* West Lafayette: Indiana University Press, 2012.

Bayly, Christopher, and Tim Harper, *Forgotten Wars: The End of Britain's Asian Empire.* London: Penguin, 2007.

Beers, Laura. "Advocating for a Feminist Internationalism between the Wars." In Carolyn James and Glenda Sluga (eds.), *Women, Diplomacy, and International Politics,* 202–21. London: Routledge, 2015.

———. *Red Ellen, The Life of Ellen Wilkinson, Socialist, Feminist, Internationalist.* Cambridge, MA: Harvard University Press, 2016.

Beinart, William, Karen Brown, and Daniel Gilfoyle. "Experts and Expertise in Colonial Africa Reconsidered: Science and the Interpenetration of Knowledge." *African Affairs* 108.432 (2009): 413–33.

Bell, Duncan. *The Idea of Greater Britain: Empire and the Future of World Order, 1860–1900.* Princeton, NJ: Princeton University Press, 2007.

Bell, Erin. "'A Most Horrifying Maturity in Crime': Age, Gender, and Juvenile Delinquency in Colonial Kenya during the Mau Mau Uprising." *Atlantic Studies* 11.4 (2014): 480–81.

Bennett, G. *British Foreign Policy during the Curzon Period, 1919–24*. Basingstoke: Palgrave, 1995.

Bennett, Huw. *Fighting the Mau Mau: The British Army and Counter-insurgency in the Kenya Emergency*. Cambridge: Cambridge University Press, 2015.

Beveridge, W. *Full Employment in a Free Society*. London: Allen and Unwin, 1944.

Beveridge, W., and A. F. Wells (eds.). *The Evidence for Voluntary Action*. London: Allen and Unwin, 1949.

Black, Maggie. *A Cause for Our Times: Oxfam, the First 50 years*. Oxford: Oxfam, 1992.

Blacker, C. "Maternity and Child Welfare Work and the Population Problem." *Eugenics Review* 31.2 (1939): 91–95.

Blackwell, Joyce. *No Peace without Freedom: Race and the Women's International League for Peace and Freedom, 1915–1975*. Carbondale: Southern Illinois University Press, 2004.

Bock, Gisela. "Antinatalism, Maternity and Paternity in National Socialist Racism." In Gisela Bock and Pat Thane (eds.). *Maternity and Gender Policies: Women and the Rise of the European Welfare States, 1880s–1950s*, 233–54. London: Routledge, 1991.

Bock, Gisela, and Pat Thane (eds.). *Maternity and Gender Policies: Women and the Rise of the European Welfare States, 1880s–1950s*. London: Routledge, 1991.

Bocking-Welch, Anna. "Imperial Legacies and Internationalist Discourses: British Involvement in the United Nations Freedom From Hunger Campaign, 1960–70." *Journal of Imperial and Commonwealth History* 40.5 (2012): 879–96.

———. *British Civic Society at the End of Empire: Decolonisation, Globalisation, and International Responsibility*. Manchester: Manchester University Press, 2018.

Bondfield, M. *A Life's Work*. London: Hutchinson, 1948.

Bornet, Jean-Marc. *Entre les lignes ennemies: Délégué du CICR, 1972–2003*. Geneva: International Committee of the Red Cross, 2011.

Boroway, Iris. *Coming to Terms with World Health: The League of Nations Health Organisation*. Berlin: Peter Lang Verlag, 2009.

Boucher, Ellen. *Empire's Children: Child Emigration, Welfare, and the Decline of the British World, 1869–1967*. Cambridge: Cambridge University Press, 2014.

Bowden, S., and D. Higgins. "British Industry in the Interwar Years." In R. Floud and P. Johnson (eds.), *The Cambridge Economic History of Modern Britain, Volume II: Economic Maturity*, 375–87. Cambridge: Cambridge University Press, 2004.

Branch, Daniel. *Defeating Mau Mau, Creating Kenya: Counterinsurgency, Civil War, and Decolonization*. Cambridge: Cambridge University Press, 2009.

Brereton, Bridget. "European Stereotypes in the Position of Women in the Caribbean: An Historical Overview." In Alan Cobley (ed.), *Crossroads of Empire: The European-Caribbean Connection, 1492–1992*, 64–79. Cave Hill, Barbados: University of the West Indies, 1994.

———. "Independence and the Persistence of Colonialism in the Caribbean." In Alan Cobley (ed.), *Crossroads of Empire: The European-Caribbean Connection, 1492–1992*, 53–63. Cave Hill, Barbados: University of the West Indies, 1994.

Briggs, Laura. "Mother, Child, Race, Nation: The Visual Iconography of Rescue and the Politics of Transnational and Transracial Adoption." *Gender and History* 15 (2003): 179–200.

Brinkley, Douglas. "Dean Acheson and the 'Special Relationship': The West Point Speech of December 1962." *Historical Journal* 33.3 (September 1990): 599–608.

British Association of Malaya. "Dealing with Juvenile Delinquency." 22.8 (December 1947).

Brown, Christopher L. *Moral Capital: Foundations of British Abolitionism*. Chapel Hill: University of North Carolina Press, 2007.

Brown, Stirling A. "Satire of Imperialism." *Opportunity: Journal of Negro Life* (March 1934): 11–12.

Buchanan, T. *Britain and the Spanish Civil War*. Cambridge: Cambridge University Press, 1997.

———. *The Spanish Civil War and the British Labour Movement*. Cambridge: Cambridge University Press, 2008.

Buekens, Pierre, and Perrine Humblet. "A 15th Century 'Bambino' Is the Symbol of Global Maternal and Child Health." *Maternal and Child Health Journal* 15 (2011): 1–4.

Bullock, Ian. *Under Siege: The Independent Labour Party in Interwar Britain*. Athabasca, AB: Athabasca University Press, 2017.

Burgwyn, H. J. *Italian Foreign Policy in the Interwar Period, 1918–1940*. Westport, CT: Praeger, 1997.

Burleigh, Michael. *Small Wars, Far Away Places: The Genesis of the Modern World, 1945–65*. Oxford: Oxford University Press, 2013.

Burlingham, Dorothy, and Anna Freud, *Young Children in War-Time in a Residential War Nursery*. London: Allen and Unwin, 1942.

Burman, Erica. *Deconstructing Social Psychology*. London: Routledge, 1994.

Burton, Andrew, and Michael Jennings, "Introduction: The Emperor's New Clothes? Continuities in Governance in Late Colonial and Early Postcolonial East Africa." *International Journal of African Historical Studies* 40.1 (2007): 1–25.

Burton, Andrew, and Paul Ocobock. "The 'Travelling Native': Vagrancy and Colonial Control in British East Africa." In A. L. Beier and P. Ocobock (eds.), *Cast Out: Vagrancy and Homelessness in Global and Historical Perspective*, 285–87. Athens: Ohio University Press, 2008.

Buxton, Charles Roden. *The Race Problem in Africa (The Metterns Lecture)*. London: Allen and Unwin, 1931.

Buxton, C. R., and D. F. Buxton. *The World after the War*. London: Allen and Unwin, 1920.

———. *The White Flame: The History of the Save the Children Fund*. London: Allen and Unwin, 1931.

Buxton, Lord Noel. *Slavery in Abyssinia: Address Given at Chatham House*. London: Chatham House, 1932.

———. "Slavery in Abyssinia." *Contemporary Review*, 141 (June 1932): 698–709.

Cabanes, Bruno. *The Great War and the Origins of Humanitarianism, 1918–1924*. Cambridge: Cambridge University Press, 2014.

Callahan, M. *A Sacred Trust: The League of Nations and Africa, 1929–1946*. Oxford: Oxford University Press, 2004.

———. *Mandates and Empire: The League of Nations and Africa, 1914–1931*. Oxford: Oxford University Press, 2008.

Campbell, Chloe. "Juvenile Delinquency in Colonial Kenya, 1900–1939." *Historical Journal* 45.1 (March 2002): 129–51.

Carothers, J. C. *The Psychology of Mau Mau*. Nairobi: Government Printer, 1954.

Ceadal, M. "The King and Country Debate, 1933: Student Politics, Pacifism and the Dictators." *Historical Journal* 22.2 (1979): 397–422.

———. *Semi-detached Idealists: The British Peace Movement and International Relations, 1854–1945*. Oxford: Oxford University Press, 2000.

Chinyaeva, Elena. *Russians outside Russia: The Émigré Community in Czechoslovakia, 1918–1938*. Munich: R. Oldenbourg Verlag, 2001.

Clarke, Sabine. "A Technocratic Imperial State? The Colonial Office and Scientific Research, 1940–1960." *Twentieth Century British History* 18.4 (2007): 453–80.

Clavin, Patricia. *Securing the World Economy: The Reinvention of the League of Nations, 1920–1946*. Oxford: Oxford University Press, 2013.

———. "The Austrian Hunger Crisis and the Genesis of International Organization after the First World War." *International Affairs* 90.2 (2014): 265–78.

Cleays, Gregory. *Imperial Sceptics: British Critics of Empire, 1850–1920*. Cambridge: Cambridge University Press, 2012.

Cloud, Y. *The Basque Children in England*. London: London: Victor Gollancz, 1937.

Colpus, Eve. *Female Philanthropy in the Interwar World: Between Self and Other*. London: Bloomsbury, 2018.

Conklin, Alice L. *A Mission to Civilize: The Republican Idea of Empire in France and West Africa, 1895–1930*. Stanford, CA: Stanford University Press, 1998.

Cooper, Frederick. *Africa since 1940: The Past of the Present*. Cambridge: Cambridge University Press, 2002.

Cooper, Frederick, and Randall Packard (eds.). *International Development and the Social Sciences: Essays on the History and Politics of Knowledge*. Berkeley: University of California Press, 1997.

———. "Introduction." In Frederick Cooper and Randall Packard (eds.), *International Development and the Social Sciences: Essays on the History and Politics of Knowledge*, 1–33. Berkeley: University of California Press, 1997.

Copsley, Nigel. "'Every Time They Made a Communist, They Made a Fascist': The Labour Party and Popular Anti-Fascism in the 1930s." In Nigel Copsey and Andrzej Olechnowicz (eds.), *Varieties of Anti-Fascism: Britain in the Inter-war Period*, 52–72. Basingstoke, UK: Palgrave, 2010.

Cox, Jeffrey. "From the Empire of Christ to the Third World: Religion and the Experience of Empire in the Twentieth Century." In Andrew Thompson (ed.), *Britain's Experience of Empire in the Twentieth Century*, 76–121. Oxford: Oxford University Press, 2011.

Craggs, Ruth, and Claire Wintle (eds.). *Cultures of Decolonisation: Transnational Productions and Practices, 1945–70*. Manchester: Manchester University Press, 2016.

Crane, Jennifer. *Child Protection in England, 1960–2000: Expertise, Experience, and Emotion*. Basingstoke, UK: Palgrave, 2018.

Cromwell, A. M. *An African Victorian Feminist: The Life and Times of Adelaide Smith Casely Hayford*. Washington, DC: Cromwell, 1992.

Crowdy, Rachel. "The League of Nations: Its Social and Humanitarian Work." *American Journal of Nursing* 28.4 (1928): 350–52.

Dale, Jennifer, and Peggy Foster, *Feminists and State Welfare*. Henley-on-Thames, UK: Routledge and Kegan Paul, 1986.

Darwin, John. *Britain and Decolonization: The Retreat from Empire in the Postwar World*. Basingstoke, UK: Palgrave, 1988.

Daughton, J. P. *An Empire Divided: Religion, Republicanism, and the Making of French Colonialism, 1880–1914*. Oxford: Oxford University Press, 2006.

Davey, Eleanor. *Idealism beyond Borders: The French Revolutionary Left and the Rise of Humanitarianism, 1954–1988*. Cambridge: Cambridge University Press, 2016.

Davey, Eleanor, John Borton, and Matthew Foley. *A History of the Humanitarian System: Western Origins and Foundations*. HPG Working Paper. London: Overseas Development Institute, 2013.

Davin, Anna. "Imperialism and Motherhood." *History Workshop Journal*, 5 (1978): 9–66.

Davis, Angela. *Pre-school Childcare in England, 1939–2010: Theory, Practice, Experience*. Manchester: Manchester University Press, 2015.

Davis, Angela Y. *Women, Race and Class*. New York: Housemans, 1981.

Dean, Mitchell. *The Constitution of Poverty: Towards a Genealogy of Liberal Governance*. London: Routledge, 1991.

de Bunsen, Victoria. *The Soul of a Turk: Record of a Trip to Baghdad*. London: John Lane, 1910.

———. *Charles Roden Buxton: A Memoir*. London: Allen and Unwin, 1948.

de Grazia, Victoria. *How Fascism Ruled Women: Italy, 1922–1945*. Berkeley: University of California Press, 1992.

De Groot, Gerard. *The Sixties Unplugged: A Kaleidoscopic History of a Disorderly Decade*. Cambridge, MA: Harvard University Press, 2008.

Desgrandchamps, Marie-Luce. "Revenir sur le mythe fondateur de Médecins Sans Frontières: Les relations entre les médecins français et le CICR pendant la guerre du Biafra (1967–1970)." *Relations Internationales* 2.146 (2011): 95–108.

———. "'Organising the Unpredictable': The Nigeria-Biafra War and Its Impact on the ICRC." *International Review of the Red Cross* 94.888 (Winter 2012): 1409–32.

Dixon, Paul. "'Hearts and Minds'? British Counter-Insurgency from Malaya to Iraq." *Journal of Strategic Studies* 32.3 (2009): 353–81.

Donnelly, Mark. *Sixties Britain: Culture, Society and Politics*. Harlow, UK: Pearson Longman, 2005.

Doron, Roy. "Marketing Genocide: Biafran Propaganda Strategies during the Nigerian Civil War, 1967–70." *Journal of Genocide Research* 16.2–3 (2014): 227–46.

Duffield, Mark. "Complex Emergencies and the Crisis of Developmentalism." *Institute of Development Studies Bulletin: Linking Relief and Development* 25.4 (1994): 37–45.

———. "The Liberal Way of Development and the Development-Security Impasse: Exploring the Global Life-Chance Divide." Security *Dialogue* 40.2 (2010): 53–76.

———. *Development, Security and Unending War: Governing the World of Peoples*. Cambridge: Cambridge University Press, 2011.

Dwork, D. *War Is Good for Babies and Other Young Children: A History of the Infant and Child Welfare Movement in England, 1898–1918*. London: Routledge, 1987.

Efron, A. *No Love without Poetry: The Memoirs of Marina Tsvetaeva's Daughter*. Evanston, IL: Northwestern University Press, 2009.

Ejikeme, Anene. "From Traders to Teachers: A History of Elite Women in Onitsha, Nigeria, 1928–1940." *Journal of Asian and African Studies* 46.3 (2011): 221–36.

Elath, Eliahu, Norman Bentwich, and Doris May (eds.). *Memories of Sir Wyndham Deedes*. London: Victor Gollancz, 1958.

Elbourne, Elizabeth. *Blood Ground: Colonialism, Missions, and the Contest for Christianity in the Cape Colony and Britain, 1799–1853*. Montreal: McGill University Press, 2002.

Elkins, C. *Imperial Reckoning: The Untold Story of Britain's Gulag in Kenya*. London: Henry Holt, 2005.

Emeh, Ikechukwu. "Dependency Theory and Africa's Underdevelopment: A Paradigm Shift from Pseudo-intellectualism, the Nigerian Perspective." *International Journal of African and Asian Studies* 1 (2013): 116–28.

Engerman, D. (ed.). *Staging Growth: Modernization, Development, and the Global Cold War*. Amherst, MA: Amherst University Press, 2003.

European Committee on Crime Problems. *Juvenile Delinquency in Post-war Europe* Strasbourg. France: Council of Europe, 1960.

Everill, Bronwen. "Bridgeheads of Empire? Liberated African Missionaries in West Africa." *Journal of Imperial and Commonwealth History* 41, Special Issue (2012): 789–805.

Fanon, Franz. *The Wretched of the Earth*. New York: Penguin, 1963.

Fassin, Didier. *Humanitarian Reason: A Moral History of the Present*. Berkeley: University of California Press, 2011.

Fast, Vera K. *Children's Exodus: A History of the Kindertransport*. London: I.B. Taurus, 2011.

Fatima, Saheed. *Protecting Children in Armed Conflict*. London: Bloomsbury, 2018.

Fehrenbach, Heide. "Children and Other Civilians: Photojournalism and Humanitarian Image-Making." In Heide Fehrenbach and Davide Rodogno (eds.), *Humanitarian Photography: A History*, 165–99. Cambridge: Cambridge University Press, 2015.

Feldman, David. *Englishmen and Jews: Social Relations and Political Culture, 1840–1914*. New Haven, CT: Yale University Press, 1994.

Ferguson, James. *The Anti-politics Machine: Development, Depoliticization, and Bureaucratic Power in Lesotho*. Minneapolis: University of Minnesota Press, 1994.

Fieldston, Sarah. *Raising the World: Child Welfare in the American Century*. Cambridge, MA: Harvard University Press, 2015.

Fink, Carole, Philipp Gassert, and Detlef Junker. *1968: World Transformed*. Cambridge: Cambridge University Press, 1998.

Fiori, Juliano, Fernando Espada, Jessica Field, and Sophie Dicker. *The Echo Chamber: Results, Management and the Humanitarian Effectiveness Agenda*. London: Save the Children, 2015.

Fisher, H. H. *The Famine in Soviet Russia, 1919–1923: The Operations of the American Relief Administration*. Berkeley: University of California Press, 1927.

Fishman, Sarah. *The Battle for Children: World War II, Youth Crime, and Juvenile Justice in Twentieth-Century France*. Cambridge MA: Harvard University Press, 2002.

Fletcher, Eileen. *Truth about Kenya: An Eye-Witness Account*. London: Movement for Colonial Freedom, 1956.

Forclaz, Amalia Ribi. *Humanitarian Imperialism: The Politics of Anti-slavery Activism, 1880–1940*. Oxford: Oxford University Press, 2015.

Forsyth, Frederick. *The Making of an African Legend: The Biafra Story*. London: Penguin, 1977.

Forsythe, David P. *The Humanitarians: The International Committee of the Red Cross*. Cambridge: Cambridge University Press, 2005.

Foucault, Michel. *Foucault on Governmentality and Liberalism: The Birth of Biopolitics; Lectures at the Collège de France, 1978–1979*. Trans. Graham Burchell. Basingstoke, UK: Palgrave, 2008.

Fourchard, Laurent. "Lagos and the Invention of Juvenile Delinquency in Nigeria, 1920–60." *Journal of African History* 47.1 (2006): 115–37.

Fowler, David. *Youth Culture in Modern Britain, c. 1920–c. 1970: From Ivory Tower to Global Movement*. Basingstoke, UK: Palgrave, 2008.

Fox, Annette Baker. *Freedom and Welfare in the Caribbean: A Colonial Dilemma*. New York: Harcourt, Brace and Co., 1949.

Fox, Grace. "The Origins of UNRRA." *Political Science Quarterly* (December 1950).

Frank, Matthew, and Jessica Reinisch. "Introduction: Refugees and the Nation-State in Europe, 1919–59." *Journal of Contemporary History* 49.3 (2014): 477–90.

Freeden, M. *Liberal Languages: Ideological Imaginations and Twentieth-Century Progressive Thought*. Princeton, NJ: Princeton University Press, 2005.

Freeman, Katherine. *If Any Man Build: The History of the Save the Children Fund*. London: Hodder & Stoughton, 1965.

Freeman, Martin. *Children's Rights: Progress and Perspectives; Essays from the International Journal of Children's Rights*. London: Routledge, 2014.

Freud, Anna. "Special Experiences of Young Children, Particularly in Times of Social Disturbance." *Mental Health and Infant Development* (1955).

Fuller, Edward. *The International Handbook of Child Care and Protection.* London: Weardale Press, 1924.

———. *The International Year Book of Child Care and Protection: The Save the Children Fund.* London: Weardale Press, 1925.

———. *The Rights of the Child: A Chapter in Social History.* London: Gollancz, 1951.

Gaitskell, D. "'Getting Close to the Hearts of Mothers': Medical Missionaries among African Women and Children in Johannesburg between the Wars." In V. Fildes, L. Marks, and H. Marland (eds.), *Women and Children First: International Maternal and Infant Welfare, 1870–1945,* 178–202. London: Routledge, 1992.

Gatrell, Peter, and Liubov Zhvanko (eds.). *Europe on the Move: Refugees in the Era of the Great War.* Manchester: Manchester University Press, 2007.

Gavitt, Philip. "Charity and State Building in Cinquecento Florence: Vincenzio Borghini as Administrator of the Ospedale Degli Innocenti." *Journal of Modern History* 69.2 (1997): 230–70.

Geidel, Molly. *Peace Corps Fantasies: How Development Shaped the Global Sixties.* Minneapolis: University of Minnesota Press, 2015.

Gelderblom, D., and P. Kok. *Urbanisation: South Africa's Challenge, Volume 1: Dynamics.* Pretoria: HSRC Publishing, 1994.

Gill, Rebecca. *Calculating Compassion: Humanity and Relief in War, Britain 1870–1914.* Manchester: Manchester University Press, 2013.

Gill, Rebecca, and Daryl Leeworthy. "Moral Minefields: Save the Children Fund and the Moral Economies of Nursery Schooling in the South Wales Coalfield in the 1930s." *Journal of Global Ethics* 11.2 (2015): 218–32.

Gleason, Mona. "Avoiding the Agency Trap: Caveats for Historians of Children, Youth, and Education." *History of Education* 45.4 (2016): 446–59.

Gleason, W. E. "The All-Russian Union of Towns and the Politics of Urban Reform in Tsarist Russia." *Russian Review* 35.3 (1976): 290–302.

George, Abosede A. *Making Modern Girls: A History of Girlhood, Labor, and Social Development in Colonial Lagos.* Athens: Ohio University Press, 2014.

George, Victor. *Social Security: Beveridge and After.* London, 1968.

Goebel, Michael. *Anti-imperial Metropolis: Interwar Paris and the Seeds of Third World Nationalism.* Cambridge: Cambridge University Press, 2015.

Gollancz, Victor. *Leaving Them to Their Fate: The Ethics of Wartime Starvation.* London: Victor Gollancz, 1946.

Gordon, Linda. "Dorothea Lange: The Photographer as Agricultural Sociologist." *Journal of American History* 93.3 (2006): 698–727.

Grant, Kevin. "Christian Critics of Empire: Missionaries, Lantern Lectures, and the Congo Reform Campaign in Britain." *Journal of Imperial and Commonwealth History* 29.2 (May 2001): 27–58.

———. *Civilised Savagery: Britain and the New Slaveries in Africa, 1884–1926.* New York: Oxford University Press, 2005.

Graves, Robert. *Good-Bye to All That.* London: Penguin, 1929.

Green, Monica. "The Save the Children Fund in the West Indies." *International Social Work* 9.2 (1966): 38–43.

Grieves, Keith. *Sir Eric Geddes: Business and Government in War and Peace.* Manchester: Manchester University Press, 1989.

Habe, Hans. *Tödlicher Friede—ein Liebesroman mit politischem Hintergrund.* Zurich: Fackelverlag, 1939.

Hacohen, Malachi. "Dilemmas of Cosmopolitanism: Karl Popper, Jewish Identity, and 'Central European Culture.'" *Journal of Modern History* 71.1 (March 1999): 105–49.

Hall, Catherine. *Civilising Subjects: Metropole and Colony in the English Imagination, 1830–1867.* Cambridge: Cambridge University Press, 2002.

Harper, Tim. *The End of Empire and the Making of Malaya.* Cambridge: Cambridge University Press, 1999.

Harris, Jose. "Political Thought and the Welfare State, 1870–1940." *Past & Present,* 135 (1992): 116–41.

Harrison, Donald Geoffrey. "Oxfam and the Rise in Development Education in England from 1959 to 1979." PhD thesis, University of London, 2008.

Hartfield, J., and D. Morely. "Efficacy of Measles Vaccine, Child Health Research Unit of the West African Council for Medical Research, Wesley Guild Hospital, Ilesa, W. Nigeria." *Journal of Hygiene,* 61 (1963): 143–47.

Haskell, Thomas L. "Capitalism and the Origins of the Humanitarian Sensibility, Parts 1 and 2." *American Historical Review* 90 (1985): 339–61, 547–66.

Haslemere Declaration Group. *The Haslemere Declaration: A Radical Analysis of the Relationships between the Rich World and the Poor World.* London: Haslemere Declaration Group, 1968.

Hayter, Teresa. *Aid as Imperialism.* London: Pelican, 1971.

Heerten, Lasse. "'A' as in Auschwitz, 'B' as in Biafra." In Heide Fehrenbach and Davide Rodogno (eds.), *Humanitarian Photography: A History,* 249–74. Cambridge: Cambridge University Press, 2015.

———. *The Biafran War and Postcolonial Humanitarianism: Spectacles of Suffering.* Cambridge: Cambridge University Press, 2019.

Hendrick, Harry. "The Child as a Social Actor in Historical Sources: Problems of Identification and Interpretation." In Pia Christensen and Allison James (eds.), *Research with Children: Perspectives and Practices,* 35–61. London: Routledge, 2008.

Herren, Madeleine. "Gender and International Relations through the Lens of the League of Nations (1919–1945)." In Carolyn James and Glenda Sluga (eds.), *Women, Diplomacy, and International Politics,* 182–201. London: Routledge, 2015.

———. "Fascist Internationalism." In Glenda Sluga and Patricia Clavin (eds.), *Internationalisms: A Twentieth-Century History,* 191–212. Cambridge: Cambridge University Press, 2017.

Hermann, Irène. *L'humanitaire en questions: Réflexions autour de l'histoire du Comité international de la Croix-Rouge.* Paris: CERF, 2018.

Hilton, Matthew. "International Aid and Development NGOs in Britain and Human Rights since 1945." *Humanity* 3.3 (2012): 449–72.

———. "Ken Loach and the Save the Children Film: Humanitarianism, Imperialism, and the Changing Role of Charity in Postwar Britain." *Journal of Modern History* 87.2 (2015): 357–94.

———. "Charity, Decolonization and Development: The Case of the Starehe Boys School, Nairobi." *Past & Present* 233.1 (2016): 227–67.

———. "Charity and the End of Empire: British Non-governmental Organizations, Africa, and International Development in the 1960s." *American Historical Review* 123.2 (2018): 493–517.

Hilton, Matthew, Emily Baughan, Eleanor Davey, Bronwen Everill, Kevin O'Sullivan and Tehila Sasson, "Humanitarianism and History: A Conversation," *Past & Present*, 241.1 (2018), online edition.

Hilton, Matthew, James McKay, Nicholas Crowson, and Jean-François Mouhot. *The Politics of Expertise: How NGOs Shaped Modern Britain.* Oxford: Oxford University Press, 2013.

Hinden, Rita. "Economic Plans and Problems in the British Colonies." *World Affairs* 112.3 (Fall 1949).

Hobson, J. A. *Imperialism: A Study.* Reprint. London: Spokesman Books, 2011.

Hodge, Joseph Morgan. *Triumph of the Expert: Agrarian Doctrines of Development and the Legacies of British Colonialism.* Athens: Ohio University Press, 2007.

———. "British Colonial Expertise, Post-colonial Careering and the Early History of International Development." *Journal of Modern European History* 8 (2010): 24–46.

Hoffman, David L. "Mothers in the Motherland: Stalinist Pronatalism in Its Pan-European Context." *Journal of Social History* 34.1 (2000): 35–54.

Hogsbjerg, C. J. "C. L. R. James and Italy's Conquest of Abyssinia." *Socialist History*, 28 (2006): 17–36.

Holloway, Kerrie. "Britain's Political Humanitarians: The National Joint Committee for Spanish Relief and the Spanish Refugees of 1939." PhD thesis, Queen Mary's University of London, 2018.

Holtby, Winifred. *Mandoa Mandoa: A Comedy of Irrelevance.* London: Virago, 1982.

Horn, Gerd-Rainer. *The Spirit of '68: Rebellion in Western Europe and North America, 1956–1976.* Oxford: Oxford University Press, 2007.

Howe, Stephen. "Labour and International Affairs." In Patricia Thane, Nick Tiratsoo, and Duncan Tanner (eds.), *Labour's First Century*, 120–50. Cambridge: Cambridge University Press, 2000.

Howell, David. *MacDonald's Party: Labour Identities and Crisis, 1922–1931.* Oxford: Oxford University Press, 2007.

Hunt, John, Colin Thornley, Brian Hodgson, and N. B. J. Huijsman. *Nigeria: The Problem of Relief in the Aftermath of the Nigerian Civil War; Report of Lord Hunt's Mission.* London: H. M. Stationery Office, 1970.

Hunt, Nancy Rose. "'Le Bebe en Brousse': European Women, African Birth Spacing and Colonial Intervention in Breast Feeding in the Belgian Congo." *International Journal of African Historical Studies* 21.3 (1988): 401–32.

Hunter, Yema Lucilda. *An African Treasure: In Search of Gladys Casely-Hayford, 1904–1950*. Accra: Sierra Leonean Writers Series, 2008.

Ignatus, Onianwa Oluchukwu. *Britain's Injurious Peace Games in the Nigerian Civil War, 1967–1970*. London: Academica Press, 2018.

Immerwahr, Daniel. *Thinking Small: The United States and the Lure of Community Development*. Cambridge, MA: Harvard University Press, 2015.

Ireton, Barrie. *Britain's International Development Policies: A History of DFID and Overseas Aid*. Basingstoke, UK: Palgrave, 2013.

Irwin, Julia. *Making the World Safe: The American Red Cross and a Nation's Humanitarian Awakening*. New York: Oxford University Press, 2013.

Isaacs, S. (ed.). *The Cambridge Evacuation Survey*. London: Routledge, 1941.

Ittmann, Karl. *A Problem of Great Importance: Population, Race, and Power in the British Empire, 1918–1973*. Berkeley: University of California Press, 2013.

Jackson, Simon, and Alanna O'Malley. "Introduction: Rocking on Its Hinges? The League of Nations, the United Nations and the New History of Internationalism in the Twentieth Century." In Simon Jackson and Alanna O'Malley (eds.), *The Institution of International Order from the League of Nations to the United Nations*. London: Routledge, 2016.

James, Carolyn, and Glenda Sluga. "Introduction: The Long International History of Women and Diplomacy." In Carolyn James and Glenda Sluga (eds.), *Women, Diplomacy, and International Politics since 1500*, 1–12. London: Routledge, 2016.

James, Harold. "State, Industry and Depression in Weimar Germany." *Historical Journal* 24.1, (1981): 231–41.

Jebb, Eglantyne. *Cambridge: A Brief Study in Social Questions*. Cambridge: Charity Organisation Society, 1906.

Jebb, Richard, "Imperial Organisation." In C. S. Goldman (ed.), *The Empire and the Century*, 332–50. London: J. Murray, 1905.

Jennings, Michael. "'Almost an Oxfam in Itself': Oxfam, Ujamaa and Development in Tanzania." *African Affairs* 101.405 (2002): 509–30.

Jerónimo, Miguel. *The "Civilising Mission" of Portuguese Colonialism, 1870–1930*. Basingstoke, UK: Palgrave, 2015.

Jobs, Richard. *Riding the New Wave: Youth and the Rejuvenation of France after the Second World War*. Stanford, CA: Stanford University Press, 2007.

Joffe, B. M. "Vocational Training of Jews in Europe." *Jewish Social Services Quarterly* 2.25 (1949): 444–51.

Johnson, B. S. (ed.), *The Evacuees*. London: Gollancz, 1968.

Johnson, J. W. De Graft. *Towards Nationhood in West Africa*. 1928. Reprint, London: Headley Bros, 1971.

Jones, Mervyn. *Two Ears of Corn: Oxfam in Action*. Oxford: Oxfam, 1965.

Jovanović, Miroslav. "Accelerated Maturity: Childhood in Emigration (Russian Children in the Balkans, 1920–1940)." In Slobodan Naumović and Miroslav Jovanović (eds.), *Childhood in South East Europe: Historical Perspectives on Growing Up in the 19th and 20th Century*, 199–214. London: Routledge, 2004.

Joyce, Patrick. *The State of Freedom: A Social History of the British State since 1800.* Cambridge: Cambridge University Press, 2013.

Kanogo, Tabitha. *Squatters and the Roots of Mau Mau, 1905–1963.* Athens: Ohio University Press, 1987.

———. "Mission Impact on Women in Colonial Kenya." In F. Bowie, D. Kirkwood, and S. Ardener (eds.), *Women and Missions: Past and Present, Anthropological and Historical Perceptions,* 165–86. Oxford: Oxford University Press, 1993.

Kelemen, P. "Modernising Colonialism: The British Labour Movement and Africa." *Journal of Imperial and Commonwealth History* 34.2 (2006): 227–28.

———. "Planning for Africa: The British Labour Party's Colonial Policy." *Journal of Agrarian Change* 7.1 (2007): 76–98.

Kelleher, Margaret. *The Feminization of Famine, Expressions of the Inexpressible?* Durham, NC: Duke University Press, 1997.

Kelly, Luke. *British Humanitarian Activity in Russia, 1890–1923.* Basingstoke, UK: Palgrave, 2018.

Kennedy, Dane. "Constructing the Colonial Myth of Mau Mau." *International Journal of African Historical Studies* 25.2 (1992): 243.

Kennedy, Dane, and Gregory Barton. "Debating the 'Global History of Britain.'" *Perspectives on History* 51.2 (February 2013)

Kent, Susan Kingsley. "The Politics of Sexual Difference: World War I and the Demise of British Feminism." *Journal of British Studies* 27.3 (1988): 232–53.

Kenyatta, Jomo. *Facing Mount Kenya: The Tribal Life of the Gikuyu.* London: Martin Secker and Warburg, 1938.

King, Laura. *Family Men: Fatherhood and Masculinity in Britain, 1914–1960.* Oxford: Oxford University Press, 2015.

King, Peter. "The Rise of Juvenile Delinquency in England, 1780–1840: Changing Patterns of Perception and Prosecution." *Past & Present,* 160 (1998): 116–66.

Klose, Fabian. *Human Rights in the Shadow of Colonial Violence: The Wars of Independence inn Kenya and Algeria.* Philadelphia: University of Pennsylvania Press, 2014.

Koren, David. *Far Away in the Sky: A Memoir of the Biafran Airlift.* Oakland, CA: Peace Corps Writers, 2011.

Koven, Seth. "Remembering and Dismemberment: Crippled Children, Wounded Soldiers, and the Great War in Great Britain." *American Historical Review* 99.4 (1994): 1167–202.

———. *Slumming: Sexual and Social Politics in Victorian London.* Princeton, NJ: Princeton University Press, 2004.

Krassowski, Andrzej. *The Aid Relationship.* London: Overseas Development Institute, 1968.

Krebs, Paula. "The Last of the Gentleman's Wars: Women in the Boer War Concentration Camp Controversy." *History Workshop Journal* 33.1 (1998): 38–56.

Kuhlman, Erika A. *Reconstructing Patriarchy after the Great War: Women, Gender, and Postwar Reconciliation between Nations.* New York: Oxford University Press, 2008.

Lacey, Janet. *Christian Aid.* London: Edinburgh House Press, 1961.

Lal, Priya. "Self-Reliance and the State: The Multiple Meanings of Development in Early Post-colonial Tanzania." *Africa: Journal of the International African Institute* 82.2 (2012): 212–34.

Lawrence, Jon. "Forging a Peaceable Kingdom: War, Violence, and Fear of Brutalization in Post–First World War Britain." *Journal of Modern History* 75.3 (2003): 557–89.

Leakey, Louis. *Mau Mau and the Kikuyu.* London: Routledge, 1952.

Legarreta, Dorothy. *The Guernica Generation: Basque Refugee Children of the Spanish Civil War.* Las Vegas, NV: University of Las Vegas Press, 1985.

Leith-Ross, Sir F. "Opening Lecture." In *War Organisation of the British Red Cross Societies and the Order of St. John of Jerusalem, Training Course of Pre-Armistice Civilian Relief Overseas, Report of Lectures, January 1943*, 1–2. London: Red Cross, 1943.

Lewis, Jane. *The Politics of Motherhood: Child and Maternal Welfare in England, 1900–1939.* London: Croom Helm, 1980.

———. "Gender and the Development of Welfare Regimes." *Journal of European Social Policy*, 2 (1992): 159–73.

———. *The Voluntary Sector, the State and Social Work in Britain: The Charity Organisation Society/Family Welfare Association since 1869.* Cheltenham, UK: Edward Elgar Publishing, 1995.

Lewis, Joanna. *Empire State-Building: War and Welfare in Kenya, 1925–1952.* Athens: Ohio University Press, 2001.

———. "Daddy Wouldn't Buy Me a Mau Mau: The British Press and the Demoralization of Empire." In E. S. Atieno Odhiambo and John Lonsdale (eds.), *Mau Mau and Nationhood: Arms, Authority, and Narration*, 235–40. Athens: Ohio University Press, 2003.

———. "The British Empire in World History." In James Midgley and David Piachaud (eds.), *Colonialism and Welfare: Social Policy and the British Imperial Legacy*, 24–32. Cheltenham, UK: Edward Elgar Publishing, 2011.

Lewis, Sophie. *Full Surrogacy Now: Feminism against Family.* London: Verso, 2019.

Li, Tania Murray. *The Will to Improve: Governmentality, Development, and the Practice of Politics.* Durham, NC: Duke University Press, 2007.

Liddington, Jill. *The Road to Greenham Common: Feminism and Anti-militarism in Britain since 1820.* Syracuse, NY: Syracuse University Press, 1989.

Light, Alison. *Forever England: Femininity, Literature, and Conservatism between the Wars.* London: Routledge, 1991.

Linstrum, Erik. *Ruling Minds: Psychology in the British Empire.* Cambridge, MA: Harvard University Press, 2016.

Lloyd, Thomas Alwyn. "'Emergency Nursery Schools': Their Planning and Design." *Perspectives in Public Health* 55.4 (1934): 202–6.

Long, Katy. "Early Repatriation Policy: Russian Refugee Return, 1922–1924." *Journal of Refugee Studies* 22.2 (2009): 133–54.

Lonsdale, John. "Mau Maus of the Mind: Making Mau Mau and Remaking Kenya." *Journal of African History* 31.3 (1990): 395–96.

———. "The Moral Economy of Mau Mau: Wealth, Poverty and Civic Virtue." In Bruce Berman (ed.), *Unhappy Valley: Conflict in Kenya and in Africa*, 360–68. Athens: Ohio University Press, 1992.

Loss, Daniel S. "The Institutional Afterlife of Christian England." *Journal of Modern History* 89.2 (2017): 282–313.

———. "Missionaries, the Monarchy, and the Emergence of Anglican Pluralism in the 1960s and 1970s." *Journal of British Studies* 57.3 (2018): 543–63.

Louis, Wm. Roger. *Imperialism at Bay: The United States and the Decolonization of the British Empire, 1941–1945*. New York: Oxford University Press, 1987.

Louis, Wm. Roger, and R. Robinson. "The Imperialism of Decolonialisation." *Journal of Imperial and Commonwealth History* 24.3 (1996): 345–63.

Lowe, Rodney. "The Second World War: Consensus and the Foundation of the Welfare State." *Twentieth Century British History*, 1 (1990): 152–82.

———. *The Welfare State in Britain since 1945*. Basingstoke: Palgrave, 2004.

Luetchford, Mark, and Peter Burns. *Waging the War on Want: 50 Years of Campaigning against World Poverty*. London: War on Want, 2003.

Lugard, F. D. *The Dual Mandate in British Tropical Africa*. 5th ed. London: Routledge, 1965.

Lunden, Walter A. *War and Delinquency: An analysis of Juvenile Delinquency in the Thirteen Nations during World War One and World War Two*. New York: United Nations, 1960.

Macardle, Dorothy. *Children of Europe: A Study of the Children of Liberated Europe, Their Wartime Experiences, Their Needs*. Boston: Beacon Press, 1951.

Macekura Stephen J., and Erez Manela, "Introduction." In Stephen J. Macekura and Erez Manela (eds.), *The Development Century: A Global History*, 1–18. Cambridge: Cambridge University Press, 2018.

MacKenzie, John. "The Persistence of Empire in Metropolitan Culture." In Stuart Ward (ed.), *British Culture and the End of the Empire*, 21–36. Manchester: Manchester University Press, 2001.

MacMillan, Margaret. *Paris 1919: Six Months That Changed the World*. New York: Random House, 2002.

MacNicol, John. "The Effect of the Evacuation of School Children on Official Attitudes to State Intervention." In Harold Smith (ed.), *War and Social Change*, 3–31. Manchester: Manchester University Press, 1986.

Magee, Gary, and Andrew Thompson (eds.). *Empire and Globalisation: Networks of People, Goods and Capital in the British World, c. 1850–1914*. Cambridge: Cambridge University Press, 2010.

Mahood, Linda. *Feminism and Voluntary Action: Eglantyne Jebb and Save the Children, c. 1876–1928*. Basingstoke, UK: Palgrave, 2009.

Maltz, Diana. *British Aestheticism and the Urban Working Classes, 1870–1900: Beauty for the People*. Basingstoke, UK: Palgrave, 2006.

Mandler, Peter. *The English National Character: The History of an Idea from Edmund Burke to Tony Blair.* Cambridge: Cambridge University Press, 2006.

———. *Return from the Natives: How Margaret Mead Won the Second World War and Lost the Cold War.* New Haven, CT: Yale University Press, 2013.

Manela, Eraz. *The Wilsonian Moment: Self-Determination and the International Origins of Anticolonial Nationalism.* Oxford: Oxford University Press, 2007.

Manji, Firoze, and Carl O'Coill. "The Missionary Position: NGOs and Development in Africa." *International Affairs* 78.3 (2002): 567–83.

Mann, Gregory. *From Empires to NGOs in the West African Sahel: The Road to Non-governmentality.* Cambridge: Cambridge University Press, 2015.

Mar, T. Banivanua. "Introduction." In T. Banivanua Mar (ed.), *Decolonisation and the Pacific: Indigenous Globalisation and the Ends of Empire,* 1–21. Cambridge: Cambridge University Press, 2016.

Markwell, Donald. *John Maynard Keynes and International Relations: Economic Paths to War and Peace.* Cambridge: Cambridge University Press, 2006.

Marrus, Michael. *The Unwanted: European Refugees in the Twentieth Century.* Oxford: Oxford University Press, 1985.

Marshall, B. "German Attitudes to British Military Government, 1945–47." *Journal of Contemporary History* 15.4 (1980): 655–84.

Marshall, Dominique. "The Construction of the Child as an Object of International Relations: The Declaration of Child Rights and the Child Welfare Committee of the League of Nations, 1900–1924." *International Journal of Child Rights,* 7 (1999): 135–36.

———. "Children's Rights in Imperial Political Cultures: Missionary and Humanitarian Contributions to the Conference on the African Child of 1931." *International Journal of Children's Rights* 12.3 (2004): 273–318.

———. "The Conference on the African Child of 1931." *International Journal of Children's Rights* 12.3 (2004): 273–318.

Matera, Marc. *Black London: The Imperial Metropolis and Decolonization in the Twentieth Century.* Oakland: University of California Press, 2015.

Mawby, Spencer. *Ordering Independence: The End of Empire in the Anglophone Caribbean, 1947–69.* Basingstoke, UK: Palgrave, 2012.

Mazower, Mark. "Minorities and the League of Nations in Interwar Europe." *Daedalus* 126.2 (1997): 47–63.

———. *Governing the World: The History of an Idea.* New York: Penguin, 2012.

McCarthy, Helen. "Parties, Voluntary Associations, and Democratic Politics in Interwar Britain." *Historical Journal* 50.4 (2007): 891–912.

———. "The League of Nations, Public Ritual and National Identity in Britain, c. 1919–56." *History Workshop Journal,* 70 (2010): 108–32.

———. *The British People and the League of Nations: Democracy, Citizenship and Internationalism, c. 1918–1945.* Manchester: Manchester University Press, 2010.

———. "Social Science and Married Women's Employment in Post-war Britain." *Past & Present* 233.1 (2016): 269–305.

———. *Double Lives: A History of Working Motherhood.* London: Bloomsbury, 2020.

McNeil, Brian. "Frontiers of Need: Humanitarianism and the American Involvement in the Nigerian Civil War, 1967–1970." PhD dissertation, University of Texas, Austin, 2016.

Metzger, Barbara. "Towards an International Human Rights Regime during the Interwar Years: The League of Nations' Combat of Traffic in Women and Children." In K. Grant, P. Levine, and F. Trentmann (eds.), *Beyond Sovereignty: Britain, Empire and Transnationalism, c. 1880–1950*, 54–79. Basingstoke, UK: Palgrave, 2007.

Milford, T. R. *The Oxfam Story*. Oxford: Oxford University Press, 1964.

Mitchell, Timothy. *Rule of Experts: Egypt, Techno-politics, Modernity*. Berkeley: University of California Press, 2002.

Mitford, Nancy. *The Pursuit of Love*. London: Penguin, 1945.

Mitrany, David. *A Working Peace System: An Argument for the Functional Development of International Organization*. Oxford: Oxford University Press, 1944.

Monie, P. W. *Toc-H Under Weigh*. London: Toc-H, 1927.

Moore, Michael. "Social Work and Social Welfare: The Organization of Philanthropic Resources in Britain, 1900–1914." *Journal of British Studies* 16.2 (1977): 85–104.

Moorehead, Caroline. *Dunant's Dream: War, Switzerland and the History of the Red Cross*. London: Carroll and Graf, 1998.

Morris, Jennifer M. *Origins of UNICEF, 1946–1953*. Lanham: Lexington Books, 2015.

Moskowitz, Kara. "'Are You Planting Trees or Are You Planting People?' Squatter Resistance and International Development in the Making of a Kenyan Postcolonial Political Order (c. 1963–78)." *Journal of African History* 56.1 (2015): 99–118.

Mulley, Claire. *The Woman Who Saved the Children: A Biography of Eglantyne Jebb, Founder of Save the Children*. London: Oneworld, 2009.

Muschik, Eva-Maria. "The Art of Chameleon Politics: From Colonial Servant to International Development Expert." *Humanity: An International Journal of Human Rights, Humanitarianism, and Development* 9.2 (2018): 219–44.

Myrdal, Gunnar. *Asian Drama: An Inquiry into the Poverty of Nations*. London: Kalyani Publishers, 1968.

Nash, Mary. "Pronatalism and Motherhood in Franco's Spain." In Gisela Bock and Pat Thane (eds.), *Maternity and Gender Policies: Women and the Rise of the European Welfare States, 1880s–1950s*, 160–77. London: Routledge, 2012.

National Planning Association. *Relief for Europe: The First Phase of Reconstruction* Washington DC: Author, 1942.

Nicolas, C. "Le CICR au secours des réfugiés russes 1919–1939." *Matériaux pour l'histoire de notre temps* 95 (2009): 13–24.

Nunan, Timothy. *Humanitarian Invasion: Global Development in Cold War Afghanistan*. Cambridge: Cambridge University Press, 2016.

Ocobock, Paul. *An Uncertain Age: Making Manhood, Maturity, and Authority in Kenya, 1898–1978*. Athens: Ohio University Press, 2017.

O'Cohrs, Patrick. *The Unfinished Peace after World War I: America, Britain and the Stabilisation of Europe, 1919–1932*. Cambridge: Cambridge University Press, 2006.

Ogborn, Miles. *Global Lives: Britain and the World, 1550–1800*. Cambridge: Cambridge University Press, 2008.

Oldfield, Sybil. *Women Humanitarians: A Biographical Dictionary of British Women Active between 1900 and 1950*. London: Continuum, 2001.

Oman, Natalie. "Hannah Arendt's 'Right to Have Rights': A Philosophical Context for Human Security." *Journal of Human Rights* 9.10 (2010): 279–302.

Orford, Anne. *Reading Humanitarian Intervention: Human Rights and the Use of Force in International Law*. Cambridge: Cambridge University Press, 2008.

Orwell, George. *Homage to Catalonia*. London: Penguin, 1938.

O'Sullivan, Kevin. "Humanitarian Encounters: Biafra, NGOs and Imaginings of the Third World in Britain and Ireland, 1967–70." *Journal of Genocide Research* 16.2–3 (2014): 299–315.

Padmore, George. *Pan-Africanism or Communism: The Coming Struggle for Africa*. London: Doubleday, 1971.

Palen, Marc-William. *The "Conspiracy" of Free Trade: The Anglo-American Struggle over Empire and Economic Globalisation, 1846–1896*. Cambridge: Cambridge University Press, 2016.

Palma, Gabriel. "Dependency: A Formal Theory of Underdevelopment or a Methodology for the Analysis of Concrete Situations of Underdevelopment?" *World Development* 6.7–8 (1978): 881–924.

Panayi, P. "Middlesbrough 1961: A British Race Riot of the 1960s?" *Social History* 16.2 (1991): 139–53.

Patenaude, Bertrand. *The Big Show in Bololand: The American Relief Expedition to Soviet Russia in the Famine of 1921*. Stanford, CA: Stanford University Press, 2002.

Pearson, C. Andrew. *Front Line Hospital: The Story of Wesley Guild Hospital Ilesa, Nigeria*. Cambridge: Cambridge University Press, 1996.

Pedersen, Susan. "National Bodies, Unspeakable Acts: The Sexual Politics of Colonial Policy-Making." *Journal of Modern History* 63.4 (1991): 647–80.

———. *Family, Dependence, and the Origins of the Welfare State: Britain and France, 1914–1945*. Cambridge: Cambridge University Press, 1993.

———. "The Maternalist Moment in the British Colonial Policy: The Controversy over "Child Slavery" in Hong Kong 1917–1941." *Past & Present* 171 (2001): 161–202.

———. *Eleanor Rathbone and the Politics of Conscience*. New Haven, CT: Yale University Press, 2004.

———. "The Meaning of the Mandates System: An Argument." *Geschichte und Gesellschaft*, 32.4 (2006): 560–82.

———. "Back to the League of Nations: Review Essay." *American Historical Review* 112.4 (2007): 1091–117.

———. *The Guardians: The League of Nations and the Crisis of Empire*. Oxford: Oxford University Press, 2016.

Pennybacker, Susan. *From Scottsboro to Munich: Race and Political Culture in 1930s Britain*. Princeton, NJ: Princeton University Press, 2009.

Peplow, Simon. *Race and Riots in Thatcher's Britain*. Manchester: Manchester University Press, 2019.

Petersson, Fredrik. *Willi Münzenberg, the League Against Imperialism, and the Comintern, 1925–1933.* Vol. 1. New York: Edwin Mellen, 2013.

Petruševa, L. I. "Le soutien du zemgor aux écoles de la diaspora." *Cahiers du Monde Russe*, 46 (2005): 831–44.

Pettiss, Susan, and Lynne Taylor. *After the Shooting Stopped: The Story of an UNRRA Welfare Worker in Germany, 1945–1947.* Trafford: Trafford Publishing, 2004.

Pine, Lisa. *Education in Nazi Germany.* New York: Berg, 2010.

Pitts, Jennifer. *A Turn to Empire: The Rise of Imperial Liberalism in Britain and France.* Princeton, NJ: Princeton University Press, 2006.

Poovey, Mary. *Making a Social Body: British Cultural Formations, 1830–1864.* Chicago: University of Chicago Press, 1994.

Porter, Andrew. "Trusteeship, Anti-slavery, and Humanitarianism." In A. Porter (ed.), *The Oxford History of the British Empire, Vol. 3: The Nineteenth Century*, 198–221. Oxford: Oxford University Press, 1999.

———. *Missionaries versus Empire: British Protestant Missionaries and Overseas Expansion.* Manchester: Manchester University Press, 2004.

———. *Religion versus Empire? British Protestant Missionaries and Overseas Expansion, 1700–1914.* Manchester: Manchester University Press, 2004.

Prashad, Vijay. *The Darker Nations: A People's History of the Third World.* New York: New Press, 2007.

Pringle, Yolanda. "Humanitarianism, Race, and Denial: The International Committee of the Red Cross and Kenya's Mau Rebellion, 1952–60." *History Workshop Journal*, 84 (2017): 89–107.

Prochaska, Frank. *Women and Philanthropy in Nineteenth-Century England.* Oxford: Oxford University Press, 1980.

Pugh, Martin. "Pacifism and Politics in Britain." *Historical Journal*, 23 (1980): 641–56.

———. *Hurrah for the Blackshirts! Fascists and Fascism in Britain between the Wars.* London: Jonathan Cape, 2005.

Pupavac, V. "Misanthropy without Border: The International Children's Rights Regime." *Disasters* 2 (2001): 95–112.

Purvis, June. "Gendering the Historiography of the Suffragette Movement in Edwardian Britain: Some Reflections." *Women's History Review* 22.4 (2013): 576–90.

Ram, Kalpana, and Margaret Jolly. "Introduction." In Kalpana Ram and Margaret Jolly (eds.), *Maternities and Modernities: Colonial and Postcolonial Experiences in Asia and the Pacific*, 1–25. Cambridge: Cambridge University Press, 1998.

Read, Róisín. "Embodying Difference: Reading Gender in Women's Memoirs of Humanitarianism." *Journal of Intervention and Statebuilding* 12.3 (2018): 300–318.

Readman, Paul. "The Place of the Past in English Culture, c. 1890–1914." *Past & Present* 186.1 (2005): 147–99.

Reinisch, Jessica. "Internationalism in Relief: The Birth (and Death) of UNRRA." *Past & Present*, 210.S6 (2011): 258–89

———. "'Auntie UNRRA' at the Crossroads." *Past & Present*, 218.S8 (2013): 70–97.

———. *The Perils of Peace: Public Health in Occupied Germany.* Oxford: Oxford University Press, 2013.

Rich, Adrienne. *Of Woman Born: Motherhood as Experience and Institution.* New York: W. W. Norton, 1986.

Ridell, N. *Labour in Crisis: The Second Labour Government, 1929–1931.* Manchester: Manchester University Press, 1999.

Riley, Charlotte L. "Monstrous Predatory Vampires and Beneficent Fairy-Godmothers: British Post-war Colonial Development in Africa." Doctoral thesis, University College London, 2013.

———. "The Winds of Change Are Blowing Economically: The Labour Party and British Overseas Development, 1940s–1960s." In Andrew Smith and Chris Jeppesen (eds.), *Legacies of Tangled Empires: British and French Decolonisation in Africa,* 43–61. London: University College London Press, 2017.

Riley, Denise. *War in the Nursery: Theories of the Child and Mother.* London: Virago, 1983.

Rist, Gilbert. *The History of Development: From Western Origins to Global Faith.* London: Zed Books, 2008.

Rooke, Patricia T., and Rudy L. Schnell. "'Uncramping Child Life': International Children's Organisations, 1914–1939." In Paul Weindling (ed.), *International Health Organisations and Movements, 1918–1939,* 176–202. Cambridge: Cambridge University Press, 1995.

Roper, Lyndal. "'Evil Imaginings and Fantasies': Child-Witches and the End of the Witch Craze." *Past & Present,* 167 (2000): 107–39.

Rose, Jaqueline. *Mothers: An Essay on Love and Cruelty.* London: Faber and Faber, 2018.

Rose, Nikolas. *The Psychological Complex: Psychology, Politics and Society in England, 1869–1939.* London: Routledge and Kegan Paul, 1985.

Rossi, Benedetta. *From Slavery to Aid: Politics, Labour, and Ecology in the Nigerien Sahel, 1800–2000.* Cambridge: Cambridge University Press, 2015.

Rowley, Michelle, and Peggy Antrobus. "Feminist Visions for Women in a New Era: An Interview with Peggy Antrobus." *Feminist Studies* 33.1 (2007): 64–87.

Rutazibwa, Olivia. "On Babies and Bathwater: Decolonizing International Development Studies." In S. de Jong, R. Icaza, and O. U. Rutazibwa (eds.), *Decolonization and Feminisms in Global Teaching and Learning,* 158–80. London: Routledge, 2018.

———. "What's There to Mourn? Decolonial Reflections on (the End of) Liberal Humanitarianism." *Journal of Humanitarian Affairs* 1.1 (2019): 65–67.

Sabaratnam, Meera. *Decolonising Intervention: International Statebuilding in Mozambique.* London: Rowman International, 2017.

Sallinen, Harri. "Intergovernmental Advocates of Refugees: The Refugee Policy of the League of Nations and the International Labour Organization in the 1920s and 1930s." PhD thesis, University of Helsinki, 2013.

Salvatici, Silvia. "'Help the People to Help Themselves': UNRRA Relief Workers and European Displaced Persons." *Journal of Refugee Studies* 25.3 (September 2012): 428–51.

Sasson, Tehila. "From Empire to Humanity: The Russian Famine and the Imperial Origins of International Humanitarianism." *Journal of British Studies* 55.3 (July 2016): 519–37.

———. "Milking the Third World? Humanitarianism, Capitalism, and the Moral Economy of the Nestlé Boycott." *American Historical Review* 121.4 (2016): 1196–224.

Sasson, Tehila, James Vernon, Miles Ogborn, Priya Satia, and Katherine Hall. "Britain and the World: A New Field?" *Journal of British Studies* 57.4 (2018): 677–708.

Sbacchi, Alberto. "Poison Gas and Atrocities in the Italo-Ethiopian War (1935–1936)." In Ruth Ben-Ghiat and Mia Fuller (eds.), *Italian Colonialism*, 47–56. Basingstoke, UK: Palgrave, 2005.

Schauer, Jeff. *Wildlife between Empire and Nation in Twentieth-Century Africa*. Basingstoke, UK: Palgrave, 2018.

Schneider, Fred D. "Fabians and the Utilitarian Idea of Empire." *Review of Politics* 35.4 (1973): 501–22.

Schofield, Camilla. *Enoch Powell and the Making of Postcolonial Britain*. Cambridge: Cambridge University Press, 2013.

Scott-Smith, Tom. "Control and Biopower in Contemporary Humanitarian Aid: The Case of Supplementary Feeding." *Journal of Refugee Studies* 28.1 (2015): 21–37.

Sellick, Patricia. "Responding to Children Effected by Armed Conflict: A Case Study of the Save the Children Fund (1919–1999)." PhD thesis, University of Bradford, 1999.

Shapira, Michal. *The War Inside: Psychoanalysis, Total War, and the Making of the Democratic Self in Postwar Britain*. Cambridge: Cambridge University Press, 2013.

Sharp, Evelyn. *The African Child: An Account of the International Conference on African Children in Geneva*. London: Longmans Green, 1931.

Shipway, Martin. *Decolonization and Its Impact: A Comparative Approach to the End of Colonial Empires*. Oxford: Oxford University Press, 2008.

Shore, Heather. *Artful Dodgers: Youth and Crime in Early Nineteenth-Century London*. London: Boydell Press, 1999.

Siegelberg, Mira. *Statelessness: A Modern History*. Cambridge, MA: Harvard University Press, 2019.

Simpson, John Hope. "The Work of the Greek Refugee Settlement Commission." *Journal of the Royal Institute of International Affairs* 8.6 (1929): 583–604.

Skinner, Rob, and Alan Lester. "Humanitarianism and Empire: New Research Agendas." *Journal of Imperial and Commonwealth History* 40.5 (2012): 729–47.

Skran, Claudena. *Refugees in Interwar Europe: The Emergence of a Regime*. Oxford: Oxford University Press, 1995.

Sluga, Glenda. *Internationalism in the Age of Nationalism*. Philadelphia: University of Pennsylvania Press, 2013.

———. "Women, Feminisms and Twentieth-Century Internationalism." In Glenda Sluga and Patricia Clavin (eds.), *Internationalisms: A Twentieth-Century History*, 63–68. Cambridge: Cambridge University Press, 2017.

Smyke, Raymond J. *Nigeria Union of Teachers: An Official History*. Oxford: Oxford University Press, 1974.

Spillers, Hortense, "Mama's Baby, Papa's Maybe: An American Grammar Book." *Diacritics* 17.2 (1987): 65–81.

Spivak, Gayatri Chakravorty. "The Rani of Sirmur: An Essay in Reading the Archives." *History and Theory* 24.3 (1985): 247–72.

Starkey, Pat. "The Feckless Mother: Women, Poverty and Social Workers in Wartime and Post-war England." *Women's History Review* 9.3 (2000): 539–57.

Steedman, Carolyn. *Childhood, Culture, and Class in Britain: Margaret McMillan, 1860–1931.* New Brunswick, NJ: Rutgers University Press, 1990.

———. *Strange Dislocations: Childhood and the Idea of Human Interiority, 1780–1930.* Cambridge, MA: Harvard University Press, 1995.

Steinacher, Gerald. *Humanitarians at War: The Red Cross in the Shadow of the Holocaust.* Oxford: Oxford University Press, 2017.

Steiner, Z. *Triumph of the Dark: European International History, 1933–1939.* Oxford: Oxford University Press, 2013.

Stewart, A. *The First Victory: The Second World War and the East Africa Campaign.* New Haven, CT: Yale University Press, 2016.

Stewart-Murray, Katherine Marjory. *Searchlight on Spain.* Middlesex: Harmondsworth, 1938.

Stoler, Ann Laura. *Along the Archival Grain: Epistemic Anxieties and Colonial Common Sense.* Princeton, NJ: Princeton University Press, 2010.

Swain, S. "Child Rescue: The Migration of an Idea." In J. Lawrence and P. Starkey (eds.), *Child Welfare and Social Action in the Nineteenth and Twentieth Centuries: International Perspectives,* 115–18. Liverpool: Liverpool University Press, 2001.

Swanwick, H. *Builders of Peace: Being Ten Years History of the Union of Democratic Control.* London: Allen and Unwin, 1924.

Sylvest, Casper. *British Liberal Internationalism, 1880–1930: Making Progress?* Manchester: Manchester University Press, 2009.

Thane, Pat. "Childhood in History." In Michael King (ed.), *Childhood, Welfare And Justice: A Critical Examination of Children in the Legal and Childcare Systems.* London: Routledge, 1984.

———. "Visions of Gender in the Making of the British Welfare State: The Case of Women in the British Labour Party and Social Policy, 1906–1945." In Gisela Bock and Pat Thane (eds.), *Maternity and Gender Policies: Women and the Rise of the European Welfare States, 1880s–1950s,* 93–118. London: Routledge, 1991.

Thomas, Keith. "Children in Early Modern England." In G. Avery and J. Briggs (eds.), *Children and Their Books,* 45–77. Oxford: Oxford University Press, 1989.

Thompson, James. "'Pictorial Lies'? Posters and Politics in Britain, c. 1880–1914." *Past & Present* 197.1 (2007): 177–210.

Thomson, Mathew. *Lost Freedom: The Landscape of the Child and the British Post-war Settlement.* Oxford: Oxford University Press, 2013.

Tilley, Helen. *Africa as a Living Laboratory: Empire, Development, and the Problem of Scientific Knowledge, 1870–1950.* Chicago: University of Chicago Press, 2011.

Titmuss, Richard. *Problems of Social Policy.* London: H. M. Stationery Office, 1950.

Todd, Selina. "Family, Welfare and Social Work in Post-war England, c. 1948–c. 1970." *English Historical Review*, 129 (2014): 362–87.

———. *The People: The Rise and Fall of the Working Class*. London: John Murray, 2014.

Todd, Selina, and Harry Hendrick. *Children, Childhood and English Society, 1880–1990*. Cambridge: Cambridge University Press, 1997.

Tomlinson, Jim. "The Commonwealth, the Balance of Payments and the Politics of International Poverty: British Aid Policy, 1958–1971." *Contemporary European History* 12.4 (2003): 413–29.

Trager, Lillian. *Yoruba Hometowns: Community, Identity, and Development in Nigeria*. Boulder, CO: Lynne Rienner, 2001.

Trentmann, Frank. "After the Nation-State: Citizenship, Empire and Global Coordination in the New Internationalism, 1914–30." In K. Grant, P. Levine, and F. Trentmann (eds.), *Beyond Sovereignty: Britain, Empire and Transnationalism, c. 1860–1950*, 34–53. Basingstoke, UK: Palgrave, 2007.

———. *Free Trade Nation: Commerce, Consumption and Civil Society in Britain*. Oxford: Oxford University Press, 2008.

Trevelyan, C. *The Union of Democratic Control: Its History and Its Policy*. London: Union of Democratic Control, 1919.

Tusan, Michelle. *Smyrna's Ashes: Humanitarianism, Genocide, and the Birth of the Middle East*. Berkeley: University of California Press, 2012.

———. "'Crimes against Humanity': Human Rights, the British Empire, and the Origins of the Response to the Armenian Genocide." *American Historical Review* 119.1 (2014): 47–77.

———. "Genocide, Famine and Refugees on Film: Humanitarianism and the First World War." *Past & Present* 237.1 (2017): 197–235.

Uche, Chibuike. "Oil, British Interests and the Nigerian Civil War." *Journal of African History*, 49 (2008): 111–35.

Unger, Cornia. "Postwar European Development Aid: Defined by Decolonization, the Cold War, and European Integration?" In Stephen Macekura and Erez Manela (eds.), *The Development Century: A Global History*, 240–60. Cambridge: Cambridge University Press, 2018.

Vernon, James. "The Ethics of Hunger and the Assembly of Society: The Technopolitics of the School Meal in Modern Britain." *American Historical Review* 110.3 (2005): 693–725.

———. *Hunger: A Modern History*. Berkeley: University of California Press, 2007.

Wagner, Kim A. "Savage Warfare: Violence and the Rule of Colonial Difference in Early British Counterinsurgency." *History Workshop Journal* 85.1 (2018): 217–37.

Wagner, R. *Clemens von Pirquet: His Life and Work*. Baltimore: Johns Hopkins University Press, 1968.

Ward, P. *The Red Flag and the Union Jack: England, Patriotism and the British Left, 1881–1924*. London: Boydell Press, 1998.

Watenpaugh, Keith David. "The League of Nations' Rescue of Armenian Genocide Survivors and the Making of Modern Humanitarianism, 1920–1927." *American Historical Review* 115.5 (2010): 1315–39.

———. *Bread from Stone: The Middle East and the Making of Modern Humanitarianism*. Berkeley: University of California Press, 2016.

Waugh, Evelyn. *Scoop*. London: Penguin, 1938.

Weber, Max. *The Protestant Ethic and the Spirit of Capitalism*. Oxford: Oxford University Press, 1920.

Webster, Wendy. "The Empire Comes Home: Commonwealth Migration to Britain." In Andrew Thompson (ed.), *Britain's Experience of Empire in the Twentieth Century*, 122–60. Oxford: Oxford University Press, 2012.

Weindling, Paul. "Fascism and Population in Comparative European Perspective." *Population and Development Review* 14 (1988): 102–21.

———. "The Role of International Organisations in Setting Nutritional Standards in the 1920s and 1930s." In H. Kamminga and A. Cunningham (eds.), *The Science and Culture of Nutrition, 1940–1940*, 319–32. Baltimore: Johns Hopkins University Press, 1995.

Wells, Karen. "Child Saving or Child Rights: Depictions of Children in International NGO Campaigns on Conflict." *Journal of Children and Media* 2.3 (2008): 235–50.

———. "The Melodrama of Being a Child: NGO Representations of Poverty." *Visual Communication* 12.3 (2013): 277–93.

———. *Childhood in Global Perspective*. London: Polity, 2014.

Welshmann, John. "Evacuation and Social Policy during the Second World War: Myth and Reality." *Twentieth Century British History*, 9 (1998): 28–53.

Westad, Odd Arne. *The Global Cold War: Third World Interventions and the Making of Our Times*. Cambridge: Cambridge University Press, 2005.

Wheatley, Natasha. "Mandatory Interpretation: Legal Hermeneutics and the New International Order in Arab and Jewish Petitions to the League of Nations." *Past & Present* 227 (2015): 205–48.

White, Elizabeth. "The Struggle against Denationalisation in Europe: The Russian Emigration and Education in the 1920s." *Revolutionary Russia* 26.2 (2013): 128–46.

White, Louise. "Separating the Men from the Boys: Constructions of Gender, Sexuality, and Terrorism in Central Kenya, 1939–1959." *International Journal of African Historical Studies* 23.1 (1990): 13–14.

Williams, H. C. "The Arrival of the Basque Children at the Port of Southampton." *British Medical Journal* (12 June 1937): 1209–10.

Williams, Jack. *Entertaining the Nation: A Social History of British Television*. Gloucestershire, UK: The History Press, 2004.

Williams, Peter. *Aid in the Commonwealth Overseas Development Institute*. London: Overseas Development Institute, 1965.

Williamson, P. *National Crisis and National Government: British Politics, the Economy and Empire, 1926–1932*. Cambridge: Cambridge University Press, 1992.

Wilson, Francesca. *In the Margins of Chaos*. New York: Macmillan, 1945.

———. *Aftermath: France, Germany, Austria, Yugoslavia 1945 and 1946*. London: Penguin, 1947.

Woolf, Virginia. *The Diary of Virginia Woolf, Volume 4: 1931–1935.* Ed. Anne Oliver Bell. London: Harcourt Brace Jovanovich, 1982.

Worley, M. *Labour Inside the Gate: A History of the British Labour Party between the Wars.* London: Bloomsbury, 2005.

Wright, P. *Iron Curtain: From Stage to Cold War.* Oxford: Oxford University Press, 2007.

Yearwood, Peter. *Guarantee of Peace: The League of Nations in British Policy, 1914–1925.* Oxford: Oxford University Press, 2009.

Young, John W. *The Labour Governments, 1964–1970, Volume 2: International Policy.* Manchester: Manchester University Press, 2003.

Zahra, Tara. *Kidnapped Souls: National Indifference and the Battle for Children in the Bohemian Lands, 1900–1948.* Ithaca, NY: Cornell University Press, 2008.

———. "'A Human Treasure': Europe's Displaced Children between Nationalism and Internationalism in Post-war Reconstruction in Europe." *Past & Present* 210.S6 (2011): 332–50.

———. *The Lost Children: Reconstructing Europe's Families after World War II.* Cambridge, MA: Harvard University Press, 2011.

Zelizer, Viviana. *Pricing the Priceless Child: The Changing Social Value of Children.* Princeton, NJ: Princeton University Press, 1985.

INDEX

Adams, Lt. Colonel Frank, 152–153, 156
Addams, Jane, 64
Ador, Gustav, 64
Alden, Percy, 60–61
Angstrom, Anna-Lenah, 32
anti-colonialism: activists and fighters, 78,
   91–98, 102, 153, 176; British Empire,
   against, 138–139, 143–144, 151, 157–162,
   166–167; decolonization. See decoloni-
   zation; independence, 4, 20, 96, 156,
   170–172; League Against Imperialism,
   91–92; Mau Mau. See Kenya, Emer-
   gency; MNLA. See Malaya, MNLA;
   Negro Commission, 92
Antrobus, Kenneth, 181, 184, *185fig.*
Antrobus, Peggy, 181–186, *182fig.*
Apponyi, Count, 70
Arendt, Hannah, 76–77
Argillo, Comte of, 120
Armenia. See refugees, Armenian
Askwith, Thomas, 162–163
Astor MP, Nancy, 108–110
Attlee, Clement, 143
Attlee, Violet, 155
Australia, 34
Austria, 53–54, 68, 76, 135, 150; annexation
   of, 127; famine in, 23, 27–28, 42;
   Vienna, 29

Baldwin, Stanley, 113
Bangladesh (East Pakistan), 204, 207
Begbie, Alison, 194

Belgium, 27–29, 64, 87, 120, 132–135, 172;
   Belgian Empire. See Congo; flag, 36
Bentinck, Lady Norah, 26–27
Bernardz, Johann, 28–29
Betts, Jimmy, 176–178
Biafra: "Biafran babies," 1–2, 192–203;
   blockade, of 192–194; Calabar, 1, 196;
   civil war. See Nigeria, civil war; famine
   in, 1–3, 46, 195, 198–201, 204, 207–209
Bibby, Jane, 151
Birch, John, 179, 187–195
Blair, Tony, 207
Blake, Alan, 155
Blue Peter, 14, 201
Boas, Franz, 93
Boer War, 5, 41–42, 80, 222n37
Bondfield, Margaret, 111
Bosnia, 207
Bowlby, John, 145
Boyce, Brigadier Tony, 142, 151, 156,
   160–163
Boyce, Nanette, 156
Brittain, Vera, 103, 134
British Empire, 6–7, 143; as a contributor
   to peace, 20, 87, 91, 201, 209, 214; end
   of, 1–4, 169–170, 206, 209. See also
   decolonization
British Honduras, 171
British Petroleum, 179
Bulgaria, 56–58, 72–74; Atolvo, *62fig.,*
   62–63; Sofia, 57; Umen, 58; Xhebba,
   62–63

Buxton MP, Charles Roden: at SCF Conference, 90, 94; friends of, 20, 71; imperial views of, 81–83, 95, 102; Nazism, sympathy for, 102, 112; political views of, 20–21, 86; Russia, visit to, 34

Buxton, Dorothy: children, attitude to, 20–24; early life, 19–20; founder of SCF. *See* SCF, foundation of; friends of, 20, 71, 86; League of Nations, attitude to, 25, 45, 63; nervous breakdown, 35; political views of, 20, 46–48, 135–136, 139, 206–208; religious views, of, 21, 33

Buxton, Lord Noel, 83–84, 99, 142; at SCF Conference, 88, 91–94; Ethiopia, visit to, 97; friends of, 87; imperial views of, 102; Nazism, sympathy for, 102, 112, 115; political views of, 86, 130

Buxton, Thomas Fowell, 20, 84

Campaign for Nuclear Disarmament, 175

Canada, 34–36

capitalism: as an inherent good, 11, 82; as dependent on the working classes, 29–31, 81, 157, 160, 203; colonial, 80, 93, 143–144, 203, 208; free trade. *See* free trade; industrialization, 79–82, 87, 90, 143, 157–159, 174

Caribbean, the (West Indies, the), 14, 78, 176, 180–186; Jamaica 180–181, 186; Trinidad, 181; West Indies Federation, 180; Windward Islands, 182–186, *182fig.*

Carothers, J. C., 162

Casely Hayford, Adelaide, 93, 96

Casely Hayford, Gladys, 93, 96

Castle MP, Barbara, 176

Chamberlain, Neville, 127

Chernigov, Boris, 36

children: abandoned, 145–146; "adoption" of, 53–55, 75, 146, 212; African, 78–104; as apolitical subjects, 39–45, 95, 154, 199; as future American workers, 112; as future colonial workers, 2, 80, 88–89, 93–94, 163, 167; as future British workers, 108, *109fig.*; as future global workers, 5–8, 23, *30fig.*, 50–51, 75–77, 145, 211; as future parents, 5–6, 43, 68, 75, 145; as future soldiers, 6, 66–69, 73, 112, 145–146, 156; as international

citizens, 51–59, 63, 66–69, 74–77, 131; as sex workers, 147–148; "assimilation" of, 58, 72, 124–125; attachment theory, 145–146, 167; childcare, 8, 131, 184; child labor. *See* labor, child; Children's Charter, 65–66; Conference on the African Child (1931), 78, *79fig.*, 85–106, 171, 178, 204, 214; Convention for the Assistance or Repatriation of Foreign Minors, 72, 76; Convention for the Protection of Children (draft), 120, 128–129; Declaration of the Rights of the Child (1924), 50, 63–78, 89, 114, 138, 210–211; Declaration of the Rights of the Child (1989), 211–212; definitions of, 162; disabled, 31, 67, 70, 76, 88; education of. *See* education; emotional stability, of, 7, 125, 145–149, 167; evacuation of, 14, 51–59, *117fig.*, 119–128, 136, 145, 202; health of, 71, 89, 99, 112, 132, 211; imprisonment of, 139, 148, 158, 161–166; infant mortality, 88–91, 94, 165, 180–181; "innocence," 23, 43–48, 56, 135, 149; "innocence," disruption of, 15, 122–123; institutionalization of, 131; Jewish, 28, 136; juvenile delinquency, 7, 144–151, 154–162, 165–167, 184; *Kindertransport,* 126–127, *126fig.*; Maternal and Child Welfare Council, 69; middle-class, 28–29; naked, 40–44; orphans and "orphans," 41–44, 65, 68, 131, 145–147, 202; parents of. *See* family; pro-natalism, 5, 112; punishment of, 139, 148, 154, 158–166, 180, 187; repatriation of, 71–73, 76, 123, 202; "right sort" of, 27–28, 40–41; Romantic view of, 7; Save the Children Fund. *See* Save the Children Fund; stateless, 51–59, 72–76; working class, 46, 69, 106–107, 110, 160

Coe, Magda, 74

Cold War, 4, 96, 139, 143–146, 174–175, 206

colonialism: after. *See* postcolonialism; anti-colonialism. *See* anti-colonialism; as a contributor to peace, 3–4, 11, 79; as a threat to peace, 80; British Empire. *See* British Empire; "civilizing" mission of, 3, 81, 87, 103–104, 159, 208; end of. *See* decolonization; "ethical" imperialism ("world responsibility"), 78–87,

Founded in 1893,
UNIVERSITY OF CALIFORNIA PRESS
publishes bold, progressive books and journals
on topics in the arts, humanities, social sciences,
and natural sciences—with a focus on social
justice issues—that inspire thought and action
among readers worldwide.

The UC PRESS FOUNDATION
raises funds to uphold the press's vital role
as an independent, nonprofit publisher, and
receives philanthropic support from a wide
range of individuals and institutions—and from
committed readers like you. To learn more, visit
ucpress.edu/supportus.